HISTORY OF METHODISM,

FROM ITS ORIGIN TO ITS HUNDREDTH ANNIVERSARY,
MDCCCXXXIX.

VOLUME I.

THE HISTORY

OF THE

Religious Movement of the Eighteenth Century,

CALLED

METHODISM,

CONSIDERED IN ITS DIFFERENT DENOMINATIONAL FORMS, AND ITS RELATIONS TO BRITISH AND AMERICAN PROTESTANTISM

By ABEL STEVENS, LL.D.

VOLUME I.

From the Origin of Methodism to the Death of Whitefield.

FIFTH THOUSAND.

New-York:
PUBLISHED BY CARLTON & PORTER,
200 MULBERRY-STREET.
LONDON: ALEXANDER HEYLIN, 28 PATERNOSTER ROW.

PREFACE.

As a great religious development of the last century, affecting largely our common Protestantism, and, unquestionably, destined to affect it still more profoundly, Methodism does not belong exclusively to the denominations which have appropriated its name. I have therefore attempted to write its history in a liberal spirit, and to consider it, not as a sectarian, but as a general religious movement, ostensibly within the Church of England, at least during the lives of the chief Methodist founders, but reaching beyond it to most of the Protestantism of England and America. I have endeavored steadily to keep this point of view till the movement was reduced into sectarian organizations.

I am not aware that this plan has been followed by any of the numerous writers on Methodism, Calvinistic or Arminian, except Isaac Taylor, and Dr. James Porter in his excellent "Compendium," our best practical manual of Methodism. If Southey's life of Wesley should be considered another exception, yet its questionable purpose, and its total misapprehension of the providential design of Methodism, have deprived it, among religious readers, of any importance, aside from the romantic interest of its facts.

This comprehensive plan is not only historically just, but it affords special advantage to the variety and interest of the narrative: for whereas the Calvinistic writers, on the one side, have had as their chief characters, Whitefield, the Countess of Huntingdon, Howell Harris, Berridge, Venn, Romaine, Madan; and the Arminian authors, on the other, the Wesleys, Grimshaw, Fletcher, Nelson; I claim them all as "workers together with God;" and the marvelous "itinerancy" of Whitefield runs parallel with the equally marvelous travels and labors of Wesley. Marking distinctly the contrasts of the Calvinistic and Arminian sections of Methodism, I have nevertheless been able to show that much more harmony existed between them, through most of their history, than has usually been supposed; that in fact the essential unity of the movement was maintained, with but incidental and salutary variations, down to the death of Whitefield. In this respect, at least, I trust my pages will teach a lesson of Christian charity and catholicity which shall be grateful to all good men who may read them; and as it is more the office of history to narrate than polemically to discuss opinions, I have endeavored not to impair the much-needed lesson in my accounts of parties. It has been as impossible as inexpedient to dissemble my own theological opinions, but it is hoped that they will not be found unnecessarily obtruded. As the Wesleyan section of the movement was the most ostensible, and took finally an organized and permanent form, it necessarily takes the lead in the earlier part of the narrative, and will almost exclusively occupy the latter part of it. I have endeavored, however, to give the fullest attention, required by the plan of the work, to other Methodist bodies.

The present volume brings the narrative down to the death of Whitefield, a period after which Calvinistic Methodism, though it will continue to receive due notice, loses its prominence, and the history of the movement becomes distinctively Wesleyan. The second volume will complete the history of British Methodism. The history of the Methodist Episcopal Church, only alluded to in the preceding volumes so far as was necessary to the integrity of the narrative, will be given in two additional volumes. While this arrangement is legitimate to the real history of Methodism, and will afford some special conveniences to the writer, it will also have the important advantage of presenting to the reader the English history, including the fullest "Life and Times of Wesley" yet published, and the history of the Methodist Episcopal Church in the United States, each in so distinct a form as not to be dependent one on the other.

I have endeavored to do justice to the Lay Preachers of Wesley, many of whom, though overshadowed by the leaders of Methodism, were its noblest heroes. Southey is the only writer who has said much respecting them; but he has referred to them in almost every instance for the purpose of citing proofs of his charges of fanaticism and insanity, though he could not disguise his admiration of their extraordinary characters, and they afford the chief romance of his volumes. He has given sketches of eight of them; I have given more than that number in the present volume; many, however, of historical importance, who were active during my present period, do not appear within it. The reader will hereafter find that I have not ignored their claims, but postponed them to more suitable points of the narrative.

The Ecclesiastical Economy, the Doctrines, Psalmody, Literature, etc., of Methodism are noticed as the narrative proceeds, their historical development being distinctly traced; but they will be more fully discussed in a book of the second volume.

I have authenticated the most important facts of the narrative by marginal references; in order, however, not to encumber the volume unnecessarily with notes, I have, in most instances, given my authority in the beginning of each chapter, without repeating it except when some intervening reference has made it necessary. The number of publications relating to early Methodism would be incredible to ordinary readers. Whether from a curious or a hostile motive, a "Catalogue of Works that have been published in Refutation of Methodism from its origin in 1729 to 1846, compiled by H. C. Decanver," was printed in Philadelphia by John Pennington in 1846. It is not complete, but comprises the titles of no less than three hundred and eighty-four publications. The compiler was a Protestant Episcopalian; "Decanver" is his *nomme de plume;* he has given his real name in the original manuscript, which, with the printed catalogue and one hundred and forty-three of the most curious of these works, he has deposited in the Library of the Theological Seminary of the Protestant Episcopal Church in New York city. Whatever may have been his design, he has done a valuable service to Methodism, and enriched the library of that institution with the best collection of such documents in the United States, perhaps the best in the world. If we add to these the works in favor of Methodism, and others bearing directly or indirectly on its history, the list can hardly be short of fifteen hundred. Of course I have not examined all these; but I know of none necessary to my purpose which have not been consulted.

None of the common portraits of Wesley are satisfactory. They lack character—at least the character which we attribute to him, from his writings and deeds. A painting has recently been discovered in England which presents him as he really was—the strong but amiable man. The portrait given in this volume is of like character. It is copied from an old engraving in the above-named library.

I am under many obligations to Rev. Drs. Whedon, (of the Methodist Quarterly Review,) Hibbard, (of the Northern Christian Advocate,) Holdich, (of the American Bible Society,) Prof. Strong of Troy, Franklin Rand, Esq., of Boston, S. B. Wickens, Esq., New York, and most especially to R. A. West, Esq., (of the New York Commercial Advertiser,) for the revision of the proofs, and important suggestions.

My task will terminate at the centenary celebration of Methodism in 1839—a period prior to the sectional disputes which have divided the Methodist Episcopal Church, and which are yet too recent for a satisfactory judgment from history.

CONTENTS.

BOOK I.

INTRODUCTION.

CHAPTER I.

STANDPOINT OF METHODISM IN THE HISTORY OF CHRISTIANITY.

Page

Christianity is Spiritual Life.... 15

The Church its Organic Form.. 16

Standpoint of Methodism....... 16

Corruption of the Church....... 16

The Reformation incomplete.... 19

Literary and Moral Aspects of England prior to Methodism.. 21

Condition of the English Church 27

Popular Demoralization........ 27

Characteristics of Methodism... 30

CHAPTER II.

THE WESLEY FAMILY.

Providential Preparations....... 33

Susanna Wesley the Foundress of Methodism 34

Her Father, Dr. Annesley...... 35

Her Marriage — Beauty — Character.......................... 36

Bartholomew Westley......... 39

John Westley.................. 40

Samuel Wesley — Remarkable Illustrations of his Character... 43

Life in the Epworth Rectory.... 51

John Wesley's Escape from Fire 59

CHAPTER III.

JOHN AND CHARLES WESLEY.

John Wesley.................. 61

Extraordinary "Noises" at Epworth......................... 62

The Wesleys at School......... 64

The Duke of Wellington....... 65

Page

The Wesleys at Oxford......... 66

Religious Inquiries 66

Kempis — Taylor — Law........ 67

"Witness of the Spirit"....... 68

"Reprobation"—"Perfection". 69

The "Holy Club"............. 72

"Methodists"................. 72

George Whitefield 74

Dispersion of the Epworth Family.......................... 77

The Moravians................ 78

The Wesleys in Georgia........ 80

Return of the Wesleys......... 82

CHAPTER IV.

GEORGE WHITEFIELD.

Whitefield's Mental Conflicts... 86

His Conversion................ 87

Effects of his Preaching........ 88

His Eloquence................. 90

He embarks for Georgia 92

Returns to England............ 92

CHAPTER V.

WESLEY AND THE MORAVIANS.

Wesley Arrives in England.... 93

His Religious Disquiet........ 93

Obligations of Methodism to the Martyrs of Constance........ 94

Zisca and his Peasant Heroes.. 95

Herrnhut — Zinzendorf........ 97

Peter Bohler.................. 100

Conversion of the Wesleys..... 101

Wesley at Marienborn......... 105

Theological Views............ 106

Scenes at Herrnhut 106

Methodism and Moravianism.. 108

BOOK II.

ORIGIN AND PROGRESS OF METHODISM, 1739-1744.

CHAPTER I.

THE WESLEYS AND WHITEFIELD ITINERATING.

Page

Wesley returns from Germany 109
Charles Wesley ... 109
London "Societies" ... 110
The Wesleys preaching ... 111
Expelled from the Pulpits ... 113
Arrival of Whitefield ... 113
He preaches in the Open Air ... 114
Wesley follows his Example ... 116
Scenes at Kingswood ... 117
Methodism in Wales ... 118
Griffith Jones—Howell Harris. 118
Whitefield in Moorfields ... 121
Extraordinary Results of his Preaching ... 122
Wesley and Beau Nash ... 123
The first Methodist Chapel ... 124
The Wesleys in Moorfields ... 125
Physical Effects of Religious Excitement ... 126
Separation from the Moravians. 129
The Foundry opened ... 131
Epoch of Methodism ... 131

CHAPTER II.

THE WESLEYS ITINERATING IN ENGLAND—WHITEFIELD ITINERATING IN AMERICA.

Susanna Wesley ... 134
Commencement of the Lay Ministry ... 136
David Taylor—Mobs ... 136
Charles Wesley mobbed in Wales ... 140
Whitefield in America ... 141
Philadelphia—Princeton College—Boston ... 141
His triumphant Passage through the Colonies ... 143

CHAPTER III.

SEPARATION OF WHITEFIELD FROM WESLEY.

The Calvinistic Controversy ... 146
Character of Wesley's Mind ... 146

Page

Arminianism as defined at Dort 148
Intellectual Character of Whitefield ... 149
Historical Importance of their Disagreement ... 151
John Cennick ... 152
Wesley's Sermon on "Free Grace" ... 153
Attempts at Reconciliation ... 155
Methodism still a Unit ... 156

CHAPTER IV.

CALVINISTIC METHODISM.

Whitefield's Tabernacle opened 157
He employs Lay Preachers ... 157
Reconciled with Wesley ... 157
Goes to Scotland ... 158
Marvelous Scenes at Cambuslang 160
Methodism in Scotland ... 161
Whitefield again in Moorfields. 162
His greatest "Field-day" ... 162
Countess of Huntingdon ... 165
Whitefield preaching in her Mansion ... 167
Chesterfield, Bolingbroke, Walpole, Hume ... 167
Lady Huntingdon's Usefulness 168
Her College at Trevecca ... 169
Its first Student ... 169
Calvinistic Methodist Societies. 170

CHAPTER V.

TRAVELS AND LABORS OF THE WESLEYS FROM 1741 TO 1744.

Susanna Wesley ... 173
Thomas Maxfield ... 174
Wesley itinerating ... 175
Introduction of Class Meetings. 176
Sketch of John Nelson ... 176
Wesley at Newcastle ... 181
Preaches on his Father's Tomb 183
The General Rules ... 185
Their Catholicity ... 187
Physical Phenomena of Religious Excitement at Newcastle 187
Wesley examines them ... 187
Pronounces them Demoniacal .. 187
Charles Wesley ... 189

Page

Is mobbed at Walsal, Sheffield, and St. Ives 189
Wesley and Nelson in Cornwall 193
Terrible Mobs 194
Progress of Methodism 198

CHAPTER VI.

EVENTS OF 1744—THE FIRST WESLEYAN CONFERENCE.

Reports against Wesley 199
Mobs in Staffordshire 200
Chas. Wesley among the Rioters 200
John Wesley in Cornwall 203
Nelson's Power over Mobs 205
He is impressed as a Soldier ... 207
The Proto-martyr of Methodism 210
The first Conference 211
Its proceedings 212
Lady Huntingdon 214
Ministerial Education approved 214
Wesley's "Appeal to Men of Reason and Religion" 216

BOOK III.

PROGRESS OF METHODISM FROM THE CONFERENCE OF 1744 TO THE CONFERENCE OF 1750.

CHAPTER I.

FROM THE CONFERENCE OF 1744 TO THE CONFERENCE OF 1745.

Charles Wesley in Cornwall ... 219
Triumphs of Methodism 220
Wesley's last Appeal to Oxford 221
Winter Itinerancy 223
Preachers impressed and imprisoned 224
Wesley arrested — Mobbed 225
Nelson itinerating 227
Methodism in the Army 229
Evans, Haime, Bond, Staniforth 229
The Battle of Fontenoy 225
Scenes on the Battle-field 235

CHAPTER II.

FROM THE CONFERENCE OF 1745 TO THE CONFERENCE OF 1750.

The Scotch Rebellion 242
Wesley abroad amid the public Alarm 243
Second part of his "Appeal" ... 244
Extensive Results of Methodism 244
Its doctrinal Liberality 244
The Wesleys itinerating 246
Thompson of St. Gennis 247
Nelson's Perils from the Mob .. 249
Vincent Perronet 257
Grimshaw's extraordinary History 258
He is mobbed with Wesley at Roughlee 261
Riot at Devizes 264
The Wesleys in Middle Life ... 266
Charles Wesley's Marriage 269
John Wesley and Grace Murray 270

CHAPTER III.

INTRODUCTION OF METHODISM INTO IRELAND.

Religious Problem of Irish History 271
Wesley comprehends it 271
Bishop Berkeley 272
Wesley arrives in Dublin 273
His Views of Irish Character ... 274
Charles Wesley in Ireland 274
Mobs and Murders in Dublin .. 275
"Swaddlers" 275
Power of Methodist Music 277
Riots at Cork 281
Charles Wesley indicted as a Vagabond 282
Success of Methodism 283
Singular Conversions 284
John Smith at Glenarm 285
A Military Veteran defending the Methodists 286
John M'Burney mobbed 286
He is martyred 287
Hard Fare of the Preachers 287
Robert Swindells 287
Sketch of Thomas Walsh 288
His Learning 288
His Labors 292
He is mobbed and imprisoned. 293
Illustrations of his Usefulness .. 295

CHAPTER IV.

LABORS OF THE CALVINISTIC METHODISTS FROM 1744 TO 1750.

Page
Whitefield's third American visit... 298
"Testimonies" against him... 299
The Cape Breton Expedition... 299
His Reception in Philadelphia.. 300
Singular Interest in Virginia... 300
He goes to Bermuda... 302
Howell Harris in Wales... 303
Lady Huntingdon in Wales.... 304
John Newton and Whitefield.. 305
Whitefield in England and Scotland... 305
Remarkable Conversions... 305
Bishop Lavington's Attacks... 306
Charles Wesley and Whitefield preaching amid the Alarms of Earthquakes in London... 308

CHAPTER V.

DEVELOPMENT OF METHODIST OPINIONS AND ECONOMY IN THE CONFERENCES FROM 1744 TO 1750.

The Conference of 1745... 310
Theological Discussions... 310
Witness of the Spirit... 311
Sanctification... 311
Page
Terrible Preaching... 311
Church Government... 312
Wesley's High-Church Views.. 314
He designed not to form a Sect 314
Session of 1746... 315
Laymen present... 315
Progress of Opinion... 315
Necessity of the Lay Ministry declared... 316
Its Divine Right acknowledged 317
Ordination anticipated... 317
Exhorters recognized... 318
Importance of Local Preachers. 318
First List of Circuits... 318
Session of 1747... 319
Free Discussion... 319
Relation of Faith to Assurance. 320
Cautions respecting Sanctification... 321
What is a Church?... 322
Divine Right of Episcopacy denied... 322
Session of 1748... 323
Formation of Societies renewed 324
Session of 1749... 325
Scheme of Union... 325
"Assistants"—"Helpers".... 325
Quarterly Meetings... 326
Book Circulation... 326
Extraordinary Results of the first Decade of Methodism... 326

BOOK IV.

PROGRESS OF METHODISM FROM 1750 TO THE DEATH OF WHITEFIELD IN 1770.

CHAPTER I.

METHODISM IN IRELAND.

Wesley again in Ireland... 329
Death of John Jane... 330
Progress of Methodism... 330
Remarkable German Colony... 332
It gives Birth to American Methodism... 333
Methodism in the Army... 333
Duncan Wright, a Military Preacher... 334
A Military Execution... 335
A Converted Surgeon... 336
Thomas Walsh... 337
His Labors... 337
His extraordinary Piety... 338
His Sickness... 340
His Mental Trouble in Death.. 341
Fletcher of Madeley... 342

CHAPTER II.

METHODISM IN ENGLAND AND SCOTLAND FROM 1750 TO 1760.

Success in Cornwall... 343
Wesley in Scotland... 345
His slight Success there... 346
State of the English Societies.. 347
Nathaniel Gilbert and Methodism in the West Indies... 351

Page
The first African Methodist.... 351
Happy Deaths of Methodists... 351
Wheatley's Defection......... 352
Bennet's Secession........... 352
Baptist Proselytism........... 353
Grace Murray................. 353
Wesley and the Calvinists..... 354
He administers the Lord's Supper to their Leaders at Lady Huntingdon's House........ 354
The Trials of Thomas Lee..... 355
Christopher Hopper........... 360
His Labors and Trials........ 362
Cownley Mobbed............. 363
The Parson and the Quaker... 363
Charles Wesley ceases to itinerate........................ 364
Death of Meriton............. 365
Fletcher joins the Methodists.. 365
Review of Success............ 367
Wesley's desire for Rest....... 368
His unfortunate Marriage...... 369
His Sickness and Epitaph...... 371
His Notes on the New Testament........................ 372
James Hervey............... 372
Wesley's Address to the Clergy 373
His views of Ministerial Qualifications...................... 373

CHAPTER III.

CALVINISTIC AND MORAVIAN METHODISM FROM 1750 TO 1760.

Whitefield "ranging"......... 375
His Good-Humor—His Health 376
His Relations with Wesley.... 378
Whitefield again in America... 379
His Visit to Ireland.......... 380
Is mobbed at Dublin.......... 381
Eminent Methodist Churchmen 382
Sketch of Berridge........... 382
Great Excitement at Everton... 383
Remarkable Conversion....... 383
Sketch of Romaine............ 385
Madan's singular Conversion.. 387
Venn........................ 388
Moravian Methodism.......... 389
Sandemanianism.............. 391
Ingham's Success and Failure. 392
Death of Lady Ingham........ 393
Ingham's Death and Character. 393

CHAPTER IV.

DEVELOPMENT OF METHODIST OPINIONS AND ECONOMY IN THE CONFERENCES FROM 1750 TO 1760.

Failure of Records............ 394
Salary of Preachers........... 395
Page
Prominent Preachers secede... 395
Tendency to Dissent.......... 396
The Perronets................ 396
Charles Wesley's High-Church Prejudices.................. 396
Critical Importance of the Session of 1755................ 397
Question of Separation from the Church.................... 397
Concession of the Preachers... 398
Was Dissent expedient?....... 399
Wesley's Twelve Reasons against it.................. 399
Wesley as a Reformer......... 400
His Opinion of John Knox..... 400
Wesley not an Anarchist...... 400
Historical Importance of his Conservatism............. 401
His Opinions at this Time..... 401
Subsequent Sessions.......... 401
Conference Examination of Characters introduced...... 401

CHAPTER V.

METHODISM FROM 1760 TO 1770.

Great Revivals............... 402
Sanctification............... 403
Writers upon it.............. 405
George Bell's Delusions....... 407
Maxfield's Separation from Wesley...................... 407
The End of the World......... 408
George Story................. 408
Fate of Bell and Maxfield..... 409
Wesley's large Congregations.. 410
Christopher Hopper........... 410
Cudworth's Letters of Hervey.. 411
Sketch of Thomas Taylor...... 411
His Adventures at Glasgow.... 413
Wright among the Highlanders 418
Dissent among Wesley's Societies........................ 418
Death of Grimshaw........... 419
Death of John Manners....... 420
Death of the oldest Lay Preacher.................... 420
Wesley and Warburton........ 421
Fletcher's Trials at Madeley... 422
His great Piety and Success.... 424
Condition of Methodism in 1770 426
Its Introduction into America.. 427
Barbara Heck—Philip Embury 427
Wesley's regard for Military Men........................ 427
Recommends Methodists to learn the Military Exercise... 428
Offers to raise Troops for the Government................ 428
Captain Webb................ 428

CHAPTER VI.

DEVELOPMENT OF METHODIST OPINIONS AND ECONOMY IN THE CONFERENCES FROM 1760 TO 1770.

Page
Minutes of Conferences........ 430
The Greek Bishop, Erasmus... 431
Union of Evangelical Clergy... 432
They decline Wesley's Terms. 433
First Census of Methodism.... 434
First Temperance Societies.... 434
Debt of the Connection....... 435
Wesley's View of his Authority 435
Preachers required to study... 436
Conference of 1767............ 436
Calvinists and Laymen present 436
Circulation of Books.......... 437
Term of Circuit Appointments.. 438
Secular Business of Preachers.. 438
John Nelson — William Shent. 438
Field Preaching — Early Rising 440
Sanctification................. 440
Preachers sent to America..... 441
Provisions for Preachers' Wives 442
Perpetuation of the Lay Ministry........................ 442
Conference of 1770............ 442
Statistics..................... 442
Preachers Families............ 443
Minute on Calvinism.......... 443
Its Historical Importance... 444

CHAPTER VII.

CALVINISTIC METHODISM FROM 1760 TO 1770.

Page
The Calvinistic Societies...... 445
Lady Huntingdon in Yorkshire 446
Attends Wesley's Conference.. 446
Venn, Grimshaw, Fletcher.... 447
Sketch of Captain Scott....... 448
Adventures of Captain Joss... 450
Scenes at Cheltenham......... 453
Lord Dartmouth — Dartmouth College.................... 454
Alliance of the Arminian and Calvinistic Leaders......... 456
Trevecca College............. 456
Expulsion of Oxford Students.. 457
Extraordinary Scenes at Trevecca...................... 458
Whitefield's declining Health.. 459
He again visits America....... 460
Returns to England........... 461
Personal Habits............... 461
Last Interviews with Wesley.. 463
Last Voyage to America...... 464
His Orphan House............ 464
Happy religious Frame........ 464
Excursion up the Hudson..... 465
Last Sermon and Death....... 466
His Eloquence and Character.. 468
Results of his Labors......... 475
Calvinistic Methodists......... 476

HISTORY OF METHODISM.

BOOK I.

INTRODUCTION.

CHAPTER I.

STANDPOINT OF METHODISM IN THE HISTORY OF CHRISTIANITY.

Christianity is Spiritual Life — The Church an Organic Form of this Life — The Philosophical Standpoint of the History of Methodism — Process of Corruption in the Early Church — The Reformation incomplete — Condition of the English Church prior to Methodism — Literary and Moral Aspects of England — Popular Degradation — Characteristics of Methodism.

HAD a studious heathen sought to ascertain the nature of the Christian religion, immediately after the completion of its canonical records, and solely from those records, he would have been surprised by its contrast with nearly all prior religious systems, in its suggestion rather than prescription of ecclesiastical arrangements, its general abstinence from ritual forms, and its total abstinence from dogmatic definitions. He would have discovered what modern Protestantism, emancipated from traditional influence, has found, that the purification of the individual man, pursued in his individual freedom, and on the responsibility of his individual conscience, was the characteristic design of Christianity — rites and creeds, as aids to faith, being left discretionary, however necessary.

Christianity is spiritual life. "The words that I speak unto you," said its Founder, "they are spirit, and they are life;"[1] and he declared the distinctive character of the new dispensation, when at the well of Sychar he said: "Believe me, the hour cometh, when ye shall neither in this mountain, nor yet at Jerusalem, worship the Father. The hour cometh, and now is, when the true worshipers shall worship the Father in spirit and in truth; for the Father seeketh such to worship him. God is a Spirit: and they that worship him must worship him in spirit and in truth."[2]

A development of Judaism, which was characterized above all other religions of antiquity by ritual forms and penal morals, Christianity, nevertheless, quickly distinguished itself by the simplicity of its ceremonies and the mild purity of its ethics, subordinating both to the interior moral life which it taught as "the regeneration,"[3] the "life of God" in the soul of man.[4]

A true Christian Church is a collective or organic form of this spiritual life; its external institutions, whether in doctrinal symbols, or modes of worship or government, are valuable only so far as they can be means to this end. And therefore any new practical measures which may be rendered expedient, by the ever-varying conditions of human history, for the effectiveness of the Church in the moral regeneration of individual men, are admissible, being in harmony with the original purpose and simplicity of the Gospel, however they may contravene ecclesiastical precedents or traditions.

Such is the standpoint which Methodism takes in the history of the Church; and such the only standpoint from which its own history can be interpreted. Throughout the extraordinary series of events which we are about to narrate from its annals, we shall find continually this recurrence to the first principles of Christianity. This is the philosophy of its history.

Ecclesiastical history records how Christianity came to lose its original spiritual simplicity, and to grow into a gigantic system of ecclesiasticism and ritualism, which was more symbolic than Judaism itself, and under the shadow

[1] John vi, 63. [2] John iv, 21, 23, 24. [3] Matt. xix, 28. [4] Eph. iv, 18.

of which personal spiritual life, and even the popular morals, withered, and seemed really, if not avowedly, superseded by Church rites.

The apostles, while yet observing some of the Judaic rites for the sake of expediency, wrote against them, nevertheless, as void under the new dispensation.[5]

In planting Christianity they adopted such forms as were found most convenient to their hands in the religious customs of their countrymen; but it is remarkable that scarcely one feature of their ecclesiastical system, if such it can be called, was borrowed from the divinely prescribed forms of the Levitical institute.

For generations the primitive Christians had no temples, but worshiped, with familiar simplicity, in private houses, or in the synagogues of converted Jews which were scattered over the Roman empire. The synagogue, unmentioned, not to say unenjoined, in the writings of Moses, afforded them also most of those simple rites and offices which afterward became technicalized and dignified into essential and even sacramental importance. When the distribution of the charities of the Church became too laborious for the apostles, they copied from the synagogue the office of Deacon. The older servants of the Church, having oversight of its Deacons and general interests, were called Elders, (Presbyters,) a title borrowed from the head of the Jewish "tribe" and the members of the Sanhedrim. The designation of these men to their offices was made by imposition of hands, a decency, but not a sacrament, derived also from the Jews, who used it in the inauguration of their municipal and provincial officers, but never in the consecration of their priests. But how soon these simple offices became essential orders, awful with divine authority, and mysterious with divine virtue! How, for more than fifteen hundred years, have controversies respecting their distinctions and prerogatives agitated Christendom! How has the simple form of the imposition of hands become the divine rite of Ordination, a sacramental

[5] Compare Acts xv, 7-31; xvi, 3; xxi, 20-26; Col. ii, 20-23.

mystery, with its fabulous but disastrous consequence of the Apostolic Succession, leading to the exclusion of the purest bodies of Christian men, who could not verify their claims to it, from the charities of the Church, and to the general perversion of Christianity by priestly and prelatical pretensions! The offices of Deacon and Elder became fundamental and unchangeable; the Elder, presiding in the assembly of his peers, as the ruler of the synagogue presided in the college of Elders,[6] became Bishop, but very different from the Scriptural "superintendent;" the Bishop became Archbishop, the Archbishop, Pope or Patriarch; the two Sacraments became seven;—the confessional and penance; the monastic life, asceticism, celibacy, and virginity; the idolatry of the host, and the worship of saints; extreme unction, purgatory, infallibility, and dogmatic symbols; the supererogative merit of works, canonization, persecution, and the inquisition,—these, with the priestly assumption of civil authority, the loss of ancient civilization, and the general degradation of the masses, make up most of the subsequent history of the Church down to the period in which the Reformation uttered its appeal back to the apostolic age.[7]

During all these ages of corruption, however, the spiritual Church existed, represented in the persons of devout men, who walked with God amid the night of error, sufferers from the evils of their times, unable to explain or to break away from them, but seeking, in their monastic cells, or in the walks of ordinary life, that purification and peace which are received only by faith; and the ecclesiastical historian finds grateful relief, as he gropes through the Dark Ages, in being able continually to point to these scattered lights which, like the lamps in Roman tombs, gleamed faintly but perennially amid the moral death of the visible

[6] As *primus inter pares.*—Vitringa, De Vet. Syn., lib. iii, cap. 16.

[7] On the origin and changes of Church government, I have followed Archbishop Stillingfleet, Irenicum; Lord King, Primitive Church; Neander, History of the Christian Religion, etc.; Archbishop Whately, Kingdom of Christ, and especially Vitringa, De Synagoga Vetere.

Church. Obscure communities also, as the Cathari of the Novatians, the Paulicians, the Albigenses, and the Waldenses, maintained the ancient faith in comparative purity, from the beginning of the fourth century down to the Reformation.

In the year 1510 an Augustinian monk walked, with desolate heart, the streets of Rome, and turning away from the pomp of her churches and the corruptions of the Vatican, sought relief to his awakened soul by ascending, on his knees, with peasants and beggars, the staircase of Pilate, which was supposed to have been trodden by Christ at his trial, and is now inclosed near the Lateran palace. While pausing on the successive steps to weep and pray, a voice from heaven seemed to cry within him, "The just shall live by faith." It was the voice of apostolic Christianity, and the announcement of the Reformation. He flew from the superstitious scene. Seven years later, the same monk nailed on the gate of the church at Wittenberg the *Theses* which introduced the Reformation. They were as trumpet blasts echoing from the Hebrides to the Calabrias, and summoning Europe to a moral resurrection.

But though the doctrine of "Justification by Faith" was thus the dogmatic germ of the Reformation, that great revolution took chiefly an ecclesiastical direction, and became more an attempt to overthrow the organic system of popery, by the reassertion of certain apostolic doctrines, than an evangelical revival of the spiritual life of the Church; hence its early loss of moral power. All Western Europe felt its first motions; but hardly forty years had passed when it reached its furthest conquests, and began its retreats. During most of the eighteenth century it could have propagated its doctrines with but little restraint in the greater part of Europe, but it had not internal energy enough to do so. Dealing ostensibly with the historical pretensions of the Church, it introduced at last the "Historical Criticism" which, notwithstanding its inestimable advantages to Biblical exegesis, degenerated, under the English deistical writings that entered Germany about the epoch of Methodism, into Rationalism, and subverted both the spiritual life and the doctrinal orthodoxy of the continental Protestant churches, and, to a great extent, substituted infidelity for the displaced popery. Besides this tendency, the Lutheran Reformation retained many papal errors, in its doctrines of the sacraments, and of the priestly offices, and erred, above all, in leaving the Church subject to the state. It did not sufficiently restore the spirituality and simplicity of the apostolic Church, and our own age witnesses the spectacle of a High-Church reaction in Germany, in which some of her most distinguished Christian scholars attempt to correct the excesses of Rationalism by an appeal, not so much to the apostolic Church as to the ante-Nicene traditions. A Puseyism as thorough as that which flourishes under the papal attributes of the Anglican Establishment, prevails in the strongholds of the German Reformation.[8]

In like manner was the English Reformation incomplete. Not only did it retain many papal errors in doctrine, especially respecting the sacraments, the priestly offices, the hierarchal constitution of the Church, and its relation to the state, but by these very errors it failed to restore adequately the primitive idea of Christianity, as "the kingdom of God within you." Hence its frequent lapses toward popery. Hardly had it been established under Henry VIII., and nourished under the brief reign of Edward VI., than it fell away under Mary, and its noblest champions, Cranmer, Latimer, Hooper, and Ridley, perished at the stake. Elizabeth restored it, but Charles I. again favored its papal tendencies. His queen was a papist. Archbishop Laud restored pictures to the churches, and embroiled the kingdom with controversies respecting copes, genuflexions, and the position of the "altar." The Court of High Commission displaced devout clergymen for not observing petty ceremonies.

[8] The evangelical world has been scandalized to find so eminent an opponent of Rationalism as Hengstenberg, leading the High-Church reaction. With him are associated such men as Stahl, Leo, and Gerlack.

After the great Rebellion, Charles II. did what he could to favor the Papists, and died one himself.[9] His brother, James II., devoted his whole reign to the restoration of Popery. The Revolution, with the accession of the Prince of Orange to the throne, alone put an end to these Papal efforts of the acknowledged "head" of the British Church, and even then many of its most influential incumbents refused to recognize the title of the new Protestant king; the Archbishop of Canterbury, with several bishops, and fourteen hundred clergymen, sacrificed their offices rather than take the oath of allegiance to him. So far was the divine right of prelacy still kindred with the divine right of royalty.

During all these Papal struggles primitive ideas of Christianity and the Church were more or less active among the people. Even before the reign of Elizabeth much popular discontent prevailed with the but partial purification of the Church from Papal errors. Her Act of Uniformity threw multitudes out of its pale, and Puritanism began its work of reformation and honest rebellion. But Puritanism, with all its virtues, had profound and inexorable vices. It early created a High-Churchism of its own, and claimed a higher Scriptural authority for Presbyterianism than the English reformers, or its great Episcopal antagonists, Sewell, Whitgift, Hooker, and others, asserted for prelacy itself.[10] The vigor of its Commonwealth has illustrated the name of England in the history of the world; but its reaction under the Restoration spread over the country as great, if not greater demoralization than had preceded it under the Papal reigns. The court became a royal brothel. The play-house became the temple of England. The drama of the day could not now be exhibited, nor even privately read without blushes. Many of the most learned and devoted clergymen, whose writings are imperishable in our religious literature, were either silenced or displaced. The

[9] Macaulay's History of England, vol. i, chap. 4.
[10] See Art. on Hooker, North British Review, 1857.

ministrations of the Church grew formal and ineffective; the Puritan Churches themselves at last fell into general decay, while the masses of the people sunk into incredible vice and brutality. A living English writer, himself a Churchman, has declared that England had lapsed into virtual heathenism, when Wesley appeared.[11]

The literature of the eighteenth century, particularly of its earlier part, is an important index to the moral character of that period. It presents a brilliant catalogue of names, among which are Addison, Steele, Berkeley, Swift, Pope, Congreve, Gray, Parnell, Young, Thomson, Rowe, Goldsmith, and Johnson, besides a splendid array in the more profound departments of knowledge. The reader may easily conceive what must have been the moral aspects of English society, when the loose wit of Congreve was the attraction of the British theater, and, as Dryden declared, "the only prop of the declining stage;" or what the respect of the people for the Church when, among the clergy, could be found men like Swift and Sterne to regale the gross taste of the age with ribald burlesque and licentious humor. And what were the popular fictions of the day? Richardson gave way before Smollett and Fielding. The latter obtained a renown which renders them still familiar; while Richardson, whom Johnson deemed "as superior to them in talents as in virtue," is barely remembered. The works of these and similar authors were the parlor-table books of the age; while on the same table lay also the erotic poets of antiquity, translated by the wits of the period, with Dryden at their head, dedicated to the first ladies of the court, and teeming with the pruriency which pervades the polite writings of that and the preceding age. Dryden died at the beginning of the century, and his works, as full of vice as of genius, were in general vogue.

The infidel works of Hobbes, Tindal, Collins, Shaftesbury, and Chubb were in full circulation, and were re-enforced by the appearance of the three greatest giants in the cause of

[11] Isaac Taylor: Wesley and Methodism.

skeptical error which modern times have produced—Bolingbroke, Hume, and Gibbon. The first was influential by his political eminence, and by the adornments which the harmonious verse of Pope gave to his opinions; the second by all the arts of insinuation, and by a style which, says Sir J. Mackintosh, "was more lively, more easy, more ingratiating, and, if the word may be so applied, more amusing than that of any other metaphysical writer;" and the last by weaving his infidel sentiments into one of the greatest works of the human intellect, a production as corrupt in its religious tendency as it is magnificent in its execution. The intelligent reader need not be reminded that the same class of writers had triumphed, and were at this time in full prevalence across the channel. The Encyclopedists had attempted the design of eradicating from the circle of the sciences every trace of Christian truth; and the polite writers of France, headed by Voltaire and Rousseau, had decked the corrupt doctrines of the day with the attractions of eloquence and poetry, humor and satire, until they swept over the nation like a sirocco, withering not only the sentiments of religion, but the instincts of humanity, and subverting at last, in common ruin, the altar, the throne, and the moral protections of domestic life. Notwithstanding the inveterate antipathies which existed between the two nations, the contagion of French opinions, both in religion and politics, infected England seriously during most of the eighteenth century. The continental infidelity had in fact sprung from the English deism, and naturally reacted upon it.

It is worthy of remark, that one of the most interesting departments of the English literature of the last century owes its birth to the alarm which the better-disposed literary men of the age took at the general declension of manners and morals, and their attempt to check it. The *British Essayists* are technically distinguished in our literature. They form a department which has become classical. They have been reprinted more extensively than any other books in our language, except the Scriptures and a few of our most popular fictions. Some of the brightest names in the catalogue of English writers owe much of their fame to these works; among them may be mentioned Steele, Addison, Berkeley, and Johnson. They were conducted as ephemeral sheets, and issued twice or thrice a week, with brief articles, which discussed the follies and vices of the times. Their character was generally humorous or sarcastic; occasionally they contained a sober rebuke of the irreligion of the day.

The first in the list is the Tattler, projected by Steele, and to which Addison was a frequent contributor. It was almost exclusively confined to the superficial defects of society, and is the best picture extant of the domestic, moral, and literary condition of the early part of that century. The Spectator, conducted jointly by Addison and Steele, followed the Tattler, and is still one of the most popular works of our language. Next appeared the Guardian, projected by Steele, and aided by Addison, Pope, and Berkeley. A long list of miscellaneous writers of the same class followed, who have not been placed, by public opinion, in the rank of the classical essayists. Dr. Johnson, in his Rambler, restored the periodical essay to its first dignity, and gave it a still higher moral tone.

Though these writers aimed, at first, more at the correction of the follies than the sins of the times, they grew serious as they grew important. It is curious to observe their increasing severity as they obtained authority by time and popularity. Steele, from a long and various study of the world, painted, with minute accuracy, its absurdities. Addison, with a style the most pure, and a humor mild and elegant, attempted to correct the literary taste of the day, and to shed the radiance of genius on the despised virtues of Christianity. He rescued Milton from the neglect which the sublime religious character of his great epic had incurred for him from the degenerate age. Pope satirized, in some admirable critiques, the literary follies of the times.

Berkeley attacked, with his clear logic and finished style, the skeptical opinions which were then prevalent; most of his articles are on "Free-thinking;" Johnson, "the great moralist," stood up a giant to battle, with both hands, against all error and irreligion, whether in high places or low places.

These writings exerted an influence upon the tastes and morals of the age; but it was comparatively superficial. Gay, who was contemporary with Addison and Steele, says it was incredible to conceive the effect they had on the town; how many thousand follies they had either quite banished or given a very great check to; how much countenance they had added to virtue and religion. Hannah More has devoted a chapter in her Education of a Princess to this interesting portion of our literature. She speaks in the highest terms of Addison's influence, and confirms these statements respecting the moral condition of the age: "At a period when religion," she says, "was held in more than usual contempt, from its having been recently abused to the worst purposes, and when the higher walks of life exhibited that dissoluteness which the profligate reign of the second Charles made so deplorably fashionable, Addison seems to have been raised up by Providence for the double purpose of improving the public taste and correcting the public morals. As the powers of imagination had, in the preceding age, been peculiarly abused to the purposes of vice, it was Addison's great object to show that vice and impurity have no necessary connection with genius. He not only evinced this by his reasonings, but he so exemplified it by his own compositions as to become, in a short time, more generally useful, by becoming more popular, than any writer who had yet appeared. This well-earned celebrity he endeavored to turn to the best of all purposes; and his success was such as to prove that genius is never so advantageously employed as in the service of virtue; no influence so well directed as in rendering piety fashionable."

But while these writers were commendable for the elevated purpose which they proposed, a purpose noble as it was novel among what are called polite authors, their influence was comparatively ineffective; it was infinitely short of what was necessary; it was moral, but not religious. It was on the side of Christianity, but had nothing to do with those great evangelical truths which are the vital elements of Christianity, and in which inheres its renovating energy. It is the diffusion of these truths among the popular mass that alone can effect any general moral elevation of men. It was reserved for the agency of Methodism to revive and spread them, with a transforming efficacy, through the British empire and much of the civilized world. Reference has been made to these authors, therefore, only as instances of the conviction felt by the better-disposed literary leaders of the day, that some new check was necessary to stop the overwhelming progress of corruption. The pictures of vice which they exhibit, and the manner in which they attempt the necessary reform, show that society was not only deplorably wicked, but that adequate means of its recovery were not understood by those who lamented its evils.

Natural religion was the favorite study of the clergy, and of the learned generally, and included most of their theology. Collins and Tindal had denounced Christianity as priestcraft; Whiston pronounced the miracles to be Jewish impositions; Woolston declared them to be allegories; and the next year after the recognized date of Methodism, Edelmann[12] and Reimarus introduced the English deism into Germany, and thus founded the Rationalism which, as developed by her "Historical" or "Negative Criticism," has nearly extinguished her religious life. The decayed state of the English Church, in which Methodism was about to have its birth, was, in fine, the cause, direct or indirect, of most of the infidelity of the age, both at home and abroad.

[12] Edelmann's "Moses mit Aufgedecktem Angesicht," was published in 1740. Art. *Criticism*, Herzog's Encyclopedia translated by Bomberger. Philadelphia, 1858.

Arianism and Socinianism, taught by such men as Clarke, Priestley, and Whiston, had become fashionable among the best English thinkers. Some of the brightest names of the times can be quoted as exceptions to these remarks; but such was the general condition of religion in England. The higher classes laughed at piety, and prided themselves on being above what they called its fanaticism; the lower classes were grossly ignorant, and abandoned to vice, while the Church, enervated by a universal decline, was unable longer to give countenance to the downfallen cause of truth.

This general decline had reached its extremity when Wesley and his coadjutors appeared. "It was," to use his own words, "just at the time when we wanted little of filling up the measure of our iniquities, that two or three clergymen of the Church of England began vehemently to call sinners to repentance."[13] His own testimony to the irreligion of the times is emphatic. "What," he asks, "is the present characteristic of the English nation? It is ungodliness. Ungodliness is our universal, our constant, our peculiar character."

From the Restoration down to the origin of Methodism, Churchmen and Nonconformists bear concurrent, and in some instances startling testimony respecting the decayed condition of religion and morals. The pathetic lamentation of Bishop Burnet, on the state of the Church, has often been quoted: "I am now," he says, "in the seventieth year of my age; and as I cannot speak long in the world in any sort, so I cannot hope for a more solemn occasion than this of speaking with all due freedom, both to the present and to the succeeding ages. Therefore I lay hold on it, to give a free vent to those sad thoughts that lie on my mind both day and night, and are the subject of many secret mournings." He proceeds to say: "I cannot look on without the deepest concern, when I see the imminent ruin hanging over this Church, and, by consequence, over the whole Reformation. The outward state of things is black enough, God

[13] Appeal to Men of Reason and Religion, Part III. Works, vol. v.

knows; but that which heightens my fears rises chiefly from the inward state into which we are unhappily fallen." Referring to the condition of the clergy, he says: "Our ember-weeks are the burden and grief of my life. The much greater part of those who come to be ordained are ignorant to a degree not to be apprehended by those who are not obliged to know it. The easiest part of knowledge is that to which they are the greatest strangers. Those who have read some few books, yet never seem to have read the Scriptures. Many cannot give a tolerable account even of the Catechism itself, how short and plain soever. This does often tear my heart. The case is not much better in many who, having got into orders, come for institution, and cannot make it appear that they have read the Scriptures, or any one good book, since they were ordained; so that the small measure of knowledge upon which they got into holy orders not being improved, is in a way to be quite lost; and then they think it a great hardship if they are told they must know the Scriptures and the body of divinity better before they can be trusted with the care of souls."[14]

Watts declares that there was "a general decay of vital religion in the hearts and lives of men;" that "this declen sion of piety and virtue" was common among Dissenters and Churchmen; that it was "a general matter of mournful observation among all who lay the cause of God to heart;" and he called upon "every one to use all possible efforts for *the recovery of dying religion in the world*."[15] Another writer asserts that "the Spirit of God has so far departed from the nation, that hereby almost all vital religion is lost out of the world."[16] Another says: "The present modish turn of religion looks as if we had no need of a Mediator, but that all our concerns with God were managed with him as an absolute God. The religion of nature makes up the darling topics of our age; and the religion of Jesus is valued only for the sake of that, and only so far as it carries on the

[14] Pastoral Care. [15] Preface to his Humble Attempt, etc.
[16] Hurrion's Sermons on the Holy Spirit.

light of nature, and is a bare improvement of that kind of light. All that is restrictively Christian, or that is peculiar to Christ (everything concerning him that has not its apparent foundation in natural light, or that goes beyond its principles) is waived, and banished, and despised."[17]

Archbishop Secker says: "In this we cannot be mistaken, that an open and professed disregard is become, through a variety of unhappy causes, the distinguishing character of the present age." "Such," he declares, "are the dissoluteness and contempt of principle in the higher part of the world, and the profligacy, intemperance, and fearlessness of committing crimes, in the lower, as must, if this torrent of impiety stop not, become absolutely fatal." He further asserts that "Christianity is ridiculed and railed at with very little reserve, and the teachers of it without any at all;"[18] and this testimony was made but one year before that which is commemorated as the epoch of Methodism. About the same time Butler published his great work on the Analogy between Religion and the Constitution and Course of Nature, as a check to the infidelity of the age. In his preface he gives a deplorable description of the religious world. He concurs with the preceding authorities in representing it as in the very extremity of decline. "It has come," he says, "to be taken for granted that Christianity is no longer a subject of inquiry; but that it is now at length discovered to be fictitious. And accordingly it is treated as if, in the present age, this were an agreed point among all persons of discernment, and nothing remained but to set it up as a principal subject for mirth and ridicule."

Southey says: "The clergy had lost that authority which may always command at least the appearance of respect; and they had lost that respect also by which the place of authority may sometimes so much more worthily be supplied. In the great majority of the clergy zeal was wanting. The excellent Leighton spoke of the Church as a fair carcass without a spirit. Burnet observes that, in his time, our

[17] Dr. Guise's Sermons at Coward's Lecture. [18] Eight Charges.

clergy had less authority, and were under more contempt, than those of any other Church in all Europe; for they were much the most remiss in their labors, and the least severe in their lives. It was not that their lives were scandalous; he entirely acquitted them of any such imputation; but they were not exemplary, as it became them to be; and in the sincerity of a pious and reflecting mind, he pronounced that they would never regain the influence they had lost till they lived better and labored more."[19]

A scarcely less prejudiced writer on Methodism admits that when Wesley appeared the Anglican Church was "an ecclesiastical system under which the people of England had lapsed into heathenism, or a state hardly to be distinguished from it;" and that Methodism "preserved from extinction and reanimated the languishing Nonconformity of the last century, which, just at the time of the Methodistic revival, was rapidly in course to be found nowhere but in books."[20]

Such was the moral condition of England when Methodism came forth from the gates of Oxford, not to revive the ecclesiastical questions over which Churchmen and Puritans had fought and exhausted each other, nor even to appeal to the Reformation, with its incomplete corrections of popery, but to recall the masses to their Bibles, which said so little about those questions, but which declared that "the kingdom of God cometh not with observation;" that it "is not meat and drink, but righteousness, peace, and joy in the Holy Ghost." Acknowledging the importance of sound doctrine, it nevertheless dealt mostly in the theology which relates to the spiritual life—Faith, Justification, Regeneration, Sanctification, and the Witness of the Spirit; these were its great ideas, and never, since the apostolic age, were they brought out more clearly. Wesley formed no creed for the English Methodists, and though some of his own writings are recognized in his chapel deeds, and by the civil courts, as the standard of Methodist doctrine, yet from their number and the great variety of subjects treated in them, a rigorous

[19] Life of Wesley, ch. 9. [20] Taylor's Wesley and Methodism, pp. 56, 59.

system of interpretation has become impossible. In providing an organization for Methodism in the New World, where it was destined to have its chief range, he so abridged the Articles of the Church of England as to exclude the most formidable of modern theological controversies, and make it possible for Calvinists, alike with Arminians, to enter its communion; he prescribed no mode of baptism, but virtually recognized all modes; and it has been doubted, incautiously perhaps, whether even a Restorationist or Universalist, if exemplary in life, could be adjudged a heretic by its creed.

Methodism reversed, in fine, the usual policy of religious sects, who seek to sustain their spiritual life by their orthodoxy; it has sustained its orthodoxy by devoting its chief care to its spiritual life, and for more than a century has had no serious outbreaks of heresy, notwithstanding the masses of untrained minds, gathered within its pale, and the general lack of preparatory education among its clergy. No other modern religious body affords a parallel to it in this respect.

Admitting the absolute necessity of Church economics, it would not admit that they were in any particular form fundamental, but that the kind and degree of moral life possessed by any body of men claiming to be a Church, constituted the proof or refutation of that claim. It admitted the Scriptural example, but not the Scriptural obligation of two orders in the ministry. It adopted but one as expedient in its English Conference, while it provided both for America. It admitted the Scriptural example of ordination by the imposition of hands, but waived it in England for the sake of peace with the National Church, and ordained its ministry simply with prayer and exhortation, until within a few years, when it was adopted, not as necessary, but as appropriate. It pretended to no Episcopal form of organization in England, but provided one for America—a Presbyterian Episcopacy—Wesley, a Presbyter, ordaining a bishop, and thus practically denying High Churchism. It founded a lay ministry of Traveling Preachers, Local Preachers, and Exhorters. It adopted the Band-meeting, the Class-meeting, the ancient Agape or Love-feast. It was, in fine, a system of vital doctrines and practical expedients—a breaking away from all old dead-weights which had encumbered the march of the Reformation—a revival Church in its spirit, a missionary Church in its organization.

Such is the standpoint of Methodism in the history of the Church; and, thus considered, its historians do not, perhaps, claim too much when, with the suggestive writer who has attempted to give us its rationale, they insist that "the Methodism of the last century, even when considered apart from its consequences, must always be thought worthy of the most serious regard; that, in fact, that great religious movement has, immediately or remotely, so given an impulse to Christian feeling and profession, on all sides, that it has come to present itself as the starting-point of our modern religious history; that the field-preaching of Wesley and Whitefield, in 1739, was *the event whence the religious epoch, now current, must date its commencement;* that back to the events of that time must we look, necessarily, as often as we seek to trace to its source what is most characteristic of the present time; and that yet this is not all, for the Methodism of the past age points forward to the next-coming development of the powers of the Gospel."[21]

[21] Isaac Taylor's Wesley and Methodism, Preface.

CHAPTER II.

THE WESLEY FAMILY.

Providential Preparations — The Epworth Rectory — Susanna Wesley, The Foundress of Methodism — Her Father, Dr. Annesley — Her Independence of Opinion — Her Marriage — Her Beauty — Her Intellectual Character — Her Religious Character — Her Husband, Samuel Wesley — His Ancestors — Bartholomew Westley and John Westley — Their Sufferings for Conscience sake — The Rector of Epworth — His Good-humor — Remarkable Anecdotes — Life at the Rectory — Characteristics of the Children — The Household Education — Mrs. Wesley conducts Religious Worship in the Rectory — Domestic Sorrows — Destruction of the Rectory by Fire — John Wesley's providential Escape.

MAN'S extremity, says Augustine, is God's opportunity. While Secker was deploring the demoralization of England, as threatening to "become absolutely fatal," and the aged Burnet saw "imminent ruin hanging over the Church," and "over the whole Reformation;" while Watts was writing that "religion was dying in the world," and Butler that "it had come to be taken for granted that Christianity was no longer a subject of inquiry, but at length was discovered to be fictitious;" when, in fine, the Anglican Church had become "an ecclesiastical system, under which the people of England had lapsed into heathenism," and "Nonconformity was rapidly in course to be found nowhere but in books,"[1] and, meanwhile, across the Channel, rationalistic infidelity was invading the strongholds of the Reformation, and the French philosophers were spreading moral contagion through Europe, God was preparing the means, apparently disconnected, but providentially coincident, which were to resuscitate the "dying" faith, and introduce the era of modern evangelism in the Protestant world. A young man, born

[1] Isaac Taylor's Wesley and Methodism.

in an inn at Bristol, and struggling for his education, as a servitor at Oxford, was seeking, in agony of spirit, for a purer faith than he could find around him, and, as he tells us, "lying prostrate on the ground, for whole days, in silent or vocal prayer." In a few years his eloquence, never, perhaps, surpassed in the pulpit, was to startle and illuminate all England, and the American Colonies from Maine to Georgia.[2] From the mountains of Wales a youth of fortune entered, later, the same university as a gentleman commoner;[3] he was to become the foreign administrator of Methodism, its first bishop in America, the founder of its missions in both Indies, and of that whole missionary scheme which, in our day, enrolls a larger number of converts from heathenism than all other Protestant missions combined. From the mountains of Switzerland came into England, meanwhile, a young man who was to become the champion of the Arminian theology of the new movement, and the intimate counselor of its leader, and whose saintly life was to leave with it a greater blessing than the works of his pen.[4]

But its chief agents were in obscure preparation in the village of Epworth, a rural community of Lincolnshire, with a population, at the time, of about two thousand souls, occupied in the cultivation and manufacture of hemp and flax. In the household of the Epworth Rectory can be traced its real origin, amid one of those pictures of English rural life which have so often given a charm to our literature, and which form, perhaps, the best example of the domestic virtues of religion that Christian civilization has afforded. An "elect lady" there trained the founder and legislator of Methodism, and to no inconsiderable degree, by impressing on him the traits of her own extraordinary character; and, under the same nurture, grew up by his side its psalmist, whose lyrics were to be heard, in less than a century, wherever the English language was spok-

[2] Gillies's Life of Whitefield. [3] Drew's Life of Coke.

[4] Benson's Life of Fletcher.

en, and to be "more devoutly committed to memory," and "oftener repeated upon a death-bed," than any other poems.[5]

The mother of the Wesleys was the mother of Methodism, says a writer who has given us the philosophy of its history,[6] and she properly belongs to the foreground of our narrative. She was "nobly related," being the daughter of Dr. Samuel Annesley, who was the son of a brother of the Earl of Anglesea.[7] She inherited from her father those energetic traits of character which she transmitted to her most distinguished child.

Dr. Annesley was one of the leading Nonconformist divines of his day. Like his grandson, he was noted at Oxford for his piety and diligence; he served the national Church as chaplain at sea, and as parish priest at Cliff, in Kent, at St. John the Apostle's and at St. Giles's, two of the largest congregations in London. Under the Act of Uniformity, the inherent energy of the family showed itself with him, as afterward with his daughter and grandson, in a calm but determined independence. He refused to "conform," and endured a series of severe persecutions, which were attended by many of those "remarkable interpositions" that distinguish the later history of the family. One of his persecutors fell dead while preparing a warrant for his apprehension. He became a leader of the Puritans during the troubles of the times, preaching almost daily, providing pastors for destitute congregations, and relief for his ejected and impoverished brethren. "O how many places," exclaims one of his contemporaries, "had sat in darkness, how many ministers had been starved, if Dr. Annesley had died thirty years since."[8] After a ministry of more than half a century, and of sore trials, under which he never once

[5] Southey's Life of Wesley, chapter 21.

[6] Taylor: Wesley and Methodism, p. 28.

[7] Adam Clarke's Wesley Family, p. 289.

[8] Dr. Daniel Williams, in Annesley's Funeral Sermon, published by Wesley, in the Arminian Magazine, vol. xv.

faltered, he died in 1696, exclaiming, "I shall be satisfied with thy likeness: satisfied, satisfied." De Foe, who sat under his preaching, has drawn his character as perfect, in an elegy. The Nonconformists considered him a second St. Paul.[9] Richard Baxter pronounced him totally devoted to God.[10] He was endeared to all who knew him intimately, and his noble relative, the Countess of Anglesea, desired, on her death-bed, to be buried in his grave.[11] He had a manly countenance and dignified person; a rich estate, which he devoted to charity; robust health, which was capable of any fatigue; and "a large soul," says Clarke, "flaming with zeal." "He was an Israelite, indeed," exclaims Calamy, "sanctified from the womb."[12] Cromwell esteemed him, and appointed him to an office at St. Paul's.

He accorded to his daughter the independence of opinion which he claimed for himself, and while yet under his roof, and not thirteen years old, she showed her hereditary spirit by examining the whole controversy between Churchmen and Dissenters, and by renouncing, in favor of the Established Church, the opinions to which her father had devoted a life of labor and suffering. The fact is characteristic; and judging from the evidence of her later history, she possessed, even at this early age, an unusual fitness for such an investigation. Devout, thoughtful, amiable, and beautiful, she was the favorite child of her father, and the change of her opinions produced no interruption of the affectionate ties which had bound them together.

She was married to Rev. Samuel Wesley about 1689, when nineteen or twenty years of age. She had been thoroughly educated, and was acquainted with the Greek

[9] Dunton's "Life and Errors," p. 95. This noted publisher, who ranks by the side of Dodsley in the English typography of the last century, was Annesley's son-in-law.

[10] Adam Clarke's Wesley Family, p. 298.

[11] Dunton, p. 280.

[12] Nonconformists' Memorial, vol. i. Anthony à Wood's sketch of him (Athenæ Oxoniensis, vol. iv,) is evidently a Jacobite caricature.

Latin, and French languages. She showed a discriminative judgment of books and men, and, without any unique trait of genius, presents, perhaps, one of the completest characters, moral and intellectual, to be found in the history of her sex. She has left us no proof of poetical talent, and the genius of her children in this respect seems to have been inherited from their father, whose passionate love of the art, and unwearied attempts at rhythm, if not poetry, may also account for the hereditary talent of the family in music.

A portrait of Susanna Wesley, taken at a later date than her marriage, but evidently while she was still young, affords us a picture of the refined and even elegant lady of the times. The features are slight, but almost classical in their regularity. They are thoroughly Wesleyan, affording proof that John Wesley inherited from his mother not only his best moral and intellectual traits, but those also of his physiognomy. Her dress and coiffure are in the simplest style of her day, and the entire picture is marked by chaste gracefulness. It lacks not, also, an air of that high-bred aristocracy from which she was descended.[13] Adam Clarke, whose uxorious fondness shows him to have been no inapt judge, says she was not only graceful, but beautiful. Sir Peter Lely, the painter of the "beauties" of his age, has left a portrait of one of her sisters, who was pronounced a woman of rare charms; "One," says Clarke, "who well knew them both, said, beautiful as Miss Annesley appears, she was far from being as beautiful as Mrs. Wesley." The learned commentator lingers with heartiest admiration before her image. He assures us that he could not repress his tears while contemplating her Christian and womanly virtues, and her more than manly struggles with adversity. "Such a woman," he says, "take her for all in all, I have not heard of, I have not read of, nor with her

[13] Clarke, (Wesley Family,) with his usual learned detail, traces the Anglesea family back beyond the Conquest. He says: "I find that Mrs. Wesley signed some of her letters with the Annesley arms."

equal have I been acquainted. Such a one Solomon has described in the last chapter of his Proverbs; and to her I can apply the summed up character of his accomplished housewife. Many daughters have done virtuously, but Susanna Wesley has excelled them all." In his comment on Solomon's sketch of the Jewish matron, he again refers to the lady of Epworth rectory as the best exemplification he knew of the Scriptural portrait.

An exact balance of faculties was the chief characteristic of her intellect. With this she combined a profound piety. Her early interest in the Nonconformist controversy shows that from her childhood, religion, even in some of its intricate questions, had engaged her thoughts. Her healthful common sense is manifest in all her allusions to the subject. Her womanly but practical mind never fell into mysticism; and when her sons were wavering under its influence at Oxford, her letters continually recalled them to wholesome and Scriptural sentiments. "I take Kempis," she writes to John, when he was poring over the pages of the "Imitation," "I take Kempis to have been an honest, weak man, who had more zeal than knowledge, by his condemning all mirth or pleasure as sinful or useless, in opposition to so many direct and plain texts of Scripture." And again she wrote: "Let every one enjoy the present hour. Age and successive troubles are sufficient to convince any man that it is a much wiser and safer way to deprecate great afflictions than to pray for them, and that our Lord knew what was in man when he directed us to pray: 'Lead us not into temptation.' I think heretic Clarke,[14] in his exposition on the Lord's Prayer, is more in the right than Castaniza concerning temptations."

With unusual sobriety on religious subjects, she united a cheerful confidence in her own religious hopes. She consecrated an hour every morning and evening to entire seclusion for meditation and prayer; her reflections at these

[14] Dr. Samuel Clarke.

times were often recorded, and present the happiest blending of good sense and religious fervor. "If," she exclaims, in one of her evening meditations; "if comparatively to despise and undervalue all the world contains, which is esteemed great, fair, or good; if earnestly and constantly to desire Thee—thy favor, thy acceptance, thyself—rather than any or all things thou hast created, be to love Thee—I do love Thee."[15]

Her independent habit of thinking led her early to Socinian opinions, but they were abandoned after matured investigations. Her letters are marked not only by just but often by profound thought. She projected several literary works, and a fragment which remains, on the "Apostles' Creed," would not have been discreditable to the theological literature of her day. She had begun a work on Natural and Revealed Religion, comprising her reasons for renouncing Dissent, and a discourse on the Eucharist, but both were destroyed by a fire which consumed the rectory.[16]

Her husband, the Rev. Samuel Wesley, was born at Whitechurch in 1662, and was her senior by seven years.[17] His character was contrasted in important respects with her own; but he shared fully her conscientious independence of opinion on religious questions. With him as with her, this seems to have been an hereditary trait, and was transmitted by them both to their children. The characteristics of the founder of Methodism were indeed continually revealing themselves in the ancestral history of the family. Samuel Wesley's grandfather, Bartholomew

15 Moore's Life of Wesley, I. 3. Clarke is very justly scandalized at the epitaph which Charles Wesley wrote for her tomb, and which represents her as in "a legal night" till her seventieth year—a period at which she attained, as we shall hereafter see, a clearer sense of her acceptance with God, while receiving the Lord's Supper from one of her sons-in-law.

16 Letter to her son, Rev. S. Wesley. Whitehead's Life of Wesley, I, 4.

17 Clarke contradicts himself at pp. 81 and 320 of Wesley Family respecting his age. Methodist writers speak with uncertainty of the year of Mrs. Wesley's birth. Clarke (p. 319) gives it as 1669 or 1670. Her epitaph, in Bunhill Fields, says she was aged 73, at her death in 1742. This determines the year of her birth as 1669.

Westley,[18] after serving the Established Church in several parishes, under Charles I., joined the Puritan party. He was ejected at the Restoration, and obstinately refusing to conform, lived by the practice of medicine, a persecuted outcast, not allowed by the Five Mile Act to approach within five miles of any of his former parishes, or any borough town, but preaching, meanwhile, as he had opportunity, till the treatment and premature death of his son, occasioned by a like conscientious independence of opinion, "brought his gray hairs with sorrow to the grave."[19] We know little else of him than these brief characteristic facts of his sufferings. Calamy says he was, when an old man, and the vigor of life had gone, "as tender hearted and affectionate as he had been pious and prudent."

His son, John Westley, under whose afflictions the veteran dissenter sunk into the grave, was true to the independent and vigorous character of his father. He was educated at

[18] Such was the original orthography of the name. Clarke thinks it may be of Arabic origin, and that the family came from Spain. Beal ("Wesley Fathers") gives it a good Saxon origin. There are traces of the name in Dorsetshire as early as the fourteenth century, a period before which, Camden tells us, surnames were not common in England, families being designated by localities. Smith (History of Wesleyan Methodism, book I, chap. 2) says there were in Dorsetshire certain portions of land formerly called *hides*, *vils*, (fields,) and *manors*, distinguished by the names Wantesleigh, Wynesleigh, Wernsley, and Westley. Hutchinson, the historian of Dorsetshire, says there is a hamlet in Broadwindsor called Wansley, Wantsley, Wantsleigh, and Wanslew, and further observes that there are twenty acres of land in Hook called West Leas. "This latter statement," remarks Smith, "probably affords a key to the whole case. *Lea*, in Saxon, signifies a place, and in English an enclosed piece of cultivated or pastured land. Such a place, designated by its bearing, would be called Westlea, and might have given the original of the family name." John de Wintereslegh, vicar of Frampton, in 1360; George Westley, treasurer of Sarum, 1403; John Westley, rector of Langton Maltravers, 1481; John Wannesleigh, rector of Bettiscomb, 1497; and John Wennesley, chaplain of Pillesdore, 1508, were all, both persons and places, in the same county and same neighborhood where the great-grandfather of John Wesley resided; there can be little doubt that they were ancestors of Samuel Westley, as the father of the founder of Methodism wrote his name at Oxford.

[19] Southey's Wesley, chap. 1.

Oxford, where he excelled in Oriental studies. He seems not to have sought ordination, but was abroad during Cromwell's power, preaching at various places, at one time to seamen, at others in rural churches. He was remarkable for his religious zeal, and, like several others of his family, kept strict notes of his interior life by a diary. At the Restoration he had scruples against the use of the Common Prayer. He was cited before the Bishop of Bristol for his irregularities, and told by the prelate that if he continued to preach, it must be according "to order, the order of the Church of England, upon ordination." "What," he replied, "does your lordship mean by an ordination? If you mean that sending spoken of in Romans x, 2, I have it." "I mean that," rejoined the bishop. "What mission had you? You must have it according to law and the order of the Church of England." "I am not satisfied in my spirit of that," was the truly Wesleyan reply; "I am not satisfied in conscience touching the ordination you speak of." He proceeded to vindicate his preaching by its good results, the approval of good men, and his entire devotion to it. "I am glad I heard this from your own mouth," replied the prelate. "You will stand to your principles, you say?" "I intend it, through the grace of God, and to be faithful to the king's majesty, however you may deal with me." "I will not meddle with you," said the bishop, perceiving, doubtless, what kind of man he was dealing with. "Farewell to you, sir," was Mr. Westley's only reply. "Farewell, good Mr. Westley," responded his lordship.[20]

Here was the germ of the ministerial system which afterward flourished under his grandson; a kind of epitome of Methodism, says Clarke. He was a "lay preacher, and he was an itinerant evangelist." "It cannot," continues Clarke, "escape the reflection of the reader, that Methodism, in its grand principles of economy, and the means by which they have been brought into action, had its specific

[20] Calamy (Nonconformists' Mem., vol. ii.) has preserved the interesting dialogue at length. Moore quotes it, Life of Wesley, I, 1.

healthy, though slowly vegetating seeds, in the original members of the Wesley family."[21]

The good impression which he left upon the mind of the Bishop of Bristol, could not save him from imprisonment shortly after. He was released by an order of the King's Council, in 1661, but was seized while leaving his church, in the next year, and again thrust into prison. A leading magistrate of the county, however, bailed him out. Soon afterward the Act of Uniformity went into effect; Wesley would not yield to it; he stood up amid his weeping people, and preaching a farewell discourse, left them, to become an outcast and a wanderer. The remainder of his history is a series of affecting sufferings; but they were borne with intrepid steadfastness. On leaving his congregation at Whitchurch, he took his family to Melcombe, but the local authorities hunted him there, imposing upon him a fine, and upon his landlady the forfeiture of twenty pounds. He took refuge in Ilminster, Bridgewater, and Taunton, living on the charity of their dissenting Churches. His sufferings at last touched the sympathies of a wealthy gentleman, who gave him a house free of rent, in the village of Preston. There he found a retreat for almost two years, when the Five Mile Act drove him out of his comfortable refuge. He sheltered his family at Poole, preaching there as he found opportunity, but living in the country to escape the new law. Four times was he imprisoned, once for half a year, and in another instance for three months. He thought of seeking shelter in America, but about the year 1690 found it in heaven. He sunk into the grave, under his many trials, at the early age of thirty-four, bearing with him the broken heart of his father, whose admiration of his independence and zeal could not sustain his own spirit in its painful sympathy with his tried and

[21] Clarke infers from the "escalop shell" on the family arms, that some of its ancestors had been in the Crusades; whether this is the fact or not, the crusading spirit seemed hereditary and ineradicable in the Wesleyan constitution.

faithful son. His sufferings, says Southey, have given him a place among the confessors of the Nonconformists. Calamy has left us evidence that John Westley was alike devout and firm, and an able theologian.[22] He lies in the church-yard of Preston; such was the spirit of the times that the vicar would not allow him to be buried in the church.[23]

Weak character is indicated as often, perhaps, by strong as by feeble opinions, for opinions are mostly prejudices; and on theological subjects, and especially on ecclesiastical questions, where so much must always be doubtful, liberality must always be more wise as well as more generous than dogmatism. It should be borne in mind, however, that if the Wesleys were tenacious of their later sentiments, this very fact proves that they were not so of their earlier opinions. They conquered, at least, the prejudices of education. Opinions on the questions for which they suffered were deemed, in their day, to be more fundamental than they have been considered since the epoch of Methodism. They were still matters of conscience, and strong souls are always strongest in matters of conscience. The opposition of Bartholomew and John Westley to the Common Prayer, and other ecclesiastical requisitions of the times, was more a protest against bigotry than bigotry itself; and by the progress of such dissent has the Anglo-Saxon mind reached its later and more forbearing liberality.

Such were the immediate ancestors of Samuel Wesley, the rector of Epworth, and father of the founder of Method-

[22] Nonconformists' Memorial, vol. ii.

[23] Southey's Life of Wesley, chap. 1. One of Wesley's circuit preachers makes an affecting reference to this good and brave man's grave: "In the church-yard no stone tells where his ashes lie, nor is there a monument to record his worth. The writer would not seem to affect anything; yet to this village (which he visits regularly, as a small Wesleyan chapel is there) he does not go without remembering the Vicar of Whitchurch. In this and that house, lonely dell, and retired spot, he seems to see the man whose spirit was *crushed*, the Christian hunted to obscurity, and the minister whose lamp, though lighted in the skies, was wickedly quenched by the triumphant spirit of persecution; and he is no stranger to the hallowed spot where his mortal part is deposited."—*Beal's Wesley Fathers.*

ism. The rector himself had a robust soul, and early proved that he inherited the ancestral spirit of his family. Designed for the ministry of the Nonconformists, and trained by so many domestic examples and sufferings to sympathize with their cause, he was appointed to prepare a reply to some severe invectives which had been published against them. In attempting the task "he conceived that he saw reason to change his opinions."[24] Rising one morning very early, and without acquainting any person with his design, he set out on foot for Oxford, and entered himself as a "poor scholar" at Exeter College. He had but two pounds five shillings in his pocket when he arrived there, and received during his collegiate life but one crown as assistance from his friends. Strong in the characteristic energy and methodical habits of his family, he successfully prosecuted his studies, supporting himself by his pen and by instructing others as a tutor. We have but few glimpses of his Oxford life; they show, however, the genuine Wesleyan character. He was laborious, devout, and not forgetful of those whom the Church of the day seemed most inclined to forget—prisoners and the wretched poor. He visited the former in the Castle, relieving their necessities and ministering to their souls; and when his sons afterward became notorious at Oxford for similar labors, he was able to write to them: "Go on, in God's name, in the path which your Saviour has directed you, and that wherein your father has gone before you."

Wesleyan in his economy as in his liberality, he was able at last to leave college for London with more than ten pounds in his pocket. Dunton, his London publisher, had married a daughter of Dr. Annesley, and introduced his young friend to the family. The acquaintance ripened at last into his marriage with Susanna Annesley. After beginning his clerical life as a curate, with twenty-eight pounds a year, and receiving a chaplaincy aboard the fleet, at seventy pounds, he took charge of a curacy in London at

[24] John Wesley: Adam Clarke's Wesley Family, p. 88.

thirty pounds, which, however, he doubled by the tireless industry of his pen. While in the city he gave a remarkable instance of his hereditary spirit. The "Declaration" of James II. was ordered to be read in the churches; and the court party, deeming Wesley a talented partisan, promised him preferment, as a motive for his support of the measure. He was poor, and living in lodgings with his wife and one child; but he spurned the overture, and believing the Declaration to be a Papal design, he not only refused to read it, but ascended the pulpit and denounced it in a sermon from the text: "If it be so, our God whom we serve is able to deliver us from the burning fiery furnace, and he will deliver us out of thy hand, O king. But if not, be it known unto thee, O king, that we will not serve thy gods, nor worship the golden image which thou hast set up."

We next find him in the curacy of South Ormsby, near Epworth, with fifty pounds a year. Here his family increased to six children; but, with true English paternity, he welcomed each addition as a gift from God, and struggled manfully to provide bread for every new comer. He says, in a letter to the Archbishop of York, that he had but fifty pounds a year for six or seven years together, and one child at least per annum. The parish had been obtained for him by the Marquis of Normanby; a characteristic instance of conduct led to its resignation. This nobleman, says John Wesley, had a house in the parish, where a woman who lived with him usually resided; she insisted on being intimate with Mrs. Wesley, but to such an intercourse the rector would not submit. Coming in one day, and finding the intrusive visitant sitting with his wife, he went up to her, took her by the hand, and unceremoniously led her out. The nobleman resented the affront, and made it necessary for Wesley to retire from the living. The dedication of one of his works to Queen Mary procured him the rectory of Epworth, where, on two hundred pounds a year, and the proceeds of his literary labors, he sustained and educated his numerous family, amounting at last to nineteen children.

His poetical mania kept him busily at work "beating rhyme," as he called it. Poem after poem came forth to the public from the rectory study. Besides his elaborate works detailing in verse which was, more rhythmical than poetical, "The Life of Christ," and "The History of the Old and New Testaments," less pretentious, but really better productions, were continually emanating from his pen. His most valuable publication was a Latin dissertation on the book of Job. He had the rare fortune of dedicating volumes to three successive queens of England; but as popular, not royal sovereignty, wields the sceptre of fate in the world of letters, the royal sanction has not been able to save them from oblivion. Their few worm-eaten remnants have no other interest than that which arises from the later historical importance of the family name. The Latin dissertation on Job evinces profound learning; and he was doubtless competent to have prosecuted successfully, under more favorable circumstances, a grand scheme which he had projected for a new edition of the original Scriptures, on the plan more lately accomplished by Bagster. Pope was intimate with the rector, and in a letter to Swift, says: "I call him what he is, a learned man, and I engage you will approve his prose more than you formerly did his poetry." Dunton says he used to write two hundred couplets a day. The current of his verse was so rapid as to carry with it all the lighter rubbish of its banks, and to sink whatever of weighty value was cast upon it.

He plied faithfully, meanwhile, his parish labors. He knew all his parishioners, and visited them from house to house, keeping a record of his visits. His preaching was pointed, and he quailed not when it gave offense. Bad livers in the parish resented it, as they did also his party politics, by wounding his cattle at night, cutting off the legs of his house-dog, breaking his doors, and by twice setting fire to his house. His conduct toward them was sometimes as prompt as in the case which occasioned his resignation at Ormsby. Many of them vexed him not a little about the tithes, and at one time they would pay only in kind. Going into a field where the tithe corn was laid, he discovered a person cutting the ears with a pair of shears, and filling with them a bag brought for the purpose. Without saying a word, he seized the astonished parishioner by the arm, and led him into the market-place of the town, where he opened the bag, turned it inside out before the multitude, and, declaring what the pilferer had done, walked quietly away, leaving him confounded before his neighbors.

He did not disguise his High Church and State principles, and his imprudent political zeal involved him in serious persecutions. Besides the injuring of his cattle, and the burning of his house, the rabble drummed, shouted, and fired arms under his windows at night. Under the pretense of a small debt, which he could not at the moment discharge, he was arrested while leaving his church, and imprisoned in Lincoln Castle, where he continued about three months. But his native spirit never failed him. "Now I am at rest," he wrote from the prison to the Archbishop of York, "for I am come to the haven where I have long expected to be; and," he characteristically adds, "I don't despair of doing good here, and, it may be, more in this new parish than in my old one." Like Goldsmith's good vicar, he immediately became a volunteer chaplain to his fellow prisoners. He read prayers daily, and preached on Sundays to them. He was consoled by the fortitude of his noble wife; "'Tis not every one," he wrote again to the archbishop, "who could bear these things; but I bless God, my wife is less concerned with suffering them than I am in writing, or than I believe your Grace will be in reading them." "When I came here," he said in another letter, "my stock was but little above ten shillings, and my wife's at home scarce so much. She soon sent me her rings, because she had nothing else to relieve me with, but I returned them." When advised to remove from Epworth, on account of his persecutions, he replied in an answer which reminds us of his son, when hooted by later mobs in his itinerant preaching: "'Tis like a coward to desert my post because the enemy fires thick upon me. They have only wounded me yet, and I believe cannot kill me."

The energy of his character and the tenacity of his opinions were, doubtless, faulty virtues. They led him into not a few unnecessary sufferings, and bordered sometimes on insanity. A fact is told of him which would be incredible if related on less authority than that of John Wesley himself. He informs us that his father, observing one evening, at the close of family prayers, that his wife did not respond "Amen" to the prayer for the king, asked her the reason. She replied that she did not believe in the title of the Prince of Orange to the throne. "If that be the case," rejoined the rector, "we must part, for if we have two kings, we must have two beds." "My mother," says Wesley, "was inflexible." Her husband went to his study, and soon after took his departure, and returned not till about a year had elapsed, when the death of the king, and the accession of Queen Anne, whose title neither questioned, allowed him to go back without violating his word. Their conjugal harmony was restored, and John Wesley himself was the first child born after their reconciliation. This very singular incident seems not to have been attended with any severe recriminations; it was as cool as it was determined and foolish; it was made a matter of conscience by both parties, and both were immovably but calmly resolute in all conscientious prejudices. As an illustration of character, it indicates worse for the good sense than the good heart of the rector, for through the robust nature of this man of sturdy opinions flowed a current of habitual good-humor, and humor, more than apparent conscientiousness itself, reveals truthfully the heart, as it is an affection, if not a virtue, which has the rare peculiarity of being necessarily genuine, and when even associated with satire, is so, more from a genial and instinctive disposition to relieve, than to add to its sting. Southey says of Samuel Wesley's early poems, that his imagination seems to have been playful, and had he written during his son's celebrity, some of his pieces might perhaps have been condemned by the godly as profane.[25] Clarke assures us that he had a large share of vivacity; that in private conversation he was very entertaining and instructive, having a rich fund of anecdote, and a profusion of witty and wise sayings. He shows that the hearty rector relished practical jokes so well as to be led sometimes to trench with them on sacred ground, where even a useful lesson could hardly redeem them.[26]

[25] Southey's EarlyEnglish Poets. AdamClarke demurs to the latter point. The veteran commentator was, however, himself not very squeamish.

[26] The Epworth parish clerk was a well-meaning and honest, but an obtrusively vain man. His master, the rector, he esteemed the greatest character in the parish, or even in the county, and himself, being second to him in church services, as only second to him, also, in importance and title to general respect. "He had the privilege of wearing Mr. Wesley's cast off clothes and wigs, for the latter of which his head was by far too small, and the figure he presented was ludicrously grotesque. The rector finding him particularly vain of one of the canonical substitutes for hair, which he had lately received, formed the design to mortify him in the presence of that congregation before which John wished to appear in every respect what he thought himself in his near approach to his master. One morning before church time Mr. W. said: 'John, I shall preach on a particular subject to-day, and shall choose my own psalm, of which I shall give out the first line, and you shall proceed as usual.' John was pleased, and the service went forward as usual till they came to the singing, when Mr. Wesley gave out the following line:

'Like to an owl in ivy bush.'

This was sung; and the following line, John, peeping out of the large canonical wig in which his head was half lost, gave out with an audible voice, and appropriate connecting twang—

'That rueful thing am I.'

The whole congregation, struck with John's appearance, saw and felt the similitude, and could not refrain from laughter. The rector was pleased, for John was mortified and his self-conceit lowered."—*Clarke's Wesley Family*. This anecdote was questioned in the Wesleyan Magazine, London, for 1824. Clarke replies "that he had it from John Wesley himself, and, as near as he can possibly recollect, in the very words given." He adds, what may be as relevant to our pages as to his own, that it is characteristic of the man, and it is from facts of this nature that the author forms a proper estimate of the character he describes. The

Adam Clarke, to whom we are indebted for our most interesting, if not most important information respecting Samuel Wesley, and who evidently found in him a kindred nature, took pains to inquire on the spot respecting his character and labors, and discovered aged parishioners to whom the memory of the man and pastor was still dear. They bore grateful testimony to his pastoral fidelity and his devoted piety, as well as his eccentricities. He had the zealous energy of his Methodist sons, and had it not expended itself in incessant literary labors, it would probably have led him into extraordinary evangelical schemes, like those which resulted in Methodism. He did, indeed, conceive a plan of gigantic missionary efforts, which, it cannot be doubted, he would have heroically prosecuted, had it not been defeated by the neglect of the government. It comprehended St. Helena, India, and China, and reached even to Abyssinia, taking in the foreign British territories as posts from which to extend the Gospel to the heathen. The written sketch of the scheme, signed by the Archbishop of York, still remains. Wesley offered to attempt it in person, if the government would sanction it, and provide a humble subsistence for his family. Clarke contends that it was entirely practicable to the English government and Church. It was an anticipation of the missionary enterprise of Methodism; but the time for it had not yet come. His wife was unconsciously preparing for it in the nursery at Epworth, while her husband was discussing it with prelates and statesmen.

A prophetic anticipation of the approaching revival

harmless weakness of the aged clerk seems to have made him quite a "character" in the Epworth circle, and the humor of the hard-working rector was doubtless often refreshed by his comicalities. Clarke says: "This is the same man who, when King William returned to London, after some of his expeditions, gave out in Epworth church, 'Let us sing, to the praise and glory of God, a hymn of my own composing:

'King William is come home, come home,
King William home is come;
Therefore let us together sing
The hymn that's called Te D'um.'"

of the Protestant faith seemed to linger in this good man's mind down to his last hour. When dying he laid his hand repeatedly on the head of his son Charles, saying: "Be steady; the Christian faith will surely revive in this kingdom; you will see it, though I shall not." And to another of his children he said: "Do not be concerned at my death, God will then begin to manifest himself to my family."[27] He died attesting the doctrine of the Witness of the Spirit, afterward so emphatically preached by the founders of Methodism. "He had a clear sense of his acceptance with God," says John Wesley. "The inward witness," he said, "the inward witness, that is the proof, the strongest proof of Christianity."[28] The family gathered around his bed to take the Lord's Supper with him for the last time; but he was hardly able to receive it. "God chastens me with strong pain," he exclaimed before departing; "but I praise him for it, I thank him for it, I love him for it." At the moment when one of his sons finished the Communion prayer he expired.

His character, sufficiently delineated in our narrative, is not without marked defects; but it is admirable for its genuine English manhood, its healthful piety, its brave independence of opinion, and the endurance of life-long struggles with poverty besides other and complicated trials.

Such were the parents and ancestors of the Wesley family.

The glimpses which we get from contemporary records of the interior life at the rectory of Epworth, give us the image of an almost perfect Christian household. If some of its aspects appear at times too grave, or even severe, they are relieved by frequent evidence of those home affections and gayeties with which the beneficent instincts of human nature are sure to resist, in a numerous circle of children, the religious austerities of riper years. The Epworth rectory presents, in fine, the picture of a domestic church, a family school, and a genuine old English household. Before the

[27] Letter of Charles Wesley: Wesley Family, p. 277.
[28] Letter of John Wesley: Ibid., p. 276.

first fire the building was a humble structure of wood and plaster, roofed with thatch, and venerable with a hundred years. It boasted one parlor, an ample hall, a buttery, three large upper chambers, besides some smaller apartments, and a study, where the studious rector spent most of his time in "beating rhymes," and preparing his sermons, leaving the rest of the house and almost all in-door affairs, as well as the management of the temporalities of the glebe and tithes, to his more capable wife, and fondly comforting himself against the pinching embarrassments of poverty with the consolation, as he expresses it in a letter to the Archbishop of York, "that he who is born a poet, must, I am afraid, live and die so, that is, poor." John Wesley expresses admiration at the serenity with which his mother transacted business, wrote letters, and conversed, surrounded by her thirteen children. All the children bore "nicknames" in the home circle, and the familiar pseudonyms play fondly through the abundant family correspondence which remains. Clarke assures us that "they had the common fame of being the most loving family in the county of Lincoln." The mother especially was the center of the household affections. John, after leaving home, writes to her at a time when her health was precarious, with pathetic endearment, and expresses the hope that he may die before her, in order not to have the anguish of witnessing her end. "You did well," she afterward writes him, "to correct that fond desire of dying before me, since you do not know what work God may have for you to do before you leave the world. It is what I have often desired of the children, that they would not weep at my parting, and so make death more uncomfortable than it would otherwise be to me." The home where such sentiments prevailed could not have been an austere one.

The children all shared this filial tenderness for the mother. Martha (afterward Mrs. Hall) clung to her with a sort of idolatry. She would never willingly be from her side, says Clarke; and the only fault alleged against the parent was her fond partiality for this affectionate child.[29] Several of the nineteen children died young, but, according to the allusion of John Wesley, already quoted, thirteen were living at one time. Some of them were remarkable for beauty, others for wit and intelligence. Samuel, the eldest son, was poetic from his childhood, and has left some of the finest hymns of the Methodist psalmody.[30] Susanna (afterward Mrs. Ellison) is described as "very facetious and a little romantic;" Mary, though somewhat deformed, as "having an exquisitely beautiful face—a legible index to a mind almost angelic," and "one of the most exalted of human characters, full of humility and goodness;" Mehetabel (Mrs. Wright) as able, in her eighth year, to read the Greek language, and as "gay, sprightly, full of mirth, good-humor, and wit, and attracting many suitors," and in later life an elegant woman, "with great refinement of manners, and the traces of beauty in her countenance." She had also an uncommon poetic talent. The few letters of Keziah that remain show vivacity and vigorous sense. Charles and John gave distinct promise, even in the nursery, of their coming greatness. The natural temper of the latter, in youth, is described as "gay, with a turn for wit and humor."[31] The former was "exceedingly sprightly and active, and so remarkable for courage and skill in juvenile

[29] Mrs. Hall's beautiful character and sad history form the most romantic and touching story in the "Wesley Family." Her affection for John was stronger than the love of woman, and she resembled him in person to a remarkable degree. Her domestic life was blighted by the deepest sorrows, which were sustained, however, with unmurmuring patience. Clarke gives their affecting details. She dined often with Dr. Johnson at Bolt-Court; he ardently admired her, and even wished her to reside in his own house with Mesdames Williams and Du Moulin. Boswell mentions his unusual deference toward her, and her striking resemblance to John Wesley, "both in figure and manner." See Boswell's Johnson, vol. ii, pp. 28, 291, 292, 374.

[30] Among them are those beginning: "The morning flowers display their sweets;" "The Lord of Sabbath let us praise;" "Hail, Father, whose creating call;" "Hail, God the Son, in glory crown'd;" "Hail, Holy Ghost, Jehovah, third," etc.

[31] Moore's Life of Wesley, II, 1. "He appeared," says the Westminster Magazine, "the very sensible and acute collegian; a young fellow of the finest classical taste, of the most liberal and manly sentiments."—*Ibid.*

encounters that he afterward obtained, at Westminster, the title of 'Captain of the school.'" Still later, he laments that he lost his first year at Oxford in diversions.[32] Martha, who lived to be the last survivor of the original Wesley family, though habitually sober, if not sad, amid the pastimes of the household circle, had an innate horror of melancholy subjects. Her memory was remarkable, and was abundantly stored with the results of her studies, especially in history and poetry. Her good sense and intelligence delighted Johnson in discussions of theology and moral philosophy. Of wit, she used to say, that she was the only one of the family who did not possess it.

Though method prevailed throughout the household, its almost mechanical rigor was relaxed at suitable intervals, in which the nursery, with its large juvenile community, became an arena of hilarious recreations, of "high glee and frolic."[33] Games of skill and of chance even, were among the family pastimes, such as John Wesley afterward prohibited among the Methodists. While the rectory was rattling with the "mysterious noises," so famous in the family history, we find the courageous daughters "playing at the game of cards."[34]

The educational system at the rectory has been the admiration of all who have written respecting the Wesley family. It had some extraordinary points. It was conducted solely by Mrs. Wesley, who thus combined the labors of a school with the other and numerous cares of her household. She has left a long letter addressed to John Wesley, in which it is fully detailed. "The children," she

[32] Smith's History of Wesleyan Methodism, I, 8.

[33] Clarke—whose monogram sketches of the family are the best, because the most "gossiping" history we have of it. My unreferred quotations are all from him. He seems to take pleasure in correcting the common impression that Wesley's early education was unduly severe. The reader will excuse me if he thinks my pages show an excess of sympathy with this design; for Epworth, not Oxford, was the cradle of Methodism.

[34] Original Letters of Rev. John Wesley and his Friends, by Dr. Priestley. Birmingham: 1791. See App. to Southey's Wesley.

says, "were always put into a regular method of living, in such things as they were capable of, from their birth; as in dressing and undressing, changing their linen, etc. The first quarter commonly passes in sleep; after that they were, if possible, laid in their cradle awake, and rocked to sleep; and so they were kept rocking till it was time for them to awake. This was done to bring them to a regular course of sleeping, which at first was three hours in the morning, and three in the afternoon; afterward two hours, till they needed none at all." When one year old, and in some cases earlier, they were taught to "cry softly," by which means they escaped abundance of correction, and that "most odious noise" of the crying of children was rarely heard in the house; but the family usually lived in as much quietness as if there had not been a child among them. Drinking and eating between meals was never allowed, unless in cases of sickness, which "seldom happened." They retired at eight in the evening, and were "left in their several rooms awake, for there was no such thing allowed in the house as sitting by a child till it fell asleep." To subdue the will of the child was one of her earliest tasks, "because," she continues, "this is the only strong and rational foundation of a religious education, without which both precept and example will be ineffectual. But when this is thoroughly done then a child is capable of being governed by the reason and piety of its parents, till its own understanding comes to maturity, and the principles of religion have taken root in the mind." Her children were taught to be quiet at family prayer, and to ask a blessing immediately after, by *signs, before they could kneel or speak.*

The family school was opened and closed with singing; at five o'clock in the afternoon all had a season of retirement, when the oldest took the youngest that could speak, and the second the next, to whom they read the Psalm for the day, and a chapter in the New Testament. She herself also conversed, each evening, with one of her children, on religious subjects, and on some evenings with two, so as to comprehend the whole circle every week.[35] Cowardice and fear of punishment, she remarks, often lead children to contract a habit of lying, from which it is difficult for them to break away in later life. To prevent this, a law was made that whoever was charged with a fault, of which he was guilty, should not be chastised if he would ingenuously confess it, and promise to amend. No child was ever punished twice for the same fault; and if he reformed, the offense was never afterward upbraided. Promises were to be strictly observed. No girl was taught to work till she read correctly; she was then kept to her work with the same application, and for the same time that she had spent in reading. "This rule," wisely remarks the mother, "is much to be observed; for the putting children to learn sewing before they can read perfectly, is the very reason why so few women can read in a manner fit to be heard." None of them were taught to read till they were five years old, except one daughter, and she was more years in learning than any of the rest had been months. The day before a child began to study, the house was set in order, every one's work appointed, and a charge given that none should come into the room from nine till twelve, or from two till five, which were the school hours. One day was allowed the pupil to learn its letters, and each of them did in that time know them all, except two, who were a day and a half at the task, "for which," she says, "I then thought them very dull." Samuel, who was the first child thus taught, learned the alphabet in a few hours. The day after he was five years old he began to study, and as soon as he knew the letters he proceeded to spell out the first chapter of Genesis. The same method was observed by them all. As soon as they acquired the knowledge of the alphabet they were put to spelling and reading one line, then a verse, never leaving it till perfect in the appointed lesson, were it shorter or longer.

[35] This fact is mentioned in the letter to her husband, February 6, 1712, in which she defends the public worship that she conducted at the rectory. Moore's Life of Wesley, I, 3.

Such was the family school at Epworth. Who can doubt that the practical Methodism of the rectory, more than any other human cause, produced the ecclesiastical Methodism which to-day is spreading the Wesleyan name around the world? It received there, also, much of its thoroughly spiritual tone. Religion impressed the habitual life of the family. Susanna Wesley was its priestess, and, more than the rector himself, ministered to the spiritual necessities of the household. During his absence she even opened its doors for a sort of public worship, which was conducted by herself. She read sermons, prayed, and conversed directly with the rustic assembly. Her husband, learning the fact by her letters, revolted, as a Churchman, at its novelty. Her self-defense is characteristically earnest, but submissive to his authority. "I chose," she says, "the best and most awakening sermons we had. Last Sunday, I believe, we had above two hundred hearers, and yet many went away for want of room. We banish all temporal concerns from our society; none is suffered to mingle any discourse about them with our reading and singing. We keep close to the business of the day, and as soon as it is over they all go home. And where is the harm of this? As for your proposal of letting some other person read, alas! you do not consider what a people these are. I do not think one man among them could read a sermon without spelling a good part of it; and how would that edify the rest? Nor has any of our family a voice strong enough to be heard by such a number of people." Her husband equally hesitated to approve or disapprove the extraordinary proceeding. Very soon she assembled round her a larger audience than had usually met at the church itself. Some of the leading parishioners, and Wesley's curate, wrote to him against the assembly as a "conventicle." Her reply is full of good sense and womanly feeling. She states that the measure was reclaiming many of the common people from immorality; that it was filling up the parish Church; that some who had not attended the latter for years were now seen there.

She prays him to relieve her from the responsibility of ending these useful services by assuming it himself, as her husband and pastor. A writer on Methodism justly remarks, that when, in this characteristic letter, she said, "'Do not advise, but command me to desist,' she was bringing to its place a corner-stone of the future Methodism. In this emphatic expression of a deep, compound feeling, a powerful conscientious impulse, and a fixed principle of submission to rightful authority, there was condensed the very law of her son's course, as the founder and legislator of a sect. This equipoise of forces, which, if they act apart, and when not thus balanced, have brought to nothing so many hopeful movements, gave that consistency to Methodism to which it owes its permanence."[36]

Thus did this truly English and Christian household pursue its course of successful self-culture. For more than forty years it rendered Epworth rectory a sanctuary of domestic and Christian virtues. Ten of the children attained adult years.[37] All these became devoted Christians, and every one of them "died in the Lord." "How powerful," remarks their biographer, in ending his almost romantic record, "is a religious education; and how true the saying, 'Train up a child in the way he should go, and when he is old he will not depart from it!'" "Such a family," he adds, "I have never read of, heard of, or known; nor, since the days of Abraham and Sarah, and Joseph and Mary of Nazareth, has there ever been a family to which the human race has been more indebted."[38]

Let us not suppose, however, that in this rare picture of Christian household life there were no shadows contrasted with its tranquil lights. It would have been less perfect without them. Samuel Wesley lived in continual conflict with poverty. He was imprisoned for debt, and died in debt. His Epworth living, though nominally valued at

[36] Isaac Taylor's Wesley and Methodism, page 28.
[37] Southey says six; Moore and Clarke say ten.
[38] Clarke's Wesley Family, p. 609.

£200, afforded but about £130, and his small adjacent parish of Wroote scarcely more than met its own expenses. The economy by which so large a family was so well sustained and educated, is one of the most remarkable facts in its history. Pressed on every side by want, suffering sometimes from severe destitution, as she has recorded in a letter to the Archbishop of York, the admirable matron of the rectory could nevertheless say, when more than fifty years old, that from the best observation she had been able to make, she had learned it was much easier to be contented without riches than with them. Keener sorrows were often added to their poverty. Death followed death until nine children had been borne away from the circle; the marriages of several of the daughters were unfortunate, and the noble mother, in a letter to her brother, writes with the anguish which only a mother can know, for the saddest sorrow of a child: "O sir! O brother! happy, thrice happy are you; happy is my sister that buried your children in infancy, secure from temptation, secure from guilt, secure from want or shame, secure from the loss of friends. Believe me, it is better to mourn ten children dead than one living, and I have buried many."

Twice was the rectory fired at night by the rabble of the parish. In the first instance it was partly consumed, in the second it was totally destroyed, together with its furniture, and the books and manuscripts of the rector. The family barely escaped with their night garments upon them. Mrs. Wesley was in feeble health; unable to climb with the rest through the windows, she was thrice beaten back from the front door by the flames. Committing herself to God, she at last waded through the fire to the street, scorching her face and hands. It was found that one child was missing. The father attempted several times to pass up the stairs to rescue him, but the consuming steps could not bear his weight. He returned in despair, and kneeling down upon the earth, resigned to God the soul of the child. Meanwhile, the latter waking from his sleep, and finding his chamber and bed on fire, flew to the window, beneath which two peasants placed themselves, one on the shoulders of the other, and saved him at the moment that the roof fell in and crushed the chamber to the ground.[39] "Come, neighbors," exclaimed the father, as he received his son, "let us kneel down; let us give thanks unto God; he has given me all my eight children; let the house go, I am rich enough." Hundreds of thousands of devout hearts have since repeated that thanksgiving. A few minutes more and the founder of Methodism would have been lost to the world. In about a quarter of a century the rescued boy went forth from the cloisters of Oxford to Moorfields, to call the neglected masses to repentance, and to begin the great work which has rendered his family historical, not only in his own country, but in all Protestant Christendom.[40]

[39] Letter of Mrs. Wesley, Whitehead's Life of Wesley, II, 1.

[40] Wesley gratefully remembered his escape, through life, and had an emblem of a house in flames engraved on one of his portraits with the motto, "Is not this a brand plucked out of the fire?"

CHAPTER III.

JOHN AND CHARLES WESLEY.

John Wesley — "Mysterious Noises" at the Rectory — Wesley at the Charter House — Charles Wesley — The Duke of Wellington — John Wesley at Oxford — Religious Inquiries — His Mother's Guidance — Thomas à Kempis — Jeremy Taylor — The Witness of the Spirit — Reprobation — William Law — Religious Habits — Scholarship — Religious Anxieties of Charles Wesley — Mysticism — The Holy Club — The Methodists — George Whitefield — Death of the Father of the Wesleys, and Dispersion of the Epworth Family — The Wesleys embark for Georgia — The Moravians — Failure of the Plans of the Wesleys — Their Errors — Their Return to England.

John Wesley was born at Epworth, on the 17th of June, 1703, old style. The domestic training which has been described, doubtless gave him those habits of method, punctuality, diligence, and piety, which afterward developed into the system of Methodism itself. His providential escape at the destruction of the Epworth rectory by fire in his sixth year, impressed him early with the sense of a special mission in the world; his mother shared the impression, and felt herself called by that event to specially consecrate him to God. Two years after it we find her making it the subject of one of her recorded evening meditations. "I do intend," she writes, "to be more particularly careful of the soul of this child, that Thou hast so mercifully provided for, than ever I have been, that I may do my endeavor to instil into his mind the principles of thy true religion and virtue. Lord give me grace to do it sincerely and prudently, and bless my attempts with good success."[1]

Writers on Methodism have been interested in tracing the influence of Wesley's domestic education on the habits of his

[1] Moore's Life of Wesley, II, 1.

manhood and the ecclesiastical system which he founded. Even the extraordinary "noises" for which the rectory became noted, and which still remain unexplained, are supposed to have had a providential influence upon his character. These phenomena were strikingly similar to marvels which, in our times, have suddenly spread over most of the civilized world, perplexing the learned, deluding the ignorant, producing a "spiritualistic" literature of hundreds of volumes and periodicals, and resulting in extensive church organizations.[2] The learned Priestley obtained the family letters and journals relating to these curious facts, and gave them to the world as the best authenticated and best told story of the kind that was anywhere extant.[3] John Wesley himself has left us a summary of these mysterious events. They began usually with a loud whistling of the wind around the house. Before it came into any room the latches were frequently lifted up, the windows clattered, and whatever iron or brass was about the chamber rung and jarred exceedingly. When it was in any room, let the inmates make what noises they could, as they sometimes did on purpose, its dead hollow note would be clearly heard above them all. The sound very often seemed in the air, in the middle of a room; nor could they exactly imitate it by any contrivance. It seemed to rattle down the pewter, to clap the doors, draw the curtains, and throw the man-servant's shoes up and down. Once it threw open the nursery door. The mastiff barked violently at it the first day, yet whenever it came afterward, he ran whining, or quite silent, to shelter himself behind some of the company. Scarcely any of the family could go from one room into another but the latch of the door they approached was lifted up before they touched it.

[2] The best account and, perhaps, the best solution of these modern wonders, have been given by Count Gasparin, of Geneva: Science versus Spiritualism, 2 vols., translated from the French. New York. See, also, Rogers's Philosophy of Mysterious Agents. Boston.

[3] Original Letters of the Rev. John Wesley and his Friends, illustrative of his Early History, with other Curious Papers, etc. By Rev. Joseph Priestley, L.L.D., F. R. S. Birmingham: 1791.

It was evidently, says Southey, a Jacobite goblin, and seldom suffered Mr. Wesley to pray for the king without disturbing the family. John says it gave "thundering knocks" at the Amen, and the loyal rector, waxing angry at the insult, sometimes repeated the prayer with defiance. He was thrice "pushed by it" with no little violence; it never disturbed him, however, till after he had rudely denounced it as a dumb and deaf devil, and challenged it to cease annoying his innocent children, and meet him in his study if it had anything to say. It replied with "a knock, as if it would shiver the boards in pieces," and resented the affront by accepting the challenge. At one time the trencher danced upon the table without any body's touching either. At another, when several of the daughters were amusing themselves at a game of cards upon one of the beds, the wall seemed to tremble with the noise; they leaped from the bed, and it was raised in the air, as described by Cotton Mather, in the witchcraft of New England. Sometimes moans were heard, as from a person dying; at others, it swept through the halls and along the stairs, with the sound of a person trailing a loose gown on the floor, and the chamber walls, meanwhile, shook with vibrations. It would respond to Mrs. Wesley if she stamped on the floor and bade it answer; and it was more loud and fierce whenever it was attributed to rats or any natural cause.

These noises continued about two months, and occurred the latter part of the time every day. The family soon came to consider them amusing freaks, as they were never attended with any serious harm; they all, nevertheless, deemed them preternatural. Adam Clarke assures us that though they subsided at Epworth, they continued to molest some members of the family for many years. Clarke believed them to be demoniacal; Southey is ambiguous respecting their real character;[4] Priestley supposed them a

[4] Though Southey avoids any explicit explanation of them in his Life of Wesley, in a letter to Wilberforce he avows his belief in their preternatural character. See Wilberforce's Correspondence, 2 vols. London.

trick of the servants or neighbors, but without any other reason than that they seemed not to answer any adequate purpose of a "miracle," to which Southey justly replies, that with regard to the good design which they may be supposed to answer, it would be end sufficient if sometimes one of those unhappy persons who, looking through the dim glass of infidelity, see nothing beyond this life, and the narrow sphere of mortal existence, should, from the well-established truth of one such story, trifling and objectless as it might otherwise appear, be led to a conclusion that there are more things in heaven and earth than are dreamed of in their philosophy. Isaac Taylor considers them neither "celestial" nor "infernal," but extra-terrestrial, intruding upon our sphere occasionally, as the Arabian locust is sometimes found in Hyde Park.[5] Of the influence of these facts on Wesley's character, this author remarks that they took effect upon him in such a decisive manner as to lay open his faculty of belief, and create a right of way for the supernatural through his mind, so that to the end of his life there was nothing so marvelous that it could not freely pass where these mysteries had passed before it. Whatever may be thought of this very hypothetical suggestion, and of its incompatibility with the disposition of this writer, and, indeed, of most of Wesley's critics, to impute to him a natural and perilous credulity, it cannot be denied that in an age which was characterized by skepticism, a strong susceptibility of faith was a necessary qualification for the work which devolved upon him, and less dangerous by far than the opposite disposition; for though the former might mar that work, the latter must have been fatal to it.

When but thirteen years old, John Wesley left the paternal home for the Charter-House School, in London. There could hardly be a misgiving of his moral safety in passing out into the world from the thorough and consecrating discipline of the rectory. His scholarship and life at the Charter-House showed a character already determinate

[5] Wesley and Methodism, p. 30.

and exalted. He suffered the usual tyranny of the elder students at the Charter-House, being deprived by them, most of the time, of his daily portion of animal food; but he preserved his health by a wise prescription of his father, that he should run round the garden three times every day. The institution became endeared to him, and on his yearly visits to London he failed not to walk through its cloisters and recal the memories of his studious boyhood, memories which were always sunny to his healthful mind. In 1720 he entered Christ Church College, Oxford, at the age of sixteen.

Meanwhile his brother, and chief coadjutor in founding Methodism, Charles Wesley, had also left Epworth, for Westminster school. Born December 18, 1708, he was the junior of John by more than five years. At Westminster he was under the tuition of his brother, Samuel Wesley, who was usher in the school. While there an incident occurred which might have changed considerably the history not only of Methodism, but of the British empire. Garret Wesley, of Ireland, who seems not to have been related to the family, proposed to adopt him and settle upon him his estate. The Rector of Epworth must have favored the offer, for money was forwarded yearly from Ireland to London for the expenses of the son. The latter, however, finally declined the proposition of his benefactor, and thus, as his brother John remarked, made "a fair escape" from fortune. Richard Colley, afterward known as Richard Colley Wesley, was adopted in his stead. This gentleman passed through several public offices, and by the time that the Wesleys were abroad founding Methodism, had entered Parliament. Under George II. he became Baron Mornington. He was the grandfather of the Marquis of Wellesley, Governor General of India, and of the Duke of Wellington, the conqueror of Napoleon.[6] Had the wish of

[6] This fact has been questioned by Maxwell, in his Life of the Duke of Wellington. Jackson, however, demonstrates its correctness; Life of Charles Wesley, I, 1. The duke's name, in the "Army List" of 1800, is the Hon. Arthur Wesley, Lieutenant Colonel of 33d Regiment.

Garret Wesley been accomplished, the name of the Duke of Wellington, and the hymns of Charles Wesley, might not to-day be known wherever the English language is spoken.

When about eighteen years old, Charles was elected to Christ Church College, Oxford. John had previously left it to become a fellow at Lincoln; the religious seriousness which had grown with his youth, now deepened into a profound anxiety to solve, by his own experience, the questions of personal religion. Healthful in his temperament, and not knowing, as he records in later years, "fifteen minutes of low spirits" during his life, he nevertheless bore, from day to day, the consciousness of a want of harmony with God. Such a harmony, "peace with God," was his ideal of personal religion. Could it not be attained? If attained, could it fail to be a matter of consciousness? Did not the Scriptures teach that "the Spirit itself beareth witness with our spirits that we are the children of God?" Was there not also a "Christian Perfection" taught in the Scriptures; a "perfect love which casteth out fear?" Not, of course, a perfection according to the absolute moral law of God, but according to the accommodated relation to that law in which our fallen race exists, under the mediatorial economy, and in which unavoidable imperfections are provided for by the Atonement, as in the case of unregenerate infancy, without the remorseful sense of guilt. If these conjectures were correct, what a deplorable condition did Christendom present? How few exemplified essential Christianity? How generally had dogmatism, ecclesiasticism, or, at best, mere ethical principles, overshadowed the spiritual life, and freedom, and beauty of genuine religion? How necesssary was it that the Christian world should be recalled from the "tithe of the mint and anise and cummin," to the spiritual life and simplicity of the Gospel, and that he, first settling these questions for himself, should proclaim them as on the housetops to his generation? These were the essential questions of "Methodism," that is to say, of primitive Christianity; and thus, while meditating in the cloisters of Oxford, was he being prepared, by the habitual pressure of such interrogations upon his own conscience, for the great mission which was before him. His vigilant mother, who seems to have been providentially guided, not only to form his character for the origination of Methodism, but to direct him, during her long life, in many of its distinct and most important stages, strengthened, by her letters, the tendencies of his mind at this time. "And now," said she, "in good earnest, resolve to make religion the business of your life; for, after all, that is the one thing that, strictly speaking, is necessary. All things besides are comparatively little to the purposes of life. I heartily wish you would now enter upon a strict examination of yourself, that you may know whether you have a reasonable hope of salvation by Jesus Christ. If you have, the satisfaction of knowing it will abundantly reward your pains; if you have not, you will find a more reasonable occasion for tears than can be met with in any tragedy."[7]

As usual in the moral discipline of good men, he was to reach the solution of the problems which now absorbed his attention, by inward struggles, the "fiery trial" which purifies. He did not yet apprehend the Scriptural simplicity of faith as the condition of justification, and also of sanctification. He pored over the pages of that marvelous book, *De Imitatione Christi*, which has lent the fragrance of its sanctity to every language of the civilized world, and which, by its peculiar appositeness to almost every aspiration, misgiving, or consolation of devout minds, has seemed more a production of Divine inspiration than any other work in Christian literature, except the Scriptures. It had been a favorite with his father, his "great and old companion." Almost perfect for its design as a monastic manual, its very adaptedness, in this respect, staggered the youthful Wesley, but it failed not to infect him with its fascinating mysticism. Its impression was deepened by Jeremy Taylor's "Holy Living and Dying." The rare poetic

[7] Southey's Wesley, chap. 2. Smith's History of Methodism, I, 3.

beauties of this work could not fail to charm his young imagination; but its piety was still more grateful to his present inquiring temper. Taylor's views of simplicity and purity of motive commended themselves to his conscience. Instantly, he says, he resolved to dedicate *all* his life to God, all his thoughts, and words, and actions—being thoroughly convinced there is no medium; that not only a part, but the whole must either be a sacrifice to God or himself, "that is, in effect, to the devil;" a sentiment that characterized his entire remaining life. The more genial light of the "Holy Living" illuminated, though it did not fully explain the pages of the "Imitation," and both books became his daily companions. His letters show their effect, and his father, perceiving it, endeavored to confirm it. "God fit you for your great work," he wrote to him; "fast, watch, and pray, believe, love, endure, and be happy, toward which you shall never want the ardent prayers of your most affectionate father." Some of Taylor's opinions provoked the dissent of the devout student, and led him more definitively to doctrines which were to be vital in the theology of Methodism. The bishop, in common with most theologians of his day, denied that the Christian could usually know his acceptance with God. Wesley replied: "If we dwell in Christ and Christ in us, which he will not do unless we are regenerate, certainly we must be sensible of it. If we can never have any certainty of our being in a state of salvation, good reason it is that every moment should be spent, not in joy, but in fear and trembling; and then, undoubtedly, in this life we are of all men most miserable. God deliver us from such a fearful expectation! Humility is, undoubtedly, necessary to salvation; and if all these things are essential to humility, who can be humble, who can be saved? That we can never be so certain of the par don of our sins as to be assured they will never rise up against us, I firmly believe. We know that they will infallibly do so, if we apostatize; and I am not satisfied what evidence there can be of our final perseverance, till we have finished our course. But I am persuaded we may know if we are *now* in a state of salvation, since that is expressly promised in the Holy Scriptures to our sincere endeavors, and we are surely able to judge of our own sincerity." [8]

Here was not only his later doctrine of the "Witness of the Spirit," but a clear dissent from the Calvinistic tenet of "final perseverance." His proclivity to Arminianism became quite decided about this time. "As I understand faith," he wrote, "to be an assent to any truth upon rational grounds, I do not think it possible, without perjury, to swear I believe anything unless I have reasonable grounds for my persuasion. Now that which contradicts reason cannot be said to stand upon reasonable grounds; and such, undoubtedly, is every proposition which is incompatible with the Divine justice or mercy. What, then, shall I say of predestination? If it was inevitably decreed from eternity that a determinate part of mankind should be saved, and none besides, then a vast majority of the world were only born to eternal death, without so much as a possibility of avoiding it. How is this consistent with either the Divine justice or mercy? Is it merciful to ordain a creature to everlasting misery? Is it just to punish a man for crimes which he could not but commit? That God should be the author of sin and injustice, which must, I think, be the consequence of maintaining this opinion, is a contradiction to the clearest ideas we have of the Divine nature and perfections." His mother confirmed him in these views, and expressed her abhorrence of the Calvinistic theology. God's prescience, she argued, is no more the effective cause of the loss of the wicked than our foreknowledge of the rising of to-morrow's sun is the cause of its rising. She prudently advised, however, abstinence from these speculations as "studies which tended more to confound than to inform the understanding."

The writings of the celebrated William Law had much influence upon him in this stage of his progress. They

[8] Moore's Wesley, II, 1, 2.

deepened his mysticism and confirmed his asceticism, leading him to depend upon his own works as the means of purification and comfort, but failing to give him just ideas of the faith "which worketh by love." And precisely here was the critical period in his history, one which must determine whether he should be the ascetic recluse at Oxford, with the "Imitation" ever before him, or the evangelist of his age, on Moorfields, and the Gwennap hills, with the Bible in his hand, *homo unius libri*, a "man of one book." With an earnestness bordering on agony, he writes to his mother, deploring the repugnance toward holiness, which he felt to be natural to him; he sought for humility, but complains that it seemed impossible to him; humility with him, however, meant at this time the ascetic self-abnegation of the "Imitation," a temper which, though it infected him temporarily afterward, was incompatible with his healthful temperament and with the destined work of his life. He implored his mother's counsels and prayers, entreating her especially to grant him the Thursday evening, which, according to her method of domestic training, she used to spend in devotional retirement with him.

His removal from Christ Church College to that of Lincoln, enabled him to change his ordinary society. He resolved to make but few acquaintances in his new residence, and none that could not aid his religious progress; and now he began that marvelous diary which so much illustrates his character, his literary opinions, and his unparalleled energy. He received the communion every week; he gave alms to the poor, and his whole life was consecrated to the attainment of the personal "holiness without which no man shall see the Lord." Meanwhile he had been admitted to orders, and preached occasionally. He had already attained a high reputation at the university, and was esteemed an excellent critic in the classic languages; his skill in logic was extraordinary; he was elected Greek lecturer and moderator of the classes in a few months after obtaining his fellowship, and when but little more than twenty-three years old. These successes were a part of his providential preparation for the career before him. Six times a week disputations were held at Lincoln College; "I could not," he writes, "avoid acquiring some degree of expertness in arguing, and especially in discerning and pointing out well-covered and plausible fallacies. I have since found abundant reason to praise God for giving me this honest art. By this, when men have hedged me in by what they call demonstrations, I have been many times able to dash them in pieces; in spite of all its covers, to touch the very point where the fallacy lay, and it flew open in a moment." He was called away much of the time to assist his father, who was sinking under years, at Epworth. On one of his occasional visits to Oxford, he found that his brother was passing through the same religious crisis as himself. Charles wrote to him, urging his return to Oxford; he describes himself as mysteriously awakened from the moral lethargy in which he had spent his youth; and attributes the Divine illumination which had been given him to the prayers of his mother. Both seemed to turn instinctively to her, rather than to their father, whenever their hearts were deeply moved by any religious anxiety or difficulty.

John, during his rural retirement at Epworth, had yielded still more to his mystical tendencies under the influence of à Kempis and Law. The turning point which was to fit or unfit him for the task of his life, had not yet been passed. He had desired at one time to try the tranquil life of the Catholic recluses; "it was the decided temper of his soul," he said. Seclusion from the world for at least some months might, he hoped, settle his thoughts and habits. A school in one of the "Yorkshire dales" was proposed. His wiser mother again stepped in to save him for his appointed career, prophetically intimating that God had better work for him to do. He tells us himself, that before his return to the university he traveled some miles to see a "serious man." Sir, said this person, as if inspired at the right moment, with the right word, for the man of Providence standing before him; Sir, you wish to serve God and go to heaven; remember you cannot serve him alone; you must therefore *find* companions, or *make* them; the Bible knows nothing of solitary religion. Wesley never forgot these words. They, perhaps, forecast the history of his life. On reaching Oxford he found "companions" already prepared for him by his brother's agency. The "Holy Club" was now known there, and the epithet of "Methodist" had already been committed to ecclesiastical history. He arrived at Oxford in November, 1729; Charles and his religious associates gathered immediately around him, recognizing at once that capacity for guidance and authority which all who approached him afterward, seemed spontaneously to acknowledge. Charles was now twenty-one years of age, a Bachelor of Arts, and a college tutor. The "Holy Club," of which he was considered the founder, at first consisted of but four members. Their names are reverently preserved by Methodist writers; they were, "Mr. John Wesley, who was fellow of Lincoln College; his brother Charles, student of Christ Church; Mr. Morgan, commoner of Christ Church, the son of an Irish gentleman; and Mr. Kirkham, of Merton College." They were closely bound together not only in their religious sympathies, but in their studies, spending three or four evenings each week in reading together the Greek Testament and the ancient classics, and Sunday evenings in the study of divinity. They received the Lord's Supper weekly, and fasted twice a week. A rigid system of self-examination was drawn up for them by Wesley, which, it has been observed, might have been appended to the spiritual exercises of Loyola, had it not mentioned the laws of the Anglican Church. The almost monastic habits of life they were forming, in which, as Wesley's biographers, Coke and Moore, remark, "the darkness of their minds as to Gospel truths is evident," was counteracted by the benevolent and active sympathies of Mr. Morgan. He had visited the prison, and brought back reports which induced the little company systematically to instruct the prisoners once or twice a week. Morgan also came to them from the bedside of a sick person of the town, and they were led to adopt a plan for the regular visitation of the sick. Meanwhile their numbers increased. In 1730 several pupils of John, and one of Charles, joined them; in 1732 Ingham, of Queen's College, and Broughton, of Exeter, and about the same time Clayton, of Brazennose, with some of his pupils, and Hervey, the author of "Theron and Aspasio" and "The Meditations," were received. Whitefield joined them in 1735. Before the return of John from Epworth, the term Methodist had been applied to them in jest, by a fellow student, and Charles was the first of the family who received the now honored title. It was suggested, doubtless, by their methodical lives; but it had been used among religious parties already. A hundred years prior to this date, we hear of "the Anabaptists and plain pack-staff Methodists."[9] A class of Nonconformists, in the days of Annesley, were designated by the epithet, for their views respecting the method of man's justification before God; and a controversial pamphlet of those times discusses the principles of the "New Methodists."[10] A class of high Calvinistic divines in England, about the time of the Wesleys, also bore the title.

Morgan, whose influence on his companions was so salutary, was of delicate constitution, but tireless beneficence. He not only visited the sick and prisoners, but collected together the peasant children of the vicinity for religious instruction, and the distribution of good books. His health failed and he retired to his home in Ireland, where, after a period of mental depression, produced by disease, he died in "great peace and resignation."

[9] Jackson's Charles Wesley, chap. 2.

[10] The controversy and the party seem to have been extensive. Dr. Williams, who preached Annesley's funeral sermon, was one of their writers. The questions in dispute were referred to the arbitration of Bishop Stillingfleet. The title of the pamphlet alluded to is, "A War Among the Angles of the Churches, wherein is shown the Principles of the New Methodists in the great Point of Justification, also a Form of Prayer according to those Principles," etc.—Ibid.

Whitefield has left us a characteristic account of his connection with the "Holy Club." He was born in 1714, at the Bell Inn, Bristol. He describes his childhood as exceedingly vicious. "If I trace myself," he says, "from my cradle to my manhood, I can see nothing in me but a fitness to be damned; and if the Almighty had not prevented me, by his grace, I had now either been sitting in darkness, and in the shadow of death, or condemned, as the due reward of my crimes, to be forever lifting up my eyes in torments."[11] Yet he alludes to intervals of deep religious sensibility in his early life. When about fifteen years old he "put on his blue apron and his snuffers," washed mops, cleaned rooms, and became a "common-drawer." Thomas à Kempis, so important with the Wesleys at Oxford, had fallen into his hands, and could not fail to impress a heart like his, which retained through life the freshness of childhood, and attained with advanced piety, the vivid but steady ardor of a seraph. He had already given evidence of his natural powers of eloquence in school declamations, and while in the Bristol Inn composed two or three sermons. Hearing of the possibility of obtaining an education at Oxford, as a servitor or "poor student," he prepared himself and went thither, and afterward provided for his expenses, chiefly by serving his fellow collegians. His mind had taken a deeply religious turn while yet at Bristol, but à Kempis had not helped him to comprehend the doctrine of Justification by Faith. He says that when he was sixteen years of age, he began to fast twice a week for thirty-six hours together, prayed many times a day, received the sacrament every ten days, fasted himself almost to death all the forty days of Lent, during which time he made it a point of duty never to go less than three times a day to public worship, besides seven times a day to his private devotions, yet, he adds, "I knew no more that I was to be born again in God, born a new creature in Christ Jesus, than if I was never born at all." He obtained Law's Serious Call at Oxford, and that

[11] Robert Philip's Life and Times of Whitefield, chap. 1.

powerful book affected him as it had the Wesleys. He says, that he now began to pray and sing psalms twice every day, besides morning and evening, and to fast every Friday, and to receive the sacrament at a parish church near his college, and at the castle, where the "despised Methodists used to receive it once a month." The Methodists were not only the common butt of Oxford ridicule, but their fame had spread as far as Bristol before Whitefield left his home. He had "loved them," he tells us, before he entered the university, and now defended them against the sarcasms of his fellow students. For a year he longed to meet them, but an opportunity seemed not to offer, though he often gazed at them with deep emotions as they passed through a satirical crowd to receive the Eucharist at St. Mary's.

He procured, at last, an introduction to Charles Wesley, who received him at once to his heart, for they were congenial spirits, being both ardent with vivid natural sympathies; the one the natural poet, the other the natural orator. He was soon introduced to the Holy Club. "They built me up daily," he says, "in the knowledge and fear of God, and taught me to endure hardness as a good soldier of Jesus Christ." Like them he now began to live by rule, to economize the very moments of his time; and whether he ate or drank, or whatsoever he did, to do all to the glory of God. Like them, he received the sacrament every Sunday, at Christ Church, and he joined them in fasting Wednesdays and Fridays. Regular retirement, morning and evening, for meditation and prayer, he says he found at first difficult, if not irksome; but it grew profitable and delightful. He was soon abroad visiting the sick and prisoners, and reading to poor families, for it had become a custom of the Methodist band to spend an hour every day in such acts of usefulness.

The morals of the university were low at this time. Infidelity prevailed, and called forth public remonstrances from the collegiate authorities. What regard was paid to religion was formal and lifeless, and the little company of earnest inquirers looked beyond their circle, in vain, for sympathy and guidance. It is not a matter of wonder, then, that some of them fell into errors. Whitefield, for a time, became a Quietist, and sought repose for his troubled spirit in seclusion from the usual meetings of the club, in walks in the fields, and in praying silently by himself. The Wesleys rescued him, and gave him directions as his "various and pitiable state required." "God gave me," he writes, with his characteristic tenderness of feeling, "God gave me, blessed be his holy name, a teachable temper, and I was delivered from those wiles of Satan."

The scene presented by these young men, thus struggling for self-purification at the greatest seat of English learning, and unconsciously preparing a new development of Protestantism, at a time of general infidelity and demoralization, cannot fail to strike any devout mind as a most impressive spectacle. It was one of those examples of Divine Providence by which the Church, in some of its darkest and most hopeless exigences, has been endowed with "power from on high," and led forth, as from the wilderness, for renewed triumphs, by means which none had anticipated, and which, notwithstanding their apparent insignificance, have surpassed the wisdom of the wise and the resources of the mighty. Voltaire predicted, about this time, that in the next generation Christianity would be overthrown throughout the civilized world; these young men defeated the prophecy, and rendered the next generation the most effective in Christian history since the days of Martin Luther.

But their preliminary training was not over. The leading agents of the coming revolution were to be cast out upon the world, to prepare themselves, in a larger arena, for the work before them. The father of the Wesleys, approaching his end, and exhorting his sons, meanwhile, to struggle on, had entreated John to become his successor at Epworth, and protect his family from dispersion at his death. The appeal was an affecting one, and the son has been reproached for not heeding it; but he was steadfast in his conviction that a different course of life devolved upon him; and his thoughtful mother seems not to have joined her husband in the attempt to divert him from it. The rector died, the family was scattered, and the Epworth rectory fades from the history of Methodism, to reappear again only when, in later years, its founder, hastening over the realm to call the neglected multitudes to repentance, and, denied the pulpit of his father, stood upon his tombstone, in the church-yard, and proclaimed his message to the villagers. The disinterestedness of his motives, in declining the Epworth living, was soon tested. General Oglethorpe, the friend and correspondent of his father, was about to conduct a reinforcement to the colony of Georgia, and the young divine, who had refused a quiet rectory, and the comforts of the parental home, consented to go, accompanied by his brother Charles, as a missionary to the American aborigines. He was to be disappointed in his main design, but was to learn, by the expedition, important lessons for the future. The charm of the mystic writers still hung about him; it was to be dispelled in the remote wilds of America, where it could do little harm, but where his failure to find religious peace, contrasted with the practical piety and spiritual enjoyment of a few simple Moravians, was to prepare him to return better qualified for the predestined work of his life.

It was still a question whether he ought to desert his widowed mother, who was now dependent upon her children. "I can be," he replied to the invitation, "the staff of her age, her chief support and comfort." His consent depended upon hers; and her reply was what might have been expected from such a woman: "If I had twenty sons, I should rejoice that they were all so employed, though I should never see them again."

On the 14th of October, 1735, the party, consisting of the two Wesleys, and Messrs. Ingham and Delamotte, left London to embark. They found on board the ship one hundred and twenty-four persons, including twenty-six German Moravians, with their bishop, David Netschman. John Wesley seems immediately, though informally, to have been recognized as the religious head of the floating community, and his methodical habits prevailed over all around him. The ship became at once a Bethel Church and a seminary. The daily course of life among the Methodist party was directed by Wesley: from four till five o'clock in the morning each of them used private prayer; from five till seven they read the Bible together, carefully comparing it with the writings of the earliest Christian ages; at seven they breakfasted; at eight were the public prayers. From nine to twelve Wesley usually studied German, and Delamotte Greek, while Charles Wesley wrote sermons, and Ingham instructed the children. At twelve they met to give an account of what each had done since their last meeting, and of what they designed to do before the next. About one they dined; the time from dinner to four was spent in reading to persons on board, a number of whom each of them had taken in charge. At four were the evening prayers, when either the second lesson of the day was explained—as the first always was in the morning—or the children were catechised and instructed before the congregation. From five to six they again retired for private prayer. From six to seven Wesley read in his state-room to two or three of the passengers, and each of his brethren to a few more in theirs; at seven he joined the Germans in their public service, while Ingham was reading between decks to as many as desired to hear. At eight they met again to exhort and instruct one another. Between nine and ten they went to bed, where, says Wesley, neither the roaring of the sea, nor the motion of the ship, could take away the refreshing sleep which God gave them.[12]

Here was practical "Methodism" still struggling in its forming process; it was Epworth rectory and Susanna Wesley's discipline afloat on the Atlantic.

The great event of the voyage, as affecting the history of Methodism, was the illustration of genuine religion which the little band of Moravian passengers gave during a

[12] Wesley's Journal, Anno 1735.

perilous storm. Wesley had observed with deep interest their humble piety, in offices of mutual kindness and service, and in patience under occasional maltreatment; but when the storm arose there was an opportunity, he says, of seeing whether they were delivered from the spirit of fear, as well as from that of pride, anger, and revenge. In the midst of the psalm with which their service began, the sea broke over the ship, split the main-sail into pieces, and poured in between the decks as if the great deep had already swallowed them up. A terrible alarm and outcry arose among the English, but the Germans calmly sung on. Wesley asked one of them: "Were you not afraid?" He answered: "I thank God, no." "But were not your women and children?" "No; our women and children are not afraid to die."

Wesley felt that he had not yet so learned Christ, and retired to lay the lesson to heart, and to urge it on the attention of their "crying, trembling English neighbors." On arriving in America it was again to be pressed upon his awakened mind by a representative of these devoted people. He met Spangenberg, one of their pastors, and consulted him respecting the best plans of ministerial labor.

"My brother," said the Moravian, "I must first ask you one or two questions. Have you the witness within yourself? Does the Spirit of God bear witness with your spirit that you are a child of God?"

Wesley was surprised, and knew not what to answer. Spangenberg observed his embarrassment, and asked: "Do you know Jesus Christ?" "I know he is the Saviour of the world," replied Wesley. "True," rejoined the Moravian; "but do you know that he has saved *you?*" "I hope he has died to save me." Spangenberg only added: "Do you know yourself?" "I do," responded Wesley; "but," he writes, "I fear they were mere words."

He was impressed by the simple beauty of the religious life of these Moravians. Delamotte and he lodged with them, and had opportunities, day by day, of observing their whole demeanor; for they were present in one room with them from morning till night, unless for the little time spent in walking for exercise. He describes them as always employed, always cheerful, always cordial to one another; "they had put away all anger, and strife, and wrath, and bitterness, and clamor, and evil-speaking; they walked worthy of the vocation wherewith they were called, and adorned the Gospel of our Lord in all things." His Churchly prejudices were rebuked by the apostolic purity of their ecclesiastical forms. They met, he says, to consult concerning the affairs of their Church; Spangenberg being about to go to Pennsylvania, and Bishop Netschman to return to Germany. After several hours spent in conference and prayer, they proceeded to the election and ordination of a bishop. The great simplicity, as well as solemnity, of the proceeding almost made him forget the seventeen hundred years between him and the apostles, and imagine himself in one of those assemblies where form and state were unknown, but Paul, the tent-maker, or Peter, the fisherman, presided, with the demonstration of the Spirit and of power.[13]

It early became manifest that he could not prosecute his designs respecting the Indians, and he continued in Savannah; but his ascetic habits and severe formalism were unsuccessful in reclaiming the demoralized colonists. A similar failure attended his brother at Frederica. They labored indefatigably, but had yet very imperfect ideas of the "way of salvation by faith." The forms of the Church were enforced with a repetition and rigor which soon tired out the people, and provoked resentments and persecutions. Charles performed four public services every day, enlarging them by an explanation of the morning and evening lessons. John, assisted by Delamotte, formed what serious persons they could find at Savannah into a society, to meet once or twice a week, in order to reprove, instruct, and exhort one another, and from them selected a

[13] Wesley's Journal, Anno 1736.

smaller number for a more intimate communion. He read the prayers according to the primitive order of his Church, beginning with the morning service at five o'clock, giving a sermon and the communion service at eleven, and the evening service at three. Between eleven and three, when the people were compelled by the heat to remain at home, he visited them from house to house. Following the primitive but obsolete Rubric, he would baptize children only by immersion, and no person was admitted as a sponsor who was not a communicant. He refused to recognize any baptism which was performed by a clergyman who had not received episcopal ordination, and insisted upon rebaptizing such children as had otherwise received that sacrament. His rigor extended even so far as to refuse the Lord's Supper to one of the most devout men of the settlement, who had not been baptized by an episcopally ordained minister;[14] and the burial service itself was denied to such as died with what he deemed unorthodox baptism.

Asceticism is usually associated with formalism, for the misled but anxious mind, failing to find comfort in the one, would add other expedients for its relief. Both the brothers denied themselves not only the luxuries, but many of the ordinary conveniences of life. They slept on the ground rather than on beds; they refused all food but bread and water; and John went barefooted, that he might encourage the poor boys of his school—a condescension better in its motive than in its example. In fine, these Oxford students, misapprehending the simplicity of the Gospel, and the liberty wherewith Christ maketh free, were groping their way, in the new world, through nearly the same deplorable errors

[14] When he escaped these "orthodox" follies, he referred to them with astonishment. In his Journal for September 29, 1749, he gives a letter from John Martin Bolzius, and adds: "What a truly Christian piety and simplicity breathe in these lines! And yet this very man, when I was at Savannah, did I refuse to admit to the Lord's table, because he was not baptized; that is, not baptized by a minister who had been episcopally ordained. Can any one carry High-Church zeal higher than this? And how well have I been since beaten with mine own staff!"

which a class of earnest men of the same university have promulgated in our day, with as little success, both as it respects their own spiritual life and the reformation of the Church. They were Puseyites.

Not only their rigorous practices, but their theological opinions defeated them. Faith, not works, as the condition of justification—faith producing works as its necessary fruits; ordinances and sacraments as only aids to faith; the conscious forgiveness of sins; peace and joy in the Holy Ghost; the sanctification, not the abnegation, of the natural affections and appetites, with cheerful thankfulness to Him "who giveth us richly all things to enjoy;" these were conceptions as yet obscure, if not foreign to their minds. How, with the Holy Scriptures in their hands, they could thus err might, indeed, be a mystery to us, were it not that the history of the human mind shows so universally the power of traditional influences, and of even apparently accidental states of opinion, to distort the interpretation of the plainest truth; so that the declaration of a profound and evangelical writer [15] of our own age may yet prove true, that ideas now admitted by the Christian world to be correct, may yet come to be repelled as intolerable and abominable.

The colonists recoiled from the earnest but erring missionaries. Gossip, backbiting, and scandal, the prevalent vices of small and isolated settlements, beset them at all points; an unfortunate "courtship" which Wesley found it prudent to abandon, occasioned the disaffection of a large family circle; open persecution followed, and an attempt was made to assassinate Charles Wesley. In about a year he returned by way of Boston, where he preached repeatedly in King's Chapel. In some fifteen months more John followed him. They had failed in their designs, but they had learned important lessons. On the sea Wesley wrote that he had bent the bow too far, by making antiquity a co-ordinate rather than a subordinate rule with Scripture; by admitting several doubtful writings; by extending antiquity too

[15] Vinet.

far; by believing more practices to have been universal in the ancient Church than ever were so; by not considering that the decrees of synods or councils were of but human authority. These considerations insensibly stole upon him, he says, as he grew acquainted with the Mystic writers, whose descriptions of union with God and internal religion made everything else appear mean and insipid. "But, in truth," he adds, "they made good works appear so too; yea, and faith itself, and what not? They gave me an entire new view of religion, nothing like any I had before. But, alas! it was nothing like that religion which Christ and his apostles taught. I had a plenary dispensation from all the commands of God; the form was thus: Love is all; all the commands besides are only means of love; you must choose those which you feel are means to you, and use them as long as they are so. Thus were all the bands burst at once; and though I could never fully come into this, nor contentedly omit what God enjoined, yet, I know not how, I fluctuated between obedience and disobedience. I had no heart, no vigor, no zeal in obeying; continually doubting whether I was right or wrong, and never out of perplexities and entanglements. Nor can I at this hour give a distinct account how or when I came a little back toward the right way; only my present sense is this—all the other enemies of Christianity are triflers; the Mystics are the most dangerous; they stab it in the vitals, and its most serious professors are most likely to fall by them."

Thus was he breaking away from the mists which had encompassed him; but he had not yet reached those higher acclivities of the religious life, where the problems which had agonized his spirit shine out in clear, serene illumination to the vision of faith. There is an earnestness which is touching in its pathos in an entry of his journal, written as the ship approached the Land's End of England: "I went to America," he says, "to convert the Indians, but O! who shall convert me? Who, what is he that will deliver me from this evil heart of unbelief? I have a fair summer religion; I can talk well, nay, and believe myself, while no danger is near; but let death look me in the face, and my spirit is troubled, nor can I say, to die is gain. I think verily, if the Gospel be true, I am safe; for I not only have given and do give all my goods to feed the poor—I not only give my body to be burned, drowned, or whatever else God shall appoint for me, but I follow after charity—though not as I ought, yet as I can—if haply I may attain it. I now believe the Gospel is true. I show my faith by my works, by staking my all upon it. I would do so again and again a thousand times, if the choice were still to make. Whoever sees me, sees I would be a Christian. Therefore are my ways not like other men's ways; therefore I have been, I am, I am content to be, a by-word, a proverb of reproach. But in a storm I think, What if the Gospel be not true? Then thou art of all men most foolish. For what hast thou given thy goods, thy ease, thy friends, thy reputation, thy country, thy life? For what art thou wandering over the face of the earth? a dream? a cunningly-devised fable? O! who will deliver me from this fear of death? What shall I do? Where shall I fly from it? Should I fight against it by thinking, or by not thinking of it? A wise man advised me some time since, 'Be still, and go on.' Perhaps this is best; to look upon it as my cross; when it comes to let it humble me, and quicken all my good resolutions, especially that of praying without ceasing; and at other times to take no thought about it, but quietly to go on in the work of the Lord."

On the 1st of February, 1738, he was again in England, and writing in his diary: "This, then, have I learned in the ends of the earth—that I 'am fallen short of the glory of God;' that my whole heart is 'altogether corrupt and abominable,' and, consequently, my whole life—seeing it cannot be that an 'evil tree' should 'bring forth good fruit;' that, 'alienated' as I am from 'the life of God,' I am a 'child of wrath,' an heir of hell; that my own works, my own sufferings, my own righteousness, are so far from reconciling me to an offended God, so far from making any atonement for the least of those sins which 'are more in number than the hairs of my head,' that the most specious of them need an atonement themselves, or they cannot abide his righteous judgment; that 'having the sentence of death' in my heart, and having nothing in or of myself to plead, I have no hope but that of being justified freely, 'through the redemption that is in Jesus;' I have no hope, but that if I seek, I shall find Christ, and 'be found in him, not having my own righteousness, but that which is through the faith of Christ, the righteousness which is of God by faith.'" Astonishing and affecting disclosures of the mysterious heart of man! Admonitory lesson to all who would successfully seek the truth, and by it be made free! Here was a man of healthful temperament, of rare intelligence, of logical astuteness, who had read every line of Holy Scripture in the very language in which prophet or apostle had penned it, and yet, with the Bible in his hand, and an anguish of earnestness in his heart, he stumbles before the most important and most simple truths of revelation. What is the solution of this mystery? Can we suppose that had he read the Scriptures only, and interpreted them as an earnest, unsophisticated peasant would have done, he could so long have failed of their simple faith and inexpressible comfort? These were all he needed; he had reached all other conditions of the Christian life; the faith to appropriate to himself the promises and consolations of the Gospel was still lacking; but could he have failed to discern this fact if he had looked into the Scriptures without the sophistications of other books and the prejudice of traditional errors? His previous references to councils, and Church decrees, and mysticism—his asceticism and ecclesiasticism in Georgia—these explain the mystery. They complicated and rendered nugatory his more direct and simple views of truth. Neither the personal history of Wesley nor the history of Methodism itself, can be comprehended without these revelations of his inward struggles. But the light was dawning, and the morning was at hand. The Moravians were again to meet him in London.

CHAPTER IV.

GEORGE WHITEFIELD.

Whitefield's Mental Conflicts — His Ascetic Errors — His Conversion — He begins to preach — He preaches in the Metropolis — Remarkable Effects of his Sermons — His Powers as an Orator — He embarks for America — His Return to England.

DURING the absence of the Wesleys in America, George Whitefield was the presiding spirit of the "Holy Club" at Oxford. He preceded the Wesleys in obtaining the peace of mind, and "assurance of faith," which they had sought together so arduously before they parted. But, like them, he passed through an ordeal of agonizing self-conflicts, in which his sensitive mind became deeply melancholy, and was betrayed into ascetic follies. He was overwhelmed with morbid horrors, and describes himself as losing at times, even the power of thinking. His memory failed; his feelings were cramped, he says, as a man bound in iron armor; he selected the poorest food, and the meanest apparel, and by dirty shoes, patched raiment, and coarse gloves, endeavored to mortify his burdened spirit. He was insulted by his fellow students, and those who employed his services discharged him, because of his self-negligence. He daily underwent some contempt at college. Students threw dirt at him in the streets. Whenever he knelt down to pray he felt great pressure both in soul and body, and often prayed under the weight of it till the sweat dripped from his face. "God only knows," he writes, "how many nights I have lain upon my bed groaning under what I felt. Whole days and weeks have I spent in lying prostrate on the ground in silent or vocal prayer."[1] During

[1] Philip's Life and Times of Whitefield, chap 1.

the forty days of lent he ate nothing but "coarse bread and sage tea," except on Saturdays and Sundays. He prayed under the trees at night, trembling with the cold, till the bell of the college called him to his dormitory, where he often spent in tears and supplications the hours which should have brought him the relief of sleep. His health sunk under these rigors; but he writes that, notwithstanding his sickness continued six or seven weeks, he trusted he should have reason to bless God for it through the ages of eternity. For about the end of the seventh week, after having undergone inexpressible trials by night and day, under the spirit of bondage, God was pleased at length to remove the heavy load, to enable him to lay hold on the cross by a living faith, and by giving him the Spirit of adoption to seal him, as he humbly hoped, even to the day of everlasting redemption. "But O!" he continued, "with what joy, joy unspeakable, even joy that was full of glory, was my soul filled, when the weight of sin went off, and an abiding sense of the pardoning love of God, and a full assurance of faith, broke in upon my disconsolate soul! Surely it was the day of my espousals, a day to be had in everlasting remembrance. At first my joys were like a spring tide, and, as it were, overflowed the banks; go where I would I could not avoid the singing of psalms almost aloud; afterward they became more settled, and blessed be God, saving a few casual intervals, have abode and increased in my soul ever since."

Healed in soul and convalescent in body, he visited his native town of Bristol, for a change of air. He met there the bishop of Gloucester, who perceived his talents and earnest spirit, and proffered him ordination. He prepared himself for the ceremony by fasting and prayer, and spent two hours the previous evening on his knees in the neighboring fields. At the ordination he consecrated himself to an apostolic life. "I trust" he writes, "I answered to every question from the bottom of my heart, and heartily prayed that God might say, Amen. And when the bishop laid his hands upon my head, if my vile heart doth not deceive me,

I offered up my whole spirit, soul, and body to the service of God's sanctuary. Let come what will, life or death, depth or height, I shall henceforward live like one who, this day, in the presence of men and angels, took the holy sacrament, upon the profession of being inwardly moved by the Holy Ghost to take upon me that ministration in the Church. I can call heaven and earth to witness, that when the bishop laid his hand upon me, I gave myself up to be a martyr for Him who hung upon the cross for me. Known unto him are all future events and contingencies. I have thrown myself blindfold, and, I trust, without reserve, into His almighty hands." His remaining life was an exemplification of these vows. He had a soul of fire, and henceforth it glowed brighter and brighter even unto the perfect day.

Fitted by every attribute of his large but simple mind to be an evangelist, but not an ecclesiastical legislator, he now went forth as the Baptist of Methodism, to prepare the way in both hemispheres for the Wesleys and their coadjutors. The good Bishop of Gloucester, who seems to have felt a genial sympathy with his ardent soul, gave him five guineas, "a great supply," wrote Whitefield, "for one who had not a guinea in the world." His first sermon was preached in the church where he had been baptized, and had received his first communion. He revealed at once his extraordinary powers. It was reported to the bishop that fifteen of his hearers had gone mad. The prelate only wished that the madness might not pass away before another Sabbath.

Returning to Oxford he forthwith resumed his "Methodist" labors, comforting his brethren, visiting the sick and prisoners, and encouraging several charity schools which the "Holy Club" had established. He was called to London to preach temporarily at the Tower. There was some scoffing at his first appearance in the pulpit, but his natural eloquence and vivid zeal burst with surprise upon the people, and he passed out amid their blessings, while the query flew from one to another, "Who is he?" For two months he continued to labor in the metropolis, visiting the soldiers in the barracks and hospitals, catechising children, reading prayers every evening in one chapel, preaching in others, and delivering one sermon a week at least at Ludgate prison. The people crowded to hear him.

Returning to Oxford he had the pleasure to see the Methodist band increasing, but he was soon away again preaching at Dummer, in Hampshire, where he spent eight hours a day in reading prayers, catechising children, and visiting the parishioners. He had received several letters from the Wesleys, in Georgia, calling him thither. "Do you ask me what you shall have?" wrote John Wesley. "Food to eat, and raiment to put on, a house to lay your head in, such as your Lord had not; and a crown of glory that fadeth not away." His heart, he says, leaped within him, and echoed to the call. Hervey, of the Oxford Club, took his place in Hampshire, and he resolved to go again to London to embark. He went first to Bristol to take leave of his friends. While there he preached indefatigably. People of all classes, and all denominations, from Quakers to High Churchmen, flocked to hear him. "The whole city," he wrote, "seemed to be alarmed." The churches were crowded, "the word was sharper than a two-edged sword, and the doctrine of the new birth made its way like lightning into the hearer's consciences." After a short absence he returned to Bristol, and found the excited people, some on foot and some in coaches, coming a mile out of the city to welcome him. They blessed him as he passed along the streets. Though preaching five times a week, he could not appease the eager crowds. It was difficult for him to make his way through them to the pulpit. Some climbed upon the roof of the church, others hung upon the rails of the organ loft, and the mass within made the air so hot with their breath, that the steam fell from the pillars like drops of rain. When he preached his farewell sermon, the irrepressible feelings of his hearers broke out into sobs and tears all over the house. They followed him weeping into the street. They kept him busy the next day, from early morning till midnight, in comforting or counseling them, and he had to escape from their importunities, secretly, during the night, for London. While delayed there by his preparations for the voyage, his unexampled eloquence produced a general sensation through the metropolitan churches. When he assisted at the Eucharist, the consecration of the elements had to be twice or thrice repeated. Charitable institutions claimed his services, and larger collections were made than had ever been received by them on similar occasions. Constables were stationed at the doors to restrain the multitude of hearers. Churches were crowded on week-days and on the autumnal Sunday mornings the streets were thronged before dawn with people, lighting their way by lanterns to hear him.

This transcendent power arose from a combination of qualities, with which he was providentially endowed for the crisis that was approaching in the history of English, and, it is not too much to say, the history of general Protestantism. A great movement was at hand, which needed, among other agencies, powers like these to usher it in on both sides of the Atlantic, and to awaken the popular sympathies to welcome it—a movement which, it has been said, has immediately, or remotely so given an impulse to Christian feeling and profession, on all sides, that it has come to present itself as the starting point of our modern religious history.[2] Wesley was approaching the coast of England while Whitefield was preparing for his embarkation; "and now," says an author who was not over credulous respecting the providential facts of Methodism, "and now, when Whitefield, having excited this powerful sensation in London, had departed for Georgia, to the joy of those who dreaded the excesses of his zeal, no sooner had he left the metropolis than Wesley arrived there, to deepen and widen the impression which Whitefield had

[2] Isaac Taylor's Wesley and Methodism, Preface.

made. Had their measures been concerted they could not more entirely have accorded."[3] In a few days Wesley was proclaiming, in the pulpits of London, "If any man be in Christ, he is a new creature."

It would be difficult, if not impossible, to define the eloquence of Whitefield. It was the utterance of the whole man—heart, head, and person. It was more; it was the "demonstration of the Spirit and of power," the utterance of a living, exulting piety. Just before these scenes in London, while in his native county, he says his spirit would make such sallies that he thought it would escape from the body. At other times he was so overwhelmed with a sense of God's infinite majesty, that he was constrained to throw himself prostrate on the ground, and offer his soul as a blank for the Divine hand to write on it what should please God. One night he describes as a time never to be forgotten. It happened to lighten exceedingly; he had been expounding to many people, and some being afraid to go home, he thought it his duty to accompany them, and improve the occasion to stir them up for the coming of the Son of man. He preached to them warnings and consolations on the highway, while the thunders broke above his head, and the lightnings sped along his path. On his return to the parsonage, while the neighbors were rising from their beds, and terrified to see the lightning run upon the ground, and shine from one part of the heavens unto the other, he and a poor but pious countryman continued in the field, praying, praising, and exulting in God, and longing for the time when Christ shall be revealed from heaven in a flame of fire! "O that my soul," he wrote, "may be in a like flame when he shall actually come to call me!"

How could such a man be other than eloquent? An untutored hearer, returning from one of his sermons, significantly said, "He preached like a lion." But with this moral power he combined most, if not all other qualifications of a popular orator. He is said to have had a perfect

[3] Southey's Wesley, chap. 4.

natural grace of manner out of the pulpit, and of gesture in it. Marvels are told about the compass and music of his voice. He was tall in person; his features were regular, and expressive of a generous and buoyant heart; his eyes were blue and luminous, though small, and a slight squint in one of them, caused by the measles, is said not to have "lessened the uncommon sweetness" of his countenance. His humble origin and occupation in the Bristol Inn, enabled him to understand and address the common people, who, while admiring that natural grace which afterward rendered him at home in aristocratic circles, felt that he was one from among themselves. He had also an aptitude for illustrations drawn from common life, and a tendency to popular humor, which, without degenerating into vulgarity, drew irresistibly toward him the popular interest; so that Wesley, who was scrupulously, though simply correct, said: "Even the little improprieties, both of his language and manner, were the means of profiting many, who would not have been touched by a more correct discourse, or a more calm and regular manner of preaching."

His passage to America was long. The ship's company, including, besides the crew, soldiers and emigrants, were mostly an immoral class; but he preached, read prayers, catechised the children, and ministered to the sick, with such zeal, that before they reached Georgia the whole moral aspect of his floating congregation was changed. He remained in the colony only about four months, but during that time traveled and labored incessantly among its settlements. A brief residence among the Indians, and an unsuccessful attempt to frame a grammar of their language, seem to have satisfied him that his call was not unto them. He found many orphan children among the colonists, and projected an asylum for them, a design which led to his early return to England. He embarked from Charleston, South Carolina, September, 1738, in time, as we shall see, for important events in the incipient history of Methodism.

CHAPTER V.

WESLEY AND THE MORAVIANS.

Wesley's Return from Georgia — His Religious Disquiet — Sketch of the Moravians — Obligations of Methodism to the Martyrs of Constance — Ziska and his Peasant Heroes — Commencement of Herrnhut — Count Zinzendorf — The Moravians in London — Peter Böhler — Conversion of Charles Wesley — Conversion of John Wesley — Wesley's Visit to Herrnhut — His Description of it — Theological Views — Obligations of Methodism to the Moravians.

THE ship which bore Whitefield from England, passed in sight of that which bore Wesley back, only a few hours before his arrival at the Downs; but neither of them knew the fact. Whitefield, liberated in spirit, and winged with zeal as with pinions of flame, was flying exultingly on his mission;[1] but Wesley, who was to be last, and yet, in an important sense, first in the new career they had been fore-casting, entered the metropolis, which was still stirred by the evangelical triumphs of his friend, bowed and broken in spirit. In placing his foot again on English soil, he repeats, with profound contrition, the record of his inward struggles: "It is now," he writes, "two years and almost four months since I left my native country, in order to teach the Georgian Indians the nature of Christianity. But what have I learned myself, meantime? Why, what I the least of all suspected, that I, who went to America to convert others, was never myself converted to God. *I am not mad*, though I thus speak, but I *speak the words of truth and soberness*, if, haply, some of those who still dream may awake, and see that as I am so are they." Were they read in philosophy? he continues, with eloquent earnestness, and in language

[1] The device of Whitefield's seal was a winged heart, soaring above the globe, and the motto, *Astra petamus.* Southey's Wesley, note 24.

which would cover boastfulness itself with shame; were they read in philosophy? so was he. In ancient or modern tongues? he was also. Were they versed in the science of divinity? he too had studied it many years. Could they talk fluently upon spiritual things? the very same could he do. Were they plenteous in alms? behold, he gave all his goods to feed the poor. Did they give of their labor as well as their substance? he had labored more abundantly. Were they willing to suffer for their brethren? he had thrown away his friends, reputation, ease, country; he had put his life in his hands, wandering into strange lands; he had given his body to be devoured by the deep, parched up with heat, consumed by toil and weariness, or whatsoever God should please to bring upon him. But, he continues, does all this, be it more or less, it matters not, make him acceptable to God? Does all he ever did, or can, *know*, *say*, *give*, *do*, or *suffer*, justify him in His sight? If the oracles of God are true, if we are still to abide by the *law and testimony*, all these things, though, when ennobled by faith in Christ, they are holy, and just, and good, yet without it are *dung* and *dross*. He refuses to be comforted by ambiguous hopes. "If," he adds, "it be said that I have faith, for many such things have I heard from many miserable comforters, I answer, so have the devils a *sort* of faith; but still they are strangers to the covenant of promise. The faith I want is a sure trust and confidence in God, that, through the merits of Christ, my sins are forgiven, and I reconciled to the favor of God."[2]

But the time of his deliverance was at hand. He had learned in anguish its preparatory lessons; his good works, his ascetism, his ritualism had failed him. It had been necessary, perhaps, that he should try them, in order to be a competent guide for the millions who were yet to be affected by his influence. Susanna Wesley had educated him for his great work, and in this respect was the real founder of Methodism, for with a different character he would have

[2] Journal, Anno 1738.

had a different history; the germinal principle of Methodism had sprung up at Oxford; but the vital element which was to give it growth and enable it to branch out over the world, was still wanting. It was to be supplied in a manner which forms one of the most extraordinary illustrations of Divine Providence afforded by the annals of the Church.

More than three hundred years had passed since the Council of Constance had sacrificed, at the stake, the two noblest men of Bohemian history, Jerome and Huss. With Wicklif, they had initiated Protestantism a century before Luther. Though Wicklif died without the honors of martyrdom, his work was apparently yet not really defeated; and his bones, dug up from the grave and reduced to ashes, were cast on the Severn, and borne by the ocean to the wide world, an emblem, says a Church historian, of the future fate of his opinions. The Papal persecutors representing Europe at Constance, deemed that in destroying Jerome and Huss they had extinguished the new movement on the continent at least; but "God's thoughts are not as man's thoughts." A spark from the stake of Constance lit up at last the flame of Methodism in England, and is extending over the world in our day like fire in stubble.

The princes and prelates had hardly retired from Constance when the people, always truer than the great of the earth in their instinctive appreciation of great truths, rose throughout Bohemia to defend the opinions and avenge the death of their martyred teachers. Armed with flails, they marched victoriously against trained armies, for they were fighting for the right of themselves and of their children to the word of God and its sacraments. A nobleman of the court, Count Ziska, placed himself at their head, and organizing them into a formidable army, fought against the Emperor Sigismund for the independence of Bohemia. He had lost one eye; the remaining one was destroyed by an arrow in battle about a year after the war began; but, when no longer able to see, he still led his triumphant peasants from victory to victory. Mounting a cask in the camp, the sightless hero prepared them for battle by his eloquent appeals. The emperor invaded Bohemia, but Ziska totally defeated him. The blind commander invaded Austria and Hungary. His victory at Arssig placed the Austrian dominions at his mercy. He founded among his peasant heroes the modern science of fortification; he held at bay the arms of all Germany; he restored the independence of Bohemia, extinguished factions, and achieved eleven victories in pitched battles. Apparently immortal in war, he fell at last by the plague; but ordered, it is said, that his skin should be converted into drum-heads, to be beat in the marches of his soldiers. Eleven years after his death did they maintain the desperate struggle. After memorable scenes of fanaticism and terror on both sides, it was concluded at last by the treaty of Prague, nearly twenty years subsequent to the martyrdom of Jerome and Huss. That treaty conceded the most important religious demands of the Bohemians; but the Papal party afterward denied them. The Hussites were depressed, persecuted, and exiled; and it seemed at times that the movement had been defeated, and that "the blood of the martyrs" could not, in this instance at least, be said to be "the seed of the Church." It is not necessary, in order to vindicate a maxim which has so often been the boast of Christian virtue and suffering, to trace the influence of the Wicklifite and Hussite movements on the "Great Reformation" a century later. The Bohemian Reformation, though repressed, was not extinguished. It had its own peculiar effect on the world, and has it to-day. Many families lingered in Bohemia and Moravia from generation to generation, retaining, in humble obscurity, the truth for which the Constance martyrs had burned. A half century after their martyrdom the prisons of Bohemia groaned with the sufferings of their faithful followers. Five years later they were again ruthlessly hunted down by persecutions. They were declared outlaws; were expatriated and despoiled of their property. The sick and aged were driven out of their homes, and many perished of cold and hunger. Some expired in dungeons, others were tortured and burned, and the remnant took refuge in the thickest forests, where, fearing discovery during the day, they kindled their fires only by night, and around them spent the hours in watchings, in reading the Scriptures, in mutual exhortations, and in prayer.[3]

It is a noteworthy fact that these persecuted Bohemians gave the first printed edition of the Bible to the world, and the oldest version in any modern language. They established presses at three different places for the purpose of printing it, and had issued three editions before Luther appeared. They hailed the Reformation under Luther; the terrible "Thirty Years' War" ensued, but failed to secure them liberty of conscience; and they wandered away to other lands to find it. One of them—Christian David, an earnest-minded carpenter—led ten persons of like mind from Schlen, Moravia, to Bertholsdorf, in Lusatia, a domain of which Count Zinzendorf, a devout young nobleman, was then lord. He was absent, but welcomed them by Heitz, his major-domo; Heitz led the little band to a piece of land, near a mound, the Hutberg or Watch-hill, where Christian David, lifting his ax, cleaved a tree, exclaiming: "Here hath the sparrow found a house, and the swallow a nest for herself, even thine altars, O Lord of hosts." On the 17th of June, 1722, the first tree was cut down; on the 17th of October the exiles entered their new home. The count was still absent, but his pious major-domo wrote him a report of their progress. A phrase in his letter has since given name to the locality, and become a household word, if not a watchword throughout the Protestant world. "May God bless the work according to his loving-kindness," wrote Heitz, "and grant that your excellency may build a city on the Watch-hill, [*Hutberg*,] which may not only stand under the Lord's guardianship, but where all the inhabitants may

[3] "Memorial Days of the Ancient Brethren's Church." The chief source of my data respecting the Bohemian Reformation is Bonnechose's Reformers before the Reformation. See also Southey's Wesley, chap. 5.

stand upon the Watch of the Lord!" [*Herrnhut.*] At the dedication of the building the good major-domo discoursed to the little company on the words of Isaiah: "I will set watchmen upon thy walls, O Jerusalem! which shall never hold their peace day nor night: ye that make mention of the Lord keep not silence, and give him no rest till he establish, and till he make Jerusalem a praise in the earth."

Thus arose *Herrnhut*—Watch of the Lord—and the Moravian Brotherhood, a religious community whose name is as "ointment poured forth," whose missions have been the admiration of all good men, and who, in our day, have the extraordinary distinction of enrolling the majority of their communicants on their lists of reclaimed pagans.

Zinzendorf, accompanied by his young wife, visited the domain some few months later, and seeing from the highway the new home of the exiles in the forest, descended from his carriage, and hastily entering it, fell upon his knees amid the group of grateful inmates, and "blessed the place with a warm heart." He had secured Roth, a diligent pastor, for his tenants at Bertholdsdorf, and his friend, the pastor Schaefer, had said at the introduction of Roth: "God will place a light upon these hills which will illuminate the whole country; of this I am assured by a living faith." The count shared this faith, and sacrificing the honors and prospects of his rank, devoted himself thenceforth to Christian labors. His friend, the Baron de Watteville, joined him; the lady Goanna de Zetzschwitz subsequently took thither a number of young women for education, and founded the famous Economy of Girls at Herrnhut, and the forest sanctuary now became the home of hundreds, not only of the remnants of the old Bohemian Protestants, but of devout men from many parts of Europe.

The government grew jealous of the new establishment, and the count was exiled, and saved his estates only by securing them to his wife. Disguised by the name of De Freydeck, one of his real but least known titles, he traveled in Germany, and became a private tutor in the family of a merchant till he could prepare himself for an examination for ordination. He succeeded, and began to preach, and journeyed as an evangelist in Sweden, Holland, Switzerland, and England. Meanwhile, under his patronage, missionaries were passing out from Herrnhut to various parts of the world. He visited in their behalf the West Indies, New-York, and Pennsylvania. Returning to revisit his Herrnhut people, he was imprisoned, was re-banished, and resumed his religious travels in various parts of Europe. Finally he found shelter again among his devoted Herrnhuters, and died at the age of sixty, amid the tears and prayers of "nearly a hundred brethren and sisters who were assembled in the room where he lay and the adjoining apartments."[4] A few hours before his departure he said to those around him: "We are together like angels; and as if we were in heaven." "Did you suppose," he asked, "in the beginning, that the Saviour would do as much as we now really see, in the various Moravian settlements, among the children of God of other denominations, and among the heathen? I only entreated of him a few first-fruits of the latter, but there are now thousands of them."

The "Reformers before the Reformation" had not then labored in vain. The Bohemian sufferers at Constance had verified the maxim so often consecrated by the tears and thanksgivings of the faithful, that "the blood of the martyrs is the seed of the Church." There gleam to-day on the darkest skies of the Pagan world reflections of light from the martyr fires of Constance; and Herrnhut, "the watch of the Lord," has become a watch-light to the world. From this people—so remarkable and fruitful in their history—was Methodism not only to copy much of its internal discipline, but to receive the impulse which was yet necessary to start it on its appointed route. Wesley had already learned much from them. In their resignation amid the storms of the Atlantic, he had seen a piety which he pos-

[4] Spangenberg's Life of Zinzendorf, translated by Samuel Jackson. London. 1838.

sessed not himself. On his landing in Georgia, the doctrine of the "Witness of the Spirit," which had dawned upon his mind from the Scriptures, while reading Jeremy Taylor at Oxford, was brought home to his conscience by the appeal of Spangenberg. His unavailing asceticism had been rebuked there by their more cheerful practical piety; his unsuccessful, because defective, preaching, by their more evangelical and more useful labors; and his rigid ecclesiasticism by the apostolic simplicity of their Church councils. And now, hardly had he landed in England from Georgia when witnesses for the truth, from Herrnhut, met him again with the appeal: "This is the way, walk ye in it."

They had established or revived several small assemblies in London and elsewhere. One of their preachers, Peter Böhler, a name which will ever be memorable to Methodists, had just arrived in the city. Wesley first met him on February 7, 1738, about a week after his own arrival—"a day much to be remembered," he writes. "From this time," he adds, "I did not willingly lose an opportunity of conversing with him."[5] He again records that "by Böhler, in the hand of the great God, I was convinced of unbelief, of the want of that faith whereby alone we are saved." At a later date he says that he was amazed more and more by the accounts which Böhler gave of the fruits of living faith—the holiness and happiness which he affirmed to attend it. Wesley began the Greek Testament anew, resolving to abide by the law and the testimony, and being confident that it would show him whether this doctrine was of God. On the first day of the following April we read in his journal: "Being at Mr. Fox's society my heart was so full that I could not confine myself to the forms of prayer which we were accustomed to use there. *Neither do I propose to be confined to them any more*, but to pray indifferently, with a form or without, as may be suitable to particular occasions." He began to see "the promise," he says, "but it was afar off." Again he records that he met

[5] Wesley's Journal, Anno, 1738.

Peter Böhler once more, and had now no objection to what the Moravian said on the nature of faith; namely, that it is—to use the words of the Anglican Church—"a sure trust and confidence which a man hath in God, that through the merits of Christ his sins are forgiven, and he reconciled to the favor of God." Neither could he deny the happiness nor holiness which Böhler described as fruits of this living faith. "The Spirit itself beareth witness with our spirit, that we are the children of God," and, "He that believeth hath the witness in himself," were texts which fully convinced him of the former, as "Whosoever is born of God doth not commit sin," and, "Whosoever believeth is born of God," did of the latter. He was staggered, however, for a time, at the Moravian doctrine of an instantaneous change of heart. Desponding under a sense of guilt, he subsequently adds: "Yet I hear a voice—and is it not the voice of God?—saying, 'Believe, and thou shalt be saved. He that believeth is passed from death unto life. God so loved the world that he gave his only-begotten Son, that whosoever believeth in him should not perish but have everlasting life.' O, let no one deceive us by vain words as if we had already attained this faith—that is, the proper Christian faith. By its fruits we shall know. Do we already feel 'peace with God,' and 'joy in the Holy Ghost?' Does 'his Spirit bear witness with our spirit that we are the children of God?' Alas, with mine he does not! O then, Saviour of men, save us from trusting in anything but thee! Draw us after thee! Let us be emptied of ourselves, and then fill us with peace and joy in believing, and let nothing separate us from thy love, in time or in eternity."

The indefatigable Böhler and his humble associates had already been guiding Charles Wesley into "the way of salvation by faith;" and as Charles was the first of the brothers who received the name of Methodist, so was he the first to learn by experience the saving truth which Methodism was destined to witness to the world. He had conversed with Zinzendorf, and had been in one of the small Moravian assemblies, where, he says, "I thought myself in a choir of angels."[6] He was entertained during a period of sickness at the house of a pious mechanic, by the name of Bray, who was an attendant of the London "Societies," and who, he says, is "now to supply Peter Böhler's place," as the latter had left England. This devoted artisan read the Scriptures to him, and was able, from his own experimental knowledge of them, to direct his troubled mind. "God sent," he says, "Mr. Bray, a poor, ignorant mechanic, who knows nothing but Christ; yet, by knowing him, knows and discerns all things." A Christian woman of the family conversed with him on the nature of faith. "Has God bestowed faith on you?" he asked. "Yes, he has." "Why, have you peace with God?" "Yes, perfect peace." "And do you love Christ above all things?" "I do, above all things incomparably." "Then, are you willing to die?" "I am, and would be glad to die this moment; for I know all my sins are blotted out; the handwriting that was against me is taken out of the way, and nailed to the cross. He has saved me by his death. He has washed me by his blood. He has hid me in his wounds. I have peace in him, and rejoice with joy unspeakable and full of glory." Her answers to the most searching questions he could ask were so full, that he had no doubt of her having received the atonement, and waited for it himself with a more assured hope.

On May 21, 1738, he inserts a remarkable passage in his journal: "I waked in hope and expectation of His coming. At night my brother and some friends came and sang a hymn to the Holy Ghost. My comfort and hope were hereby increased. In about half an hour they went. I betook myself to prayer, the substance as follows: 'O, Jesus, thou hast said, *I will come unto you.* Thou hast said, *I will send the Comforter unto you.* Thou hast said, *My Father*

[6] Jackson's Life of Charles Wesley, chapter iv. I cannot too strongly commend this work. It has been our best *history* of Methodism. It is to be regretted that the American edition omits many of its best specimens of Charles Wesley's poetry. The English edition is a mosaic set with the gems of his genius.

and I will come unto you and make our abode with you. Thou art God, who canst not lie. I wholly rely upon thy most true promise. Accomplish it in thy time and manner." Having thus prayed he was composing himself to sleep in quietness and peace, when he heard some one say, "In the name of Jesus of Nazareth, arise, and believe, and thou shalt be healed of all thy infirmities." The words were so appropriate to his state of mind that they "struck him to the heart." He said within himself, "O that Christ would but speak thus to me!" and lay "musing and trembling for some time." Then ringing the bell for an attendant he sent to ascertain who had uttered the words, feeling in the mean time "a strange palpitation of heart," and saying, yet fearing to say, I believe, I believe. The devout woman who had before given him so positive a testimony respecting the knowledge of the forgiveness of sins, came to him and said: "It was I, a weak, sinful creature, that spoke; but the words were Christ's. He commanded me to say them, and so constrained me that I could not forbear." He sent for his pious host, and asked him whether it would be right for him to dare to presume that he now had Faith? Bray answered, that he ought not to doubt of it; it was Christ that spoke to him; he knew it, and wished them to pray together. "But first," said he, "I will read what I have casually opened upon: 'Blessed is the man whose transgression is forgiven, whose sin is covered. Blessed is the man to whom the Lord imputeth not iniquity, and in whose spirit there is no guile.'" "Still," says Wesley, "I felt a violent opposition and reluctance to believe; yet still the Spirit of God strove with my own and the evil spirit, till, by degrees, he chased away the darkness of my unbelief. I found myself convinced, I knew not how nor when, and immediately fell to intercession. I now found myself at peace with God, and rejoiced in hope of loving Christ. My temper was for the rest of the day mistrust of my own great but unknown weakness. I saw that by faith I stood, and the continual support of faith kept me from falling, though of myself I am ever sinking into sin. I went to bed still sensible of my own weakness; I humbly hope to be more and more so, yet confident of Christ's protection."

Three days after Charles had thus attained "rest to his soul," John also found it. He records that he continued to seek it, though with strange indifference, dullness, and coldness, and unusually frequent relapses into sin, till Wednesday, May 24. About five o'clock on the morning of that day he opened his Testament on these words: "There are given unto us exceeding great and precious promises, even that ye should be partakers of the divine nature." 2 Peter i, 4. Just as he went out he opened it again on the passage, "Thou art not far from the kingdom of God." In the evening he went very unwillingly to a society in Aldersgate-street, where a layman was reading Luther's preface to the Epistle to the Romans; about a quarter before nine, while listening to Luther's description of the change which the Spirit works in the heart through faith in Christ, "I felt," writes Wesley, "my heart strangely warmed. I felt I did trust in Christ, Christ alone for salvation, and an assurance was given me that he had taken away my sins, even mine, and saved me from the law of sin and death. But it was not long before the enemy suggested, 'This cannot be faith, for where is thy joy?' Then was I taught that peace and victory over sin are essential to faith in the Captain of our salvation; but that, as to the transports of joy which usually attend the beginning of it, especially in those who have mourned deeply, God sometimes giveth, sometimes withholdeth them, according to the counsels of his own will. After my return home I was much buffeted with temptations, but cried out and they fled away. They returned again and again; I as often lifted up my eyes, and He sent me help from his holy place. And herein I found the difference between this and my former state chiefly consisted. I was striving, yea fighting with all my might under the law as well as under grace. But *then* I was sometimes, if not often, conquered; *now* I was always conqueror." Thus had the feet of both the brothers been directed into the path of life by the instrumentality of the London Moravians.

Wesley's mother, who was residing in London, was still his guide and counselor. He read to her a paper recording his late religious experience. She strongly approved it, and said "she heartily blessed God who had brought him to so just a way of thinking."[7] Thus, in the thirty-fifth year of his age, after twenty-five years, as he elsewhere informs us,[8] of religious solicitude and struggles, did he, by a clearer apprehension of the doctrine of justification by faith, find rest to his soul, and feel himself at last authorized to preach that blessing to all contrite men, from his own experimental proof of its reality. But had he not faith before? Doubtless he had; at another time he declared that he had, but that it was "the faith of a servant" rather than "of a child." The animadversions of Southey and Coleridge on his present experience are conclusively met by the direct question whether that experience was in accordance with the Scriptures or not. Was his previous state of inward struggle and desolation, or his present one of settled trust and peace, most in harmony with the Scriptural description of a regenerated soul, which has "peace with God through our Lord Jesus Christ," having "not received the spirit of bondage unto fear, but the spirit of adoption, whereby we cry, Abba, Father?" Any further question than this is not one of Christian experience, but of Christianity itself.

The interest which these and previous events had given him for the Moravians, induced him to visit Herrnhut. In about a fortnight he set out on the journey, accompained by his friend, Ingham, and six others. At Marienborn they met Zinzendorf, who had organized there a brotherhood of about fifty disciples from various countries. "I continually met," says Wesley, "with what I sought for, living proofs of the power of faith; persons saved from inward as

[7] Compare his Journal, June 8, 1738, with June 13, 1739. These references effectually correct Southey's misrepresentations of her opinion on the subject.

[8] Smith's History of Methodism, II, 1.

well as outward sin, by the love of God shed abroad in their hearts; and from all doubt and fear, by the abiding witness of the Holy Ghost given unto them." He sums up the views which Zinzendorf gave him concerning justification, as follows: 1. Justification is the forgiveness of sins. 2. The moment a man flies to Christ he is justified. 3. And has peace with God, but not always joy. 4. Nor, perhaps, may he know he is justified till long after. 5. For the assurance of it is distinct from justification. 6. But others may know he is justified by his power over sin, by his seriousness, by his love of the brethren, and his "hunger and thirst after righteousness," which alone prove the spiritual life to be begun. 7. To be justified is the same thing as to be born of God. ("Not so," interpolates Wesley.) 8. When a man is awakened he is begotten of God, and his fear and sorrow, and sense of the wrath of God, are the pangs of the new birth.

He passed to Herrnhut, which he reached August 1, 1738. He describes it as lying in Upper Lusatia, on the border of Bohemia, and containing about a hundred houses, built on a rising ground, with evergreen woods on two sides, gardens and cornfields on the others, and high hills in the back ground. It had one long street, through which the great road from Zittau to Lobau extended. Fronting the middle of this street was the orpnan house, in the lower part of which was the apothecaries' shop; in the upper the chapel, capable of containing six or seven hundred people. Another row of houses ran, at a small distance, from the orphan house, which accordingly divided the rest of the town, besides the long street, into two squares. At the east end of it was the Count's house, a small, plain building like the rest, having a large garden behind it, which was well laid out, not for show but for the use of the community. Wesley spent there about a fortnight. He found at Herrnhut defects, doubtless, but his best expectations were surpassed. "God," he says, "has given me at length the desire of my heart. I am with a Church whose conversation is in heaven, in whom is the mind that was in Christ, and who walk as he walked. As they have all one Lord and one faith, so they are all partakers of one spirit, the spirit of meekness and love, which uniformly and continually animates all their conversation. O how high and holy a thing Christianity is, and how widely distant from that which is so called, though it neither purifies the heart nor renews the life, after the image of our blessed Redeemer." He heard there, with admiration, Christian David, who had cleaved with his ax the first tree for the mansion of the colony. Of justification this Christian mechanic said: "The right foundation is not your contrition—though that is not your own, not your righteousness, nothing of your own, nothing that is wrought in you by the Holy Ghost; but it is something without you, the righteousness and the blood of Christ. For this is the word: 'To him that believeth on God, that justifieth the ungodly, his faith is counted for righteousness.' This, then, do if you would lay a right foundation. Go straight to Christ with all your ungodliness; tell him, 'Thou whose eyes are as a flame of fire, searching my heart, seest that I am ungodly; I plead nothing else. I do not say I am humble or contrite, but I am ungodly; therefore bring me to him that justifieth the ungodly, Let thy blood be the propitiation for me.' Here is a mystery, here the wise men of the world are lost; it is foolishness unto them."

He was struck by the peculiarity of almost everything about this Christian community. Some of its customs were questionable, but most appeared to him peculiar only in the sense of being thoroughly Christian. Even what might be called their recreations were religious. He saw, with agreeable surprise, all the young men march around the town in the evening, "as is their custom," singing praise with instruments of music, and gathering into a circle on a neighboring hill to join in prayer. Returning with resounding songs, they concluded the evening, and made their mutual adieus by commending one another to God in the great square. He was affected by their simple burial rites. Their graveyard was "God's Acre." They bore thither the dead with hymns. Little children led the procession, and carried the bier of a deceased child. He saw a bereaved father, a humble mechanic, looking upon the grave of his infant, and wishing to console him, found it unnecessary, for he had a higher comforter. Wesley inquired respecting his affliction. "Praised be the Lord," was the parent's reply; "praised be the Lord, he has taken the soul of my child to himself; I know that when his body is raised again both he and I shall be ever with the Lord."

"I would gladly," says Wesley, "have spent my life here, but my Master calling me to labor in other parts of his vineyard, I was constrained to take my leave of this happy place." He returned as he came, on foot, bearing with him lessons which were to be available in all his subsequent career.

Methodism owes to Moravianism special obligations. First it introduced Wesley into that regenerated spiritual life, the supremacy of which over all ecclesiasticism and dogmatism it was the appointed mission of Methodism to reassert and promote in the Protestant world. Second, Wesley derived from it some of his clearest conceptions of the theological ideas which he was to propagate as essentially related to this spiritual life; and he now returned from Herrnhut not only confirmed in his new religious experience, but in these most important doctrinal views. Third, Zinzendorf's communities were based upon Spener's plan of reforming the Established Churches, by forming "little Churches within them,"[9] in despair of maintaining spiritual life among them otherwise; Wesley thus organized Methodism within the Anglican Church. And, fourth, not only in this general analogy, but in many details of his discipline can we trace the influence of Moravianism.

He reached England in September, 1738. After these providential preparations, he was ready to begin his great career, though as yet without a distinct anticipation of its historical importance.

[9] Spangenberg's Life of Zinzendorf.

BOOK II.

ORIGIN AND PROGRESS OF METHODISM. 1739—1744.

CHAPTER I.

THE WESLEYS AND WHITEFIELD ITINERATING.

Wesley returns from Germany — Charles Wesley — Religious "Societies" in London — Wesley takes Refuge in them when expelled from the Churches — He preaches to the Prisoners at Newgate — His Tenacity for Church Order — Whitefield arrives — He is denied the City Pulpits — He goes to Bristol — Is excluded from the Pulpits there — Preaches in the open Air at Kingswood — Wesley at Bristol — He begins to preach in the open Air — Vast Congregations — Whitefield's Departure — Scenes at Kingswood — Methodism in Wales — Griffith Jones — Howell Harris — Whitefield in Moorfields — Extraordinary Effects of his Preaching — Wesley's Labors — He encounters Beau Nash at Bath — The First Methodist Chapel — Wesley in Moorfields — Marvelous Effects on his Hearers — Examples — Charles Wesley threatened with Excommunication — He preaches in Moorfields — The Foundry opened for Worship — Separation from the Moravians — Epoch of Methodism.

WHILE Wesley was returning to England on the German Ocean, Whitefield was also returning on the Atlantic. They were about to meet, to lay permanently, though unconsciously, the foundations of Methodism.

Charles Wesley had been preaching with increased zeal during his brother's absence. Several clergymen had embraced his improved views, and converts were multiplied daily by his labors. When he preached the houses were generally crowded with eager hearers, but church after church was closed against him. He had taken charge of the curacy of Islington, but was ejected from it, not so much because of his doctrine, as for the earnestness with which he uttered it. He frequented Newgate, and ministered to the convicts; and his fervid spirit rejoiced in the simple but lively devotions of the small assemblies which the Moravians had revived in London. These societies were formed in 1667, under the labors of two London clergymen, Horneck and Smithies, and the auspices of Bishop Hopkins, during a period of extraordinary religious interest. More than thirty years later Dr. Woodward published an account of them. He reports that there were, in his day, forty in London and its neighborhood, besides several in the country and nine in Ireland. They seem to have had no other affiliation than a common purpose and the ties of a more intimate religious sympathy than the formal means of grace in the Established Church afforded. They became active in Christian philanthropy, and originated, it is said, no less than twenty associations for the suppression of vice and the relief of suffering, some of which grew into sufficient importance to command the interest of several bishops and of the queen of William III.[1] They had latterly much declined, but the visits of the Moravians to London renewed a few of them. They seemed a providential preparation for the approaching development of Methodism; for when the Wesleys were expelled from the pulpits of the Establishment, they found refuge and audiences in these humble assemblies, and they afforded at last the nucleus and form of the more thoroughly organized Methodist "Societies" in several parts of the kingdom.

When Wesley reached the metropolis, on returning from Germany, he flew to them as to an asylum. He arrived on Saturday night. The next day "I began," he says, "to declare in my own country the glad tidings of salvation, preaching three times, and afterward expounding to a large

[1] Mary, not Anne as Smith says, History of Methodism, II, 2. Philip's Life of Whitefield, chap. 4.

company in the Minories. On Monday I rejoiced to meet our little society, which now consisted of thirty-two persons. The next day I went to the condemned felons in Newgate, and offered them a free salvation. In the evening I went to a society in Bear Yard, and preached repentance and remission of sins. The next evening I spoke the truth in love at a society in Aldersgate-street; some contradicted at first, but not long; so that nothing but love appeared at our parting. Thursday, 21st, I went to a society in Gutter-lane, but I could not declare the mighty works of God there, as I did afterward at the Savoy, with all simplicity, and the word did not return empty. On Saturday, 23d, I was enabled to speak strong words both at Newgate and at Mr. E.'s society, and the next day at St. Anne's, and twice at St. John's, Clerkenwell, so that I fear they will bear with me there no longer."[2]

Thus he entered upon the great career of his life, for these incessant labors were no consequence of a febrile or temporary zeal; they are an example of what was thereafter to be almost his daily habit till he fell, in his eighty-eighth year, at the head of more than a hundred and fifty thousand followers, and five hundred and fifty itinerant preachers, who were stimulated by his unabated zeal to similar labors in both hemispheres. And now those marvelous "Journals" which have afforded so much inspiration to the devout, so much matter of criticism to the learned, and of astonishment and scorn to the skeptical, open before us as a new book of wonders, calm themselves, but hurrying us along, year after year, with an almost feverish excitement. He began by "expounding," nearly every day, in the London "Societies." On Sundays he preached in the churches, but at the end of almost every sermon he records it to be the last time; not that his manner was clamorous, or in any way eccentric; nor that his doctrine was heretical, for it was clearly that of the Homilies and other standards of the Church; but it was brought out too forcibly and presented too vividly for the

[2] Journal, Sept. 17, 1738.

state of religious life around him. He went from the closed pulpits not only to the "Societies," but to the prisons and the hospitals, where his message was received with gratitude and tears, and was attended with the demonstration of the Spirit and of power. "Friday, November 3, 1738," he writes, "I preached at St. Antholin's; Sunday, five in the morning, at St. Botolph's, Bishopsgate; in the afternoon at Islington; and in the evening to such a congregation as I never saw before, at St. Clement's in the Strand. As this was the first time of my preaching here, I suppose it is to be the last. On Wednesday my brother and I went, at their earnest desire, to do the last good office to the condemned malefactors." He describes the scene at their execution as the most affecting instance he ever saw of faith triumphing over sin and death. Observing the tears running down the cheeks of one of the criminals, while his eyes were steadily fixed upward, a few moments before he died, Wesley asked, "How do you feel now?" He calmly replied: "I feel a peace which I could not have believed to be possible; and I know it is the peace of God which passeth all understanding." His brother improved the occasion by declaring the Gospel of peace to a large assembly of publicans and sinners. "O Lord God of my fathers," exclaimed Wesley, "accept even me among them, and cast me not out from among thy children." In the evening he was preaching at Basingshaw church, and the next morning at St. Antholin's.

The Wesleys were still tenacious of "Church order;" they had done nothing, nor did they yet intend to do anything, which was contrary to that order. They had consultations with the Bishop of London and the Archbishop of Canterbury, and were found by these prelates to be even too rigid in some of their ecclesiastical opinions. The former approved their doctrine of Assurance as explained in his presence, but had to reprove them for their readiness to rebaptize Dissenters. The latter gave them sensible advice. "Keep," he said, "to the doctrines of the Church; avoid all exceptionable phrases; preach and expound only the essentials of religion; other things, time and the providence of God only can cure."

Denied the city pulpits, the brothers went not only to the "Societies" and prisons, but to and fro in the country, preaching almost daily. Whitefield was needed to lead them into more thorough and more necessary "irregularities." He arrived in London December 8, 1738. Wesley hastened to greet him, and on the 12th "God gave us," he writes, "once more to take sweet counsel together." The mighty preacher who had stirred the whole metropolis a year before, now met the same treatment as his Oxford friends. In three days five churches were denied him. Good, however, was to come out of this evil. He also had recourse now to the "Societies," and his ardent soul caught new zeal from their simple devotions as from his new trials. Wesley describes a scene at one of these assemblies, which reminds us of the preparatory Pentecostal baptism of fire, by which the apostles were "endued with power from on high," for their mission. He says, January 1, 1739, that Messrs. Hall, Kinchin, Ingham, Whitefield, and his brother Charles were present with him at a love-feast in Fetter-lane, with about sixty of their brethren. About three in the morning, as they were continuing instant in prayer, the power of God came mightily upon them, insomuch that many cried out for exceeding joy, and many fell to the ground. As soon as they had recovered a little from the awe and amazement which the presence of the Divine Majesty had inspired, they broke out with one voice, "We praise thee, O God; we acknowledge thee to be the Lord." Whitefield exclaims: "It was a Pentecostal season, indeed." And he adds, respecting these "Society meetings," that "sometimes whole nights were spent in prayer. Often have we been filled as with new wine, and often have I seen them overwhelmed with the Divine Presence, and cry out, 'Will God, indeed, dwell with men upon earth? How dreadful is this place! This is no other than the house of God, and the gate of heaven!'"[3]

[3] Gillies's Life of Whitefield, chap. 4, note.

In this manner did the three evangelists begin together the memorable year which was afterward to be recognized as the epoch of Methodism. On the 5th Whitefield records an occasion which foreshadowed the future. A "conference" was held at Islington with seven ministers, "despised Methodists," concerning many things of importance. They continued in fasting and prayer till three o'clock, and then parted "*with a full conviction that God was about to do great things among us.*"[4]

Whitefield wished to take collections for his projected Orphan House, but the churches were soon generally closed against him; only two or three still remained at his command for a few days. Preaching in one of them with "great freedom of heart and clearness of voice," while nearly a thousand people stood outside the edifice, and hundreds had gone away for want of room, he was struck with the thought of proclaiming the word, as Christ did, in the open air. He mentioned it to some friends, who looked upon it as a fanatical notion. "However," he writes, "we knelt down and prayed that nothing may be done rashly. Hear and answer, O Lord, for thy name's sake."

He went to Bristol, his native city, which had formerly received him with enthusiasm. The churches were open to him at his arrival, but in a fortnight every door was shut, except that of Newgate prison; and this, also, was soon after closed against him, by the authority of the mayor. Not far from Bristol lies Kingswood, a place which has since become noted in the history of Methodism. It was formerly a royal chase, but its forests had mostly fallen, and it was now a region of coal mines, and inhabited by a population which is described as lawless and brutal, worse than heathens, and differing as much from the people of the surrounding country in dialect as in appearance.[5] There was no church among them, and none nearer than the suburbs of Bristol, three or four miles distant. Whitefield found here an unquestionable justification of field

[4] Philip's Life and Times of Whitefield, chap. 4.
[5] Southey's Wesley, chap. 6.

preaching, and on Saturday, February 17, 1739, he crossed the Rubicon, and virtually led the incipient Methodism across it, by the extraordinary irregularity of preaching in the open air. Standing upon a mount, he proclaimed the truth to about two hundred degraded and astonished colliers. He took courage from the reflection that he was imitating the example of Christ, who had a mountain for his pulpit, and the heavens for a sounding-board; and who, when his Gospel was refused by the Jews, sent his servants into the highways and hedges. "Blessed be God," he writes, "that the ice is now broke, and I have now taken the field. Some may censure me, but is there not a cause? Pulpits are denied, and the poor colliers are ready to perish for lack of knowledge."

He repeated his labors at Kingswood with continually increasing hearers; two thousand were present at his second sermon; from four to five thousand at his third; and they rapidly grew to ten, fourteen, and twenty thousand. His marvelous powers found their full play in this new arena, and his poetic spirit felt the grandeur of the scene and its surroundings. He speaks of the sun shining very brightly, and the people standing in such "an awful manner around the mount," and in such profound silence, as to fill him with a "holy admiration." The trees and hedges were full. All was hushed when he began; and he preached for an hour with great power, and so distinctly that all could hear him. "Blessed be God," he writes, "Mr. ——— spoke rightly; the fire is kindled in the country." To behold such crowds standing together in solemn silence, and to hear the echo of their singing resounding over the mighty mass, suggested to him the scene of the general assembly of the spirits of just men made perfect, when they shall join in singing the song of Moses and the Lamb in heaven! The moral effect of these occasions still more deeply impressed him. Having no righteousness of their own to renounce, the poor colliers were glad to hear that Christ was a friend to publicans, and came not to call the righteous, but sinners to repentance. He could see the effect of his words by the white gutters made by the tears which trickled down their blackened cheeks, for they came unwashed out of the coal pits to hear him. Hundreds after hundreds of them were brought under deep religious impressions, which, as the event proved, happily ended in sound and thorough conversions. The change was soon visible to all. As the scene was quite new, and Whitefield had just begun to preach extempore, it often, he says, occasioned him inward conflicts. Sometimes, when twenty thousand people were before him, he had not, in his own apprehension, a word to say either to God or to them. "But," he continues, "I was never totally deserted, and frequently (for to deny it would be lying against God) so assisted that I knew by happy experience what our Lord meant by saying, 'Out of his belly shall flow rivers of living water.'" The open firmament above him, the prospect of the adjacent fields, with the sight of thousands beyond thousands, some in coaches, some on horseback, and some in the trees, and at times "all affected and drenched in tears together," presented a scene which was sublime and at times overpowering to his vivid imagination, especially when the grand picture was impressed with the solemnity of the approaching evening. "It was then," he writes, "almost too much for, and quite overcame me." [6]

He soon began to preach boldly on a large bowling-green in Bristol, and as thousands flocked to the novel scene, he wrote to Wesley to come to his aid. Wesley arrived on Saturday evening, April 31, 1739. He could hardly reconcile himself at first, he says, "to this strange way of preaching in the fields, of which he set me an example on Sunday, having been all my life, till very lately, so tenacious of every point relating to decency and order, that I should have thought the saving of souls almost a sin, if it had not been done in a church." The next evening, Whitefield being gone, he began expounding to a small "Society" the Sermon on the Mount; "one pretty remarkable precedent," he writes,

6 Gillies's Whitefield, chap. 4.

"of field-preaching, though I suppose there were churches at that time also." Monday, 2d of May, at four in the afternoon, he "submitted to be more vile," he says, and proclaimed in the open air the glad tidings of salvation, from a little eminence in a ground adjoining the city, to about three thousand people. His text befitted the occasion: "The Spirit of the Lord is upon me, because he hath anointed me to preach the Gospel to the poor. He hath sent me to heal the broken-hearted; to preach deliverance to the captives, and recovery of sight to the blind; to set at liberty them that are bruised; to proclaim the acceptable year of the Lord." In a few days more he was standing on the top of Hannam Mount, in Kingswood, proclaiming, "Ho, every one that thirsteth, come ye to the waters: . . yea, come, buy wine and milk without money and without price;" and in the afternoon he again stood up amid five thousand, and cried, "If any man thirst let him come unto me and drink." He too had now crossed the Rubicon, and all who knew him knew that with him there could be no retreat.

Driven out of the churches, the new evangelists had evidently taken possession of the people. Whitefield committed his out-door congregations to Wesley, and left for other fields. The multitude sobbed aloud at his farewells; crowds gathered at his door when he departed, and twenty accompanied him out of the city on horseback. His exit was hardly less triumphant than at his former visit, notwithstanding his different treatment from the clergy and authorities. As he passed through Kingswood the grateful colliers stopped him; they had prepared an "entertainment" for him, and offered subscriptions for a charity school to be established among them. He was surprised at their lavish liberality; and laying, at their urgent request, a corner-stone for the building, knelt down on the ground among them, and prayed that the gates of hell might not prevail against it, to which their rough voices responded a hearty "Amen." Breaking away from them at last, he passed into Wales.

Religion and morals had sunk as low in the Principality, during this century, as in other parts of the country. A contemporary witness[7] represents that spiritual darkness hung over the land. The morals of both high and low were generally corrupt, drunkenness, gluttony, and licentiousness being everywhere prevalent. Saturday night was spent, usually to the dawn of the Sabbath, in the *Nosweithian Cann*, or song singing to the harp, accompanied with dancing; and Sunday afternoon at the *Achwaren-Gamp*, athletic sports and rustic dances, which drew together the population of towns and villages; while the *Bobl gerdded*, or walking people, a vagabond class, infested the country, living by beggary. The Church, meanwhile, is represented as almost totally inert, and "nothing would appear more improbable than that Methodism could find proselytes" among a people so thoughtless, reckless, and profligate. Many papal superstitions still lingered among the peasantry, and Wesley, at his first visit, said "they were as little versed in the principles of Christianity as a Creek or Cherokee Indian," a condition which Methodism was destined totally to revolutionize.

The moral desolation of the country induced Griffith Jones, who, though he lived and died a clergyman of the Establishment, became noted as a Methodist, to attempt some extraordinary means for its improvement. He established the Welsh "circulating schools," an itinerant system of religious education, conducted by an organized corps of instructors, who were distributed over the country to teach the common people to read the Scriptures in Welsh, and to instruct them in the catechism and in psalmody. They passed from one district to another, pausing sufficiently in each to teach such persons as they found willing to receive them, and revisiting them for the same purpose at intervals. This novel scheme was soon extended over the whole country. Jones was meanwhile

[7] See "An Account of Religion in Wales about the Middle of the Eighteenth Century." Philip's Whitefield, chap. 6. It was taken from the mouth of a very old Welsh Methodist, and published in 1799, in the Trysorva, edited by Rev. Thomas Charles, of Bala.

the most indefatigable preacher in Wales; and while the Wesleys and Whitefield were beginning their extraordinary labors in England, he was making preaching tours, and extending his itinerant schools, through a large portion of the Principality. He sometimes preached from tombstones, and on the green sward, for the churches could not accommodate the people. About the time of Whitefield's visit, one hundred and twenty-eight of his schools were in operation; and they had been established in almost every parish when their venerable founder died, in 1761. Though a faithful Churchman, the impulse which he gave to religion in Wales resuscitated and greatly promoted evangelical Dissent. His teachers became the earliest native Methodist preachers; and their travels as instructors, as also his own preaching tours, opened the way for the Methodist itinerancy. He co-operated afterward with Wesley and Whitefield, met in their Conferences in London, and is entitled to be considered one of the Methodist founders.

The name of Howell Harris is as dear to evangelical Welshmen as that of Griffith Jones. He was born at Trevecca in 1714. In 1735 he went to Oxford to study for the Church, but disgust at the infidelity and immorality which prevailed there drove him away. Returning to Wales, he began to exhort the neglected poor in their cottages, and was so successful that in a few months he formed several societies among them, thus affording another of those providential coincidences which mark the religious history of the times. Thirty of these organizations were sustained by him at the time of Whitefield's arrival, and in three years more they numbered three hundred. He lived and died a Churchman, but received little sympathy from the established clergy, and until the visits of the Methodist founders, pursued his evangelical labors almost alone, apparently without anticipating that they would result in a widespread evangelical Dissent. In 1715 there were only thirty Dissenting chapels in the Principality, and in 1736 only six in all North Wales;[8]

[8] Philip's Life and Times of Whitefield, chap. 6.

in 1810 they numbered nearly a thousand; they have increased to more than two thousand.[9]

Harris was a lay preacher; he applied repeatedly for ordination, but was denied it by the bishops on account of his irregular modes of labor. Whitefield passed from Kingswood to Cardiff, and there saw him for the first time. Their souls met and blended like two flames, and "set the whole Principality in a blaze."[10] For three years had the laborious layman traveled, and preached twice nearly every day. Seven counties had he gone over, calling the people to repentance, addressing them in fields, from tables, walls, or hillocks. "He is full of the Holy Ghost," wrote Whitefield; "blessed be God, there seems a noble spirit gone out into Wales." And he expresses himself as not doubting that Satan envied the happiness of their first meeting, and as believing that they should make his kingdom shake throughout the Principality. They held public meetings immediately in Cardiff, preaching amid weeping crowds within and a scoffing rabble without.

The next day they were at Newport, where Whitefield addressed a large assembly. He found, he said, Wales well prepared for the Gospel; new schools were opening every day, on the plan of Griffith Jones, and the people readily came twenty miles to hear a sermon. Husk, Pontypool, Abergavenny, Carlean, and Treleck were rapidly visited. In some instances the churches were opened to him, and when they could not accommodate the crowd he preached a second sermon in the open air. All the way, he says, he could think of nothing so much as of Joshua, going from city to city and subduing the devoted nations. Mobs threatened him, but he hesitated not. At Treleck, being

[9] According to the official statistics of the British Government for 1857, they were about 2,300. Over one million, or nearly the whole Welsh population, now attend public worship some part of the day every Sabbath. There is now a church, National or Dissenting, to nearly every three square miles of Wales. (Article by Rev. J. G. Evans in New-York Observer, May 1, 1858.) Methodism, which, as we shall hereafter see, made but slight impression on Scotland, has elevated the popular religious condition of Wales above that of Scotland.

[10] Philip's Whitefield, chap. 6.

denied the church, he stood upon a horseblock before the inn and delivered his message. At Carlean Harris had been assailed by the rabble, who beat a drum and huzzaed around him. Whitefield considered it to be a challenge which he himself ought to accept. He stood up amid "many thousands," but "God suffered them not to move a tongue." He preached with unusual power, and "was carried out beyond himself." Harris followed the English discourses of Whitefield with exhortations in Welsh. They were congenial spirits, and their co-operation gave an impulse to the religious spirit of Wales which has not only been felt down to our day, but promises to be perpetual.

Returning to England, Whitefield traversed a large portion of the country, preaching at bowling-greens, market-crosses, and on the highways. After thus preparing the way for the Wesleys, by arousing the popular attention of the rural districts, he went to London, where, while opening the services at Islington church, he was silenced by a church-warden, but stood upon a tomb in the church-yard, and proclaimed the truth to the willing people.

Excluded from all the churches, he resolved to preach at Moorfields on the next Sunday. His friends admonished him of danger from the rabble which frequented that noted resort; two of them, however, had courage enough to accompany him. Arm in arm, they pushed their way through the multitude; but he was separated from his companions by the pressure, and borne along through a lane which the mob formed for him to the center of the fields. A table placed there for his pulpit was broken to pieces; he was then pressed to a wall, mounting which he preached to the swarming thousands with such effect that they were soon tamed down to the quiet and decorum of a church. "The word of the Lord," he writes, "runs and is glorified; people's hearts seem quite broken; God strengthens me exceedingly; I preach till I sweat through and through."

He went the same evening to Kennington Common, and addressed a vast multitude. These labors he continued with increasing interest. Scores of carriages, hundreds of horsemen, and thirty or forty thousand on foot, thronged around him.[11] Their singing could be heard two miles off, and his own voice a mile. Wagons and scaffolds were hired to the throng that they might the better hear and see the wonderful preacher, who, consecrated and gowned as a clergyman of the national hierarchy, had broken away from its rigid decorum, and, like his divine Master, had come out into the highways and hedges to save their neglected souls. The genuine popular heart recognized him as a true apostle; and in the collections, made after these field sermons, for his Orphan Asylum, the poor people gave their half-pence so liberally that he was wearied down in receiving them, and a single man could not carry the amount home for him. He records a contribution, of which nearly one half consisted of but little short of ten thousand pieces of copper. After the collection had been taken, the crowd gathered around his carriage throwing their mites into the windows. Such are the people at heart, whatever their voices and fists may declare in the mob.

Wesley, meantime, was greatly successful at Bristol, where he had formed "Bands;" and at Kingswood, where the school, begun by Whitefield, was rising under his care. He made excursions, also, to other towns, and his journals afford, on almost every page, examples of incredible labors. Astonishing effects began to attend his word. While preaching at Newgate, Bristol, on the words, "He that believeth hath everlasting life," he was led, without any previous design, to declare strongly and explicitly that God willeth "all men to be thus saved," and to pray that if this were the truth of God, he would "bear witness to His word." Immediately one, and another, and another, sank to the earth; "they dropped on every side as thunderstruck." And the next day he records "that all Newgate rang with the cries of those whom the word of God cut to the heart."[12] His own

[11] He gives one estimate of nearly sixty thousand in Moorfields. Philip's Life, etc., chap. 4.

[12] Journal, Anno 1739.

spirit grew mighty in the consciousness of the moral power he was now wielding by the word of God. On one occasion, he says, his soul was so enlarged that he thought he could have cried out, in another sense than Archimedes, "Give me where to stand and I will shake the earth." The same day he stood amid hundreds of people on Rose Green, and taking for his text, "The God of glory thundereth," etc., preached to them in a storm of lightning and rain, which could not disperse them from his magical presence.

In one of his excursions to Bath, about this time, he encountered the noted Beau Nash, the presiding genius of its gayeties. The incident is interesting, as being the first of those public interruptions of his ministry which were soon to degenerate into mobs, and agitate most of England and Ireland. The fashionable pretender hoped to confound the preacher and amuse the town, but was confounded himself. Wesley says there was great public expectation of what was to be done, and he was entreated not to preach, for serious consequences might happen. The report gained him a large audience, among whom were many of the rich and fashionable. He addressed himself pointedly to high and low, rich and poor. Many of them seemed to be surprised, and were sinking fast into seriousness, when their champion appeared, and, coming close to the preacher, asked by what authority he did these things? By the authority of Jesus Christ, conveyed to me by the now Archbishop of Canterbury, when he laid hands upon me and said, Take thou authority to preach the Gospel, was the reply. This is contrary to act of parliament; this is a conventicle, rejoined Nash. Sir, said Wesley, the conventicles mentioned in that act, as the preamble shows, are seditious meetings; but this is not such; here is no shadow of sedition; therefore it is not contrary to that act. I say it is, replied Nash; and, besides, your preaching frightens people out of their wits. Sir, asked Wesley, did you ever hear me preach? No. How, then, can you judge of what you never heard? Sir, by common report. Common report is not enough; give me leave, sir, to ask, is not your name Nash? My name is Nash. Sir, continued Wesley, I dare not judge of *you* by common report. The irony was too pertinent to fail of effect. Nash paused awhile, but, having recovered himself, said, I desire to know what these people come here for? One of "the people" replied, Sir, leave him to me; let an old woman answer him: you, Mr. Nash, take care of your body; we take care of our souls, and for the food of our souls we come here. His courage quailed before the sense and wit of the common people, and, without another word, he retreated in haste. As Wesley returned the street was full of people hurrying to and fro, and speaking emphatic words. But when any of them asked, Which is he? and he replied, I am he, they were awed into silent respect.

He had already undesignedly become an "Itinerant;" his ordinary employment in public, he says, was now as follows: every morning he read prayers and preached at Newgate; every evening expounded a portion of Scripture to one or more of the societies. On Monday, in the afternoon, he preached abroad, near Bristol; on Tuesday at Bath and Two-mile Hill, alternately; on Wednesday, at Baptist Mills; every other Thursday, near Peneford; every other Friday, in another part of Kingswood; on Saturday afternoon and Sunday morning, in the Bowling Green, (which lies near the middle of Bristol;) on Sunday, at eleven, near Hannam Mount; at two, at Clifton; and at five, on Rose Green; and "hitherto," he adds, "as my days, so my strength hath been."

His societies in Bristol grew so rapidly that he was compelled to erect a place of worship for their accommodation; and thus was another step taken forward in the independent career upon which he was being unconsciously led by the providence of God. On the 12th of May, 1739, the corner-stone "was laid with the voice of praise and thanksgiving." This was the first Methodist chapel in the world. He had not the least design of being personally engaged either in the expense or the direction of the work, having appointed "eleven feoffees," on whom he supposed the burden would fall; but, becoming involved in its entire financial responsibility, he was constrained to change this arrangement. And as to the direction of the undertaking, he says he presently received letters from his friends in London, Whitefield in particular, (backed with a message by a person just from the metropolis,) that neither he nor they would have anything to do with the building, nor contribute anything toward it, unless he would instantly discharge all feoffees and do everything in his own name. Many reasons they gave for this course; but one was decisive with him, namely, that such feoffees always would have it in their power to control him, and, if he preached not as they liked, to turn him out of the house he had built. He accordingly yielded to their advice, and, calling all the feoffees together, canceled, without opposition, the instrument made before, and took the whole management into his own hands. Money, he says, it is true, he had not, nor any human prospect of procuring it; but he knew "the earth is the Lord's, and the fullness thereof," and in his name set out, nothing doubting. In this manner was it that the property of all his chapels became vested solely in himself during the early part of his career, a responsibility which was necessary in his peculiar circumstances, which he never abused, and which he transferred, in prospect of his death, by a "deed of declaration," to his Legal Conference. Decisions in the Court of Chancery, made under this document, have given security to the property, and stability to the whole economy of Wesleyan Methodism down to our day.

Charles Wesley was laboring, meantime, incessantly in many parts of London, and Ingham in Yorkshire. Whitefield lingered in London, as if detained to thrust out Wesley before the multitudes there. Wesley arrived from Bristol, and the next day accompanied him to Blackheath, to hear him preach. Between twelve and fourteen thousand people were present. Whitefield urged him to address them; he recoiled, but at last consented, and thus became known as a field-preacher at the metropolis. Whitefield felt that he himself had done a good work that day. He says: "I went to bed rejoicing that another fresh inroad was made into Satan's territories, by Mr. Wesley following me in field-preaching in London as well as in Bristol."

After accompanying Wesley to Bristol, Kingswood, and Gloucester, and visiting other places as a field-preacher, Whitefield embarked again for America August 14, 1739. He had a work of preparation to do there also, for, in a few years, Wesley's itinerants were to follow on his track.

Most English religious writers of our day, who have treated of these events, have come to acknowledge the utility, if not the necessity, of the irregular labors of Whitefield and the Wesleys in the condition of the Church and of the degraded masses of their time, for the beneficial results are inscribed on all the land and on much of the world; but they have not been equally liberal in excusing the marvelous phenomena which attended the zealous evangelists, and which surprised them as much as their enemies. It was impossible that such extraordinary exertions should not be accompanied by extraordinary excitement, and it was, perhaps, equally impossible that the extraordinary excitement should not occasion correspondent physical effects. Some of these effects have already been mentioned. The most singular fact about them is, that for a considerable time the superior ardor and eloquence of Whitefield did not produce them, while, under the calmer and more logical preaching of Wesley, people dropped on every side as if thunderstruck. It is also noteworthy, that from the date of his return from Germany down to this time, not one of his texts, as recorded in his Journals, was of a severe or terrific character, but they were, as in most of his life, selected from the "great and precious promises," or related to the nature and means of personal religion. Yet under such preaching did hardened, as well as sensitive hearers, fall around him like men shot in battle. While preaching on the Common, at Bristol, from the words, "When they had nothing to pay, he frankly forgave them both," a young woman sank down in violent agony, as did five or six persons at another meeting in the evening. Many were greatly offended by their cries. The same offense was given during the day by one at "Theaner's Hall," and by eight or nine others at "Gloucester-lane." One of these was a young lady, whose mother was irritated at the scandal, as she called it, of her daughter's conduct; but "the mother was the next who dropped down and lost her senses in a moment, yet went home with her daughter full of joy, as did most of those who had been in pain." Such "phenomena" increased continually. Bold blasphemers were instantly seized with agony, and cried aloud for the divine mercy, and scores were sometimes strewed on the ground at once, insensible as dead men. A traveler at one time was passing by, but on pausing a moment to hear the sermon was directly smitten to the earth, and lay there apparently without life. A Quaker, who was admonishing the bystanders against these strange scenes as affectation and hypocrisy, was himself struck down, as by an unseen hand, while the words of reproach were yet upon his lips. A weaver, a great disliker of Dissenters, fearing that the new excitement would alienate his neighbors from the Church, went about zealously among them to prove that it was the work of Satan, and would endanger their souls. A new convert lent him one of Wesley's sermons; while reading it at home he suddenly turned pale, fell to the floor, and roared so mightily that the people ran into the house from the streets, and found him sweating, weeping, and screaming in anguish. He recovered his self-possession, and arose rejoicing in God. On one occasion great numbers fell around the preacher, while he was inviting them to "enter into the Holiest by a new and living way." A woman opposed them as giving way to an agitation which they might control, and endeavored to escape from the assembly. Scarcely had she got three or four yards when she fell down in as violent agony as the rest.

Not until July, 1739, when Whitefield was again with Wesley, did any such phenomena attend his own preaching. "Saturday, 9th," says Wesley, "I had an opportunity to talk with him of those outward signs which had so often accompanied the inward work of God. I found his objections were chiefly grounded on gross misrepresentations of matter of fact. But the next day he had an opportunity of informing himself better, for no sooner had he began to invite all sinners to believe in Christ than four persons sank down close to him, almost in the same moment. One of them lay without either sense or motion. The third had strong convulsions all over his body, but made no noise unless by groans. The fourth, equally convulsed, called upon God with strong cries and tears. From this time I trust we shall all suffer God to carry on his own work in the way that pleaseth him."

These marvels were not peculiar to Methodism; they had occurred in "Religious Revivals" from the Reformation down to this time. Edwards recorded them as common under his ministry in New England.[13] Gillies shows them to have been frequent in Scotland and other sections of the Church.[14] They have occurred in our day, with even an epidemic prevalence, in many parts of America. Charles Wesley discountenanced them. John considered them at first with favor, as proofs of the power of the truth, but afterward discouraged them. Most Methodists agree with Watson, "that in no such cases does the occasional occurrence of noise and disorder prove that an extraordinary work in the hearts of men was not then carrying on by the Spirit of God; that by the exercise of a firm discipline, then most of all to be exerted, they are to be as far as possible repressed, for the power of the work does not lie in them; and that yet discipline, though firm, ought to be discriminating, for the

[13] See his Treatise on the Religious Affections, and his Narrative of the New England Revival.

[14] Gillies's Historical Collections; see also Watson's Observations on Southey's Life of Wesley. Isaac Taylor's solution of these affections is quite apologetic, but perhaps equally fantastic: Wesley and Methodism, p. 44

sake of the real blessing with which, at such seasons, God is crowning the administration of his truth." They will come under our consideration more fully hereafter.

The new movement had now advanced too far for a retreat, and had acquired too much energy to stand still; it must go forward with increasing "irregularities" and isolation from the Church. Charles Wesley was cited to Lambeth, and threatened by the Archbishop with excommunication; for while his brother was preaching in the open air at Bristol, and Whitefield in Moorfields, he had followed their example in Essex, Thaxted, and other places. He was somewhat intimidated by the menace of the Archbishop; but Whitefield, whose agency seems to have been always opportune throughout this stage of Methodism, was at hand for his rescue, and exhorted him to take his stand openly in Moorfields the following Sunday. He did so, preaching there to ten thousand hearers. He preached elsewhere in the afternoon, and still later on the same day, to "multitudes upon multitudes," at Kennington Common. At night he sought consolation at the Moravian society, in Fetter-lane. He, too, was now fully committed to the "irregularities" of the new movement.

Apparently adverse events hastened its development. Peter Böhler had formed the constitution of the Fetter-lane Society. Wesley, though virtually recognized as its guide, had not interfered with its regulations. But dangerous errors were creeping into it: some of its members denounced the institution of the Christian ministry, and some all religious ordinances; others became Antinomians; quietism prevailed among them. Some of the customs and hymns introduced by the Moravians were exceptionable. Molther, a Moravian recently from Germany, promoted these errors with unwearied enthusiasm, and inculcated especially "True Stillness" as a substitute for external means of grace. Wesley hastened to London, and found, he says, "every day the dreadful effects of our brethren's reasoning and disputing with each other. Scarcely one in ten retained his first love, and most of the rest were in the utmost confusion, biting and devouring one another." He entreated them to stand in the old paths, and no longer to subvert one another by idle controversies and strife of words. He left them apparently reconciled, and Molther acceded to his counsels; but scarcely had he returned to Bristol before information reached him of new troubles. Again he visited and admonished them, but was not successful. On Sunday, July 20, 1740, he read to the society his objections, and being resisted, took final leave of it. He was followed by about a score of its members, to whom nearly fifty were soon after added, comprising most of the female "Bands." "We gathered up," says Charles Wesley, "our wreck *raré nantes in gurgile vasto*, floating here and there on the vast abyss, for nine out of ten were swallowed up in the dead sea of stillness. O why was not this done six months ago! How fatal was our delay and false moderation!"

Attempts were made by the Moravians for a reunion. Peter Böhler arrived soon after the separation; Wesley revered him more, perhaps, than he did any other man then living, but, as his objections applied not so much to the Moravians in general as to local evils among them in England, and these could not be remedied, he could not follow the counsels of his old friend. "I marvel," he says, "how I refrain from joining these men; I scarce ever see any of them but my heart burns within me; I long to be with them, and yet I am kept from them." Spangenberg,[15] his friend in Georgia, and finally Zinzendorf himself, came to London to repair the division; but it was irreparable, and it is well, perhaps, that it was so. Time allayed the irritations of both parties. Each had its peculiar mission in the world; each has since cordially recognized the other; but had it not

[15] Latrobe, in a note to Spangenberg's Life of Zinzendorf, examines the Moravian difficulties in London very candidly, in reply to Whitefield's charges. They seem to have been temporary errors, and not chargeable to the Church elsewhere. Wesley however believed, with Whitefield, that they were inherent in the Moravian system, and he attacked them often afterward. Zinzendorf was certainly inclined to defend them. I take, however, with pleasure, Latrobe's explanations.

been for this temporary disturbance, Wesley and his associates might have been merged in the Moravian body,[16] and assuredly not with the advantages which have resulted to the world from the distinct organization of Methodism.

Wesley had previously secured the foundry in Moorfields, a building which the government had used for the casting of cannon, but which was deserted and dilapidated. At the invitation of two strangers he preached in it, and at their instance, and by their assistance, opened it for regular public worship on the 11th day of November, 1739, some eight months before his separation from the Fetter-lane Society. This date has been considered the epoch of Methodism, for thenceforward the Foundry was its head-quarters in London. In his "Church History," Wesley assigns it other dates, as the formation of "the Holy Club," at Oxford, in 1729; and the meeting of himself and others, by the advice of Peter Böhler, in Fetter-lane, May 1, 1738; but in his introduction to the "General Rules of the Society," he says: "In the latter end of the year 1739 eight or ten persons came to me in London and desired that I would spend some time with them in prayer, and advise them how to flee from the wrath to come; this was the rise of the UNITED SOCIETY." "This," he tells us, "was soon after the consecration of the Foundry." Twelve came the first night, forty the next, and soon after a hundred.[17] Though he continued in fraternal relations with the Moravians till the separation of July 20, 1740, the society formed the preceding year was organized and controlled by himself, and has continued in unbroken succession down to our day.[18] The date of its origin was celebrated with

[16] At a later period Charles Wesley was deterred from joining the Moravians, and adopting their English Quietism, only by the strenuous remonstrances of his brother and Lady Huntingdon. Jackson attempts to disprove the fact, but Smith successfully corrects him. Jackson's Charles Wesley, chap. 8: Smith's Hist. of Methodism, II, 2.

[17] Jackson's Life of Charles Wesley, chap. 7.

[18] Dr. Smith (History of Wesleyan Methodism, II. 2,) argues in favor of the date of the separation from the Moravians in 1740. His reasons do not, however, justify such a deviation from the acknowledged opinion of

centenary solemnities by all the Methodist communities of the world in 1839. It was signalized not only by the organization of the Society, and by the opening of the Foundry for worship, but by the erection at Bristol of the first Methodist chapel, by the organization of "Bands" in that city, and by the publication by the Wesleys of their "Hymns and Sacred Poems," the beginning of that Methodistic psalmody which has since been of inestimable service to the denomination wherever it has extended.[19]

The purely accidental, or, rather, providential manner in which Methodism had reached this stage of its progress, is too obvious to need much remark. Excluded from the churches, and with "Bands" of converted men in London, Bristol, and Kingswood under his care, Wesley was compelled to provide places for their assemblies and regulations for their government. He did so only as the necessity was thrust upon him, not knowing what result would follow. Neither at this period, nor indeed at any subsequent time, did he think of deviating from the national Church. It was the practical and summary philosophy of his life to do the duty nearest to him, assured that all others would come in their due order. His least partial biographer has justly said, that whither his plans at this time were to lead he knew not, nor what consistence the societies he was collecting would take, nor where he was to find laborers as he enlarged his oper-

all Methodist bodies throughout the world. There can hardly be a dispute respecting the real epoch of Methodism. The same affirmation cannot be made, however, respecting the locality of its origin. "Bands" were formed by Wesley, and the "New Room," or chapel, was commenced at Bristol, some months before the opening of the Foundry and the formation of the "Society" in London. Myles (Chronological History of the Methodists, chap. 1) says: "The first preaching-house was *built* in Bristol; the first which was *opened* was in London." The italics are his own.

[19] At their return from Georgia they published a similar work, but it was less adapted to public use. The two volumes issued in 1739 spread rapidly among the new "Societies." Two editions were issued during the first year; they introduced that popular church music which has ever since been characteristic of Methodism, and one of the most potent means of its success.

ations, nor how the scheme was to derive its financial support. But these considerations troubled him not. God, he believed, had appointed it, and God would always provide means for His own ends.[20] English Methodist writers have deemed it desirable to defend him against imputations of disregard for the authority and "order" of the national Church. The task is not difficult, as will be seen in the course of our narrative; but it may hereafter be a more difficult one to defend him, before the rest of the Christian world, for having been so deferential to a hierarchy whose moral condition at the time he so much denounced, and whose studied policy throughout the rest of his life was to disown, if not to defeat him.

[20] Southey's Life of Wesley, chap. 9.

CHAPTER II.

THE WESLEYS ITINERATING IN ENGLAND; WHITE FIELD ITINERATING IN AMERICA.

Susanna Wesley — Her Counsels and Encouragements to her Son — Beginning of the Lay Ministry — David Taylor — Mobs — Charles Wesley itinerating — Is mobbed in Wales — Whitefield itinerating in America — Effects of his Preaching in Philadelphia — Princeton College — His Reception in Boston — His triumphant Passage through the Colonies.

During these important events Susanna Wesley was providentially still at hand, though in extreme age, to counsel and encourage her son. She had approved his field-preaching, and accompanied him to Kennington Common, where she stood by his side amid twenty thousand people.[1] Her son Samuel Wesley, with whom she had resided at Westminster since the dispersion of the family from Epworth, remonstrated against her sanction of the irregular labors of his brothers; but she saw the overruling hand of God in the inevitable circumstances which compelled them to their extraordinary course. A consultation was held in her presence respecting their separation from the Fetter-lane Society, and she approved that necessary measure. She had been led, about this time, by a clearer faith, to sympathize more fully than ever with their new views of the spiritual life. John Wesley records a conversation with her on the subject, in which she remarked that till lately she had rarely heard of the present conscious forgiveness of sins, or the Witness of the Spirit, much less that it was the common privilege of all true believers. "Therefore," she said, "I

[1] Wesley's Journal, Anno 1739.

never durst ask for it myself. But two or three weeks ago, while my son Hall, in delivering the cup to me, was pronouncing these words: 'The blood of our Lord Jesus Christ which was given for thee,' they struck through my heart, and I knew that God, for Christ's sake, had forgiven *me* all *my* sins." Wesley asked whether her father (Dr. Annesley) had not the same faith, and if she had not heard him preach it to others. She answered, he had it himself, and declared, a little before his death, that for more than forty years he had no darkness, no fear, no doubt at all of his being "accepted in the Beloved;" but that, nevertheless, she did not remember to have heard him preach even once explicitly upon it; whence she supposed he also looked upon it as the peculiar blessing of a few, and not as promised to all the people of God.[2]

Doubtless she had enjoyed before this time a genuine Christian experience; her writings incontestably prove this; her misgivings related to the degree of confidence which attended a true faith. The doctrine of Assurance, or the Witness of the Spirit, as Wesley called it, had always been admitted by the Puritan divines of both Old and New England; but, as she remarked, it had not been considered the privilege of all true believers. It was a logical consequence of the Calvinistic theology, that it should be assurance of eternal as well as of present salvation, and the perilous liabilities of such an inference rendered it a rare and almost esoteric opinion in Calvinistic Churches. Arminianism alone could therefore safely restore this precious truth as a common privilege to the Church. And herein is seen the providential necessity of Arminianism as the theological basis of the Methodist movement; for what would Methodism have been without its most familiar doctrine, the "Witness of the Spirit" as the common right and test of Christian experience?

Under the stirring events of these times the aged mother of Wesley was, after a long and faithful pilgrimage, enabled,

[2] Journal, Sept. 3, 1739.

"with humble boldness," to claim the consolation of that "assurance" which she had so long hesitated to accept. Such is the only possible explanation of the case.

In changing the foundry into a chapel, he had prepared an adjacent house as a residence for himself and his assistants in London. Hither his mother now removed, and here she spent her remaining days, sustained by his filial care, and counseling him in his new responsibilities.

After his separation from the Moravians, Wesley resumed his itinerant ministrations with unabated zeal. He had appointed John Cennick, a layman, to take charge of the Kingswood society, and to pray, and expound the Scriptures, though not to preach, during his absence. Thomas Maxfield, one of his converts at Bristol, was appointed to the same duties at the Foundry in London, and about the same time John Nelson (a memorable name in the annals of Methodism) began to exhort in public, working as a mason for his bread by day, and holding meetings at night; and thus, as will hereafter be seen, originated, without design on the part of Wesley, that "lay ministry" which has spread and perpetuated Methodism in both hemispheres.

During the years 1740 and 1741 Wesley traversed many parts of the kingdom, preaching almost daily, and sometimes four sermons on the Sabbath. Ingham, his companion in America, was abroad also, itinerating in Yorkshire, where he formed many societies. Howell Harris pursued his labors successfully in Wales, and John Bennet preached extensively in Derbyshire and its surrounding counties. David Taylor, a man of signal usefulness, also began to travel and preach about this time. He was a servant to Lord Huntingdon. Converted through the instrumentality of the Methodists, with whom Lady Huntingdon was now openly identified, he was encouraged by her to pursue his labors in the hamlets around her residence at Donnington Park. He had some education, sound sense, and good ability as a preacher. He went, under the direction of the countess, to Glenfield and Ratby, in Leicestershire, where his preaching in the open air excited extraordinary interest, and attracted great assemblies of the rustic population. Samuel Deacon threw down his scythe in the field, and wended his way with the multitude to the preaching place; he returned to his home deeply impressed with the truth, and eventually became a distinguished preacher at Barton-fabis, in Leicestershire; his labors and church extended out into Hugglescote, Melbourne, Loughborough, Derby, Leicester, (where a decayed Church was resuscitated,) Nottingham, and other places. All the neighboring regions, in fine, were pervaded by the Methodistic influence thus introduced, and the salutary results continue to our day.[3]

[3] The Churches thus formed, together with others in Cambridge and Yorkshire, were united, in 1770, into a "connection," with Baptist principles. In 1840 it comprised one hundred and thirteen churches, eleven thousand three hundred and fifty-eight members, five district home missionary societies, a foreign missionary society, and two academies. The author of the "Life and Times of Lady Huntingdon" (vol. i, p. 44) says: "The principal strength of the New Connection of General Baptists is in the Midland Counties, and Barton-fabis is considered the 'mother of them all.' In 1802, the Midland Conference included twenty-one churches. In 1816, the Warwickshire churches, six in number, formed themselves into a separate conference; as also in 1825, four or five churches in the north of Nottinghamshire were formed into what was called the North Midland Conference. The Midland Conference, in 1832, included forty-two churches. These *forty-two* churches in the Midland Counties probably contain seven thousand members; many of the chapels are large and well attended; the Sunday schools attached have many hundred children in them. As the little one has become a thousand, may the small one at home and abroad become a strong nation! These details, when viewed in connection with the itinerant labors of a servant belonging to the Countess of Huntingdon, sent forth under her patronage, are peculiarly interesting. But for those labors, and the benediction of the Spirit resting upon them, giving maturity and reproduction to the seed sown, what would have been the state of thousands in those villages and towns? Coventry is a home missionary station of this district, as are also Northampton, Mansfield, Ashbourne, Macclesfield, Manchester, etc." Such is an example of that evangelical influence of Methodism, beyond its denominational limits, which has been asserted in our narrative as a part of its providential mission.

Mobs began to assail the traveling evangelists, but they often "melted away like water, and were as men that had no strength," before Wesley's appeals. The rabble met him in throngs as he descended from the coach at the door of the Foundry, preventing his entrance; but on taking his stand in the street and preaching to them of "righteousness and judgment to come," they became a quiet and attentive congregation, and dismissed him with many blessings. Many more, he says, who came into the Foundry as lions in a short time became as lambs, the tears trickling apace down the cheeks of those who at first most loudly contradicted and blasphemed. A few days later a riotous multitude entered the building, and attempted to drown his voice by their outcries. But soon "the hammer of the word brake the rocks in pieces; all quietly heard the glad tidings of salvation." On the following Sunday when he came home he found an innumerable mob around the door, who raised a simultaneous shout the moment they saw him. He sent his friends into the house, and then walking into the midst of the crowd, proclaimed "the name of the Lord, gracious and merciful, and repenting him of the evil." They stood staring one at another. "I told them," he says, "they could not flee from the face of this great God, and therefore besought them that we might all join together in crying to him for mercy." To this they readily agreed. His peculiar power was irresistible; he prayed amid the awe-struck multitude, and then went undisturbed to the little company within.

While he was passing and repassing between London and Bristol, with continual deviations to Windsor, Southampton, Leicester, Ogbrook, Nottingham, Bath, and Wales, Charles Wesley was scarcely less active. He also was assailed by persecutors. In March, 1740, he was beset by a mob at Bengeworth; he says "their tongues were set on fire of hell." One in the crowd proposed to take him away and duck him. He broke out into singing with Thomas Maxfield, and allowed them to carry him whither they would. At the bridge end of the street they relented and left him. But instead of retreating, he took his stand there, and singing,

"Angel of God, whate'er betide,
Thy summons I obey,"

preached to some hundreds who gathered respectfully around him, from the text, "If God be for us, who can be against us?" He had fairly won the field. "Never," he says, "did I feel so much what I spoke. The word did not return empty, as the tears on all sides testified."

He passed to Evesham, Westcot, Oxford, and other places, preaching, and withstanding the clamors of the people, till he arrived again in London, where the Foundry, Moorfields, and Kennington Common were his arenas. While in the city he was tireless also in pastoral labors, devoting three hours daily to "conferences" and to the "bands." In June, 1740, he was again abroad among the rural towns, accompanied by his faithful assistant, Thomas Maxfield. He preached in Bexley, Blendon, Bristol, and Kingswood. At the latter place he was especially refreshed by the good results of the Methodist labors. Methodism had already commenced those demonstrations of its efficacy among the demoralized masses which have since commanded for it the respect of men who have questioned its merits in all other respects. "O what simplicity," he exclaims, "is in this childlike people! A spirit of contrition and love ran through them. Here the seed has fallen upon good ground." And again, on the next Sabbath, he writes: "I went to learn Christ among our colliers, and drank into their spirit. O that our London brethren would come to school to Kingswood! God knows their poverty; but they are rich, and daily entering into rest, without first being brought into confusion. Their souls truly wait still upon God, in the way of his ordinances. Ye many masters, come, learn Christ of these outcasts, for know, 'except ye be converted, and become as little children, ye cannot enter into the kingdom of heaven.'" He questions whether Herrnhut could afford a better example of Christian simplicity and purity; and yet these reclaimed colliers were repelled from the Lord's Supper by most of the regular clergy of the churches of Bristol, because their reformation had been effected by the "irregular" labors of the Methodists.

From Kingswood he made a preaching excursion into Wales, where he spent three weeks, co-operating with Howell Harris, who, though differing from him on the "Five Points" of the Calvinistic controversy, welcomed him cordially. His last night in the Principality was one of stormy riot. He was at Cardiff, expecting to depart by water the next day; Howell Harris and a company of devout people had assembled with him there for some days, and the interest of their meetings had diverted the public attention from the players of the theater. The latter, joined by the populace, and led on by a physician who had taken offense at one of Wesley's sermons, assailed the assembly. Many, it is said, had bound themselves by an oath to prevent his further preaching. At night the mob attacked the house; the physician struck Wesley with his cane, but was tripped down in the confusion, and after injuring several persons, and raving like a demoniac, was carried out; but the house was quickly again broken open by two magistrates, who, however, found it desirable to retire after some inquiries. The players then beset it. "We sang on unconcerned," he writes, "though they were armed, and threatened to burn the house. The ground of their quarrel is, that the Gospel has starved them." After midnight one of the actors got into the house, sword in hand: the weapon was wrested from him, and he thrust out. "When the sword was brought in," says Wesley, "the spirit of faith was kindled at the sight of the danger. Great was our rejoicing within, and the uproar of the players without, who strove to force their way after their companion." The hour had arrived for him to go on board the vessel; against the remonstrances of many of his friends, he resolutely walked out through the midst of the rabble; he was unmolested, and passed calmly to the water side, where many of his friends standing on the shore, joined him in hearty thanksgiving. The vessel being delayed, he returned on shore after some hours, and found Howell Harris and others still assembled. He preached to them again while some of his fiercest opposers stood weeping around him. He afterward waited on a magistrate, and presented to him, as a trophy, the sword taken from the player the preceding night. Such is an illustrationof the trials and the spirit of the founders of Methodism.

Returning to Bristol and Kingswood, he resumed his labors there, and visited the neighboring towns, preaching indefatigably. He records even five sermons a day. During the summer of 1741 he made three more excursions into Wales. His travels were rapid, his discourses incessant and powerful, his trials from persecutors not a few, but his success was immediate. He formed many societies, and opened broadly the way for the later progress of Methodism.

While the Wesleys were thus definitively founding Methodism in England, Whitefield was traversing the colonies of North America, promoting that more general but salutary influence among existing Churches which was so important a part of its mission on both sides of the Atlantic, and which forms an essential feature in its early history.[4]

He left England, as we have seen, on his second voyage to America, in August, 1739, and landed at Philadelphia in the beginning of November. His eloquence set the city astir immediately; its effects are described as "truly astonishing." People of all denominations, Quakers, Presbyterians, Baptists, as well as Churchmen, thronged the churches, and after he had departed public service was held twice every day, and three and four times on Sundays for about a year, and the city, though then comparatively small, kept up twenty-six societies for social prayer.[5] Though the churches were at his command, he preached often in the open air, for the

[4] See Isaac Taylor's Methodism. Much of this able but unsatisfactory work discusses "Methodism" as distinguished from "Wesleyanism."

[5] Memoirs of Mrs. Hannah Hodge. Philadelphia, 1806.

eager multitudes could not find room in any building. The favorite place for his out-door preaching was the balcony of the old court-house (since Market-house) in Market-street. His powerful voice was heard on the opposite shore of New Jersey, and the crews of vessels on the Delaware could distinguish his words.[6]

He passed to New-York, and on his route through New-Jersey proclaimed his message in the principal towns to thousands, who gathered from all the surrounding regions. A general religious interest had been previously excited among them by the labors of Frelinghuysen, the Tennents, Blair, and Rowland.[7] He records that Tennent and his brethren had begun an institution for the education of pastors. The building in which the young men were then studying was a log-house, about twenty feet long and nearly as many broad. From this "despised place" seven or eight worthy ministers of Christ had been sent forth, and a foundation was being laid for the instruction of many others. The work, he was persuaded, was of God, and "therefore would not come to naught." Thus arose the theological fame of Princeton. Nassau Hall received a Methodistic baptism at its birth. Whitefield inspirited its founders, and was honored by it with the title of A.M.; the Methodists in England gave it funds; and one of its noblest presidents was the correspondent of Wesley, and honored him as a "restorer" of the true faith.[8]

[6] Note to American edition of Gillies's Life of Whitefield. Philadelphia, 1854.

[7] Physical effects like those which had attended the Methodist preaching in England had already occurred in New-Jersey under the ministration of Rowland; the hearers "fainted away," and numbers were carried out of the church in a state of insensibility. Gillies's Whitefield, chap. 5.

[8] When Davies and Gilbert Tennent were in England soliciting aid for the college, fifteen years later, Tennent called on Wesley in London. The latter alludes to the visit with an expression of his characteristic catholicity. "He informed me," he writes, "of his design, now ready to be executed, of founding an American college for Protestants of every denomination; *an admirable design if it will bring Protestants of every denomination to bear with one another.*"—*Journal*, Anno 1754. Princeton has verified Wesley's doubt rather than his hope—and from

He spent a week in New-York, preaching thrice a day in churches and in the open air.[9] Returning on land to Georgia, he preached throughout his route sometimes to ten thousand people. Many enthusiastic Philadelphians accompanied him as a cavalcade sixty miles from the city. About the middle of January he was with his family at the Orphan House, where forty children were soon gathered under his protection. In a short time he found it necessary to resume his travels, in order to collect funds for their support. Taking passage for Newcastle, Delaware, he was before long again addressing thousands in Philadelphia. "Societies for praying and singing" were multiplied "in every part of the town;" and a hundred and forty of his converts were organized into a Church on one day by Gilbert Tennent. His route through New-Jersey was attended, as before, by vast congregations. Since his previous visit a general outward reformation had become visible. Many ministers had been quickened in their zeal

necessity as much, perhaps, as from choice. American sects have derived but questionable advantages from such combinations. President Davies corresponded with Wesley, and addressed him in language which Methodists have not usually had the pleasure to receive from their Calvinistic brethren. "Though you and I," he said, "may differ in some little things, I have long loved you and your brother, and wished and prayed for your success, as zealous revivers of experimental Christianity. If I differ from you in temper and design, or in the essentials of religion, I am sure the error must be on my side. Blessed be God for hearts to love one another! How great is the honor God has conferred upon you in making you a restorer of declining religion!" See his letter in Wesley's Journal, Anno 1757.

[9] The English Church was denied him. He preached usually in Dr. Pemberton's Presbyterian meeting-house on Wall-street, the only one of that denomination in New-York, and in front of the old Exchange on Broad, near Water-street; and still later at the "Brick Meeting," which was then "in the fields;" the effect of his labors was such that Pemberton's church had to be repeatedly enlarged. In this city occurred the well-known illustration of his dramatic power, when, preaching to a large number of sailors, he introduced a description of a storm and shipwreck, carrying away their imaginations so irresistibly that in the climax of the catastrophe they sprang to their feet, exclaiming: "Take to the long boat!" Conant's Narratives of Remarkable Conversions and Revival Incidents, etc. New-York, 1858.

to preach the word in season and out of season, and their congregations were greatly enlarged. Several preachers, prompted by his example, went forth traveling and laboring among the towns. After visiting New-York with unabated success, he again returned to Savannah. But his fame had spread to New-England, and Rev. Drs. Colman and Cooper, of Boston, sent letters to Georgia, urging him to visit them. Again he took passage for the north, and arrived at Newport, Rhode Island, September 14, 1740. He began immediately his usual course of incessant preaching. His sermons on his way to Boston spread his reputation, and when within ten miles' distance he was met by the governor's son and a train of the clergy and chief citizens, who escorted him into the city. Belcher, the governor, received him heartily, and became his warm friend. He was denied "King's Chapel," the English Church; but Webb, Foxcroft, Prince, Sewall, and all the other Puritan divines, welcomed him. His preaching had its usual effect. "It was Puritanism revived," said old Mr. Walter, the successor of Eliot, the apostle to the Indians. "It was the happiest day I ever saw in my life," exclaimed Colman, after his first sermon. He "itinerated" northward from Boston, traveling one hundred and seventy miles, and preaching sixteen times in about a week. On his return the whole city seemed moved. High and low, clergymen and municipal officers, professors and students from the neighboring college of Cambridge, and people from the country towns, thronged to hear him, and appeared ready to "pluck out their eyes for him." Twenty thousand hearers crowded around him when he delivered his farewell discourse under the trees of the Common, where Lee, the founder of Methodism in New-England, was afterward to preach his first sermon in Boston. "Such a power and presence of God with a preacher," wrote one who heard him, "I never saw before. Our governor has carried him from place to place in his coach, and could not help following him fifty miles out of town."

He directed his course westward to Northampton, where he met a congenial spirit in Jonathan Edwards. Pulpits were open to him on all the route, and a "divine unction" attended his preaching. From Northampton he passed down to New Haven, addressing as he journeyed vast and deeply affected congregations. He arrived there October 23, when the Colonial Legislature was in session, and on the Sabbath preached before them and an immense throng, some of whom had come twenty miles to hear him. The aged governor was so deeply affected that he could speak but few words; with tears trickling down his cheeks like drops of rain, he exclaimed: "Thanks be to God for such refreshings on our way to heaven!"

By November 8 he was again in Philadelphia, preaching in a house which had been erected for him during his absence, and which afterward became the Union Methodist Episcopal Church. On the 14th of December he reached the Orphan House, near Savannah. In seventy-five days he had preached a hundred and seventy-five sermons, and received upward of seven hundred pounds sterling for his orphans. "Never," he writes, "did I see such a continuance of the Divine presence in the congregations to which I have preached." Never had preacher or any other orator led the masses more triumphantly. He had stirred the consciences of tens of thousands from Maine to Georgia, and doubtless, by these and his subsequent travels, did much to prepare the soil for that harvest of Methodism which in our day has "shaken like Lebanon" along all his course.

On the 16th of January, 1741, he again embarked at Charleston for England.

CHAPTER III.

SEPARATION OF WHITEFIELD FROM WESLEY.

The Calvinistic Controversy — Character of Wesley's Mind — The Difficulties of Calvinism to such a Mind — Arminianism, as defined at the Synod of Dort — Intellectual Character of Whitefield — His Adoption of Calvinistic Opinions — Historical Importance of the Dispute between Wesley and Whitefield — Wesley excludes it from his Societies — It disturbs them in London — Difficulties at Kingswood — John Cennick — Wesley's Sermon on "Free Grace" — Whitefield's Return to England — His Separation from Wesley — Unsuccessful Attempts at Reconciliation.

WHILE these good and great men were thus abroad, laboring exclusively for the moral recovery of souls, and confining themselves to those vital truths which alone were essential to this end, a serious occasion of discord occurred between them; but the painful record of their partial alienation, which the fidelity of history requires, is relieved by the fact, acknowledged by both Wesley and Whitefield, that the important movement in which they were engaged took a wider sway from their differences of opinion. These differences related to the problem of Predestination—the insoluble difficulties which for so many ages have been fruitful causes of contention and bigotry among good men, and must continue to be so till they are transferred from Dogmatic Theology to their more legitimate place in the sphere of Metaphysics.

Wesley, as we have seen, early and definitively took the Arminian view of these questions, and was confirmed in that view of them by the correspondence of his mother while he was yet at Oxford. If, as some of his critics say, his intellect was more logical than philosophical, this was, perhaps, one of his chief qualifications for his appointed work. What was needed in the theological development of Methodism was clear, pointed definitions, rather than philosophic generalizations, of those elementary evangelical truths which are most essential to the personal salvation of men; for, in its positive bearing, Methodism was to be a spiritual, rather than a dogmatic or ecclesiastical reform, its effects on the dogmatic and ecclesiastical errors of the times being chiefly negative, and the more effective for being such. No thinker in the modern Church has excelled Wesley in the direct logic, the precision, the transparent clearness, and popular suitableness with which he presented the experimental truths of Christianity. Faith, Justification, Regeneration, Sanctification, the Witness of the Spirit, these were his themes, and never were they better defined and discriminated by an English theologian; and the keen faculty and practical directness with which he thus treated theological ideas was, perhaps, equally important in guiding him to those effective expedients of church government which have won for him, from the greatest historian of his country, the eulogy of having had "a genius for government not inferior to that of Richelieu."[1]

It was impossible that a mind thus addicted to precise conceptions and direct conclusions, rather than generalizations, should hesitate which side to take in the Calvinistic controversy. Even the modern qualifications of Calvinism, stated in the pious, compromising spirit of Baxter, could not satisfy him. It was vain to say to such a thinker that in predestinating the elect to be saved, God had only passed by the reprobates, leaving them to their own natural wickedness and fate. His prompt reply would be that, according to his opponents, the foreknowing God created the reprobate in his wickedness, and under his inevitable doom, and he would devolve upon them the formidable task of showing how then the unassisted offcast could be held responsible for his fate. He would require them, also, to reconcile with

[1] Macaulay's Review of Southey's Colloquies, Edinburgh Review, 1850. See also his Miscellanies, vol. i, p. 283.

such a condition of, perhaps, nine-tenths of the human race, the Divine beneficence; the Scriptural warnings and invitations addressed to them; the universal redemption made for them, or, if that were denied, the explicit Scriptural offers of it; their responsibility for their moral conduct, which, if alleged to be voluntary, is so, nevertheless, because their volitions are bound by an eternal decree, or, at least, by the total absence of that Divine grace by which alone the will can be corrected. The inevitable salvation of the elect, according to the dogma of Final Perseverance, he would also insist to be logically dangerous to good morals. The philosophical predestinarian would not admit the logical pertinency of these difficulties; it is not the province of the historian to discuss them polemically; it is sufficient to say that such was the character of Wesley's mind, and such the consequences which he drew from the Calvinistic theology. And yet, as we shall presently see, he was already too conscious of the peculiar mission of Methodism as a spiritual development of the Reformation, to attach fundamental importance to the question, or make it a condition of member ship in his societies.

In avowing Arminian opinions, and in giving that title to the magazine which he subsequently established,[2] he did not adopt the perversions which many of the disciples of Arminius have taught in Europe, and which have too often since been confounded with Arminianism by its opponents. He found in the writings of that great and devout theologian an evangelical system of opinions, as he thought, and Arminianism, as stated by the Remonstrants at the Synod of Dort, he did heartily receive, namely: 1. That God did decree to confer salvation on those who, he foresaw, would maintain their faith in Christ Jesus inviolate until death; and, on the other hand, to consign over to eternal punishment the unbelieving who resist his invitations to the end of their lives. 2. That Jesus Christ, by his death, made expiation for the sins of all and every one of mankind; yet that none but

[2] He commenced the Arminian Magazine in 1778.

believers can become partakers of its divine benefit. 3. That no one can of himself, or by the powers of his free will, produce or generate faith in his own mind; but that man being by nature evil, and incompetent (*ineptus*) both to think and to do good, it is necessary he should be born again and renewed by God, for Christ's sake, through the Holy Spirit. 4. That this divine grace or energy, which heals the soul of man, perfects all that can be called truly good in him, yet that this grace compels no man against his will, though it may be repelled by his will. 5. That those who are united to Christ by faith are furnished with sufficient strength to overcome sin; but that it is possible for a man to lose his faith and fall from a state of grace.[3]

While Wesley's mind was severely dialectic, and in some cases, doubtless, too much so, Whitefield's was quite the reverse. He seldom or never attempts a logical statement of his opinions; his logic was in his heart rather than in his head; and his feelings, happily of the purest temper, and guided by the conscience rather than the reason, usually determined his opinions. But the logic of the feelings, though the most important in ordinary life, that upon which the most responsible relations and duties are devolved by nature herself, is baffled in the presence of these theological mysteries. An accidental bias may make a man like Whitefield a bigot through life, for or against them. Had Whitefield thought of the controversy, for the first time, while preaching with tears before twenty thousand neglected and depraved hearers in Moorfields; had the question whether the Atonement comprehended them all, and whether all could "turn and live," come up then for an answer, he would have shouted the affirmative to the wretched multitude, and been an unwavering Arminian ever after.[4] But he saw the contro-

[3] The last proposition was left undecided at the time of the Synod, but adopted by the Arminians afterward. See Murdock's Mosheim, Seventeenth Century.

[4] He seems, indeed, not to have liked the public preaching of Predestination down to the time of his breach with Wesley. Before the crisis of the dispute he proposed silence to Wesley, and assured him that what-

versy from a different standpoint. He felt himself to have been so vile a sinner that he could not but ascribe his salvation to infinite and sovereign grace. Wesley would have granted this, but would also have asked the question, Why not exalt this sovereign grace still more by allowing that it has provided for all men? Whitefield saw thousands not more depraved than he had been, yet unreclaimed; his grateful heart, therefore, assumed, not with egotism, but with contrition, that a special grace had mysteriously plucked him out from the lost multitude. "Free grace," he exclaimed, in a letter to Wesley, "free, indeed, because not to all; but free, because God may withhold or give it to whom and when he pleases." And his ebullient spirit found so much delight in the hope of his final salvation, that the doctrine of "Final Perseverance" was eagerly seized by him, with apparently no hesitancy at its possible bad consequences to men of less conscientious fervor. In all his letters to Wesley, during the dispute that now occurred between them, we find but one allusion to "Reprobation;" that was an aspect of the subject which he seemed inclined not to think of; it was "Electing Grace" which absorbed his thoughts—"Final Perseverance"—the inestimable mercy of God in rescuing even elect souls from perdition, without a reference to his severity in creating and then abandoning forever the lost masses of reprobates. He had not read, he says, a single work of Calvin; he was "taught the doctrine of God;" he even had "the Witness of the Spirit" respecting it, and pronounces Wesley no proper "judge of its truth," as he had not received that witness on the question.[5] "God himself," he says, in another letter, "God himself, I find, teaches my friends the doctrine of election. Sister M. has lately been convinced of it; and, if I mistake not, dear and honored Mr. Wesley will be hereafter convinced also." Wesley was

ever had been his own opinions on the question he had never preached them.

[5] See the correspondence, quite impartially given, by Southey, Life of Wesley, chap. 11.

affected by the tender spirit of the correspondence. He replied: "The case is quite plain; there are bigots both for predestination and against it; God is sending a message to either side, but neither will receive it unless from one who is of their own opinion. Therefore for a time you are suffered to be of one opinion and I of another. But when his time is come, God will do what men cannot, namely, make us both of one mind." The prediction was fulfilled in its best sense, for, though never one in opinion, they became one in heart, and their separate courses in public life verified Wesley's opinion of the providential design of their theological divergence.

The dispute between them at this time is not without historical importance, as it doubtless led to the later controversy between Fletcher and his opponents, which has influenced Methodist opinions throughout the world, and which, it can be wished, more perhaps than hoped, may be the last great struggle on the question, before it shall be finally consigned by theologians over to the unavailing studies of metaphysicians, a suggestion which dogmatists will be slow to receive, but which, nevertheless, the popular good sense of Christendom is irresistibly forcing upon them.

Tenacious as Wesley was of his personal opinions, we have said that he did not insist on the Arminian doctrines as a condition of membership in his societies. All he required was that disputes respecting them should not be obtruded into devotional meetings by either party. His first trouble on the subject was from a member of one of the London societies, by the name of Acourt, who would debate it in the meetings of his brethren. Charles Wesley forbade his admission. He presented himself at a subsequent meeting, when John was present, and inquired if he had been excluded for his opinions? "Which opinions?" asked Wesley. "That of election," he replied. "I hold that a certain number are elected from eternity, and they must and shall be saved, and the rest of mankind must and shall be damned!" He asserted that others of the society so believed.

Wesley replied that he never questioned their opinions; all he demanded was that they should "only not trouble others by disputing about them." "Nay, but I will dispute about them," responded the hearty Calvinist; "you are all wrong, and I am determined to set you right." "I fear," said Wesley, "that your coming with this view would neither profit you nor us." "I will go then," replied Acourt, "and tell all the world that you and your brother are false prophets, and I tell you that in a fortnight you will all be in confusion."[6] Wesley was not a man to be subdued by such logic.

What induced him to take at last a decisive course respecting this controversy was the discovery that John Cennick, his "helper" at Kingswood, had attacked his Arminianism publicly. The school at Kingswood was entirely distinct from the seminary which afterward became noted there as Wesley's school for "preachers' sons." Whitefield had performed the ceremony of laying its foundation stone, but left the institution immediately in the hands of Wesley. "I bought the ground where it stands," says Wesley, "and paid for building it, partly from the contributions of my friends, partly from the income of my fellowship."[7] John Cennick was employed by him as teacher, and though a layman, was authorized by him to expound the Scriptures to the society which Wesley himself had gathered in the vicinity, and which met in the seminary. Cennick was an earnest, pious young man. He first met the Wesleys in London, in 1739, and being poor, and without employment, was sent to Kingswood at the instance of Charles Wesley. He did well there for some time. In 1740 he dissented from the preaching of "Universal Redemption," which, however, he had publicly approved before, on a visit of Charles Wesley. He raised a party against the doctrine and his patrons. He wrote letters to Whitefield, in America, urging his immediate return to suppress the heresy. Wesley was justly indignant at this

[6] Wesley's Journal, June 19, 1740.

[7] Works, vol. v, p. 283.

treatment, from a man whom he himself employed, and who attempted to "supplant him in his own house." The harmony of the society was disturbed; many efforts were made to restore it; but Cennick was obstinate, and insisted that himself and his adherents, while retaining their membership, should also "meet apart." After unavailing delays and overtures of peace, Wesley read publicly a paper declaring, "by the consent and approbation of the Band Society of Kingswood," that Cennick and his followers "were no longer members thereof." One of the accused asserted that it was not for any strife or disorder that they were expelled, but only for holding the doctrine of election. Wesley replied that they knew in their own consciences this was not the case; that there were several predestinarians in the societies, both in London and Bristol, nor did he "ever yet put any one out of either because he held that opinion." About fifty persons adhered to Cennick, and upward of ninety to Wesley.

Cennick afterward united with the Whitefield Methodists, but did not continue long with them. He became at last a Moravian. He was a good though weak man, and his subsequent earnest and laborious life shows that he deserves more lenience than has usually been accorded to him by Methodist writers.[8]

These events convinced Wesley that it was time to protest against the Calvinistic doctrines publicly. He immediately preached in Bristol the most impassioned of his sermons, containing passages as eloquent as the pulpit literature of our language affords.[9] It was printed, and was the third of his published discourses; the first was issued on

[8] Jackson treats him impartially: Life of Charles Wesley, chap. 8. The eccentric Matthew Wilks published his sermons, with a "Life" prefixed, and says: "He possessed a sweet simplicity of spirit, with an ardent zeal in the cause of his divine Master."

[9] When the late Earl of Liverpool read its peroration in Southey, he declared that in his judgment it was the most eloquent passage he had ever met with in any writer, ancient or modern. Jackson's Life of Charles Wesley, chap. 8.

his embarkation for Georgia, a farewell message to his friends on "The Trouble and Rest of Good Men;" the second was on "Salvation by Faith," preached and printed soon after his own conversion; the present discourse was on "Free Grace." It was sent by his opponents to Whitefield, who was then in America. Whitefield wrote frequent letters to him, remonstrating against his opinions, but still sincerely proposing mutual peace. His intercourse with the New-England clergy had, however, deepened his interest for the Calvinistic opinions. Assisted by his American friends, he composed an answer to Wesley, and had it printed at Boston, and also in Charleston, South Carolina.

On the 11th of March, 1741, Whitefield again reached England, and the next Sabbath was preaching in the open air at Kennington Common. But his reception was disheartening. His Calvinistic sentiments had become known by his correspondence. A letter from him against Wesley's opinions had been surreptitiously printed before his arrival, and circulated at the door of the Foundry. Wesley stood up in the desk with a copy of it in his hand, and referring to its disingenuous publication, said he would do what he believed his friend, the writer, would, were he present, and tore it into pieces. The congregation spontaneously did so with the copies which had been given them at the door.

A violent prejudice now spread against Whitefield, and the people refused to hear him. He still wished for peace with the Wesleys. He hastened to Charles Wesley, who was in London, and says it would have melted any heart to have seen them weeping, "after prayer that the breach might be prevented." He soon began to believe, however, that he was sacrificing the truth by not preaching election, and when John Wesley returned to the city, Whitefield declared that they preached two different Gospels, that he could no longer give the Wesleys the right hand of fellowship, but must preach against them. When reminded that he had just before promised and prayed for peace, he pronounced his promise an error, a weakness, and retracted it.[10]

Whitefield's strength was also his weakness. The ardor which made him powerful when right, rendered him impetuous when wrong, and he now committed some grave but temporary errors. He preached against the Wesleys by name in Moorfields, not far from the Foundry, where his old friends were preaching at the same time. He addressed them a letter finding fault with petty details in the chapel furniture at Kingswood; but when approached by them, his better feelings revived. They invited him to preach at the Foundry; yet there, before thousands of hearers, and with Charles Wesley by his side, he proclaimed the absolute decrees in a most peremptory and offensive manner.[11] Wesley had repeated interviews with him, and sought for a reconciliation; but the attempt was useless. Wesley protests, at a later period, that the breach was not necessary; that those who believed Universal Redemption had no desire to separate, but those who held Particular Redemption would not hear of any accommodation. "So," he adds, "there were now two sorts of Methodists, those for particular and those for general redemption."[12] He insists, at another time, that had it not been for the "manner" in which the Calvinistic party maintained their doctrine, the division might have been avoided; that difference of doctrine need not have created any difference of affection, but Whitefield "might have lovingly held particular redemption, and we general to our lives' end."[13]

Thus did Methodism divide into two currents, but thereby watered a wider range of the moral wilderness. Both flowed from the same source and in the same general direction. Both parties still adhered to the Church of England, availing themselves of the historical if not literal ambiguity

10 Wesley's Journal, March, 1741.

11 John Wesley's Letter to Rev. Thomas Maxfield. London, 1778. Jackson's Life of Charles Wesley, chap. 8.

12 Wesley's Short History of Methodism. Works, vol. v, p. 247.

13 Letter to Maxfield. Jackson's Charles Wesley, chap. 8.

of its seventeenth Article. Neither yet thought of forming a distinct ecclesiastical organization, and both soon after entered into cordial relations, though pursuing their common work in separate courses. Methodism, in fine, still continued to be a general evangelical movement, ostensibly within the English Church, though not hesitating to reach into any opening beyond it. Its history, therefore, if properly written, must still be a unit.[14]

[14] The anonymous author of "The Life and Times of the Countess of Huntington," has abused the Wesleys by many false details in his sketch of this dispute. I have not deemed it necessary to encumber my pages with them. The reader will find them fully answered in Jackson's Life of Charles Wesley, chap. 8.

CHAPTER IV.

THE CALVINISTIC METHODISTS.

Whitefield's Tabernacle opened — He employs Lay Preachers — Is reconciled with Wesley — Goes to Scotland — Wonderful Effects of his Preaching — Scenes at Cambuslang — Slight Success of Methodism in Scotland — Remarkable Scene at Moorfields — The Countess of Huntingdon — Whitefield preaching at her Mansion — Noble Hearers: Chesterfield, Bolingbroke, Walpole, Hume — The Countess erects Chapels — Her Liberality — The School of the Prophets at Trevecca — Her Followers become Dissenters.

THE loss of Whitefield's popularity in London could be but temporary. His zeal and eloquence could not fail to triumph over popular disaffection. Evangelical Calvinists gathered about him, and some of them proposed to erect for him a place of worship. A lot of ground was secured near Wesley's Foundry, and the celebrated Tabernacle quickly rose upon it. The new building was immediately crowded, and, following Wesley's example, which he had before disapproved, Whitefield secured the assistance of lay preachers. Cennick and Humphreys, both of whom had been Wesley's "helpers," joined him, and soon after Howell Harris came to his aid from Wales.

Though operating thus at separate batteries, and in near proximity, Wesley and Whitefield did not long maintain opposing fires, but turned them against the common enemy. "All," says Whitefield, "was wonderfully overruled for good, and for the furtherance of the Gospel."[1] They were soon personally reconciled; cordial letters passed between them; brotherly meetings took place, and they preached in each other's pulpit. "May you be blessed in bringing

[1] Gillies's Whitefield, chap. 8.

souls to Christ more and more," wrote Whitefield to Charles Wesley. "Our Lord exceedingly blesses us at the Tabernacle. Behold what a happy thing it is for brethren to dwell together in unity." The poet of Methodism responded in one of his noblest lyrics.[2] "Bigotry," said John Wesley, writing of Whitefield at a later date, when distinguished Calvinists were patronizing him; "bigotry cannot stand before him, but hides its head wherever he comes. My brother and I conferred with him every day; and let the honorable men do what they please, we resolved, by the grace of God, to go on hand in hand through honor and dishonor."

It would be impossible to detail, within our appropriate limits, the marvelous labors and successes of Whitefield during the three years of his present sojourn in England. Though separated from Wesley, he desired not to establish a sect; he knew that he was not competent to do so; he lacked the requisite legislative capacity; but as he represented Calvinistic Methodism, Calvinistic clergymen and Churches encouraged his labors. The Erskines of Scotland, distinguished as leaders of the Scotch Secession, invited him thither, and he made two excursions beyond the Tweed before his next return to America. The Erskines and their brethren of the Associate Presbytery were staunch zealots for the Solemn League and Covenant, which forms so interesting a feature in not only the ecclesiastical, but the civil history, and even the romantic literature of the country. They could make no compromise with English Churchmen, or any others who differed from them. Soon after his arrival at Dunfermline, where Ralph Erskine resided, Whitefield was surprised by a grave but ludicrous scene; ludicrous by its very gravity. He found himself introduced into the presence of several venerable members of the Associate Presbytery, who proposed to proceed to busi-

[2] Hymn for the Rev. Mr. Whitefield and Messrs. Wesley. See Jackson's Life of Charles Wesley, chap. 8, English edition. This spirited poem is unfortunately omitted in the American edition.

ness in formal session. He inquired for what purpose. They gravely replied, to consult and set him right about Church order, and the Solemn League and Covenant. He assured them they might save themselves that trouble; that he had no difficulties about either subject, and to intermeddle with either was not within "his plan." Yielding to his devout feelings, he proceeded to relate his Christian experience, and how Providence had led him into his present catholic course of action. Some of them were deeply affected by the singular narrative. Ebenezer Erskine entreated their forbearance with him as a good man who had unfortunately been born and bred in England, and had never studied the Solemn League and Covenant. One of the Associate divines replied, that he was the less excusable on this account, for England had revolted most in regard to Church government, and he should be acquainted with the important matters in debate. Whitefield insisted that he had never made them a subject of study, being too busy with more important interests. Several of the sturdy Scotchmen repelled the hint. "Every pin in the Tabernacle," they said, was important. He begged them to do good in their own way, and to allow him to proceed in his. They dissented; he then entreated them to say what they would have him do. They demanded that if he could not forthwith sign the Solemn League and Covenant, he should at least preach only for them till he was better enlightened, for they were the people of the Lord. It was even suggested that two of their brethren should be deputed with him to England to settle a Presbytery there, and two more to accompany him to America for a similar purpose.

He declined to take sides with either of the Scotch parties, but was determined to preach, as he had opportunity, for both. "If the pope himself," he said to the astonished Ralph Erskine, "if the pope himself would lend me his pulpit I would gladly declare the righteousness of Jesus Christ therein." The Seceders, absorbed by local controversies and the Solemn League and Covenant, could not comprehend him, and left him to himself. One of them mounted the pulpit, and preached against the English Church, declaring that any one who held communion with it or with "the backslidden Church of Scotland could not be an instrument of reformation." They afterward appointed a day of fasting and prayer against him.[3] He preached, however, with great success in the kirks of some thirty towns and cities, delivering from two to seven sermons a day, and left them in a general religious revival.

On his second visit, in the spring of 1742, he was received with enthusiasm. Multitudes met him at the landing at Leith, weeping for joy, and welcoming him with blessings. They followed his coach to Edinburgh, and crowded around him when he alighted, pressing him in their arms. His preaching stirred the whole city. The churches could not contain the people, and an amphitheater, under awnings, had to be constructed in the Park for their accommodation. He was called to the west, and made a tour of several weeks through its principal towns, preaching daily, and leaving a profound sensation wherever he went.

At Cambuslang the popular interest reached a height which was never equaled elsewhere under his labors. He preached three times on the day of his arrival to many thousands. The third discourse was at nine o'clock at night,

[3] Gillies's Whitefield, chaps. 8, 10. A violent pamphlet, characteristic of the times, was issued against him, entitled, "A Warning against countenancing the Ministrations of Mr. George Whitefield. Together with an Appendix upon the same Subject, wherein are shown that Mr. Whitefield is no Minister of Jesus Christ; that his Call and Coming to Scotland are scandalous; that his Practice is disorderly and fertile of Disorder; that his whole Doctrine is, and his success must be Diabolical; so that People ought to avoid him from Duty to God, to the Church, to themselves, to Fellow-Men, to Posterity, to him. By ADAM GIB, Minister of the Gospel at Edinburgh. Edinburgh, 1742." This curious publication is noticed in Philip's Whitefield, p. 278, American edition. A copy of it (the only one perhaps in America) is in the Library of the General Theological Seminary of the Protestant Episcopal Church, New-York.

and continued till eleven, "amid such a commotion," he says, "as scarcely ever was heard of." A fellow-clergyman relieved him at eleven, and preached on till one in the morning. All night the voice of prayer and praise could be heard in the fields. This remarkable introduction soon brought all the surrounding population to hear him. A "brae" or hill near the manse, was occupied instead of the church. "The people," he writes, "seem to be slain by scores. They are carried off, and come into the house like soldiers wounded in and carried off a field of battle. Their cries and agonies are exceedingly affecting." At another time a great sacramental occasion was held, in imitation of Hezekiah's Passover. More than twenty thousand people were present. Three tents were set up for the administration of the Supper, and twenty clergymen assisted in the service. There was preaching all day to such as could not get access to the administrators, and at nightfall Whitefield preached to the whole mass. Though usually occupying but about half an hour in his sermons, he now stood up for an hour and a half, speaking with irresistible power. The next morning, he says, "I preached again to near as many, but such a universal stir I never saw before. The motion fled as swift as lightning from one end of the auditory to the other. You might have seen thousands bathed in tears, some at the same time wringing their hands, others almost swooning, and others crying out and mourning over a pierced Saviour."

By these and subsequent labors in Scotland did Whitefield promote the mission of Methodism to that land. In no section of Europe had the Reformation more thoroughly wrought its work among the common people. An intelligent, frugal, and religious population, they needed, less than any other, the provocations of zeal which are usually furnished by new sects. Wesley marveled at their insusceptibility to Methodism; but Methodism at this time was more important as a general moral movement, pervading the old churches and the whole public mind, than as a sectarian development more or less organized. In the former sense it did a good work in Scotland. The revivals under Whitefield's preaching spread new energy through much of the Kirk, and since the era of Methodism, Scotland has shared that mighty influence of the movement which has been manifest in the religious progress of the whole United Kingdom. Her increased spiritual life, her foreign missions, her scarcely paralleled fidelity to the independence and integrity of the Church in the organization of her grand "Free Kirk," show that she has felt profoundly the religious spirit of our times. Arminian Methodists may condemn her tenacious Calvinism, but they should remember that Methodism itself proposes to ignore the Calvinistic controversy as a condition of Church communion. If Methodism regrets its little progress in Scotland, it may at least console itself that there is less reason for this regret there than in any other country in the world.

At London Whitefield could not long be content with his spacious Tabernacle, but took again the open field. The most riotous scenes at Moorfields were usually during the Whitsun holidays. The devils then held their rendezvous there, he said, and he resolved "to meet them in pitched battle." He began early in order to secure the field before the greatest rush of the crowd. At six o'clock in the morning he found ten thousand people waiting impatiently for the sports of the day. Mounting his field pulpit, and assured that he "had for once got the start of the devil," he soon drew the whole multitude around him. At noon he again took the field. Between twenty and thirty thousand swarmed upon it. He described it as in complete possession of Beelzebub, whose agents were in full motion. Drummers, trumpeters, merry-andrews, masters of puppet shows, exhibitors of wild beasts, players, were all busy in entertaining their respective groups. He shouted his text, "Great is Diana of the Ephesians," and boldly charged home upon the vice and peril of their dissipations. The craftsmen were alarmed, and the battle he had anticipated and challenged now fairly began. Stones, dirt, rotten eggs, and dead cats were thrown at him. "My soul," he says, "was among lions;" but before long he prevailed, and the immense multitude "were turned into lambs." At six in the evening he was again in his field pulpit. "I came," he says, "and I saw; but what? Thousands and thousands more than before." He rightly judged that Satan could not brook such repeated assaults in such circumstances, and never, perhaps, had they been pushed more bravely home against the very citadel of his power. A harlequin was exhibiting and trumpeting on a stage, but was deserted as soon as the people saw Whitefield, in his black robes, ascend his pulpit. He "lifted up his voice like a trumpet, and many heard the joyful sound." At length they approached nearer, and the merry-andrew, attended by others, who complained that they had taken many pounds less that day on account of the preaching, got upon a man's shoulders, and advancing toward the pulpit, attempted several times to strike the preacher with a long, heavy whip, but always tumbled down by the violence of his motion. The mob next secured the aid of a recruiting sergeant, who, with music and straggling followers, marched directly through the crowd before the pulpit. Whitefield knew instinctively how to manage the passions and whims of the people. He called out to them to make way for the king's officer. The sergeant, with assumed official dignity, and his drum and fife, passed through the opened ranks, which closed immediately after him, and left the solid mass still in possession of the preacher. A third onslaught was attempted. Roaring like wild beasts on the outskirts of the assembly, a large number combined for the purpose of sweeping through it in solid column. They bore a long pole for their standard, and came on with the sound of drum and menacing shouts, but soon quarreled among themselves, threw down their pole and dispersed, leaving many of their number behind, "who were brought over to join the besieged party."[4] At times, however, the tumult rose like the noise of many waters, drowning the

[4] Gillies's Whitefield, chap. 9.

preacher's voice; he would then call upon his brethren near him to unite with him in singing, until the clamorous host were again charmed into silence. He was determined not to retreat defeated; preaching, praying, singing, he kept his ground until night closed the strange scene. It was one of the greatest of his field days. He had won the victory, and moved off with his religious friends to celebrate it at night in the Tabernacle; and great were the spoils there exhibited. No less than a thousand notes were afterward handed up to him for prayers, from persons who had been brought "under conviction" that day; and, soon after, upward of three hundred were received into the society at one time. Many of them were "the devil's castaways," as he called them. Some he had to marry, for they had been living together without marriage; and "numbers that seemed to have been bred up for Tyburn were at that time plucked as brands from the burning." It may be doubted whether the history of Christianity affords a more encouraging example of the power of the Gospel over the rudest minds, and in the most hopeless circumstances. The moral sense will respond to Divine truth from the depths of the most degraded soul, and amid the wildest tumults of mobs. The response may not be heard; it may be stifled; but it is felt. Apostles knew the fact, and ancient heathenism fell before the confidence with which it inspired their ministrations. The charge of enthusiasm applies doubtless to these labors of Whitefield; but it is a compliment rather than a detraction. In less urgent circumstances such enthusiasm might appear to be fanaticism, but here it was legitimate. How were these heathen masses to be otherwise reached by the Gospel? Thousands of them never entered the churches of London. Clothed in rags, their very persons labeled with the marks of vice and wretchedness, they would have hardly found admission into them had they sought it. Moorfields must be invaded if it were to be conquered, and no less energetic invasions than those which Whitefield and Wesley made there, could be successful. They were successful; and the suppression, at last, of the enormous scenes of that and similar resorts in England, is attributable greatly to the moral triumphs of Methodism among the degraded classes of the common people.

Besides his labors in London and Scotland, Whitefield traveled extensively in England before his next embarkation for Georgia, in 1744. His popularity had fully returned. At Bristol assemblies more numerous than ever attended his preaching. Even in the minor towns ten or twelve thousand were his frequent estimates of his hearers, for the population of all neighboring villages usually thronged to the places of his out-door sermons. He made repeated tours through Wales, and each time with increased success. In one of these visits, employing three weeks, he traveled four hundred English miles, preached forty sermons, and spent three days in attending Associations of the new societies. "At seven in the morning," he writes, "have I seen perhaps ten thousand from different parts, in the midst of a sermon, crying *Gogunniant bendytti*, ready to leap for joy." "The work begun by Mr. Jones spreads far and near in North and South Wales."

Though Whitefield designed not to establish a Methodist sect, circumstances compelled him, after his separation from Wesley, to give a somewhat organized form to the results of his labors among the Calvinistic adherents who gathered about him. Lady Betty Hastings had patronized the little band of Methodists at Oxford; Lady Margaret Hastings, her sister, had adopted, through her influence, the Methodist sentiments, and afterward married Ingham, who was one of the Oxford Methodists, and the companion of Wesley in Georgia. Her influence over her sister-in-law Selina, the Countess of Huntingdon, led the countess, during a serious sickness, to a religious life, and to a strong sympathy with the Methodists. Bishop Benson, who had ordained Whitefield, and had been tutor to her husband, the Earl of Huntingdon, was called by the latter to restore his wife to a "saner" mind. The good bishop failed in the attempt, and expressed regret that he had ever laid his hand on Whitefield. "Mark my words, my lord," replied the countess, "when upon your dying bed, that will be one of the ordinations upon which you will reflect with pleasure." The prediction was fulfilled. The bishop, when he came to die, sent Whitefield a present of ten guineas, and asked an interest in his prayers. Lady Huntingdon, though remotely related to the royal family, and moving in the highest circles of aristocratic life, frequented the Moravian societies in London, and at the separation of Wesley from them, co-operated with the Methodist party. She invited him to her residence at Donnington Park, where he often preached. She adopted heartily his doctrine of Christian Perfection. "The doctrine," she wrote him, "I hope to live and die by; it is absolutely the most complete thing I know."[5] She encouraged him in his extraordinary labors, and especially in the promotion of a lay ministry as the great necessity of the times. Her Calvinistic opinions led her to patronize Whitefield when he separated from Wesley, and her talents, wealth, and influence placed her at the head of Calvinistic Methodism; but she endeavored to secure a good understanding between the great evangelists. She wrote to each, recommending their closer co-operation, and not without effect. Whitefield preached in Wesley's chapel, Wesley reading the prayers; and the next Sunday Wesley officiated at the Tabernacle, assisted by Whitefield. Twelve hundred persons received the Lord's Supper at the conclusion of the sermon. The reconciliation was further strengthened by a powerful sermon to an overflowing assembly at Wesley's chapel the next day, by Howell Harris, the Welch colaborer of both the great leaders.[6] Their personal friendship remained uninterrupted during the rest of their lives. "Thanks be to God," wrote the countess, "for the love and unanimity which have been displayed on this occasion. May the God of peace and harmony unite us all in the bond of affection."

It is not irrelevant to notice here, though with the anticipa-

[5] Lady Huntingdon Portrayed, chap. 3. New York, 1857.

[6] Life and Times of Selina, Countess of Huntingdon, vol. i, chap. 8.

tion of some dates, the early development of this part of the Methodistic movement. At the death of her husband, Lady Huntingdon devoted her life actively to religious labors, and in 1748 invited Whitefield to preach in her mansion at Chelsea, near London, hitherto a resort for the highest classes of the fashionable and aristocratic world, and she soon after appointed him one of her chaplains. Paul preached privately to those that were of reputation, thought Whitefield; he therefore concurred in her ladyship's proposal to combine with his public labors among the crowds at the Tabernacle, and the ten thousands at Moorfields, private sermons at the Chelsea mansion. Notable men heard there the truth from his eloquent lips. Chesterfield listened to him with delight, and gave him one of his courtly compliments: "Sir, I will not tell you what I shall tell others, how I approve you." He opened for the evangelist his chapel at Bretby Hall. Several of his noble relatives were claimed by Whitefield as his spiritual trophies. His wife and her sister, the Countess Delitz, died in the faith. Horace Walpole heard him with admiration, though his rampant wit trifled with him behind his back. Hume listened with wonder, and said he would go twenty miles to hear him. Bolingbroke complimented him, approved his Calvinism, and received his sermons and his visits; his brother, Lord St. John, became a convert, and died in the hope of the Gospel.[7] Many ladies of the highest aristocratic rank became "devout women," and ornaments to the Christian Church. The Marchioness of Lothian arrived in London in a dying condition about this time, and united with the Countess of Leven, Lady Balgonie, Lady Frances Gardiner, Lady Jane Nimmo, and Lady Mary Hamilton, in establishing a meeting for prayer and the reading of the Scriptures, to be held alternately at each other's houses, which continued to be well attended and singularly useful for many years. It was confined to a select circle of women of high station, many of whom adorned the doctrine which they professed by a life of holiness and self-

[7] Life and Times of Selina, Countess of Huntingdon, vol. i, chap. 7.

denial amid their distinguished associates. Still later, the Countess of Northesk and Hopetown, the daughters of Lord Leven, the Countess of Buchan, Lady Maxwell, Lady Glenorchy, Wilhelmina, Countess of Leven, (formerly Lady Balgonie,) with her sisters, Lady Ruthven and Lady Banff, Lady Henrietta Hope, and Sophia, Countess of Haddington, were devoted members of this select band.[8] Thus while Methodism was gathering its societies from the humblest classes, at the Tabernacle and the Foundry, it bound together, in similar assemblies, a few of the "noble" in the aristocratic quarter of the metropolis.

Meanwhile Whitfield's success opened the way for the utmost zeal and liberality of the countess. She gave away, for religious purposes, more than five hundred thousand dollars.[9] She sold all her jewels, and by the proceeds erected chapels for the poor. She relinquished her aristocratic equipage, her expensive residences and liveried servants, that

[8] "These have all long since joined the general assembly and church of the redeemed from among men, and are now uniting in ascriptions of praise to Him who hath redeemed them to God by his blood." (Life and Times of Selina, Countess of Huntingdon, vol. i, chap. 7.) Many flocked from the court circle to the Park-street mansion to hear Whitefield; and, as might be expected, found the truth too novel and keen to be endured. This author (himself "a member of the House of Shirley and Hastings") gives an example which had its parallel almost daily under the Methodist preaching among the lowest classes. "Mr. Whitefield's lectures to the 'brilliant circle' at Lady Huntingdon's were evidently as faithful as they were eloquent. The well-known Countess of Suffolk found them so. Lady Rockingham prevailed on Lady Huntingdon to admit this beauty to hear her chaplain; he, however, knew nothing of her presence; he drew his bow at a venture, but every arrow seemed aimed at her. She just managed to sit out the service in silence, and when Mr. Whitefield retired she flew into a violent passion, abused Lady Huntingdon to her face, and denounced the sermon as a deliberate attack on herself. In vain her sister-in-law, Lady Betty Germain, tried to appease the beautiful fury, or to explain her mistake; in vain old Lady Eleanor Bertie and the Duchess Dowager of Ancaster, both relatives of Lady Suffolk, commanded her silence: she maintained that she had been insulted. She was compelled, however, by her relatives who were present, to apologize to Lady Huntingdon. Having done this with a bad grace, the mortified beauty left the place to return no more." She was the female favorite of the court of George II., and Pope's celebrated "Mrs. Howard."

[9] Life and Times of Selina, Countess of Huntingdon, vol. i, chap. 7.

her means of usefulness might be more ample. She purchased theaters, halls, and dilapidated chapels in London, Bristol, and Dublin, and fitted them up for public worship. New chapels were also erected by her aid in many places in England, Wales, and Ireland. Distinguished Calvinistic clergymen, Churchmen as well as Dissenters, co-operated with her plans, and were more or less under her direction. Romaine, Venn, Madan, Berridge, Toplady, Shirley, Fletcher, Benson, and a host of others, shared her beneficent labors. She met them in frequent conferences, attended sometimes by the Wesleys. She made tours through parts of England and Wales, accompanied by like-minded noble ladies and by eminent evangelists, who preached wherever they went, in the churches and in the open air. She mapped all England into six districts or circuits, and sent out six "canvassers" from among her most successful adherents, to travel them, and to preach in every community, large or small, which was not pre-occupied by similar laborers; and at the time of her death, her influence had extended over the four sections of the United Kingdom.

Her zeal and munificence provided places of worship faster than they could be supplied by her preachers, especially in Wales. A college for the preparation of clergymen was therefore opened, in a romantic and dilapidated castle of the twelfth century, at Trevecca, the birth-place of Howell Harris, the Welsh evangelist. Its preparation for the purpose exhausted all the available means of the countess; but Ladies Glenorchy and Chesterfield, with other aristocratic but devout friends, gave her large contributions. Wesley heartily approved her plan. She submitted it also to Fletcher of Madeley; at the close of the day on which he received her letter he retired to his rest in prayerful meditation respecting it. In the dreams of the night the scheme was revolving through his thoughts, and a young man, "James Glazebrook, collier and getter-out of iron-stone in the woods of Madeley," appeared as in a vision before him—a suitable student with whom to begin "the school of the prophets." "To my great surprise," wrote Fletcher to the countess, "he came into Madeley the next morning. I found, upon inquiry, that he was as much drawn to come as I to speak of him." He had been seven years converted, had "no mean gift in singing and prayer," and his "judgment and sense were superior to his station." Such was the first pupil of Trevecca.[10]

Fletcher himself became its president; and at a later date Joseph Benson, the Wesleyan commentator, was appointed its head master. Students soon flocked to the school. Religious opinions were not made a test for admission; but candidates who professed to have been truly converted to God, and were resolved to devote themselves to the ministry, in either the Established Church or any denomination of Dissenters, were welcomed, and provided, at the countess's expense, with board, tuition, and a yearly suit of clothes.

Lady Huntingdon's "Connection" holds an important place in the history of these times. It spread the Methodist movement effectively among British Calvinists, whether within or without the Church, and thus contributed inestimably to that general but potent influence which impartial Churchmen and Dissenters acknowledge to have been exerted by Methodism on the whole later progress of religion in Great Britain.[11] Like Wesley, Lady Huntingdon, with Whitefield, Howell Harris, and most of

[10] Lady Huntingdon Portrayed, chap. 8. Glazebrook became one of Wesley's preachers, and subsequently, by the aid of Fletcher and Lady Huntingdon, obtained ordination in the Established Church. He died vicar of Belton, Leicestershire. He was distinguished for his piety and usefulness, and also for his satirical humor. Works from his pen on extemporary preaching, infant baptism, and other subjects, as also a posthumous volume of sermons, were published. A memoir of him appeared in the Evangelical Register (England) in 1836.

[11] It is significant, however, that Doddridge, Watts, and other great Dissenters in the early times of Methodism, showed publicly but little sympathy with Whitefield, though they acknowledged much privately. They forfeited their right to an honorable place in the history of the new movement. The reason of the fact may be seen in Philip's "Life and

her preachers, was strongly attached to the Church of England. They wished not to be classed with Dissenters; but in order to protect her chapels from suppression, or appropriation by the Established Church, she had to avail herself, in 1779, of the "Toleration Act," a law by which all religious societies that would not be subject to the established ecclesiastical power, could control their own chapels by an avowal, direct or virtual, of Dissent. Her "Connection" thus took its place among the Dissenting Churches, and Romaine, Townsend, Venn, and many others of her most influential colaborers belonging to the Establishment, ceased to preach in her chapels.

At the extreme age of eighty-four this remarkable woman died, uttering with her last breath: "My work is done. I have nothing to do but to go to my Father." She left twenty thousand dollars for charities, and the residue of her fortune for the support of sixty-four chapels which she had helped to build in various parts of the kingdom. No one of her sex, perhaps, in the history of the Church, certainly none of modern times, has done more by direct labors and liberality for the promotion of genuine religion.

Times of Whitefield," chap. 10. They were endeavoring to repeat the scheme of "comprehension" which Bates, Manton, and Baxter had attempted in vain with Bishop Stillingfleet. Sympathy toward Methodism might have compromised them with the Establishment, whose favor they were seeking. The facts, as given by Philip, though unfortunate for these great and good men, are irrefutable.

CHAPTER V.

TRAVELS AND LABORS OF THE WESLEYS FROM 1741 TO 1744.

Lay Preaching — Thomas Maxfield — Susanna Wesley — Her Death — Wesley itinerating — Introduction of Class-Meetings — John Nelson — His History — Wesley visits him in Yorkshire — Wesley in the North of England — Newcastle — Its degraded Poor — Wesley preaching on the Tombstone of his Father — General Rules of the United Societies — Their Catholicity — Physical Phenomena of the Excitement at Newcastle — Wesley considers them Demoniacal — Charles Wesley mobbed at Sheffield — He goes to Cornwall — Is mobbed at St. Ives — John Wesley and John Nelson in Cornwall — Their Privations — Wesley mobbed at Wednesbury — Charles Wesley at Wednesbury — Progress of Methodism.

WE have followed Whitefield in his ministerial travels from the date of his separation from Wesley in 1741, to his embarkation for America in 1744. This interval was filled with extraordinary itinerant labors by the Wesleys and their coadjutors, and was followed by a memorable event, the first session of the Wesleyan Methodist Conference.

Notwithstanding the disturbances occasioned by the Calvinistic dispute, and the separation of Whitefield, the year 1742 was attended with increased success. It was, however, a period of severer trials than the Methodist evangelists had hitherto encountered. Methodism had achieved moral miracles among the degraded colliers of Kingswood. It could point for its noblest demonstration to such abysses of popular degradation, into which it had borne the cross, as almost into the gates of hell. Its satirists were compelled to acknowledge its marvelous and salutary power over classes which had been considered hopelessly beyond the reach of any moral influence that either the Church or the Dissenters could then exert. But the lower classes of England generally were sunk in scarcely less degradation, and there were especially other mining regions of the kingdom, as Newcastle and Cornwall, whose demoralization was notoriously extreme. Wesley and his colaborers resolved to invade them at any risk. They knew that in the condition of these sections, at the time, violent opposition must be expected. The magistrates would probably be hostile; the clergy, incapable in their stately churches and formalism of reaching the wretched multitudes, would probably denounce the intruders, a fact which was found to be too true; but what were all such consequences, compared with the results of the continued moral neglect of these perishing masses? The evangelical itinerants directed their course, therefore, toward the mining populations of the north and west, prepared for mobs, and, if need be, for martyrdom. We shall see that they recoiled not from either, but steadily pushed forward their conquests, amid scenes which sometimes resembled the tumults of battle-fields.

Hitherto Wesley's lay "helpers" had been but "exhorters," and readers and "expounders" of the Scriptures; but "lay preaching" was now formally begun. Thomas Maxfield, occupying the desk of the Foundry in Wesley's absence, had been led to deviate from these restrictions. Wesley received a letter at Bristol informing him of the fact. His prejudices for "church order" were still strong, and he hastened to London, with no little alarm, to check the new irregularity. His mother was still at hand, however, to guide him. Retired in the parsonage of the Foundry, lingering at the verge of the grave, and watching unto prayer over the marvelous developments which were occurring in the religious world around her, through the instrumentality of her family, she read the indications of the times with a wiser sagacity than her son, and was now to accomplish her last controlling agency in the Methodist movement, and to introduce an innovation by which, more than by any other fact in its ministerial economy, it has been sustained and extended in the world. She perceived on his arrival that his countenance expressed dissatisfaction and anxiety, and inquired the cause. "Thomas Maxfield," he replied, with unusual abruptness, "has turned preacher, I find." She reminded him of her own sentiments against lay preaching, and that he could not suspect her of favoring anything of the kind. But take care, she added, what you do respecting that young man; he is as surely called of God to preach as you are. She counseled him to examine what had been the fruits of Maxfield's preaching, and to hear him also himself. He heard him: "It is the Lord, let Him do what seemeth to Him good," was all he could further say, and Thomas Maxfield became the first of that host of itinerant lay preachers which has since carried the standard of the Gospel more triumphantly over the world than any other class of the modern Christian ministry.

Maxfield was not the first of Wesley's lay assistants, but the first of his lay preachers. John Cennick and others probably preceded him in the former capacity. Wesley, in his last Journal, mentions Joseph Humphrys as being the first lay preacher that assisted him "in England, in the year 1738," but doubtless refers to him as an exhorter and expounder, for his scruples in the case of Maxfield prove that he would not have tolerated formal preaching by Humphrys at that earlier date; and in the Conference Minutes of 1766, he names Maxfield as the first layman who desired to help him "as a son in the Gospel." "Soon after," he adds, "there came a second, Thomas Richards, and a third, Thomas Westall."

Lady Huntingdon, also, had the good sense to encourage this important innovation. She heard Maxfield, and wrote to Wesley in the warmest terms respecting him. "He is," she said, "one of the greatest instances of God's peculiar favor that I know. He has raised from the stones one to sit among the princes of his people; he is my astonishment; how is God's power shown in weakness!"[1]

Having lingered till her seventy-third year, counseling and encouraging her sons, and having at last aided in securing the prospects of Methodism indefinitely, if not for all time, by the introduction of a lay ministry, Susanna Wesley died this year on the premises of the Foundry, within sound of the voices of prayer and praise which were ascending almost daily from that memorable edifice—the first Methodist chapel opened in the world, the scene of the organization of the first of the "United Societies," and of the first session of the Wesleyan Methodist Conference. It was a befitting place for the departure of the mother of the Wesleys from the church on earth to the church in heaven. She had, says Wesley, no doubt, or fear, or any desire but to depart and be with Christ.[2] He and five of her daughters stood around her bed when she expired, on the 23d of July, 1742. When no longer able to speak, but apparently still conscious, her look, calm and serene, was fixed upward, while they commended her to God in prayer. She died without pain, and at the moment of her departure her children, gathering close around her, sung as she had requested with her last words, "a psalm of praise to God." Followed by an innumerable concourse of people, Wesley committed her remains to the grave, among the many illustrious dead of Bunhill-fields.

Wesley's lay ministry comprised during the year no less than twenty-three itinerants, besides several local preachers.[3] They were distributed among his increasing societies, and traveled and preached continually in the adjacent towns and villages, he himself affording them in his incessant labors an example which none of them could exceed. He made a

1 Moore's Life of Wesley, IV, 3. Life and Times of Lady Huntingdon, vol. i, chap. 3. This writer represents that she induced Maxfield to take this new step.

2 Journal, July, 1742.

3 Smith's History of Methodism, II, 2. Myles's Chronological History of the Methodists, chap. 11.

rapid tour in Wales during the early part of the year, preaching often in the open air, and assailed by mobs, but was successful in building up and multiplying the societies. He visited Bristol repeatedly, and formed there the first "Methodist class-meeting," and, on returning to London, introduced the same improvement into the metropolitan societies. "This," he says, "was the origin of our classes in London, for which I can never sufficiently praise God. The unspeakable usefulness of the institution has ever since been more and more manifest." The Watchnight was also held this year for the first time in the London societies.

Under Wesley's first sermon in Moorfields John Nelson, an honest Yorkshire mason, of extraordinary character and powers of mind, had received the truth, and having returned to his home in Birstal, was now producing no little sensation by his exhortations and prayers among his rustic neighbors. Wesley set out in May for Yorkshire, to visit and direct him.

Nelson had led an upright life from his youth, being trained in steady habits of morality if not piety, by religious parents. His faculties were strong, and marked not only by good common sense, but an aptitude to grapple with those agonizing problems respecting the soul and its destiny, evil and good, which the greatest minds can neither solve nor evade. He had a humble but a happy home, a good wife, good wages, good health, and a stout English heart; but though addicted to no immoralities, he was distressed by the sense of moral wants, which his life failed to meet. "Surely," he said, "God never made man to be such a riddle to himself, and to leave him so."[4] Something he believed there must be in true religion to meet these wants of the soul, otherwise man is more unfortunate than the brute that perishes. Absorbed in such meditations, this untutored mechanic wandered in the fields after the work of the day, discussing to himself questions which had employed and ennobled the thoughts of Plato in the groves of the Cephissus,

[4] Nelson's Journal, p. 12, American edition.

and agitated by the anxieties that had stirred the souls of Wesley and his studious associates at Oxford. His conduct was a mystery to his less thoughtful fellow-workmen. He refused to share in their gross indulgences; they cursed him because he would not drink as they did. He bore their insults with a calm philosophy; but having as "brave a heart as ever Englishman was blessed with,"[5] he would not allow them to infringe on his rights; and when they took away his tools, determined that if he would not drink with them he should not work while they were carousing, he fought with several of them until they were content to let him alone in his inexplicable gravity and courage. He went also from church to church, for he was still a faithful Churchman, but met no answer to his profound questions. He visited the chapels of all classes of Dissenters, but the quiet of the Quaker worship could not quiet the voice that spoke through his conscience, and the splendor of the Roman ritual soon became but irksome pomp to him. He tried, he tells us, all but the Jews, and hoping for nothing from them, resolved to adhere steadily to the Church, regulating his life with strictness, spending his leisure in reading and prayer, and leaving his final fate unsolved. Whitefield's eloquence at Moorfields, however, attracted him thither, but it did not meet his wants. He loved the great orator, he tells us, and was willing to fight for him against the mob, but his mind only sunk deeper into perplexity. He became morbidly despondent; he slept little, and often awoke from horrible dreams, dripping with sweat, and shivering with terror. Wesley came to Moorfields; Nelson gazed upon him with inexpressible interest as he ascended the platform, stroked back his hair, and cast his eye

[5] Robert Southey, Life of Wesley, chap. xiv. John Nelson's whole life proved that such a eulogy was not undeserved from the biographer of Lord Nelson. The naval conqueror would have admired the evangelical hero, and have acknowledged him his equal in both English courage and English good sense. Southey delays on the history of John Nelson with much particularity and interest. He was evidently the poet's favorite among the many heroes of early Methodism.

directly upon him. "My heart," he says, "beat like the pendulum of a clock, and when he spoke I thought his whole discourse was aimed at me." "This man," he said to himself, "can tell the secrets of my breast; he has shown me the remedy for my wretchedness, even the blood of Christ." He now became more than ever devoted to religious duties, and soon found the peace of mind he had so long been seeking. He records with dramatic interest the discussions and efforts of his acquaintances to prevent him from going too far in religion. They seem to have been mostly an honest, simple class like himself; they thought he would become unfit for business, and that poverty and distress would fall upon his family. They wished he had never heard Wesley, who, they predicted, would "be the ruin of him." He told them that he had reason to bless God that Wesley was ever born, for by hearing him he had become sensible that his business in this world was to get well out of it. The family with whom he lodged were disposed to expel him from the house, for they were afraid some mischief would come on either themselves or him, from "so much praying and fuss as he made about religion." He procured money and went to pay them what he owed them, and take his leave; but they would not let him escape. "What if John is right, and we wrong?" was a natural question which they asked among themselves. "If God has done for you anything more than for us, show us how we may find the same mercy," asked one of them. He was soon leading them to hear Wesley on Moorfields. One of them was made partaker of the same grace, and he expresses the hope of meeting both in heaven.

With much simplicity, but true English determination, he adhered to his religious principles at any risk. His employer required work to be done during the Sabbath on the Exchequer building, declaring that the king's business required haste, and that it was usual, in such cases, to work on Sunday for his majesty. Nelson replied that he would not work on the Sabbath for any man in England, except to quench fire, or something that required the same immediate help. His employer threatened him with the loss of his business. He replied that he would rather starve than offend God. "What hast thou done that thou makest such an ado about religion?" asked the employer; "I always took thee for an honest man, and could trust thee with five hundred pounds." "So you might," replied the sturdy Methodist, "and not have lost one penny by me." "But I have a worse opinion of thee now than ever," resumed the employer. "Master," replied Nelson, "I have the odds of you there, for I have a much worse opinion of myself than you can have." The honest man was not dismissed, nor again asked to work on Sunday, nor were any of his fellow-workmen.

He now wrote to his wife, who was in the country, and to all his kindred, explaining his new method of life, and exhorting them to adopt it. He fasted once a week, and gave the food thus saved to the poor. He even hired a fellow-workman to hear Wesley; and his liberality was effectual, for the mechanic afterward assured him that it was the best deed, both for himself and his wife, that any one had ever done for them. He read the Scriptures with increased ardor, and was soon abundantly furnished with apt texts for his opponents, and consoling promises for his own inward trials. He had formerly had frightful dreams of contests with Satan, and was usually worsted in the combat; but he now became the victor in these imaginary conflicts. He dreamed that he saw the great adversary rampant among the people, in the form of a red bull; he seized his horns with good courage, threw him upon his back, and trod triumphantly upon his neck.

Such was John Nelson, a man from the lowest grade of English life, but whose brave heart and immovable integrity fitted him to have taken a place among the noblest martyrs, had he been called to it; and whose fervent piety, steadfast zeal, and Saxon energy, made him one of the apostles of early Methodism. His natural magnanimity, good sense, clear apprehension of Scripture, apt style, and simple manners, rendered him a favorite and successful preacher among a class which few educated clergymen could have reached. A Yorkshireman by birth, he became the chief founder of Methodism in that county, a section of England in which it has had signal success down to our day.

As his family resided in Birstal, he started, after his conversion, to visit them and his neighbors, that he might recommend to them his new views of religion in person, as he had done in letters. They met him with no little opposition; they could not well consider him a maniac, he had too much good English sense and sobriety for such a suspicion; but he might be under a strange delusion of the devil! After no little hesitancy, and a vast amount of rustic polemics, his two brothers, an aunt, and two cousins yielded, and became his disciples. He sat in his own house reading, exhorting, and praying with such of his neighbors as came to hear. The number increased so much that he had soon to stand at the door and address them without and within. Six or seven were converted weekly; the ale-houses were deserted, and the moral aspect of the whole town was changed.[6] His exhortations became more topical as the inquiries of his hearers became more specific, and soon, without anticipating it, he was addressing them in formal discourses. He had, in fact, become a Preacher, and his sermons, from being quite private, had become public, and were attended with such extensive results that Wesley started from London, as we have seen, to visit and direct him.

On arriving at Birstal Wesley was surprised to find a society and a preacher awaiting him. He addressed them and hundreds of others on the top of Birstal Hill. He

[6] Wesley says, (Short History of the People called Methodists, sect. 20:) "Many of the greatest profligates in all the country were soon changed; their blasphemies were turned to praise. Many of the most abandoned drunkards were now sober; many Sabbath breakers remembered the Sabbath to keep it holy; the whole town wore a new face. Such a change did God work by the artless testimony of one plain man! And from thence his word sounded forth to Leeds, Wakefield, Halifax, and all the West Riding of Yorkshire."

recognized Nelson as one of his "Helpers," and his band of rustic followers as one of his United Societies. Methodism thus took root in Birstal, and has since spread into every village of Yorkshire.

The Moravians, with their London errors, thronged about the sturdy mason, and perverted many of his converts; but he himself was more than a match for them, with his apt quotations of Scripture. His sound though untutored mind could not be seduced by their sophistries.

Wesley had not hitherto visited the north of England. Leaving Nelson, with full confidence in his steadfast discretion and further success, he hastened to Newcastle, one of those degraded mining regions which Methodism proposed to invade the present year. He walked into the town, and never, he says, had he witnessed so much drunkenness, cursing, and swearing, from the mouths of little children as well as adults, in so short a time. "Surely," he exclaimed, "this place is ripe for Him who 'came not to call the righteous but sinners to repentance.'"[7]

At seven o'clock on Sunday morning he walked down to Sandgate, the most degraded part of the town, and standing at the end of the street with a religious friend, began to sing the Hundredth Psalm. Three or four persons came out to see what was the matter; they soon increased to four or five hundred; before he had closed twelve or fifteen hundred stood around him. He discoursed to them, as usual when he addressed the vicious poor, on one of the most consolatory texts: "He was wounded for our transgressions; he was bruised for our iniquities; the chastisement of our peace was upon him, and by his stripes we are healed." When he had concluded, the wretched multitude, who had never before had the offers of the Divine compassion thus brought to them in their very streets, stood, he writes, "gaping and staring" upon him with astonishment. "If you desire to know who I am," he cried, "my name is John Wesley; at five in the

[7] For our citations from John Wesley throughout this chapter, see his Journals, 1742-3-4.

evening, with God's help, I will preach here again." At five o'clock the hill upon which he designed to preach was covered from top to bottom. He says he never saw such a multitude, either in Moorfields or at Kennington Common. He knew that one half could not hear him, though he had them all in range of his view, as he stood at the apex of the living pyramid. It was an occasion to inspire such a man. The "south had not kept back;" it seemed now that "the north was about to give up" to the little band which had so lately commenced its march from the gates of Oxford, and had already spread its evangelical triumphs in England, Wales, and America. His text was again a proclamation of mercy, for these poor multitudes, he believed, were not the worst of sinners; he knew that under their rude and boisterous vices were hidden crushed but living consciences; longings for better things; generous sensibilities that would respond to the voice of God or man whenever they could hear it speaking to their wants and sorrows. "I will heal their backslidings; I will love them freely," were the gracious words which he shouted to them as his text. The effect justified his wisdom. After hearing his message of mercy, the "poor people," he says, "were ready to tread me under foot out of pure love and kindness." It was some time before he could make his way out of the eager throng. He had to escape by another street than that by which he came, but, on reaching his inn, he found that several of his hearers had got there before him. They vehemently entreated him to stay with them at least a few days, or, if that could not be, yet only one day more; but he could not; he had promised to be with Nelson again immediately, and was compelled to leave them clamoring around him for the bread of life. His brother came among them in a short time, and before the year closed Wesley again visited them; he saw their degradation more thoroughly than before; he found, he writes, that he had got into the very Kingswood of the north. Twenty or thirty "wild children" ran around him as soon as he entered the Common to preach. He describes them as neither clothed nor naked. "One of the largest (a girl about fifteen) had a piece of a ragged dirty blanket some way hung about her, and a kind of cap on her head, of the same cloth and color." He was deeply affected by the sight of his miserable audience, and they looked, he says, as if they would have "swallowed him up," especially while he was applying to them the words: "Be it known unto you, men and brethren, that through this man is preached unto you forgiveness of sins." He immediately began the erection of a chapel among them. One of those "Societies" which he had providentially found ready for him in London, Bristol, and other towns, had maintained a lingering existence in Newcastle. It now became the nucleus of Methodism there, and a profound but remarkably tranquil religious interest spread through the surrounding regions. "I never saw," he writes, "a work of God in any other place so evenly and gradually carried on; it continually rises, step by step." Instances, however, of excitement, and its physical effects, afterward appeared at Newcastle, as at other places, and required the exercise of his best prudence.

On his return he passed rapidly through many towns, preaching daily. He stopped at an inn in Epworth, the parish of his father and his own birthplace. The curate, who was a drunkard, refused him the pulpit. David Taylor, Lady Huntingdon's servant, was with him, and announced, as the congregation retired from the church, that Wesley would preach in the graveyard in the afternoon. He accordingly stood upon his father's tombstone, and preached to such a congregation as Epworth had never seen before. For one week he daily took his stand above the ashes of his father, and "cried aloud to the earnestly attentive congregations." He must have deeply felt the impressive associations of the place, but paused not to record his emotions. His one great work of preaching, preaching day and night, seemed wholly to absorb him. His hearers, however, felt the power of his word and of the scene. God bowed their hearts, he says, and on every side, as with one accord, they lifted up their voices and wept; several dropped down as dead. A gentleman came to hear him who boasted that he was of no religion, and had not been in a church for thirty years. The striking scene of the churchyard could probably alone have brought him to hear Wesley. He was smitten under the sermon, and when it was ended stood like a statue, looking up to the heavens. Wesley asked: "Are you a sinner?" "Sinner enough," he replied, with a broken voice, and remained gazing upward till his friends pressed him into his carriage and took him home. Ten years later Wesley saw him, and was agreeably surprised to find him strong in faith, though fast failing in body. For some years, he said, he had been rejoicing in God without either doubt or fear, and was now waiting for the welcome hour when he should depart and be with Christ.

Wesley found in Epworth an old servant of his father, and several poor people, who had adopted the Methodistic views, and were living by faith, and he organized societies throughout a wide circuit of neighboring towns, in which he preached daily before the hour of his evening sermons at his father's tomb. These societies were mostly composed of the lowest people; but such salutary effect had Methodism on their daily lives as to commend it often to the respect of the higher classes, and almost everywhere a few of "the noble" shared its blessings.[8]

[8] While on his present visit to Epworth, he says he rode over to a neighboring town to wait upon a justice of the peace, a man of candor and understanding, before whom their angry neighbors had carried a whole wagon load of these new heretics. But when the magistrate asked what they had done there was a deep silence, for that was a point their conductors had forgot. At length one said: "Why they pretend to be better than other people; and besides, they pray from morning till night."

The justice asked: "But have they done nothing besides?"

"Yes, sir," said an old man; "an it please your worship, they have *convarted* my wife. Till she went among them she had such a tongue, and now she is as quiet as a lamb."

"Carry them back! carry them back!" replied the magistrate, "and let them convert all the scolds in the town."

Wesley's Journal abounds with similar facts.

The foundations of Methodism had now been laid in much of the land. Societies were springing up in all directions; Classes were generally introduced among them; itinerant lay preachers were multiplying; chapels had already been built in Bristol, London, Kingswood, and Newcastle. It became obvious that better defined terms of membership were necessary for the growing societies. Wesley, therefore, in consultation with his brother, formed the memorable "General Rules of the United Societies," a document which has become a part of the constitutional law of the Methodist Episcopal Church of America. It defines the "United Society" to be "no other than a company of men having the form and seeking the power of godliness; united in order to pray together, to receive the word of exhortation, and to watch over one another in love, that they may help each other to work out their salvation." Members are required to be distributed into classes, about twelve to each class, one of whom is styled the leader. He is to meet them once a week for religious inquiry and conversation, and for the collection of their contributions toward the expenses of the Society, reporting the result to the preacher and stewards regularly. But one condition is previously required of such as wish admission to the classes—"a desire to flee the wrath to come, and to be saved from their sins;" but this desire is to be shown, first, *by doing no harm;* by avoiding evil in every kind, especially that which is most generally practiced; such as taking the name of God in vain; profaning the Sabbath, either by doing ordinary work thereon, or by buying or selling; drunkenness, buying or selling spirituous liquors, or drinking them, unless in cases of extreme necessity; fighting, quarreling, brawling, brother going to law with brother; returning evil for evil, or railing for railing; using many words in buying or selling; buying or selling uncustomed goods; giving or taking things on usury; uncharitable or unprofitable conversation, particularly speaking evil of magistrates or of ministers; doing to others as they would not have others do unto them, and doing what they know is not for the glory of God; as the putting on of gold, or costly apparel; the taking such diversions as cannot be used in the name of the Lord Jesus; the singing those songs, or reading those books that do not tend to the knowledge or love of God; softness, and needless self-indulgence; laying up treasure on earth; borrowing without a probability of paying, or taking up goods without a probability of paying for them. Secondly, the sincerity of their profession was to be shown *by doing good*, by being in every kind merciful after their power, as they had opportunity; doing good of every possible sort, and as far as possible to all men; to their bodies, of the ability that God giveth, by giving food to the hungry, by clothing the naked, by visiting or helping the sick, and prisoners; to their souls, by instructing, reproving, or exhorting all they had any intercourse with; *trampling under foot that enthusiastic doctrine of devils, that we are not to do good unless our hearts be free to it;* by doing good, especially to them that are of the household of faith, or groaning so to be; employing them preferably to others; buying one of another; helping each other in business, and so much the more, because the world will love its own, and them only; by all possible diligence and frugality, that the Gospel may not be blamed; by running with patience the race that was set before them, denying themselves, and taking up their cross daily; submitting to bear the reproach of Christ; to be as the filth and offscouring of the world, and expecting that men should say all manner of evil of them falsely for the Lord's sake. Thirdly, by attending on all the ordinances of God, such as public worship, the ministry of the word, either read or expounded, the Lord's Supper, family and private prayer, searching the Scriptures, and fasting or abstinence. "These," add the two brothers, "are the general rules of our societies; all which we are taught of God to observe, even in his written word, the only rule both of our faith and practice; and all these we know his Spirit writes on every truly awakened heart. If there be any among us who observes them not, who habitually breaks any of them, let it be made known unto them who watch over that soul, as they must give an account. We will admonish him of the error of his ways; we will bear with him for a season. But then if he repent not, he hath no more place among us. We have delivered our own souls."

Such was the original platform of Methodism. It comprises not one dogmatic statement, nor hardly what could be called an ecclesiastical requisition. All earnest inquirers after religious truth and spiritual purification throughout the world could approve it with scarcely a qualification. It was a purely catholic and apostolic expression of Christianity. At a later date Wesley exclaims in his Journal: "O that we may never make anything more or less the term of union with us, but the having the mind that was in Christ, and the walking as he walked."[9]

During the year 1743 Wesley repeated his excursions to Wales, and also to the north of England. He visited Epworth, and again preached on the tomb of his father. He was now not only denied the pulpit, but even the sacrament of the Lord's Supper. He was again with Nelson at Birstal, and returned thence to London, proclaiming his message at Sheffield, Wednesbury, Stratford-on-Avon, Evesham, and Bristol. On the 14th of February he directed his course toward the north, and in five days was preaching at Newcastle, where he found that his previous visit had left a wide-spread sensation. He perceived, in visiting the adjoining towns, the necessity of reducing his "itinerancy" to a more methodical arrangement, and "resolved not to strike one stroke in any place where he could not follow the blow;" thence sprung up his regular "circuit system," which was subsequently extended to the labors of all his assistants.

While at Newcastle he made a special investigation of the remarkable physical effects which had occurred there, as elsewhere, under his preaching. He found, first, that all per-

[9] Journal, September 29, 1745.

sons who had been thus affected were in perfect health, and had not before been subject to convulsions of any kind. Second, that these new affections had come upon them in a moment, without any previous notice, while they were either hearing the preaching, or thinking on what they had heard. Third, that they usually dropped down, lost their strength, and were seized with violent pain. Their feelings they described differently. Some said they felt as if a sword was running through them; others thought a great weight lay upon them, as if it would press them into the earth. Some said they were quite choked, and found it difficult to breathe, that their hearts swelled ready to burst; others that the whole body seemed rending to pieces. These symptoms he still attributed to a preternatural agency. "I can no more impute them," he writes, "to any natural cause than to the Spirit of God." But they were not divine; they were demoniacal; "it was Satan tearing them as they were coming to Christ."[10] His Journal abounds in candid records of such phenomena; and the curious who would study these extraordinary effects (repeated so often in our own day) for the purpose of discovering a physiological or any other solution of them, can find no better data than he records.

Charles Wesley, who attached less importance to these marvels, subsequently found, at Newcastle, that the propensity to morbid imitation, which played so many and such epidemic follies in the ecclesiastical history of the Middle Ages, had not a little to do with them. He also detected among them many deliberate counterfeits. One, who came drunk from an ale-house, was pleased, he writes, to fall into a fit for his entertainment, and beat himself heartily. Wesley thought it a pity to hinder him, and, instead of singing

[10] As late, however, as 1781, when he published his Short History of the People called Methodists, he gives an important qualification to this opinion. "Satan," he says, "*mimicked* this part of the work of God, in order to discredit the whole, and yet it is not wise to give up this part any more than to give up the whole." Wesley seemed always to be puzzled by these problems; his opinions respecting them were throughout his life exceedingly vague if not contradictory.

over him, as had often been done, left him to recover at his leisure. A young woman began to cry aloud; he ordered her to be carried away; her convulsions were so violent as to deprive her of the use of her limbs, till they laid and left her without the door. She there immediately found her strength and walked off. Some very unquiet women, who always took care to stand near him, and try which should cry loudest, became "as quiet as lambs" when removed out of his sight. The first night he preached in the town half his words were lost through their outcries. Before he began on another evening, he gave public notice that whoever cried so as to drown his voice should, without any man's hurting or judging them, be gently carried to the farthest corner of the room. His porters had no employment during the meeting; "yet," he writes, "the Lord was with us, mightily convincing of sin and righteousness."[11]

John Wesley returned to his lay fellow-laborer, Nelson, at Birstal, and went with him to Leeds, where Wesley preached his first sermon in that great center of northern Methodism.[12] A society had already been formed there, probably by John Nelson himself.

On Wesley's return to Bristol, his brother set out for the north, preaching in almost every town on his route, and was repeatedly beset by ferocious mobs. At Wednesbury he found that Methodism was accomplishing its salutary work among the colliers. More than three hundred had been reformed and gathered into the Society, while others raged against the itinerants, like untamed beasts of the forest. He walked with his Wednesbury brethren to Walsal, singing as they went; but as they passed through the streets of the latter place, they were hailed by the shouts of the rabble. He took his stand on the steps of the market-house, where a host of excited men rallied against him, and bore down like a flood to sweep him away. Stones flew fast and thick. Many struck without hurting him. He

[11] Jackson's Life of Charles Wesley, chap. 10.

[12] Smith's History of Methodism, II, 2.

kept his ground till he was about to close his discourse, when the raging stream bore him from the steps. He regained them, and was pronouncing the benediction when he was again swept down; but a third time he took his position, and returned thanks to God, after which he passed through the midst of the rioters, menaced on every hand, but untouched.

He went to Sheffield, where worse scenes awaited him. He says: "Hell from beneath was moved to oppose us." As soon as he was in the desk, "the floods began to lift up their voice." A military officer contradicted and blasphemed, but the preacher took no notice of him, and sang on. Stones were thrown, hitting the desk and people. To save them and the house, he gave notice that he should preach out of doors, and look the enemy in the face. "The whole army of aliens followed me," he says; their leader laid hold of him and reviled him; he gave the enraged soldier "A Word in Season, or Advice to a Soldier," one of the tracts of his brother; he then prayed particularly for the king, and preached on amid the contention, though often struck in the face by stones. After the sermon he prayed for sinners as servants of their master, the devil, upon which the officer ran at him with great fury, threatening revenge for his abuse, as he called it, of the king, his master. He forced his way through the crowd, drew his sword, and presented it to the preacher's breast. Wesley threw open his vest, and fixing his eye on his assailant, calmly said: "I fear God, and honor the king." The captain's countenance fell in a moment; he put up his sword and quickly retreated from the scene. Wesley returned to the house of a friend; but the rioters followed, and exceeded in their outrage anything he had seen before. Those of Moorfields, Cardiff, and Walsal, were lambs, he says, compared to these. They resolved to pull down the preaching-house, "and they set to their work," he writes, "while we were praying and praising God. It was a glorious time with us. Every word of exhortation sunk deep, every prayer was sealed, and many found the Spirit of glory resting on them." The mob pressed hard to break open the door. Wesley would have gone out to them, but his brethren would not suffer him. The rabble raged all night, and by morning had pulled down one end of the house. "Their outcries often waked me in the night," he writes; "yet I believe I got more sleep than any of my neighbors." This disgraceful tumult he ascribes to sermons preached against the Methodists by the clergy of Sheffield.

The next morning he was expounding at five o'clock, and later the same day he preached in the heart of the town. The mob shouted from afar, but troubled him not. On returning to his lodging he passed the ruins of the chapel; not one stone remained upon another. The rioters again rallied, and following him, smashed in the windows of his lodging, and threatened to tear down the dwelling, but the preacher, fatigued and courageous, fell asleep "in five minutes in the dismantled room." "I feared no cold," he writes, "but dropped asleep with that word, 'Scatter thou the people that delight in war.'" Charles Wesley often acknowledged himself to have been constitutionally a timid man, but his religious feelings made him heroic whenever danger menaced him in the path of duty.

The next morning at five o'clock he counseled and comforted the little company of his brethren, and went on his way to other labors and perils. He saluted John Nelson at Birstal, and proclaimed his message in that and neighboring towns to many thousands. He preached in the streets at Leeds, and found there a society of fifty members. At Newcastle, Sunderland, Shields, and other places, his labors were successful, and he returned to London nothing daunted by the stormy trials he had encountered.

Though bold as a lion in perils, Charles Wesley was not only naturally timid, but subject, like most men of poetic sensibility, to attacks of melancholy. He found relief in activity, and in a short time was again on his route from London to Cornwall. Pausing to preach at Bristol, Exeter, and Bodmin, he arrived by the middle of July at St. Ives, which had become the center of Methodism in the West. One of those societies which had been formed in London before the date of Methodism, had been kept up in the town, and opened the way for the Methodist evangelists. A lay "Helper" was on hand to receive him. The mob was also waiting for him here, and in several neighboring places. At St. Ives the chapel was attacked, its windows smashed in, its seats torn up, and the fragments borne away, with the shutters, poor-box, and all but the stone walls. Wesley stood silently looking on. They swore bitterly that he should not preach there again, an assertion which he immediately disproved by proclaiming that Christ had died for them all. Several times they lifted their hands and clubs to strike him, but an unseen arm restrained them. They beat and dragged about the women, particularly one of a great age, and trampled on them without mercy. Wesley bade the people stand still and see the salvation of God, resolving to continue with them until the end of the strife. After raging about an hour, the ruffians fell to quarreling among themselves; broke the head of the town-clerk, who was their captain, and drove one another out of the room. "Having kept the field, the society gave thanks for the victory."

The converted miners were a courageous class, and were unappalled by these trials. The next day Wesley writes: "I cannot find one of this people who fears those that can kill the body only." Some of their bitterest persecutors were won by their meek endurance, and became standard-bearers of the Cross among them.

Similar assaults were made in other places. At Poole a drunken hearer attempted to drag the preacher from his stand, and a church-warden, heading the rabble, drove him and his congregation out of the parish. The church record bears to this day an entry of expenses at the village inn for drink to the mob and its leader, for driving out the Methodists.[13] Several weeks, however, did Charles Wesley pur-

[13] Smith's History, etc., II, 2.

sue his labors successfully in almost every part of West Cornwall. Thousands heard the word amid the din of riots; hundreds from the most degraded classes were converted into devout Christians and exemplary citizens, and Cornwall has since become the most successful arena of Methodism in England. Nowhere, perhaps, in the world has it more strikingly demonstrated its beneficent power over the common people.

Soon after the return of Charles Wesley from Cornwall, John Wesley arrived there, accompanied by Nelson. They found about a hundred and twenty members in the society at St. Ives. Nelson worked during the day at his trade, and at night aided Wesley and Shepherd, another lay assistant, in preaching among the population of the peninsula of West Cornwall. Methodism had not yet penetrated into many of the villages, and the itinerants sometimes suffered for want of the common comforts of life. Nelson relates, in characteristic style, examples of these hardships. "All this time," he says, "Mr. Wesley and I lay on the floor; he had my great-coat for his pillow, and I had Burkitt's Notes on the New Testament for mine. After being here nearly three weeks, one morning, about three o'clock, Mr. Wesley turned over, and finding me awake, clapped me on the side, saying, 'Brother Nelson, let us be of good cheer; I have one whole side yet, for the skin is off but one side.' We usually preached on the commons, going from one common to another, and it was but seldom any one asked us to eat or drink. One day we had been at St. Hilary Downs, where Mr. Wesley preached from Ezekiel's vision of dry bones, and there was a shaking among the people while he preached. As we returned Mr. Wesley stopped his horse to pick the blackberries, saying, 'Brother Nelson, we ought to be thankful that there are plenty of blackberries, for this is the best country I ever saw for getting a stomach, but the worst that ever I saw for getting food. Do the people think we can live by preaching?' I said: 'I know not what they may think; but one asked me to eat something as I came from

St. Just, when I ate heartily of barley bread and honey.' He said: 'You are well off; I had a thought of begging a crust of bread of the woman where I met the people at Morvah, but forgot it till I had got some distance from the house.'"[14]

Such were not uncommon privations among the primitive Methodist itinerants of both hemispheres. No clergymen, however, fare better than have Methodist preachers in Cornwall since that day; and even then, wherever the common people were gathered into the new societies, they were ready to share all they possessed with the devoted men who brought to their mines and hovels the bread of life. They received the Gospel with a heartiness and devotion which have never been surpassed. Wesley records that on the morning which was to close his present visit, he was waked between three and four o'clock by a group of miners, who, eager for the five o'clock sermon, were waiting and singing hymns beneath his windows.

Leaving Nelson to supply the societies, Wesley made rapid visits to Bristol and Wales, and returned again to the north. At Wednesbury he was attacked by an overwhelming mob of colliers and others. He was pushed along in their midst from one magistrate to another within, and two miles beyond, the town, during several hours of the night, and under a pelting storm of rain. These guardians of the peace were in bed, and refused either to hear or to disperse the mob. A second crowd from Walsal came down upon the first, and, dispersing it, bore him off. A stout woman, who had headed the first mob, now tried to rally them again for his defense, and swearing that none should touch him, ran in among the new assailants, and knocked down three or four men one after another, but was soon herself overpowered. The Walsal rabble dragged him from one end of the town to the other. In descending a steep and slippery part of the road an attempt was made to throw him down; had it been suc-

[14] Nelson's Journal, p. 85.

cessful he would probably have been trodden to death. One of the female members of the society was thrown into the river. A strong man behind Wesley aimed several blows with an oak bludgeon at the back of his head. One of them would probably have been fatal, but they were all turned aside, Wesley says he knows not how. He was struck by a powerful blow on the chest, and by another on the mouth, making the blood gush out; but felt no more pain, he affirms, from either than if they had touched him with a straw; not certainly because he was over excited or alarmed, for he assures us that from the beginning to the end he was enabled to maintain as much presence of mind as if he had been sitting in his study, but his thoughts were entirely absorbed in watching the movement of the rioters. The noise on every side, he says, was like the roaring of the sea. Many cried: "Knock his brains out! down with him! kill him at once! crucify him!" "No, let us hear him first," shouted others. He at last broke out aloud into prayer. The ruffian who had headed the mob, a bear-garden prize-fighter, was struck with awe, and turning to him said: "Sir, I will spend my life for you; follow me, and not one soul here shall touch a hair of your head." Several others now rallied for his protection. An honest butcher cried out for him, and laying hold bravely on four or five of the most violent of the rioters, thrust them away. The people fell back, as if by common consent, and, led on through their opened ranks by the champion of the rabble, he safely escaped to his lodgings.

Notwithstanding the manifest usefulness of Methodism to the lower classes of the English population, proved in the reformation of hundreds of them at Wednesbury, as elsewhere, the clergy and magistrates favored the mob. The former had instigated it, and the latter refused to suppress it. The Methodists of the town had endured intolerable wrongs before the riot reached this frightful crisis. Women and children had been knocked down and dragged in the gutters of the streets; their houses had been attacked, their windows broken, their furniture demolished.[15] Such was the condition of the English police in that day that the rioters were assembled by the blowing of a horn, and virtually usurped the control of the laws for nearly half a year. They drew up a form of recantation, which they declared all Methodists should sign; and such as refused to do so were beaten, and placed in peril of their lives. Wesley, with his usual courage and sagacity, had gone to Wednesbury to confront this formidable opposition. He knew that if Methodism were of God, it had a mission to perform toward these colliers, and their long-neglected and brutalized class throughout the land; that in approaching them it would unavoidably provoke such hostilities, and that its only policy was to meet and conquer them till it should open a clear field for itself among the lower classes generally. No man could have less natural disposition for what some might deem the ministerial heroism or romance of such adventures than he. The scholar, the accomplished divine, the well-bred gentleman, fastidiously nice, even, in matters of apparel and personal manners, these scenes of popular derision and ruffianism must have been most repugnant to him. He certainly never had the fanatical folly to court them, but he never feared them. Calm in temper, keen in sagacity, and apposite in remark, he knew how to meet them. He had come to Wednesbury expressly to do so in this instance, and he succeeded. The mob had yielded, and its very leaders had become his defenders. A less sagacious man would have supposed it well to remain on the field now that he had won it; but Wesley left the next morning. He knew that though the mass had been conquered, the fermentation in some minds had not yet entirely subsided, and might easily again break out; but that a few days of delay and town talk over the sufferings of the Methodists, and the cool bearing of their

15 Many Methodist families in Wednesbury still preserve fragments of furniture as precious memorials of the sufferings of their fathers. Watson's Life of Wesley, chap. 7.

leader, could not fail to promote the favorable turn which the popular feelings had taken toward them. He therefore rode away the next day, but passed through the town, and says that "every one I met expressed such cordial approbation that I could scarce believe what I saw and heard."

He went to Nottingham, where Charles Wesley was preaching. "He looked," says the latter, "like a soldier of Christ. His clothes were torn to tatters." Charles soon after visited Wednesbury to comfort the persecuted society. He found its members assembled, nothing terrified by their adversaries, and preached to them from, "Watch ye, stand fast in the faith; quit yourselves like men; be strong." "Jesus," he says, "was in the midst, and covered us with a covering of his Spirit. Never was I before in so primitive an assembly. We sang praises lustily, and with a good courage, and could all set our seal to the truth of our Lord's saying: 'Blessed are they that are persecuted for righteousness' sake.' We laid us down and slept, and rose up again. We assembled before day to sing hymns to Christ, as God." As soon as it was light he walked down into the town, and preached boldly on, "Fear none of those things which thou shalt suffer. Behold, the devil shall cast some of you into prison that ye may be tried; and she shall have tribulation ten days. Be thou faithful unto death, and I will give thee a crown of life." "It was," he says, "a most glorious time; we longed for our Lord's coming to confess us before his Father and his holy angels. We now understood what it was to receive the word in much affliction, and yet with joy in the Holy Ghost."

He received several new members into the society, and among them was the late captain of the mob. This depraved man was not without generous feelings; he had been constantly in deep religious contrition since the night on which he had attacked and rescued Wesley. Charles asked him what he thought of his brother. "Think of him," said he; "that he is a mon of God; and God was on his side when so many of us could not kill one mon."[16] Thus did Methodism pluck "brands from the burning," and lift them up before the astonished mobs and magistrates as its best trophies.

John Wesley was soon again in Newcastle, and the remainder of the year was spent in undiminished labors. The persecutions which broke out in many places increased the popular interest in the new movement and aroused the energy of its laborers. The year closed with forty-five itinerants in the field, besides many local preachers. Societies had sprung up in many of the principal towns; their membership cannot be ascertained, but it must have included many thousands. There were more than two thousand in London alone.[17] Wesley saw that a great work had begun; that it could not fail to affect the whole kingdom if it went on, and that it was now no time to succumb before mobs or any other difficulties. Mobs, he knew, could not last long; the laws, if nothing else, must sooner or later suppress them, and they could only result in greater impetus to the new movement. They afforded the most conclusive proof of the moral degradation of the common people, and therefore the best justification of the extraordinary efforts by which Methodism attempted to awaken the inert conscience of the land. Steadfast perseverance in these efforts was what the times required; with Wesley that could never be wanting, and it could never fail among his subordinate laborers while their leader bore their standard courageously forward. The next year was to open with new "fights of affliction," but with still greater victories.

[16] Wesley's Journal, Anno 1743. Jackson's Charles Wesley, chap. 10.
[17] Jackson's Charles Wesley, chap. 11.

CHAPTER VI.

EVENTS OF 1744: THE FIRST WESLEYAN CONFERENCE.

Reports against Wesley — Terrible Mobs in Staffordshire — Charles Wesley among the Rioters — John Wesley in Cornwall — Scenes at St. Ives — Wesley preaching at Gwennap — John Nelson — His Power over the Mob — He is impressed for the Army — Characteristic Incidents — Thomas Beard, the Protomartyr of Methodism — The First Wesleyan Conference — Its Proceedings — Its Policy — Lady Huntingdon — Ministerial Education approved — Wesley's Earnest Appeal to Men of Reason and Religion.

The year 1744 was to be signalized in the history of Methodism not only by the first session of the Wesleyan Conference, but by formidable trials. Before the Conference Wesley made rapid excursions into various parts of England and Wales. The country was in general commotion, occasioned by threatened invasions from France and Spain, and by the movements of the Scotch Pretender. Reports were rife that the Methodist preachers were in collusion with the papal Stuart. All sorts of calumnies against Wesley flew over the land. He had been seen with the Pretender in France; had been taken up for high treason, and was at last safe in prison awaiting his merited doom. He was a Jesuit, and kept Roman priests in his house at London; he was an agent of Spain, whence he had received large remittances, in order to raise a body of twenty thousand men to aid the expected Spanish invasion. He was an Anabaptist; a Quaker; had been prosecuted for unlawfully selling gin; had hanged himself; and, at any rate, was not the genuine John Wesley, for it was well known that the latter was dead and buried. That he was a disguised Papist, and an agent for the Pretender, was the favorite slander; and when a proclamation was made requiring all Roman Catholics to leave London, he stayed a week in the city to refute the report. He was summoned by the justices of Surrey, London, to appear before their court, and required to take the oath of allegiance to the king, and to sign the Declaration against Popery. Charles Wesley was actually indicted before the magistrates in Yorkshire, because in a public prayer he had besought God to "call home his banished ones." This, it was insisted, meant the House of the Stuarts; and he had to explain, at the tribunal, the purely spiritual meaning of the phrase, before he was acquitted.

Mobs raged, meanwhile, in many places. In Staffordshire the Methodists were assailed not only in their assemblies, but in the streets, and at their homes. At Walsal the rioters planted a flag in public and kept it flying during several days. In Darlston women were knocked down, and abused in a manner, says Wesley, too horrible to be related.[1] Their little children, meanwhile, wandered up and down, no neighbor daring to take them in lest he should hazard his own life. Houses were broken into, and furniture destroyed and thrown out into the street. One of the Methodists says that he was denied shelter in his own father's dwelling, the latter fearing it would be torn down. Charles Wesley, as we shall hereafter see, could, at a later date, distinguish the houses of Methodists by their "marks of violence," as he rode through the town. In Wednesbury the disorders were again frightful; and for nearly a week the mob reigned triumphant. They were gathering all Monday night, and on Tuesday began their riotous work, sanctioned, if not led on, by gentlemen of the town. They assaulted, one after another, all the houses of those who were called Methodists. They first broke the windows, suffering neither glass, lead, nor frames to remain. Then they made their way in, and all the tables, chairs, chests of drawers, with whatever was not easily movable, they dashed in pieces, particularly shop

[1] Journal, Anno 1744.

goods and furniture of every kind. What they could not well break, as feather beds, they cut in pieces, and strewed about the room. The wife of a Methodist was lying in, but that was nothing; they pulled away her bed and cut it in pieces. Wearing apparel and things which were of value or saleable were carried away, every man loading himself with as much as he could well bear of whatever he liked best. All this time none offered to resist them. Men and women fled for their lives; only the children remained, not knowing whither to go. Some of the gentlemen who had instigated these dreadful scenes, or threatened to turn away collier or miner from their service if he did not take part in them, now drew up a paper for the members of the society to sign, importing that they would never invite nor receive any Methodist preacher again. On this condition it was promised that the mob should be checked at once, otherwise the victims must take what might follow. The pledge was offered to several; but the faithful sufferers declared, one and all, "We have already lost all our goods, and nothing more can follow but the loss of our lives, which we will lose too, rather than wrong our consciences."

The mob divided into several companies, and marched from village to village within a range of four or five miles, and the whole region was in a state little short of civil war.

Wesley was justly indignant to find these outrages described the next week, in the London newspapers, as perpetrated by the Methodists themselves, who, "upon some pretended insults from the Church party," had risen in "insurrection" against the government. He hastened from London to sustain the persecuted societies in the riotous districts, for it was his rule, he wrote, "always to face the mob." At Dudley he learned that the lay preacher had been cruelly abused at the instigation of the parish minister; the peaceable itinerant would probably have been murdered, had not an honest Quaker enabled him to escape disguised in his broad-brimmed hat and plain coat.[2] At Wednesbury he

[2] Jackson's Life of Charles Wesley, chap. 11.

found none of the magistrates willing to protect the Methodists. One of these functionaries declared that their treatment was just, and offered five pounds to have them driven out of the town. The spirit of the converted colliers was rising, and Wesley had difficulty in restraining them from self-defense. One of the magistrates refused to hear a Methodist who came to take oath that his life was in danger. Another delivered a member of the society up to the mob, and waving his hand over his head, shouted, "Huzza, boys! well done! stand up for the Church!" The sound of family worship in the evening was the signal for breaking into the Methodist houses. At Walsal Charles Wesley found "the enemy's head-quarters;" the flag of the rioters waved in the market-place. He passed to Nottingham, and there also the war had begun. The Methodists were driven from the chapel and pelted in the streets. They would have avenged their wrongs had it not been for the restraining efforts of another good Quaker. The mayor passed by laughing, while Charles Wesley was preaching at the town-cross amid flying missiles from the mob. At Lichfield "all the rabble of the county was gathered together and laid waste all before them;" not one, however, of the Methodists "had resisted evil; they took the spoiling of their goods joyfully." At Sheffield and Thorpe he found the mob had relented, and the societies enjoyed rest. At the latter place a persecutor had died in despair, and the rabble had been appalled into quiet. Some of them had even joined the society. At Wakefield and Leeds he learned that the Methodists had been excluded from the Lord's Supper at the parish churches. At Birstal he found John Nelson's hill quite covered with hearers; in the midst of his discourse a gentleman "came riding up, and almost over the people." Speaking of temperance and judgment to come, Wesley turned and said, "'Thou art the man.' His countenance fell, and he fled before the sword of the Spirit. The power of God burst forth, and a cry was heard throughout the congregation."

He pursued his way to Newcastle, where disturbances

were also breaking out. Taking his stand in the public square, he proclaimed, "Ye shall be hated of all men for my name's sake." He afterward found "a great mob" at the chapel, and "spending an hour in taming them," exhorted them for two hours more. "The rocks," he says, "were melted on every side, and the very ringleaders of the rebels declared they would make a disturbance no more." The next day, however, the storm raged again among another class. The people had given themselves up to drunkenness, in honor of a supposed victory of the British over the French.[3] They thronged about the chapel, struck several of the brethren, and threatened to pull down the pulpit. He afterward learned that at the same hour the chapel at St. Ives was pulled down. At Epworth he met on the common a lay preacher, Thomas Westall, who was driven away from Nottingham by "the mob and mayor." Wesley immediately preached to the panic-struck society and the noisy crowd on the text, "Enter into the rock, and hide yourselves as it were for a little moment, until the indignation be overpast." As he passed through Birstal again the mob was tearing down John Nelson's house, but fled away as Wesley and his companions approached with singing. He returned to London, and collected funds for the relief of the persecuted societies. Some of his finest lyrics were composed during his travels amid these tumults. He often recited and sometimes sung them among the raging crowds. Four of them were written "to be sung in a tumult," and one was a "prayer for the first martyr;" it was soon to be found appropriate.

The storm meanwhile swept over Cornwall also. The chapel at St. Ives was entirely destroyed. John Wesley went thither; and on arriving at the home of one of the

[3] Such was the state of English morals at this period, that drunkenness was a fashionable vice. Nearly thirty years later Johnson said to Boswell: "I remember when all the *decent* people in Lichfield [Johnson's native town] got drunk every night, and were not thought the worse for it." Boswell's Johnson, vol. i, p. 340.

Methodists, where the society was waiting for him, he was received, he writes, "with a loud though not bitter cry; but they soon recovered, and we poured out our souls together in praises and thanksgivings." As soon as they went out they were saluted with huzzas, stones, and dirt. He was agreeably surprised at the Christian meekness and patience with which the converted miners, once degraded and violent men themselves, now endured persecution for righteousness' sake. Some who had been the worst of the rabble, had become the most exemplary sufferers. He records that "the Methodists of St. Just had been the chief of the whole country for hurling, fighting, drinking, and all manner of wickedness; but many of the lions had become lambs, and were continually praising God, and calling their old companions in sin to come and magnify the Lord together." Such had been the general state of religion in the country, that many intelligent men could not comprehend these changes. They were anomalies and madness to them. One of the clergy in Cornwall, a person, says Wesley, of unquestioned sense and learning, and a doctor of divinity, some of whose most abandoned parishioners had been reclaimed, asked a devout Methodist "who had been made the better by this preaching?" "The man before you," was the reply; "one who never before knew any work of God in his soul." "Get along," cried the learned divine; "you are all mad, crazy-headed fellows," and seizing him by the shoulders thrust him out the door.

On the public fast-day, appointed for the safety of the nation against the menaced invasion, Wesley listened to a sermon in the Church of St. Ives, in which the Methodists were denounced as enemies of the Church and state, Jacobites, and Papists. But the sun of the same day went down upon him, as he stood controlling the troubled elements at Gwennap. "I stood," he says, "on the wall, in the calm still evening, with the setting sun behind me, and almost an innumerable multitude before, behind, and on either hand. Many likewise sat on the little hills, at some distance from the bulk of the congregation. But they could all hear distinctly while I read: 'The disciple is not above his Master,' and the rest of those comfortable words which are day by day fulfilled in our ears."[4]

Thus did he maintain his ground: to retreat, was to abandon this demoralized populace to its moral wretchedness; to persevere, he knew would conquer its turbulence in spite of the influence of the clergy. He did persevere, and at last won the well-deserved victory. Methodism prevailed through all Cornwall, and in his old age his journies through its towns and villages were like "royal progresses" or triumphal marches. The descendants of those who had mobbed him crowded his routes, and filled the steps, balconies, and windows, to see and bless him as he passed;[5] and in our day Cornwall witnesses in all its towns and hamlets, to the power of the Gospel as preached by Wesley and his persecuted itinerants.

After spending three weeks in the west he went to Epworth, where he found that one of his preachers, John Downes, had been impressed as a soldier, and placed in Lincoln jail. An "inexpressible panic," he says, prevailed in all places. He passed to Birstal, the home of John Nelson, but there learned that this heroic man had also been seized for the army, and carried off to prison. Soon after he heard that Thomas Beard, another assistant, had shared the same fate.

John Nelson had been traveling about the land, working by day and preaching at night. His good sense, cool courage, sound piety, and apt speech, secured him success wherever he went. He had spread out Methodism exten-

[4] The Gwennap amphitheater must have presented a grand spectacle on such occasions; an engraving representing Wesley preaching there is extant; in the latter part of his life, aged, and venerated by the people, he still occupied it for preaching at his annual visits. "I think," he wrote, "this is one of the most magnificent spectacles which is to be seen on this side heaven." The Methodist singing there especially was sublime to him. "No music," he said, "is to be heard on earth comparable to the sound of many thousand voices," as he there heard them, "all harmoniously joined in singing praises to God and the Lamb."

[5] Watson's Life of Wesley, chap. 7.

sively in Yorkshire, Cornwall, Lincolnshire, Lancashire, and other counties. He was a man of such genuine spirit and popular tact that his worst opposers usually became his best friends, and the rudest men delighted to hear him. He passed through Wednesbury soon after the terrible riots there, and preached in the open air. The mob came, but would not molest him. At Nottingham several persons tried to throw squibs into his face and at his feet while he was preaching, but others threw them back; and a sergeant of the army came to him with tears, and said: In the presence of God and all this people I beg your pardon, for I came on purpose to mob you; but when I could get no one to assist me I stood to hear you, and am convinced of the deplorable state of my soul; I believe you are a servant of the living God. "He then kissed me," says Nelson, "and went away weeping."[6] No evidence could better prove the power of the artisan preacher. He journeyed on to Grimsby, where the parish clergyman hired a man to beat the town drum, and went before it, gathering together the rabble, and giving them liquor to go with him and "fight for the Church." When they came to Nelson's lodgings they set up three huzzas, and their clerical leader cried out to them to pull down the house; but no one offered to touch it till Nelson had done preaching; they then broke the windows, leaving not one whole square of glass in the building. The people were assailed as they went out; but the mob began to fight one another, and thus allowed the preacher and his hearers to escape. Not long after the minister gathered the rioters together again, and gave them more drink. They then came and broke the stanchions of the windows, pulled up the paving in the streets, threw the stones into the house, and demolished its furniture; but they again quarreled among themselves, and dispersed after five hours of tumult. The clergyman, who was a representative of a large class of his profession at that day, hired the town drummer to disturb the evangel-

[6] Nelson's Journal, p. 90.

ist again the next morning; but after beating his drum around the congregation for three quarters of an hour, he yielded under Nelson's eloquence, threw away the drum, and stood listening with the tears running down his cheeks. Such was the power of this extraordinary man over his rudest hearers.

He went to Epworth; both the clerk and clergyman of that parish were drunkards; the former ran, as Nelson was preaching in the open air, and cried to the congregation to make way that he might reach the itinerant and carry him before his master, who was at the village ale-house. The people stood up, however, for the eloquent mason, and bade the clerk hold his peace and go about his business. He chose to become still ruder, when a sturdy yeoman took him up and threw him on a dung-hill.

At Pudsey the people were afraid to admit him to their houses, as they had heard that constables were searching for him. Nelson sat upon his horse in the street and exhorted them. "The Lord," he assured them, "would build the walls of Jerusalem in these troublesome times." He passed on to Leeds, where he "kept hewing stone by day and preaching every night." The Methodists of Leeds may justly boast of him as their founder and apostle. On reaching his home at Birstal, he was met with warnings that he should be impressed for the army if he did not immediately escape. The ale-house keepers complained of the loss of their customers by his preaching, and the parish clergyman wished not such a rival near him. "I cannot fear," said the brave Yorkshireman; "I cannot fear, for God is on my side, and his word hath added strength to my soul this day." He was seized the next day while preaching at Adwalton. He was much esteemed among his fellow-townsmen, and one of them offered five hundred pounds bail for him, but it was refused, and he was marched off to Halifax, where the Birstal vicar was on the bench as one of the Commission. Nelson's neighbors came to bear witness for him, but the commissioners declined to hear any other than their clerical associate, who reported him to be a vagrant, without visible means of living. Nelson, who had always been an industrious workman, repelled the charge manfully. "I am as able to get my living by my hands," he said, "as any man of my trade in England is, and you know it." He was ordered to Bradford. On leaving Halifax many of the common people wept and prayed for him as he passed through the streets. "Fear not," he cried to them; "God hath his way in the whirlwind, and he will plead my cause; only pray for me that my faith fail not." At Bradford he was plunged into a dungeon, into which flowed blood and filth from a slaughter-house above it, so that it smelt, he says, "like a pig-stye; but my soul," he adds, "was so filled with the love of God that it was a paradise to me." There was nothing in it to sit on, and his only bed was a heap of decayed straw. But even there his manly spirit won him friends; a poor soldier wished to become responsible for him; and an opposer of the Methodists offered security for him that he might be allowed to sleep in a bed. The people handed him food, water, and candles through a hole in the door, and stood outside joining him in hymns most of the night. He shared their charities with a miserable fellow-prisoner, who might have starved had it not been for his kindness.

Nelson's excellent wife came to him early the next morning, and showed that she was worthy of him. She had two young children to provide for, and expected soon another, but addressing him through the hole in the door, said: "Fear not; the cause is God's for which you are here, and he will plead it himself. Therefore be not concerned about me and the children, for He that feeds the young ravens will be mindful of us. He will give you strength for your day; and after we have suffered awhile he will perfect what is lacking in our souls, and bring us where the wicked cease from troubling and where the weary are at rest."

"I cannot fear," responded the brave man; "I cannot fear either man or devil so long as I find the love of God as I now do."

The next day he was sent to Leeds. Multitudes flocked to see him, and he thought, he says, of the Pilgrim's Progress, for hundreds of people in the street stood and looked at him through the iron gate, and were ready to fight about him. Several would have bailed him out. A stranger offered a hundred pounds security, but it was refused. At night a hundred persons met in the jail, and joined him in worship. In a short time he was marched off to York, where violent hostility prevailed against the Methodists. While he was guarded through the streets by armed troops, it was, he says, as if hell was moved from beneath to meet him at his coming. The streets and windows were filled with people, who shouted and huzzaed as if he had been one who had laid waste the nation. "But," he adds sublimely, "the Lord made my brow like brass, so that I could look upon them as grasshoppers, and pass through the city as if there had been none in it but God and me." Here he was again sent to prison, but ceased not to admonish the officers and others about him whenever they swore, and they often shrank before his word and his glance. He was ordered to parade. The corporal who was commanded to give him a musket, and gird him with his military trappings, trembled as if he had the palsy. Nelson said he would wear them "as a cross," but would not fight as it was not agreeable to his conscience, and he would not harm his conscience for any man on earth. He reproved and exhorted all who approached him. At one time "a great company" gathered to see him, and wished to hear his opinions. He preached to them, and they retired, declaring "this is the doctrine which ought to be preached, let men say what they will against it." Before long he was preaching in the fields and the streets, and no remonstrances of his officers could stop him. He replied to them always with respectfulness, but with an invincible though quiet firmness.

He was subjected to maltreatment, which his brave spirit would have resented had it not been for his Christian principles. A stripling ensign, especially, took pleasure in tormenting him. This officer had him put in prison for reproving his profanity and for preaching, and when he was let out threatened to chastise him. Nelson records that "it caused a sore temptation to arise in me, to think that a wicked, ignorant man should thus torment me, and I able to tie his head and heels together. I found an old man's bone in me; but the Lord lifted up a standard, when anger was coming on like a flood, else I should have wrung his neck to the ground and set my foot upon him."

He was at last released by the influence of Lady Huntingdon with the government, after having been marched about the country with his regiment for nearly three months. He immediately resumed his labors as a good soldier of the Lord Jesus. On the night of his discharge he was preaching at Newcastle; several of his military comrades came to hear him, and parted from him with tears. We shall meet him again amid severer scenes, but always sublime in the calmness, simplicity, and courage of his noble nature.

Thomas Beard, his fellow evangelist, had also been his fellow-sufferer in the regiment, and met a sadder fate. He maintained a brave spirit under his sufferings, but his health failed. He was sent to the hospital at Newcastle, "where," says Wesley, "he still praised God continually." His fever became worse and he was bled, but his arm festered, mortified, and had to be amputated. A few days later he died, the protomartyr of Methodism.[7]

It is not surprising that the scholarly mind of Wesley sometimes revolted from such scenes. "I found," he writes, "a natural wish, O for ease and a resting-place! Not yet, but eternity is at hand." Amid these very agitations he was planning for a still more energetic prosecution of the

[7] Wesley refers to him in his Journal, 1744, with much feeling, and quotes the lines:

"Servant of God, well done! well hast thou fought
The better fight; who singly hast maintained,
Against revolted multitudes, the cause
Of God, in word mightier than they in arms."

Charles Wesley wrote two of his best hymns on the death of Beard.

great work which was manifestly henceforth to occupy his life. He wrote letters to several clergymen, and to his lay assistants, inviting them to meet him in London, and to give him "their advice respecting the best method of carrying on the work of God."[8] And thus was called together the *first Methodist Conference* on Monday, the 25th of June, 1744. It was held in the Foundry, London. On the preceding day, the regular clergymen and lay preachers who had responded to the call took the Lord's Supper together. On the morning of the first session Charles Wesley preached before them.[9] Besides the Wesleys there were present four ordained ministers of the Church of England: John Hodges, rector of Wenvo, Wales, a friend and colaborer of the Wesleys in the Principality, who not only opened his own pulpit to them, but accompanied them in their different routes and out-door preaching; Henry Piers, the vicar of Bexley, a convert of Charles Wesley, and whose pulpit and home were ever open to him and his brother; Samuel Taylor, vicar of Quinton, whose church the Wesleys always occupied when passing through that parish, and who himself was known as an itinerant evangelist; and John Meriton, a clergyman from the Isle of Man, who itinerated extensively in both England and Ireland.[10] It has usually been supposed that these six regular clergymen composed the first Wesleyan Conference.[11] There were present, however, from

8 The Large Minutes. See also Wesley's Works, vol. v, p. 220.

9 Jackson's Charles Wesley, chap. 11.

10 Ibid.

11 Jackson commits this mistake. (Life of Charles Wesley, chap. 11.) The error arises from the fact that the names of the lay preachers present were not given in the current Minutes. Wesley's first edition of the Minutes of his Conferences was issued in Dublin, about five years after this session. He published them in two pamphlets, one containing the deliberations of the sessions on doctrinal subjects, the other, discussions of matters of discipline. The first was afterward comprised in the current Minutes, and was supposed to contain the only remaining record of the early conferences. The second was entitled the "Disciplinary Minutes." Its existence was forgotten until both tracts were found, bound with a copy of the early hymn book, at a London book-stall, by Rev. Joseph Hargreaves, from whom they came into the hands of Dr. George Smith, who has made important use of them in his History of Methodism, (book. II, chap. 3.) There can be

among the lay preachers, Thomas Maxfield, Thomas Richards, John Bennet, and John Downes.[12]

The Conference being opened, regulations were immediately adopted for its own government. They were marked by the simplicity and purely evangelical character with which the Methodistic movement had thus far been characterized, and also by that charitable freedom of opinion which it has ever since been at least an indirect tendency of Methodism to promote. "It is desired," said these good men, "that everything be considered as in the immediate presence of God, that we may meet with a single eye, and as little children who have everything to learn; that every point may be examined from the foundation; that every person may speak freely what is in his heart, and that every question proposed may be fully debated and 'bolted to the bran.'" It was a question formally proposed, How far does each agree to submit to the unanimous judgment of the rest? The answer is worthy of perpetual remembrance. "In speculative things each can only submit so far as his judgment shall be convinced; in every practical point, so far as we can, without wounding our several consciences." Should they be fearful, it was asked, of thoroughly debating every question which might arise? "What are we afraid of? Of overturning our first principles? If they are false, the sooner they are overturned the better. If they are true, they will bear the strictest examination. Let us all pray for a willingness to receive light to know every doctrine whether it be of God."[13]

no doubt of the genuineness of this interesting document. Its internal evidence is conclusive. Its value to the Methodist historian is inestimable, as it gives information of Conferences respecting which we have no other account whatever.

[12] "Disciplinary Minutes." Smith's History of Methodism, II, 3.

[13] Minutes of the Methodist Conferences, from the first held in London, by the late Rev. John Wesley, A.M., in the year 1744; vol. i. London: 1812. As the Minutes of the first Conference were not published till 1749, they include some proceedings which took place at other sessions prior to this date. When it is important that their chronological order should be observed, I refer them to their real dates, as shown in the "Disciplinary Minutes," according to Dr. Smith's quotations.

Having settled its own regulations, the conference suspended its business for an interval of prayer, after which it proceeded to consider, first, What to teach; second, What to do, or how to regulate the doctrine, discipline, and practice of the ministry and the Society. These propositions comprehended the scope of its further deliberations. The first two days were spent in discussions of the theology necessary to be maintained in their preaching; and the whole record of the debate vindicates the representation already made[14] of the disposition of the Methodist founders to avoid unnecessary Dogmatics, by confining their instructions to those vital truths which pertain to personal religion. Repentance, Faith, Justification, Sanctification, the Witness of the Spirit were defined with precision. No other tenets were discussed except as they were directly related to these.

On the third, fourth, and fifth days, questions of discipline and methods of preaching were examined. The relations of the Methodist Societies to the Church of England were considered. Secession from the Establishment was discountenanced, but evidence was given that Wesley's opinions of "church order" had already undergone a liberal improvement. To the question, How far is it our duty to obey the bishops? the answer is, "In all things *indifferent;* and on this ground of obeying them, we should observe the Canons as far as we can with a safe conscience." Intimations are given in the "Disciplinary Minutes" of a classification of the Methodists of that day, which was doubtless very speedily changed, for, besides the United Societies and Bands, there were "Select Societies" and "Penitents," phrases which seldom or never afterward appear in Methodist records. The rules of the United Societies and also of the Bands were approved. The suggestions of the Conference on the "best general method of preaching" were excellent for the lay preachers. They were: 1. To invite; 2. To convince; 3. To offer Christ; lastly, To build up; and to do this in some measure in every sermon. Very precise rules were

[14] See Book I, chap. 1.

prescribed for lay assistants. Wesley was still, however, reluctant to encourage a lay ministry. To the question whether lay assistants are allowable? the Minutes reply, "Only in cases of necessity." He was yet hopeful that the clergy of the national Church would be so generally reached by the extending revival as to supersede that necessity. "We believe," say these Minutes, "that the Methodists will either be thrust out or will leaven the whole Church." The assistants were instructed to preach against Formality. The questions, "Is it lawful to bear arms?" and "Is it lawful to use the law?" were decided affirmatively.

It is a fact of peculiar interest to the advocates of ministerial education among Methodists, that as early as this, the first Conference of the denomination, their views were asserted by their great founder, and apparently without a dissent from his associates. It was formally asked, "Can we have a seminary for laborers?" Methodism was not yet sufficiently mature, especially in its finances, for the important design; the answer was, therefore, "If God spare us till another Conference." Accordingly, at the next session it was asked, "Can we have a seminary for laborers yet?" "Not till God gives us a proper tutor," was the reply.[15] The inquiry was made at subsequent Conferences, and never abandoned till it was effectively answered by the establishment of the present two well-endowed "Theological Institutions" in England, and the two "Biblical Institutes" in America. Methodism, like the "Great Reformation," commenced its work within a university, and has always, in its public capacity, zealously promoted useful knowledge and educational institutions. Objections to even theological education have been comparatively modern and mostly personal.

During the session all the Conference were received at Lady Huntingdon's mansion in London, for the countess still considered Methodism a common cause. Wesley preached

[15] Watson's Wesley, chap. 9. "Wesley looked to Kingswood school," says Watson, "as subsidiary to this design," . . . "so that the institution was actually resolved upon, and delayed only by circumstances."

there from a befitting text: "What hath God wrought?" Piers, of Bexley, and Hodges, of Wenvo, took part in the service; while Maxfield, Richards, Bennet, and Downes, sat around them, recognized as genuine, though unordained embassadors of Christ. This was the first of those household sermons which afterward, under Whitefield, gave to her ladyship's residence in London the character of a chapel.

On Friday the little band dispersed, to proclaim again their message through the country. They made no provision for future sessions; they apparently had no definite conceptions of the great work in which they found themselves involved, except the suggestion of their spiritual faith, that God would not allow that work to come to naught without first morally renovating the Churches of the land. Any organic preparations for its future course would probably have interfered with the freedom and efficiency of its development. History teaches that men raised up for great events are usually endowed with wisdom and energy for their actual circumstances, and seldom effect momentous changes on hypothetical schemes; and that even the constitutions of states are best when they arise from gradual growths. Great men are God's special agents, and they are not only good, but great, in proportion as they are co-workers together with Him, using to the utmost their present resources, and trusting the result to his foreseeing wisdom. Such an anticipation of the result as might fit them intellectually to forecast it, might unfit them morally to achieve it. We behold with admiration the prodigious agency of Luther in the modern progress of the world, but we can hardly conceive that he could have anticipated it without being thereby morally disqualified for it. Most of the practical peculiarities of Methodism would have been pronounced impracticable if suggested before the exigencies which originated them. To have supposed that hundreds of thousands of the common people could be gathered, and kept from year to year, in weekly Class-meetings, for direct conversation and inquisition respecting their personal religious experience, and that such a fact should become the basis of one of the most extended sections of English Protestantism; that a ministry for these multitudes could be raised up among themselves, a ministry without education, many of its members, according to their critics, eccentric, and predisposed to enthusiasm, if not fanaticism, and yet kept from doctrinal heresies; that they could be trained to habits of ministerial prudence and dignity, and to the most systematic methods of evangelical labor known in the modern Church; that with uncertain salaries, and generally with severe want, they should devotedly adhere to their work; that generation after generation they should consent to the extraordinary inconveniences of their ministerial itinerancy, to be torn up with their families every two or three years from their homes and churches, and dispatched they knew not whither—such unparalleled measures, proposed beforehand, would have seemed, to thoughtful men, preposterous dreams. Yet more than a hundred years have shown them to be not only practicable, but effective beyond any other contemporary means of religious progress. That Wesley did not seek to anticipate the wants of Methodism, except in the most obvious instances, was both a reason and a proof of his practical ability to meet them when they came.

In this year he published his "Earnest Appeal to Men of Reason and Religion." It is mostly a defense of the opinions and practice of the Methodists. It is eloquently written, and appeals, with justifiable confidence, to the striking results which had already attended the Methodistic movement. "Behold," he writes, "the day of the Lord has come! He is again visiting and redeeming his people. Having eyes, see ye not? Having ears do ye not hear, neither understand with your hearts? At this hour the Lord is rolling away our reproach. Already his standard is set up. His Spirit is poured forth on the outcasts of men, and his love shed abroad in their hearts. Love of all mankind, meekness, gentleness, humbleness of mind, holy and heavenly affections, do take the place of hate, anger, pride, revenge, and vile or vain affections. Hence, wherever the power of the Lord spreads, springs outward religion in all its forms. The houses of God are filled; the table of the Lord is thronged on every side; and those who thus show their love of God, show they love their neighbor also, by being careful to maintain good works, by doing all manner of good, as they have time, to all men. They are likewise careful to abstain from all evil. Cursing, Sabbath-breaking, drunkenness, with all the (however fashionable) works of the devil, are not once named among them. All this is plain, demonstrable fact. I insist upon the fact; Christ is preached, and sinners are converted to God. This none but a madman can deny. We are ready to prove it by a cloud of witnesses. Neither, therefore, can the inference be denied that God is now visiting his people."

Of the objections to the Methodists he says: "This only we confess, that we preach inward salvation, now attainable by faith. And for preaching this (for no other crime was then so much as pretended) we were forbid to preach any more in those churches where, till then, we were gladly received. This is a notorions fact. Being thus hindered from preaching in the places we should first have chosen, we now declare the 'grace of God which bringeth salvation in all places of his dominion;' as well knowing that God dwelleth not only in temples made with hands. This is the real, and it is the only real ground of complaint against us. And this we avow before all mankind, we do preach this salvation by faith. And not being suffered to preach it in the usual places, we declare it wherever a door is opened, either on a mountain, or a plain, or by a river side, (for all which we conceive we have sufficient precedent,) or in prison, or, as it were, in the house of Justus, or the school of one Tyrannus. Nor dare we refrain. 'A dispensation of the Gospel is committed to me; and wo is me if I preach not the Gospel.'"

Of the conduct of the national clergy, as contrasted with that of the Methodists, he says: "Which of you convinceth us of sin? Which of you (I here more especially appeal to my brethren, the clergy) can personally convict us of any ungodliness or unholiness of conversation? Ye know in your own hearts, (all that are candid men, all that are not utterly blinded with prejudice,) that we 'labor to have a conscience void of offense both toward God and toward man.' Brethren, I would to God that in this ye were even as we. But indeed (with grief I speak it) ye are not. There are among yourselves ungodly and unholy men; openly, undeniably such; drunkards, gluttons, returners of evil for evil, liars, swearers, profaners of the day of the Lord. Proof hereof is not wanting, if ye require it. Where then is your zeal against these? A clergyman, so drunk he can scarce stand or speak, may, in the presence of a thousand people, (at Epworth, in Lincolnshire,) set upon another clergyman of the same Church, both with abusive words and open violence. And what follows? Why, the one is still allowed to dispense the sacred signs of the body and blood of Christ: but the other is not allowed to receive them, because he is a field preacher. O ye pillars and fathers of the Church, are these things well pleasing to Him who hath made you overseers over that flock which he hath purchased with his own blood? O that ye would suffer me to boast myself a little! Is there not a cause? Have ye not compelled me? Which of your clergy are more unspotted in their lives, which more unwearied in their labors, than those whose 'names ye cast out as evil,' whom ye count 'as the filth and offscouring of the world?' Which of them is more zealous to spend and be spent for the lost sheep of the house of Israel? Or who among them is more ready to be offered up for their flock 'upon the sacrifice and service of their faith?'"[16]

[16] Works, vol. v, pp. 23, 24, 32.

BOOK III.

PROGRESS OF METHODISM FROM THE CONFERENCE OF 1744 TO THE CONFERENCE OF 1750.

CHAPTER I.

FROM THE CONFERENCE OF 1744 TO THE CONFERENCE OF 1745.

Charles Wesley in Cornwall — Triumphs of Methodism — John Wesley preaches for the last Time before the University of Oxford — Winter Itinerancy — Impressment and Imprisonment of Preachers — Meriton — Bennet — Maxfield — Wesley arrested — He is mobbed at Falmouth — Success in Cornwall and Wales — John Nelson itinerating — He conquers his Persecutors — Methodism in the British Army in Flanders — John Evans — John Haime — Samson Staniforth — Mark Bond — Remarkable Scenes in the Battle of Fontenoy — Triumphant Deaths of Methodist Soldiers — Deaths of Haime and Staniforth.

The Conference of 1744 had no sooner adjourned than Charles Wesley, accompanied by another of its members, the Rev. John Meriton, a clergyman from the Isle of Man, set out for Cornwall. The storm of persecution which had broken upon that region rendered it necessary that one of the Wesleys should be frequently present to comfort and advise the societies. On the arrival of the travelers at Middlesey they met John Slocomb, a young lay preacher who had just escaped from the fate of Nelson, Beard, and Downes, having been imprisoned as a vagrant and impressed for the army. After being detained some time he was brought before the Commissioners, who not only found no just charge against him, but discovered also that he was of too small a stature, too nearly "a Zaccheus," for the military rules, and allowed him to resume his Christian labors. He became a useful itinerant preacher, and, many years later, John Wesley mentions him as falling in the work at Clones, Ireland, "an old laborer worn out in the service of his Master."[1]

As they entered Cornwall they found that the field in the West had yielded a rich harvest. On arriving at Gwennap, Wesley writes: "Here a little one has become a thousand; what an amazing work has God done in one year! The whole country is alarmed, and gone forth after the sound of the Gospel; in vain do the pulpits ring of popery, and madness, and enthusiasm. Our preachers are daily pressed to new places, and enabled to preach five or six times a day. Persecution is kept off till the seed takes root. Societies are springing up everywhere, and still the cry from all sides is, 'Come and help us.'" Methodism had produced in all parts of Cornwall a manifest improvement in the moral condition of the people. Many who had not joined the societies had, nevertheless, abandoned their gross vices. "The whole country," continues Wesley, "is sensible of the change." At the preceding assize there was a "jail delivery," but not one felon was to be found in the prisons, a fact which he informs us was unknown before in the memory of man. At their last public revel enough men could not be rallied to make a wrestling match, "all the Gwennap men being struck off the devil's list, and found wrestling against him, not for him." When he took his leave of the reclaimed populace of this town, they came forth by thousands to the field preaching, covering all the green plain and hills of the natural amphitheater; "they hung," he says, "upon the word of life." He spake for three hours, yet knew not how to stop. "Such sorrow and love as they there expressed the world will not believe, though a man declared it unto them." With much difficulty he was able at last to make his way through them, and pass on his

[1] Jackson's Charles Wesley, chap. 12.

journey; and several of his hearers, women as well as men, kept pace with the horses for two or three miles of the road, then "parted in body, not in mind."[2] The miners came out unwashed from their subterranean dens, some still to oppose, but most by this time to welcome and hear him. At Crowan he preached to between one and two thousand, who "seemed started out of the earth; several hid their faces and mourned inwardly, being too deeply affected to cry out." "The poor people," he added, "were ready to eat us up, and sent us away with many a hearty blessing." The storm of persecution had lulled everywhere. Even at St. Ives, where the chapel lay in ruins, the societies had rest, and welcomed him with grateful tears. At St. Just he found more than two hundred converts gathered into the classes. "Our Lord," he wrote, "rides on triumphant through this place." The parish church itself had become crowded with Methodist hearers. At Morvah he found a hundred and fifty in the society, and a chapel commenced. The Gospel had broken the ranks of the mob, hosts of rioters had become Methodists; and at Gulval he received into the society one who had been the greatest persecutor in all Cornwall.

Still accompanied by Meriton, he left Cornwall for Wales, where they traveled and preached several days. Returning by way of Bristol and Kingswood, and proclaiming the word daily as they journeyed, they reached Oxford, where they met John Wesley, and Henry Piers, another clerical member of the late Conference. An interesting event drew them to this celebrated seat of learning, the scene of the early studies and first labors of the Methodist founders, and where they had received the derisive name which they were to render honorable throughout the religious world. According to usage it was John Wesley's turn, as a Fellow of Lincoln College, to preach before the University, and as it would probably be the last opportunity of the kind allowed

[2] His beautiful and affecting lyric, "Naomi and Ruth, adapted to the Ministry and People," was suggested by this scene.

him, his friends gathered there to witness the occasion. It was the season of the races. Oxford was crowded with strangers, and Wesley's notoriety as a field preacher excited a general interest to hear him. Such was the state of morals at the time, that clergymen, gownsmen, and learned professors shared, with sportsmen and the rabble, the dissipations of the turf. Charles Wesley went in the morning to the prayers at Christ Church, and found men in surplices talking, laughing, and pointing, as in a playhouse, during the whole service. The inn where he lodged was filled with gownsmen and gentry from the races. He could not restrain his zeal, but preached to a crowd of them in the inn court-yard. They were struck with astonishment, but did not molest him. Thence he went to St. Mary's Church, with Meriton and Piers, to support his brother in his last appeal to their Alma Mater. Wesley's discourse was heard with profound attention. The assembly was large, being much increased by the races. "Never," says Charles Wesley, "have I seen a more attentive congregation. They did not let a word slip them. Some of the heads of colleges stood up the whole time, and fixed their eyes on him. If they can endure sound doctrine like his he will surely leave a blessing behind him. The vice-chancellor sent after him and desired his notes, which he sealed up and sent immediately. We walked back in form, the little band of us four, for of the rest durst none join us." Wesley's sermon on this occasion has been published. It is entitled "Scriptural Christianity," and is a calm and able discussion of the subject, and of the means of diffusing genuine religion over the land. It concludes with a close, and powerful, but dignified application to the university dignitaries, to the fellows, tutors, and under-graduates, referring distinctly but not invidiously to the prevalence of formality and worldliness among them, and to the decay of Scriptural piety throughout the Church. In his journal of that day he says: "I preached, I suppose, the last time at St. Mary's! Be it so. I am now clear of the blood of these men. I have fully delivered my own soul." It was

St. Bartholomew's day, and failed not of suggestive memories. He was well pleased, he says, that it should be the very day on which, in the preceding century, near two thousand burning and shining lights were put out at one stroke; "yet what a difference is there between their case and mine," he adds; "they were turned out of house and home, and all that they had, whereas I am only hindered from preaching, without any other loss, and that in a kind of honorable manner, it being determined that when my next turn to preach comes they would pay another person to preach for me."[3] This they did twice or thrice, till, in fine, he resigned his Fellowship. Such was the treatment he received from the university, to which he has given more historical importance than any other graduate of his own or subsequent times, and more perhaps than any other one ever will give it.[4]

The same day he left the venerable town, the scene of so many of his early reminiscences; left it with his final testimony, to pursue his apostolic career among the ignorant and neglected populace, and before the day closed was preaching again at Wycomb.

Methodism had extended over England from Land's End to Newcastle, and Wesley was now continually traversing the country, establishing order and discipline among the new societies, and preaching two and often three sermons daily, beginning almost invariably at five o'clock in the morning. The latter part of the year he spent in the north, amid the severities of an unusual winter. Turnpikes were then unknown in that section of England, and the snows were deep. He and his itinerant companions were often compelled to walk, leading their horses. "Many a rough journey," he says, "have I had before, but one like this I never

[3] Short History of the People called Methodists, section 30. Works, vii, 354, American edition.

[4] The legislators of England have ordered a statue of Wesley, to adorn the walls of the new Parliament House; Oxford still declines him any honorable recognition. Such is the difference of progress between Church and state in England. Parliament has had in our day its Peel, Oxford its Pusey.

had, between wind, and hail, and rain, and ice, and snow, and driving sleet, and piercing cold; but it is past; those days will return no more, and are therefore as though they had never been." His brother passed through similar trials during this inclement season; unable to ride on the obstructed roads, and sometimes too chilled and enfeebled to walk. They relaxed not their energy, however; every city, town, and village they considered their parish, and wherever they were delayed their work went on.

They had also to brave severer trials. In most of the localities where riotous persecutions had prevailed, the societies were now enjoying comparative rest; but mobs broke out in other places, and several of the lay preachers were driven from their fields, and some imprisoned. Meriton, accompanied, by a youthful itinerant, was interrupted, while preaching at Shrewsbury, by a constable, who seized the young man to impress him for the king's service. Meriton himself was imprisoned, and his companion escaped only by running from street to street, and finally taking refuge at a private house, where he was compassionately locked up in a closet till midnight, when, disguised in female dress, he made his way out of the town, passing sentinels who were appointed to watch for him on the bridge.

John Bennet, another itinerant, was "impressed" with three of his lay brethren in Cheshire. His good courage and prudence disheartened his persecutors, and they released him, but his companions had to stand a legal trial. Thomas Maxfield and seven or eight members of the society at Crowan were seized for the army. He was sent in a boat to Penzance, thrust into a dungeon, and offered to the com mander of a ship of war then in Mount Bay, but the officer was shrewd enough to know that such a recruit would be of questionable service on shipboard. "I have no authority," he said, "to take such men as these, unless you would have me give them so much a week to preach and pray." A humble Cornish preacher was pulled down by a constable while preaching at Corlam, and borne off to the House of

Correction at Bodmin. A warrant was got out for John Wesley himself in Cornwall. He was taken into custody, but his persecutors were surprised to find him a gowned clergyman and a well-bred gentleman. Instead of conducting him to the magistrate they escorted him with awkward politeness to his inn, with a promise to call for him the next day. They took good care, however, to trouble him no more. He took his stand the same evening in the open air at Gwennap, and while preaching to a great assembly, three gentlemen, so called, rode furiously into the crowd shouting, "Seize him! seize him for his majesty's service!" The people would not obey them, but sang a hymn. Many of them were struck meanwhile by the infuriated riders. One of the horsemen seized Wesley by the cassock, and dismounting dragged him away by the arm. In a short time he perceived that he was dealing with no fanatic, but a gentleman and scholar, and insisting that he meant no harm, requested Wesley's company at his own house. Wesley declined the dubious politeness. His persecutor then ordered a horse for each of them, and drove back with the preacher to the place whence he had taken him.[5]

The next day a more serious scene awaited him at Falmouth. An innumerable multitude assailed the dwelling where he was staying. A louder or more confused noise, he says, could hardly occur at the taking of a city. The terrified family escaped, leaving only Wesley and a servant maid in the house. The rabble forced open the door and filled the passage. Only a wainscot partition remained between them and their victim. Wesley, supposing the wall would soon fall, showed his coolness at the moment by taking down a large looking-glass which hung against it. The mob, with terrible imprecations, began to attack the partition. "Our lives," he says, "seemed hardly worth an hour's purchase." The servant entreated him to hide himself in a closet. "It is best," he replied, "for me to stand just where I am." The crews of some privateers,

[5] Journal, Anno 1745.

which had lately arrived in the harbor, were in the street, and being impatient at the slow progress of the rioters within, drove them out, and undertook the assault themselves. Putting their shoulders against the door, and shouting, "Avast, lads! avast!" they prostrated it upon the floor of the room. Wesley stepped forward immediately into their midst, bareheaded, and said: "Here I am. Which of you has anything to say to me? To which of you have I done any wrong? To you? or you? or you?" He continued speaking till he reached the middle of the street; there he took his stand, and addressed them as his "neighbors and countrymen." He had his usual success. Several of the crowd cried out: "He shall speak. Yes! yes!" Others swore that no man should touch him. He was conducted in safety to a house, and soon after left the town in a boat.

Passing along from town to town, he describes the societies as in "great consternation." All kinds of reports and alarms were spread. The news of former mobs created general apprehensions of continued riots; but the courageous perseverance and patient endurance with which they had been met were fast subduing them. St. Ives was now "the most still and honorable post," so greatly had the times changed. At Trewint he heard that Francis Walker had been driven thence, but had since been an instrument of great good wherever he had gone. "Indeed," he adds, "I never remember so great an awakening in Cornwall wrought in so short a time among young and old, rich and poor, from Trewint quite to the seaside." He passed into Wales. The truth had spread with mighty effect through most of the Principality. "We are here," he wrote, "in a new world, as it were, in peace, and honor, and abundance; how soon should I melt away in this sun shine; but the goodness of God suffers it not."

While the Wesleys were thus traversing the country, preaching the word through evil report and good report, their lay coadjutors were stimulated by their example to scarcely less indefatigable labors. Several of them, as we have seen, were mobbed, impressed, or imprisoned; but their numbers continually multiplied, and their itinerant preaching began to awaken the whole country with interest for or against the Methodistic movement.

John Nelson had been released from his impressment about the middle of the preceding year. He forthwith resumed his evangelical travels, preaching with great power, mastering extraordinary rencounters, sometimes polemical, sometimes mobocratic; and almost always subduing his opponents by his robust sense, his calm, pious courage, and a natural adroitness which seldom failed to excite the admiration of the rabble, and convert them into clamorous friends. The very day of his release from his regiment he preached, as we have seen, at Newcastle. He returned thence to his home at Birstal, where he found that his former converts had been seriously perverted by Antinomian teachers during his absence. He went out, and mounting a table in the midst of a great assembly, recalled them to their former faith. He was esteemed as an apostle by the simple multitude, and an extraordinary effect was produced by his exhortation. "A trembling," he says, "spread among them; many fell to the ground, and cried out, 'Lord, save or I perish.'"[6] Many came to him with tears, acknowledging that they had been deluded in his absence, and begging him to pray for them. Nelson was a thorough student of the Bible, and, in the best sense, a good theologian, though not much of a polemic. His sound judgment and wholesome sentiments soon prevailed, and restored the society at Birstal. Having achieved this salutary work he went to York, in the streets of which he had been hooted, while led to prison by soldiers, six months before. He had spoken some words of exhortation, and scattered some small books there at that time, and now he was welcomed by almost a score of persons, who had found peace with God, and thrice as many who were seeking it, the result of those casual

[6] Nelson's Journal, p. 61.

efforts, for no one had been there to instruct them since. He received a letter from Sunderland, inviting him thither. Two men had conversed with him as his regiment passed through that town; his exhortations had taken effect upon their hearts also, and they now opened the way for Methodism among their neighbors. On his return from Sunderland he preached at Nottingham Cross. His eloquence subdued the crowd, but a few individuals attempted to burn his face with squibs. They failed, however, and burning themselves, left him to finish his discourse in quiet. When he had concluded, a military man came to him, and, kneeling on the earth, beseeched him with tears to pray that God would have mercy upon his soul, for he had come there to pull him down; "but your words," he continued, "have come as a sword to my heart, and I am convinced you are God's servant. I hope I shall begin to lead a new life from this hour." Nelson's peculiar power was continually producing such effects, and none seemed to feel it more readily than soldiers and rude, hard-hearted men. At another visit to Nottingham about this time, a mob rushed into the house where he was preaching and drowned his voice with outcries. He endeavored to speak on, but one of the rioters came behind him and filled his mouth with dirt. "I think," he says, "I never felt myself so near being choked in my life; but when I had got the dirt out I spoke on." He had not proceeded long before the ringleader turned about, and said: "Let him alone, for he is right and we are wrong; and if any of you touch him I will knock you down." He guarded Nelson to his lodgings, and bore many blows for him, and desired the faithful preacher to pray for him, that he might not rest till he had found peace with God, for he was sure he had fought against the truth, but would do so no more.

Nelson returned again to Sunderland, and standing in deep snow preached to the greater part of the town, who remained patiently in the cold to hear him. At Wednesbury he found that several of the fiercest persecutors were now content to bear themselves the reproach of the Gospel. In Birstal, in Somersetshire and Wiltshire, and in many other places, did this good and courageous man thus pursue his incessant labors, subduing the rudest minds by his homely sense and natural eloquence.

Meanwhile Wesley was surprised by extraordinary news from the Continent. Methodism had broken out in the British army in Flanders, and was achieving in camps and on battle-fields the moral miracles which it had effected among the miners of Cornwall, Kingswood, and Newcastle.[7] Some six or seven soldiers had begun to preach, places of worship had been established in different camps, and congregations of a thousand hearers at a time gathered in them; several hundreds of converts had been formed into societies, and many of them died triumphing in the faith amid the carnage of battle.

John Evans had heard Wesley on Kennington Common. His religious convictions, which had been strong from his childhood, could not be dissipated in the camp. At the battle of Dettingen the balls flew thick about him; his comrades fell on either hand; but he was spared, and felt that his remaining life must be consecrated to God. He found an old Bible in one of the baggage-wagons and began to study it; the pains of hell, he wrote Wesley, got hold upon him, and he dared no longer commit any outward sin. He met John Haime, a Methodist soldier, who instructed him and led him into the path of life. He and his religious comrades opened two places of worship in Ghent, and services were held by them there every day. "He continued," says Wesley, "to preach and live the Gospel till the battle of Fontenoy." He fought bravely on that field, and died there, as we shall presently see, a death full of religious heroism.

[7] Letters from John Evans and John Haime, in Wesley's Journal, 1744–5. Haime's four letters are given with only his initials, as he was living when Wesley published them; but their contents, compared with his autobiography, (Lives of Early Methodist Preachers, vol. i,) prove beyond doubt that they were his.

John Haime, the chief if not the first agent in these extraordinary scenes, was afterward noted among Wesley's lay preachers. He was one of those remarkable men who, like Nelson, Bradburn, and Bramwell, were raised up by Methodism from humble life to eminent usefulness, and who characterized its early lay ministry by their own strongly-marked traits.

He had not Nelson's robust healthfulness of mind; his moral sensibilities were often rendered morbid by constitutional nervous disease, and unquestionably took at times the aspect of partial insanity; but this fact only renders more admirable the religious courage with which he combated his own infirmities, and persevered through a long and afflicted life, with fidelity to his conscience and his duty. In his childhood he was inclined to religious meditation, and, like Nelson, "wandered about on the river sides and through woods and solitary places, looking up to heaven many times with a heart ready to break."[8] The morbid tendency of his mind led him to despondence, which he at last endeavored to dissipate by plunging into gross immoralities. Suicide itself was an alternative of which he often thought in these accesses of diseased feeling. He believed that he had passed beyond the reach of the Divine compassion, and represents himself as tempted to blaspheme God and die. At one time having a stick in his hand, "I threw it," he says, "toward heaven against God with the utmost enmity." He sought relief to his troubled spirit in the army, and enlisted as a dragoon; but serious thoughts and gross excesses alternated in his life from day to day. Bunyan's "Grace abounding to the chief of Sinners" fell into his hands. The Bedford pilgrim had passed through similar morbid trials, and his book was prized by the perplexed and desponding soldier as "the best he had ever seen," for it comforted

[8] Lives of Early Methodist Preachers, written by themselves, vol. i, p. 150. London, 1837. These autobiographical sketches were first published by Wesley in his Arminian Magazine. Many of them possess extraordinary interest, both as illustrations of character and of early Methodism.

him "with some hopes of mercy." But his despondence was not past; his feelings took the intensity of terror; the "hand of the Lord," he says, "came upon me with such weight as made me roar for very anguish of spirit." He now read and fasted, and went to church, and prayed seven times daily. One day, as he walked by the Tweed side, he cried aloud, "being all athirst for God, 'O that thou wouldst hear my prayer, and let my cry come up before thee!'" "The Lord," he writes, "heard; he sent a gracious answer; he lifted me up out of the dungeon. He took away my sorrow and fear, and filled my soul with peace and joy in the Holy Ghost. The stream glided sweetly along, and all nature seemed to rejoice with me. I was truly free; and had I had any one to guide me, I need never more have come into bondage."

Such a guide he needed above all things; an intelligent, devoted, healthful mind, sympathizing with and counseling his broken and lacerated spirit, would have saved him from years of anguish; but the only religious comrade he found in his barrack met his grateful acknowledgments of the grace of God, with the admonitory lesson, "Take care, for Satan can transform himself into an angel of light;" and his sensitive mind, always prompt with self-suspicions, sank again into darkness. He met in the street at Deptford John Cennick, who as we have seen had left Wesley to join Whitefield in the Calvinistic controversy. Haime told him the distress of his soul. "The work of the devil is upon you," said Cennick, and rode away. "It was," writes the heart-broken soldier, "it was the tender mercies of God that I did not put an end to my life. I cried, 'O Lord, my punishment is greater than I can bear.'" Before many days, however, he was again comforted with peace in believing. He passed over to the Continent with his regiment. Alternating between despondence and joy, he was, meanwhile, strict in his religious habits; he reproved vice among his fellow-soldiers, and became practically an evangelist in the camp. He went into the battle of Dettingen exclaiming: "In Thee have I trusted; let me never be confounded." "My heart," he adds, "was filled with love, peace, and joy more than tongue can express. I was in a new world. I could truly say: 'Unto you who believe he is precious.'" Seven hours he stood amid the perils of the field, while his comrades fell around him; the one at his left hand was struck dead, but Haime came out of the battle safe, and triumphant in his faith.

Soon after this combat Sampson Staniforth, another memorable name in the catalogue of Wesley's lay preachers, arrived with his regiment in the camp. Unlike Haime, his youth had been spent with scarcely a religious impression. He had heard the Bible read in the family of his employer, but says that he knew not what it meant, nor why it was called the word of God, nor why people went to church. He records that, during his early life, he never once thought, What was I born into the world for? What is my business in it? Or where shall I go when I leave it? He plunged into the worst excesses, and felt not the least remorse for any of his sins, "being as perfectly without God in the world as the beasts that perish."[9] He enlisted as a soldier, and in one of his marches heard Whitefield preach, but with little effect upon his conscience; down, indeed, to his arrival in the camp in Flanders, when he was twenty-five years old, he had never uttered a prayer. His vices in the camp were excessive, and several times periled his life. He was the last man in the army whom his Methodist comrades could have hoped to reclaim, much less to send back into England as a worthy and heroic recruit for the host of lay evangelists which was then gathering around the founders of Methodism. In camps, however, are found those contrasts of character which we detect in all disguises, and in all scenes of this our inexplicable life; and while many men plunge into the excitements of a military career, like Staniforth, from sheer recklessness, others, like Haime, seek in them relief from the restlessness of their moral sensibilities. Methodism has

[9] Lives of Early Methodist Preachers, vol. ii, p. 148.

never made better converts than among soldiers. In the regiment of Staniforth was Mark Bond, his contrast in all respects. Bond had feared God from his third year; in his seventh year he thought he was tempted to curse him, and went under a hedge and uttered the supposed blasphemy. From that time till he met the Methodists in the army he lived in daily despair of the Divine mercy. Afraid to commit suicide, he enlisted, with the hope of being killed in battle. "His ways," says Staniforth, "were not like those of other men;" he would not take drams; he was always sorrowful; he read much, prayed often in private, and sent his money home to his friends. This afflicted man, bound down so many years under a terrible delusion, was to reclaim the reprobate Staniforth. Bond went to hear Haime, Evans, Clement, and other Methodists of the camp. "With them he found," writes Staniforth, "what he wanted. God soon spoke peace to his soul, and he rejoiced with joy unspeakable." By some mysterious sympathy he could not keep away from Staniforth, but followed him continually with exhortations and warnings, till he brought him to the meetings of the Methodist soldiers.

There Staniforth was surprised, the first time in his life, with religious thoughts; the tears flowed down his cheeks, the rock was rent. "I was knocked down," he says, "like an ox. I had nothing to plead, having never had either the power or the form of godliness. No works, no righteousness was mine. I could only say: 'God be merciful to me a sinner!'" He immediately broke away from all his vices. His "dear companion," as he now always called Bond, asked him if he had a Bible, or any good book. He replied that he had none, and had never read any in his life. Bond had but a piece of an old Bible, and gave it to him; it was doubtless the dearest gift he could make, short of his own life, but "I can do better without it than you," was his just remark. Bond took him as his comrade, put his own pay with his, to help him out of debt, and treated him with the tenderness and care of a parent toward a child.

Staniforth, however, saw the enormous vices of his life in such a light as appalled him; he thought he must have committed the unpardonable sin; but Bond was prepared for him on that point, having vanquished the same delusion after years of despair. At last, in secret prayer, he was enabled to believe his sins forgiven. His intense thoughts portrayed Christ on the cross, amid the opening clouds, as in a vision. "All guilt," he says, "was gone, and my soul was filled with unutterable peace."

The change in Staniforth's life wrought "quite an alarm" throughout his regiment; he had been their leader in vice, and no one could gainsay his conversion; at least ten of his immediate comrades were converted through his example, and "the flame spread through all the camp, so that we had," he writes, "many hearers, and more and more were continually added to the society." The army was divided, but the new military evangelists were also providentially distributed; Haime and Evans went to Bruges, and Clements and others to Ghent. The number of converts increased daily; there were some in almost every regiment. At least three hundred were united in societies, and seven preachers were almost daily proclaiming the word among them. Haime preached usually five times a day at different places, walking frequently between twenty and thirty miles. He hired others to do his camp duties, that he might have more time for these religious services. Tabernacles containing several rooms, for various meetings, were erected in the camps. "I had now," he says, "three armies against me: the French army, the wicked English army, and an army of devils." The latter beset him yet with religious perplexity and dejection, but could not subdue him.

At Bruges the English general gave him permission to preach every day in the English church; the Methodist soldiers marched on Sundays in procession to the service, and their good singing charmed thither the officers and their families.

A severe test awaited these devoted men, but they met it as became "good soldiers of the Lord Jesus." They had become marked men throughout the army, by their abstinence from the immoralities of the camp, and their earnest recommendation of religion as a fitness for life and a preparation for death. On the 1st of May, 1745, the battle of Fontenoy required them to face death in the ranks with their forty-six thousand comrades, and there was no little interest felt among officers and men to see how their religion would bear the trial. The day before, Staniforth, who was now firm in his faith, was in the ranks, ready to be led on. "I stepped out of the line," he says, "and threw myself on the ground, and prayed that God would deliver me from all fear, and enable me to behave as a Christian and good soldier. Glory be to God, he heard my cry, and took away all my fear. I came into the ranks again, and had both peace and joy in the Holy Ghost." They lay on their arms all night. Bond, his "dear companion," was by his side, for their friendship had become like that of Jonathan and David. "We had," says Staniforth, "sweet communion together, having constant and strong confidence in God." At dawn they were advancing toward Fontenoy, and already the terrors of battle confronted them; the dead were strewn along their march; they charged the trenches of the French, and many of the Methodists fell; but the two friends survived the day, though Bond received two musket balls, one striking him on the right thigh, and hitting two pieces of coin which were in his pocket, the other striking a clasp-knife, and bending the blade, but doing no other harm. "I neither desired life nor death," says Staniforth, "but was entirely happy in God."

Meanwhile Haime and his companions were in similar perils on other parts of the field. One of his brethren, believing his death at hand, went into battle, exclaiming: "I am going to rest in the bosom of Jesus!" and was in heaven before night. "Indeed," writes Haime, "this day God was pleased to prove our little flock, and to show them his mighty power. They showed such courage and boldness in the fight as made the officers, as well as soldiers, amazed. When wounded, some cried out: I am going to my Beloved! Others, Come, Lord Jesus, come quickly! And many that were not wounded earnestly desired to be dissolved and to be with Christ." When Clements, one of the preachers, had his arm broken by a musket-ball, they would have carried him out of the battle, but he said, "No; I have an arm left to hold my sword; I will not go yet." When a second shot broke his other arm, he said: "I am as happy as I can be out of paradise." John Evans, now a preacher also, having both his legs taken off by a chain-shot, was laid across a cannon to die; where, as long as he could speak, he was praising God, and exhorting all around him. Haime stood the hottest fire of the enemy for several hours. He believed he should not die that day. After about seven hours a cannon-ball killed his horse under him. An officer cried out: "Haime, where is your God now?" He answered: "Sir, he is here with me, and he will bring me out of this battle;" presently a cannon-ball took off the officer's head. Haime's horse fell upon him, and one cried out: "Haime is gone!" But he replied: "He is not gone yet." He soon disengaged himself, and walked on, praising God. "I was exposed," he says, "both to the enemy and to our own horse; but that did not discourage me at all, for I knew the God of Jacob was with me. I had a long way to go, through all our horse, the balls flying on every side; and all the way lay multitudes bleeding, groaning, or just dead. Surely I was as in the fiery furnace, but it did not singe a hair of my head. The hotter the battle grew the more strength was given me; I was as full of joy as I could contain." As he was quitting the field he met one of his brethren, seeking water, and covered with blood, so that he could not at first recognize him. The wounded Methodist smiled, and said: "Brother Haime, I have got a sore wound." "Have you got Christ in your heart?" asked Haime. "I have," was the reply; "and I have had him all this day. I have seen many good and glorious days, with much of God; but I never saw more of it than this day. Glory be to God for all his mercies!"

Four preachers and many members of the societies fell on the field. In a later battle, near Maestricht, Staniforth lost Bond, his companion and guide. He was shot through the leg by a musket ball; as his friend carried him away the dying man exhorted "him to stand fast in the Lord." Staniforth had to leave him and resume his place in the ranks, but on a retreat found him where he had laid him. By this time he had received another ball through his thigh. They were obliged to part, for the enemy was pressing on; but, writes Staniforth, "his heart was full of love, and his eyes full of heaven." "Here fell," he adds, "a great Christian, a good soldier, and a faithful friend."

Staniforth returned to England, and became a devoted Methodist preacher.

Haime continued his labors in the army for some time; but having gone to Antwerp for forage, he made some small purchases there for his comrades on Sunday, a custom almost universal among both Papists and Protestants on the Continent. He was suddenly seized with the thought that he had apostatized by this act. His morbid sensibilities were so affected by the impression, that for twenty years he suffered despair itself, not daring even to pray much of that time. He maintained, however, the strictness of his external life, and he ceased not to preach, though bending under despondency. "Frequently," he says, "as I was going to preach, the devil has set upon me as a lion, telling me he would have me just then, so that it has thrown me into a cold sweat. In this agony I have caught hold of the Bible, and read, 'If any man sin, we have an advocate with the Father, Jesus Christ the righteous!' I have said to the enemy, 'This is the word of God, and thou canst not deny it!' Thereat he would be like a man that shrunk back from the thrust of a sword. But he would be at me again. I again met him in the same way; till at last, blessed be God, he fled from me. And even in the midst of his sharpest assaults God gave me just strength enough to bear them. When he has strongly suggested, just as I was going to preach, 'I will have thee at last!' I have answered, (sometimes with too much anger,) 'I will have another out of thy hand first!' And many, while I was myself in the deep, were truly convinced and converted to God." On returning to England he entered the Methodist ministry; Wesley endeavored to meet the peculiar necessities of his case; and, in advanced age, the suffering soldier, who had shown his good courage on the field and in the itinerant ministry, conquered his constitutional dejection, the terrible foe before which his brave spirit had so often recoiled but never succumbed. During nearly twenty years more of life he presented an example of Christian enjoyment which should be an encouraging lesson to all similar sufferers. The comfort which Methodism brought to Bond and Haime, it has afforded to thousands of such despondent minds; its generous theology disowns the delusion which depressed them; and its vivid spirit, inspiring the heart with confidence in the Divine love, and exalting the sensibilities with devotional and joyful emotion, affords the best moral support against the influence of mental disease.

Many of these Methodist soldiers, awaiting the morning of the resurrection, sleep in Christ on the battle-fields of the continent; many returned home when the war ended, some to strengthen the growing Methodist Societies, some the itinerant ministry. Six months after the battle of Fontenoy Charles Wesley, then in London, wrote in his journal: "We had twenty of our brethren from Flanders to dine with us at the Foundry."[10] Still later he met a number of them at the camp at Deptford, on their way to suppress the Northern Rebellion. They assembled in the society there. "We solemnly commended them," he says "to the grace of God before they set out to meet the rebels. They were

[10] Journal of Rev. Charles Wesley, etc., vol. i, p. 407. London, 1849.

without fear or disturbance, knowing the hairs of their head are all numbered." Several others, on arriving in London, were presented by Colonel Gumley (one of Whitefield's converts) to Lady Huntingdon. "I was truly amazed," says the countess, "with the devotional spirit of these poor men, many of whom are rich in faith and heirs of the kingdom."[11] Whitefield met some of them in Edinburgh more than three years after the battle of Fontenoy, and formed them into a society. On leaving that city he addressed them an affectionate pastoral letter.

Thomas Rankin, one of Wesley's earliest missionaries to America, formed in his youth a society of them at Dunbar, his native town in Scotland. They had hired a room and met for worship every morning and evening. A great religious interest extended through the town from these meetings, and many of the inhabitants were converted and gathered into their little company.[12] They were dragoons of John Haime's regiment. At Musselborough also they had formed a society, and were instrumental in the spread of vital religion among the townsmen. Wesley's preachers visited them and formed them into regular "appointments." The first Methodist Societies of Scotland were the two at Dunbar and Musselborough.[13] Wesley found them prospering twelve years later, and the invitation which led to his first visit to that country came from a military officer who was in quarters at Musselborough. Some who were in the same regiment with Haime, but resisted if they did not resent his exhortations, joined the Methodists after they returned to England. Eight years later Wesley found seventeen of Haime's fellow-dragoons in the society at Manchester, where they were "patterns of seriousness, zeal, and all holy conversation."[14] Nearly ten years later he met at Trowbridge one who found peace with God while a soldier in Flanders,

[11] Life and Times of Selina, Countess of Huntingdon, chap. 7.

[12] Life of Thomas Rankin, in Lives of Early Methodist Preachers, written by themselves, vol. iii, pp. 8–20.

[13] Coke and Moore's Life of Wesley, chap. 2, sec. 2.

[14] Wesley's Journal, Anno 1753.

and having been much prospered in business since his discharge, had built a preaching house at his own expense. He was ambitious that Wesley should preach the first sermon in it, but it was so excessively crowded before the introductory hymn was finished, that he had to disappoint the generous soldier, by going out and preaching at the door to a "multitude of hearers, rich and poor."

A quarter of a century after the battle of Fontenoy an aged preacher wrote to John Wesley that "all the promises of Scripture were full of comfort to him, *particularly this: 'I have chosen thee in the furnace of affliction;'*" that "the Scriptures were all precious to his soul as the rain to the thirsty land;" that he "could now truly say, '*The Lord is my shepherd, therefore shall I lack nothing; he maketh me to lie down in green pastures; he leadeth me beside the still waters; he restoreth my soul; he leadeth me in the paths of righteousness for his name's sake.*'" It was the despondent but brave John Haime who thus wrote. By the grace of God he had conquered both himself and the devil, and was now ready to conquer "the last enemy."

In the Arminian Magazine for 1784 we read: "On the 18th of August, 1784, died, at Whitechurch, in Hampshire, that faithful soldier of Christ, John Haime, in the seventy-eighth year of his age. He preached as long as he was able to speak, and longer than he could stand without support." When his sight and speech had nearly failed, he exclaimed: "When my soul departs from this body a convoy of angels will conduct me to the paradise of God."

More than forty years after the battle of Fontenoy, another veteran preacher wrote to Wesley: "I am now in the sixty-third year of my age, and glory be to God, I am not weary of well-doing! I find my desires after God stronger than ever; my understanding is more clear in the things of God, and my heart is united more than ever both to him and his people. I know their religion and mine is the gift of God through Christ, and the work of God by his Spirit." It was Sampson Staniforth; and in the Arminian Magazine for

1799 we read: "Thus died Sampson Staniforth, who had steadily walked with God for nearly sixty years. He preached the Gospel for almost fifty years, and finished his course in the seventy-ninth year of his age. He possessed his soul in patience, and looked to the hour of his dissolution with joyful expectation of being forever with the Lord. He was neither molested with gloomy doubts nor painful fears, nor was the enemy of souls permitted to distress him; but as his heart stood fast, believing in the Lord, so his evidence for heaven continued unclouded to the last moment of life."

Such is one of the most extraordinary passages in the history of not only Methodism, but of Christianity in any age; one of the most striking proofs of the inherent and inextinguishable power of the religious instinct in the most degraded natures and in the most adverse circumstances; one of those demonstrations of it which confirm the hope of good men who labor for the final and universal triumph of Christianity. It seemed indeed a part of the providential design of Methodism that it should multiply these demonstrations, as preparatory for that deepened faith, and those great enterprises of Christian propagandism which have arisen from the impulse that it gave to British and American Protestantism. It had wrought out such demonstrations among the colliers of Kingswood and Newcastle, the miners of Cornwall, the peasants of Yorkshire, and the drunken multitudes of Moorfields and Kennington Common; it now presented another amid the vices of the camp and the carnage of battle, rescuing scores and hundreds of ignorant and corrupt men, whom it was to record as triumphing in death amid the horrors of war, or as life-long examples of Christian purity and usefulness. If its history teaches any one lesson as paramount to all its other suggestions, it is that good men, laboring and suffering for the salvation of their race, should "have faith in God" by having it in humanity.

CHAPTER II.

FROM THE CONFERENCE OF 1745 TO THE CONFERENCE OF 1750.

The Rebellion under Charles Stuart — Wesley abroad amid the Public Alarm — His Preaching at Newcastle — He publishes the concluding part of his Appeal to Men of Reason and Religion — Extensive Results of Methodism — Its Exemption from Heresy — Its Doctrinal Liberality — Charles Wesley — John Wesley in Cornwall — In the North — John Nelson — He encounters terrible Mobs — Wesley itinerating — Mobs subdued — Success of Methodism — Vincent Perronet — William Grimshaw — His Eccentricities — His extraordinary Labors — He is mobbed with Wesley at Roughlee — Charles Wesley itinerating — Extraordinary Riot at Devizes — The Wesleys in Middle Life — Marriage of Charles Wesley — John Wesley and Grace Murray.

The second conference met in Bristol on the first day of August, 1745. Methodism advanced rapidly during the ensuing ecclesiastical year, notwithstanding the general agitation of the public mind, occasioned by the attempt of Charles Stuart to regain for his family the British throne. He had taken Edinburgh, and threatened England with invasion. The plans of Cope, commander of the government troops, were feebly conceived and as feebly executed. The possession of Edinburgh and the victory of Preston Pans inspired the rebels with confidence, and spread alarm through the whole country. As the Pretender was a Papist, and a pensioner of France, the liberties of England and her Protestant faith would be endangered by his success, notwithstanding his specious promises. Christian Englishmen could not, therefore, but consider his movements as imminently perilous to the country, and an alarming retribution from God for its sins. The Wesleys went through the land distributing admonitory tracts and hymns, and calling the people to repentance in daily sermons. Newcastle, situated far in the north, was especially exposed to the enemy, and was in great commotion. John Wesley went thither immediately after the Conference, that he might be with its Methodist society amid the agitation.[1] When he arrived he found that all householders were summoned to meet the mayor to devise means of protection. As he was not a townsman he did not go, but sent a loyal letter. The people were placed under arms; the walls were fortified, and the gates filled up. "Many," he says, "began to be much concerned for us because our society house was without the walls. But the Lord is a wall of fire to all that trust in him."

Day by day the news from the north became more alarming. Citizens who had the necessary means, and especially the gentry, were constantly removing their goods and hastening to the south. Wesley meanwhile preached day and night in the streets and in neighboring villages, encouraging the loyalty of the people, and calling upon them to repent of their sins, and put their trust in God. News came that the enemy was in full march, and would reach the city the next day. Instead of fleeing away for safety with the many who were leaving, Wesley stayed in the city. "At eight o'clock," he says, "I called on a multitude of sinners in Gateshead to seek the Lord while he might be found. Mr. Ellison preached another earnest sermon, and all the people seemed to bend before the Lord. In the afternoon I expounded part of the lesson for the day—Jacob wrestling with the angel. The congregation was so moved that I began again and again, and knew not how to conclude. And we cried mightily to God to send his majesty King George help from His holy place, and to spare a sinful land yet a little longer, if haply they might know the day of their visitation." A person from the north was apprehended and put in prison; he attempted to cut his throat, but was saved

[1] Journal, Anno 1745.

from death by the physicians, and disclosed plans of the rebels which, if successful, must have been fatal to the city. To their detection Wesley ascribes its escape. Believing the danger over for the present, he directed his course elsewhere.

Until the next Conference his time was spent in unremitted travels and preaching. He prepared, also, during this interval the concluding part of his "Appeal to Men of Reason and Religion." It is eloquent in its earnestness. After describing the extreme demoralization which had prevailed through the nation, he writes: "The grace of God which bringeth salvation, present salvation, from inward and outward sin, hath abounded of late years in such a degree as neither we nor our fathers had known. How extensive is the change which has been wrought on the minds and lives of the people! Know ye not that the sound is gone forth into all the land; that there is scarce a city or considerable town to be found where some have not been roused out of the sleep of death, and constrained to cry out in the bitterness of their soul, 'What must I do to be saved?' that this religious concern has spread to every age and sex; to most orders and degrees of men; to abundance of those in particular who in time past were accounted monsters of wickedness, drinking in iniquity like water, and committing all uncleanliness with greediness."[2]

He contends that this remarkable reformation was attended by no important outbreaks of heretical opinions or popular superstition. "In former times," he remarks, "wherever an unusual concern for the things of God hath appeared, on the one hand strange and erroneous opinions continually sprung up with it; on the other, a zeal for things which were no part of religion, as though they had been essential branches of it. But it has not been so in the present. No stress has been laid on anything, as though it were necessary to salvation, but what is undeniably contained in the word of God. And of the things contained therein, the stress laid on each has

[2] Wesley's Works, vol. v, p. 145.

been in proportion to the nearness of its relation to what is there laid down as the sum of all—the love of God and our neighbor. So pure from superstition, so thoroughly Scriptural, is that religion which has lately spread in this nation." He further asserts that the new movement was singularly exempt from bigotry. "The Methodists are in nowise bigoted to opinions. They do indeed hold rigid opinions, but they are peculiarly cautious not to rest the weight of Christianity there. They have no such overgrown fondness for any opinions as to think those alone will make them Christians, or to confine their affection or esteem to those who agree with them therein. There is nothing they are more fearful of than this, lest it should steal upon them unawares. They contend for nothing trifling, as if it was important; for nothing indifferent, as if it were necessary; but for everything in its own order."

Such was the very genius of Methodism. In an eloquent concluding passage Wesley asserts its liberality with still greater emphasis. He asks his opponents why they will persist in opposing a work of God like this? "If you say, 'Because you hold opinions which I cannot believe are true,' I answer, Believe them true or false, I will not quarrel with you about any opinion. Only see that your heart be right toward God, that you know and love the Lord Jesus Christ; that you love your neighbor, and walk as your Master walked, and I desire no more. I am sick of opinions, I am weary to hear them. My soul loathes this frothy food. Give me solid and substantial religion; give me an humble, gentle lover of God and man, a man full of mercy and good fruits, without partiality and without hypocrisy; a man laying himself out in the work of faith, the patience of hope, the labor of love. Let my soul be with these Christians wheresoever they are, and whatsoever opinion they are of. 'Whosoever' thus 'doeth the will of my Father which is in heaven, the same is my brother, and sister, and mother.' Inexcusably infatuated must you be if you can ever doubt whether the propagation of this religion be of

God. Only more inexcusable are those unhappy men who oppose, contradict, and blaspheme it."

Casting forth this noble appeal before the nation, he went forward prosecuting his evangelical labors among the common people in almost every city, town, and village on his course from the Tweed to Land's End. Charles Wesley spent the year in equal labors. A great religious interest prevailed at Shepton-Mallet; he hastened from the Conference at Bristol to promote it; but in going to the place of preaching he slipped, and injured one of his legs so severely that he was unable to walk for some time. He was carried about, however, from place to place, preaching daily on his knees. At Cardiff a man who had been the most violent persecutor of the Methodists of that town, sent his Bath-chair to bear the disabled evangelist to his next appointment. "Indeed," he writes, "the whole place seems at present turned toward us."[3] During several weeks he could walk only by the aid of crutches, but preached twice a day with great effect. "The word of God," he wrote, "is not bound if I am, but runs very swiftly. I have been *carried* to preach morning and evening." In Wales and Cornwall, in London, Bristol, Kingswood, and many other places, did he pursue his labors with continually increasing success till the session of the next Conference.

The third Conference was held on the twelfth of May,[4] 1746. It detained the itinerant laborers but two days from their fields. Wesley did not allude to it in his Journal, but hastened forth on his ministerial routes, which now extended over the whole of England and Wales. In August he traversed a large part of the Principality, preaching in churches, on tombstones, and on the highways, to greater congregations than he had ever addressed in that part of the kingdom. He was mobbed but once during this excursion. In September he was again itinerating in Cornwall,

[3] Jackson's Life of Charles Wesley, chap. 12.

[4] Not the thirteenth, as the bound Minutes state. See Smith's History, II, 3.

where the miners still crowded to hear him. The amphitheater at Gwennap presented greater hosts than ever, and peace prevailed everywhere. He was not disturbed in a single instance during this visit, and the worst persecutors had now become the most devoted converts. The societies were not only enjoying rest from their late terrible trials, but were gathering strength daily, and extending to all the towns and villages. Methodism was, in fine, taking universal and ineradicable root among the Cornish population. The clergy, however, very generally stood aloof. There was one notable exception. Thompson, the tolerant and zealous rector of St. Gennis, was known as thoroughly Methodistic, and as the friend of Wesley, Whitefield, and Lady Huntingdon. He was a man of genius, and had been a favorite among the gentry and clergy, though debauched in morals while in the ministry. A terrible dream, twice repeated, led him to reflection. He reformed his life, and began to preach in earnest, and his parishioners were generally awakened and reformed. He befriended Wesley amid the Cornish persecutions, and was soon himself honored as a "Methodist." All the neighboring clergy closed their pulpits against him, and he was cited at last before Lavington, his diocesan, the noted opponent of Methodism, to give an account of his conduct. Lavington threatened to "strip the gown from him" for his Methodistic practices. Thompson stripped it off himself, and casting it at the prelate's feet, said, "I can preach the Gospel without a gown," and left him astonished at his independence. On recovering from his amazement, Lavington recalled him, and soothed him with explanatory remarks. The zealous rector remained faithful to his Methodist friends till death, and did much for the moral improvement of Cornwall.[5]

[5] He died in 1782. Wesley says, (Journal, 1782,) "I preached in the street at Camelford. Being informed here that my old friend Mr. Thompson, rector of St. Gennis, was near death, and had expressed a particular desire to see me, I judged no time was to be lost; so borrowing the best horse I could find, I set out and rode as fast as I could." He found the rector just alive, and troubled, like Bunyan's pilgrim, with inward con-

During the winter Wesley directed his course toward the north, through severe storms. He instituted a thorough pastoral examination of the societies on his route; a small one at Tetney he pronounced the best in the country. Its class-paper showed an extraordinary liberality for so poor a people. "Are you the richest society in England?" he inquired. "All of us," replied the class-leader, "who are single persons, have agreed together to give both ourselves and *all we have* to God; and we do it gladly, whereby we are able, from time to time, to entertain all the strangers that come to Tetney, who often have no food to eat nor any friend to give them a lodging." At Osmotherly, a large congregation gathered around him, and "those," he wrote, "who had been the most bitter gainsayers seemed now to be melted into love." At Newcastle he was encouraged to find the society alive with zeal, and in perfect harmony. "They are," he writes, "of one heart and of one mind. I found all in the house of the same spirit, pouring out their souls to God many times in a day together, and breathing nothing but love and brotherly kindness." Many from the higher classes assembled at the society's place of worship. "Surely," he wrote, "God is working a new thing in the earth. Even to the rich is the Gospel preached; and there are, of these also, who have ears to hear, and hearts to receive the truth as it is in Jesus." At Blanchland he preached in the church-yard to a great crowd, gathered from the lead mines of all the neighboring country as far as Allendale, six miles distant. They drank in his words as if athirst for the truth. At Sunderland, where John Nelson had founded Methodism, as we have seen, by a passing word of exhortation, while led through the place in his regiment, Wesley now preached in the streets to a multitude which reminded him of the living seas at Kennington Common. He sought out the neglected and degraded towns and ham-

flicts. Wesley proved a comforter to him; they took the Lord's Supper together for the last time; "and I left him," writes he, "much happier than I found him, calmly waiting till his change should come."

lets, and penetrated especially into the mining villages. At Hexham, he says, "a multitude of people soon ran together, the greater part mad as colts untamed. Many had promised to do mighty things. But the bridle was in their teeth. I cried aloud: 'Let the wicked forsake his way, and the unrighteous man his thoughts.' They felt the sharpness of the two-edged sword, and sunk into seriousness on every side, insomuch that I heard not one unkind or uncivil word, till we left them standing and staring one at another." Happily he was now able, by means of the lay ministry, to send laborers into the fields wherever he thus broke up the fallow ground; men who had been plucked by Methodism from the midst of these same heathen crowds, and knew how to approach them.

John Nelson was unquestionably at the head of this growing corps of lay evangelists. Wesley unexpectedly met him about this time at Osmotherly, whither the good stonemason had just escaped from perils such as he had never before encountered, and which could not have failed to crown him with the honors of martyrdom, had it not been for the Herculean vigor of his frame. Since we last parted from him he had been pursuing his itinerant labors with unfaltering energy and success at Birstal, and in Somersetshire and Wiltshire. He spent four months in these localities, and gathered numerous converts into societies at Poulton, Coleford, Oakley, Shepton-Mallet, Rood, and Bearfield. "So God doth work," wrote the brave man, amid these successes; "so God doth work, and none can hinder, though the instruments be ever so weak; if he bids, a worm shall shake the earth."[6] In his own town of Birstal, contrary to the usual fate of prophets, he was held in high honor, and saw Methodism spread out on the right and left. No bishop of the realm could have wielded a stronger influence among his humble fellow-townsmen. He was called about this time to witness there an affecting instance of the power of religion. An "old gentleman" who had been among his opposers, and

[6] Nelson's Journal, p. 165. Am. ed.

had aided in his impressment, was prostrated by mortal sickness, and now sent, with contrition, for his prayers and instructions. Nelson says, "he trembled and wept bitterly, and I found him under as great convictions as I ever saw a man." After his third visit the aged sufferer was comforted with peace in believing, and for five weeks that he remained on earth he was not a day without some divine consolation, and continued to utter praises to God, and exhortations to his family and visitors till he expired. "He seemed," says Nelson, "to be sanctified body, soul, and spirit." He requested Nelson to preach over his corpse. The scene exhibited by the humble itinerant as he stood at the grave of the old but reclaimed persecutor must have been sublime. He had gathered many similar trophies from the ranks of his enemies while they were in the fullness of life and health, but here was one plucked from the very grasp of death. The discourse was attended with extraordinary effect. Many of his former enemies were smitten under it with remorse; and a "great awakening," he writes to Wesley, "followed throughout the town."[7]

In the former strongholds of the mob quiet now prevailed, for the itinerants had won the field. But Nelson was a pioneer, continually penetrating into new regions, and almost everywhere riotous outrages were enacted at his coming. No man, not even Wesley himself, had more success in mastering such hostilities; but sometimes they were uncontrollable, and his escape from death seemed miraculous. As he advanced about this time toward the course of Wesley, he was assailed at Harborough by almost the "whole town, men, women, and children." The young men and apprentices had previously combined with the determination to seize the first Methodist preacher who should come among them, and drag him, with a halter round his neck, to

[7] This incident is not related in his Journal, but in a letter to Wesley, published by the latter in the first volume of the Arminian Magazine, (1778,) p. 259.

the river to drown him, thereby deterring any others, as they hoped, from troubling the town. A son of the parish clergyman was leader of the mob. A partially insane man had been appointed to put the halter on the preacher's neck, and now assailed Nelson with one in his hand. A butcher stood with a rope to aid in dragging him to the stream. But Nelson's power over his hearers was invincible; while his voice was heard the leaders of the mob could do nothing. They procured six large hand-bells as the best means of breaking the spell of his eloquence. They succeeded in drowning his voice, when the madman rushed in and put the halter to his throat. Nelson pushed it back, and the maniac fell to the ground as if "knocked down by an ax." The butcher stood trembling with awe, and dared not touch him. A constable who was disposed to favor the rioters came, but on approaching the preacher "turned pale," took him by the hand, led him through the mob, and helping him to mount his horse, bade him "go on in the name of the Lord." "O my God!" exclaimed the delivered evangelist, "hitherto thou hast helped me!"

Nelson was to encounter, however, worse perils immediately after at Hepworth Moor. He was assailed there with a shower of stones while preaching on a table in the open air. All who were around him fled, leaving him as a mark for the flying missiles, but none touched him. When he descended and was departing, he was struck on the back of his head with a brick, and fell bleeding to the earth. He was unable to rise for some time, but being lifted up, staggered away, the blood running down his back and filling his shoes, and the mob following him with shouts and menaces that they would kill him as soon as he passed the limits of the town. "Lord," cried the periled Methodist, as he tottered along, "thou wast slain without the gate, and canst deliver me from the hands of these bloodthirsty men." An honest man opened his door and took him in; a surgeon dressed his wound, and the same day he was on his way to preach at Acomb. There his trials were to culminate. A coach drove up crowded within and without by young men, who sang bacchanalian songs and threw rotten eggs at the women of the assembly. Two of the strongest of the rioters approached him, one of them swearing that he would kill him on the spot. Handing his coat and wig to his associate, he rushed at the preacher crying, "If I do not kill him I will be damned." Nelson stepped aside and the assailant pitched on his head; on rising he repeated the attempt, and rent away Nelson's shirt collar, but again fell. In a third assault he prostrated the preacher, and leaping with his knees upon him, beat him until he was senseless, opening meanwhile the wound on his head, which bled freely. The ruffian supposed he was dead and returned to his associates, seizing as he passed one of Nelson's friends, whom he threw against a wall with such violence as to break two of his ribs. The rest of the mob doubted whether Nelson had been completely dispatched, and twenty of them approached him. They found him bleeding profusely, and lifted him up. The brother of the parish clergyman was among them, and denouncing him, said: "According to your preaching, you would prove our ministers to be blind guides and false prophets; but we will kill you as fast as you come." Another said: "If Wesley comes on Tuesday he shall not live another day in this world." When they had got him into the street they set up a huzza, and a person caught hold of his right hand "and gave him a hasty pluck;" at the same time another struck him on the side of his head and knocked him down. As he arose they again prostrated him. No less than eight times did they fell him to the earth. His robust frame alone saved him from death. When he lay on the ground unable to rise again, they took him by the hair of his head and dragged him upon the stones for nearly twenty yards, some kicking him, meanwhile, with merciless rage. Six of them stood upon him, to "tread the Holy Ghost out of him," as they said. "Then they let me alone a little while," he writes, "and said one to another, 'We cannot kill him.' One said, 'I have heard that a cat hath nine lives, but I think that he hath nine score.' Another said, 'If he has he shall die this day.' A third said, 'Where is his horse, for he shall quit the town immediately.' And they said to me, 'Order your horse to be brought to you, for you shall go before we leave you.' I said, 'I will not, for you intend to kill me in private, that you may escape justice; but if you do murder me it shall be in public; and it may be that the gallows will bring you to repentance, and your souls may be saved from the wrath to come." They attempted then to drag him to a well and thrust him into it, but a courageous woman who was standing near it, defended him, knocking several of his persecutors down. These ruffians passed in the community for gentlemen, and while still harassing Nelson at the well, they were recognized by two ladies in a carriage from the city, whom they knew; they slunk away confounded, and their victim escaped.

Such was John Nelson's most perilous itinerant adventure. He certainly deserved for it the honors, though he escaped the fate of martyrdom. His powerful constitution rallied immediately from the effect of this terrible treatment, and the very next day the heroic man rode forty miles, and stood, with unbroken spirit, at evening, resting himself against a tombstone in Osmotherly churchyard, listening to Wesley as he proclaimed from it the word of life to the assembled population of the town. "I found," he writes, "his word to come with power to my soul, and was constrained to cry out, 'O Lord I will praise thee for thy goodness to me, for thou hast been with me in all my trials; thou hast brought me out of the jaws of death; and though thou didst permit men to ride over my head, and laid affliction on my loins, yet thou hast brought me through fire and water into a wealthy place.'" He assures us that in all these perils his soul was kept in peace, so that he felt neither fear nor anger, and adds with grateful emphasis: "So far, Lord, I am thy witness; for thou dost give strength for our day according to thy word, and grace to help in time of need. O my dear

Redeemer, how shall I praise thee as thou oughtest to be praised? O let my life be a living sacrifice to thee, for it is by thee alone that I have escaped both temporal and eternal death." His meekness was equal to his courage, and both were surpassed only by his charity.

The good seed scattered by this noble evangelist amid the mobs of Yorkshire, sprang up, however, under the very storm, in rich harvests. His fiercest persecutors became often the most zealous Methodists; they were sometimes smitten by their consciences in the act of assailing or burlesquing him and his fellow-laborers. John Thorp was a frequenter of an ale-house in Yorkshire, where such burlesques were the entertainment of a bacchanalian company. One after another mounted a table, and, with the Bible in hand, recited a text, and mimicked the itinerant preachers. Three had done so when Thorp took his stand, declaring he would excel them all by an imitation of Whitefield. He opened the book by hazard for his text, and read Luke xiii, 3: "Except ye repent ye shall all likewise perish." The passage struck his conscience like a bolt from heaven. He was terrified at his own guilt, but proceeded with his discourse, to the astonishment of his drunken associates, who were spellbound with awe, and dared not interrupt him. Some of his sentences, he says, made his own hair stand erect. "If ever I preached in my life," he added, "by the assistance of the Spirit of God, it was at that time." Finishing his discourse, he dismounted from the table, and returned home without another word to his companions; he forsook them forever and immediately joined the Methodist Society. During two years he suffered under deep anguish, but at last found peace in believing, and became one of Wesley's preachers.[8]

Wesley and Nelson took counsel and comfort together at

[8] "He was successful wherever he went," says a writer in the Arminian Magazine. He afterward ministered to an Independent church, and died in 1776. A brother clergyman says: "He was a very holy man, much respected during his life, and made a glorious end."

Osmotherly over their afflictions and successes, and separated immediately for other trials and triumphs. At Leeds, where Nelson had successfully established Methodism, Wesley found an extraordinary interest, and preached to an immense assembly, hundreds of whom went away unable to hear his voice. At Birstal, Nelson's home, the multitude was scarcely less numerous. At Keighley, where, during a previous visit, he had formed a society of ten members, he now met more than a hundred. At Manchester, where Nelson had preached the first Methodist lay sermon in 1743, he again met that noble lay laborer. Nelson had announced his coming through the city, and gathered a vast multitude to hear him. Wesley passed on to Plymouth, where he was again mobbed. A lieutenant, with drummers, and a retinue of soldiers and rabble, greeted him with huzzas. He rode into the midst of them and conquered, as usual. He took the lieutenant by the hand, and subdued him by a few gentle words. "Sir," exclaimed the soldier, "no man shall touch you; I will see you safe home. Stand off! Give back! I will knock the first man down that touches him!" and led him safely to his lodgings. "We then parted," says Wesley, "in much love." After the officer had left him he still kept his ground, and for half an hour addressed the astonished people, who, he says, "had forgotten their anger, and went away in high good-humor." The next day he preached on the common to a "well-behaved and earnest congregation."

He went again into Cornwall. There the field had been severely contested, but, as we have seen, was won at last. At St. Ives, he says, "we walked to church without so much as one huzza. How strangely has one year changed the scene in Cornwall! This is now a peaceable, nay, honorable station. They give us good words almost in every place. What have we done that the world should be so civil to us?" His favorite preaching place, the natural amphitheater at Gwennap, was again filled with an immense audience. At Bray, he says, "neither the house nor the yard could contain the congregation, and all were serious;

the scoffers are vanished away; I scarce saw one in the county. I preached in the evening at Camborne to an equally serious congregation; I looked about for the champion who had so often sworn I should never more preach in that parish; but it seems he had given up the cause, saying, one may as well blow against the wind." There were eighteen exhorters in the county, some of whom had good talents, and did valuable service for the Societies. At a few new points he met with mobs, but they succumbed quickly before him. Returning to Bristol, he found the largest congregation he had ever seen there. "What," he writes, "has God wrought in this city! And yet, perhaps, the hundredth part of his work does not now appear." From Bristol he passed into Wales, and thence over to Ireland, where he spent more than a month.

During the remainder of our present period, down to the Conference of 1750, he traveled and preached with augmented activity. He made several visits to Ireland. In England and Wales he found Methodism everywhere advancing, and proving its evangelical power by its salutary results. At Coleford, he writes, "the colliers of this place were 'darkness,' indeed, but now they are light." At Wednesbury, formerly the scene of the worst riots, he preached to vast congregations, "every man, woman, and child," he says, "behaving in a manner becoming the Gospel." Even in London a favorable change appeared. St. Bartholomew's Church was again opened to him, and Bateman, the rector, had become known as a "Methodist." "How strangely is the scene changed!" he writes; "what laughter and tumult was there among the best of the parish when we preached in a London church ten years ago! And now all are calm and quietly attentive, from the least even to the greatest." The congregation in Moorfields, he adds the next day, was greatly enlarged, and their seriousness increased with their numbers, so "that it was comfortable even to see them." At his native town of Epworth he was once more allowed to receive the Lord's Supper. He preached in the open air at the Cross, for the church could not contain the people had it been open to him. Almost the whole town were present. "God has wrought," he says, "upon the whole place. Sabbath-breaking and drunkenness are no more seen in these streets; cursing and swearing are rarely heard; wickedness hides its head already. Who knows but, by and by, God may utterly take it away?" At Grimsby, where the mob had repeatedly triumphed, his hearers crowded not only the large society room, but adjacent apartments, the stairs, and the street, for "the fear of God had spread in an uncommon manner among this people also." At Newcastle, where he again spent considerable time, he found not only a great increase of members in the society, but also more spiritual life and zeal than he had ever witnessed there; and the same, he records, was true in all the neighboring country societies. At Bolton tranquillity prevailed after a violent storm of several weeks, during which many were beaten and wounded, but none turned from their steadfastness. At Bristol the society had increased to more than seven hundred members. At Leeds and Birstal his congregations were so immense that two thirds of them could not hear his voice. "Who," he asks, "would have expected such an inconvenience as this, after we had been twelve years employed in the work. Surely none will now ascribe the number of the hearers to the novelty of field preaching."

Wesley received important assistance during these times from Rev. Vincent Perronet, vicar of Shoreham, a man of saintly piety, who became his confidential counselor, and gave two sons to the itinerant ministry. Perronet's house was often the resort of both the Wesleys for consultation. He adopted their strongest views of personal religion, and wrote several pamphlets in defense of Methodism. Wesley dedicated to him the "Plain Account of the People called Methodists." During a long life, this venerable man maintained unbroken friendship with the Methodist founders, and co-operated with them in their extraordinary plans of evangelization, though they were condemned by most of the regular clergy as dangerously eccentric if not insanely fanatical. So important were his counsels in the early stages of Methodism, that Charles Wesley used to call him its Archbishop.[9]

A still more active coadjutor of the Wesleys among the regular clergy, at this time, was Rev. William Grimshaw, curate of Haworth, in Yorkshire. He had studied at Cambridge, and went from the university to his clerical duties, corrupt in his morals and unsound in his opinions. Content with the perfunctory attendance on his parish duties, he considered himself a fair example of the clerical manners of the times; especially as it is said that he refrained, as much as possible, from gross swearing, unless "in suitable company," and when he got drunk would take care to sleep it off before he went home.[10] In the twenty-sixth year of his age he was arrested in this negligent and depraved course of life by powerful religious impressions. After ten years spent in orders, and a protracted period of mental anguish, which sometimes seemed to verge on insanity, he found consolation and purification in those vital doctrines which were distinctive of the theology of Methodism, though he had not yet heard a Methodist preacher, or read a Methodist publication. In 1742 he took charge of the curacy of Haworth, and three years afterward gave in his adhesion to Wesley as one of his "Assistants."[11] He retained his parish at Haworth, but superintended two Methodist circuits which included it and extended over many towns in Yorkshire, Lancashire, and Cheshire. So thorough were his labors on these districts that they usually bore the name of "Grimshaw's circuits," and the lay itinerants the title of "Grimshaw's preachers." He regulated the Classes, renewed the Tickets, conducted the Love-feasts, and did all the other duties of a Methodist preacher. He took part in the proceedings of Wesley's Conference once in three years, when it was held at Leeds. When it sat in Bristol or

[9] Jackson's Centenary of Methodism, chap. 5.
[10] Grimshaw's Life, by Myles.
[11] Smith's History of Methodism, II, 3.

London, his incessant itinerant preaching would not admit of his attendance.[12]

He was an original character, but his eccentricities generally took a useful direction, and were combined with much humility, and with unusual charity. His Haworth parishioners are said to have been as ignorant and brutal as their country is wild and rugged, but he thoroughly reformed them. His congregations increased so much that they could not get into the church, but crowded the doorways, windows, and adjacent fields. They often melted under his preaching, and many of his hearers fell to the earth as dead men. Four hamlets were comprised in his parish; besides his regular church services, he preached in these villages four times monthly, in order to reach the aged and infirm, and such as were not disposed to attend the regular service. Frequently he would preach before the doors of such as neglected the parish worship. "If you will not come to hear me at the church," he would say on these occasions, "you shall hear me at home; if you perish you shall perish with the sound of the Gospel in your ears." He traveled over his two circuits every two weeks, often preaching thirty times a week, and whenever he was at Haworth he held a meeting in the parsonage at dawn or before it. If idlers loitered in the churchyard during worship, when the building was not crowded, he would go out while the congregation was singing, and compel them to go in. Sometimes he would escape from the church to the streets and ale-houses, and hunting out the delinquents, would drive them before him to the service. He held a Sunday evening meeting expressly for such parishioners as excused themselves from the day worship on account of their poor clothes. He sometimes disguised himself, that he might go out among his parishioners and detect and reprove their vices. To a family who were noted for their supposed liberality to the poor, he went in the character of an aged beggar and asked a night's lodging, but was

[12] By Wesley's regulations the Conference sessions were held for some years only at London, Bristol, and Leeds.

turned away with harshness: he knew how to address them afterward. He was devoted to Wesley's itinerants; his house was their home; he performed even menial services for them, and when the parsonage was crowded, as it often was by them and their religious followers, he would give up his bed and sleep in the barn. He cleaned their shoes; he opened his kitchen for their preaching; and as the rules of the Church would not allow them to be introduced into his pulpit, he built a chapel and preaching-house for them in his parish. When one of them had preached with great effect, he fell down at his feet, declaring that he was not worthy to stand in the presence of the unordained evangelist. Another he took in his arms with grateful admiration, exclaiming: "The Lord bless thee! this is worth a hundred of my sermons." He was almost recklessly liberal, denying himself of everything but the sheerest necessities of life that he might aid the poor. It was his frequent boast, "If I should die to day, I have not a penny to leave behind me." He was as honest as liberal, however, and, contrary to the expectation of his friends, died without debt. He usually rose at five o'clock in the morning, and the hour was made known through the parsonage by his voice singing the Doxology of Ken:

"Praise God from whom all blessings flow."

He lived constantly as at the gate of heaven and about to enter it; standing in the midst of his household at the close of the morning devotions, he took formal leave of them as for the last time, with the benediction, "May God bless you in your souls, and in your bodies, and in all you put your hands to-day. Whether you live or die, may the Lord grant that you may live to him, and for him, and with him forever." He was a natural orator, and often sublimely eloquent, though always intelligible to the rude population around him. He was, says one who knew him well, "the most humble walker with Christ I ever met."[13] There was a sort of reckless and boundless generosity about his eccentric nature, and it

[13] Arminian Magazine, 1795.

infected and won all who approached him. Wesley and Whitefield often visited him; and on these occasions he rallied the population of all the neighboring country. The prayers were read in the church, but as only a small portion of the assemblies could get within it, a platform was erected without for the preaching. The Lord's Supper was usually administered afterward at the altar, the congregation filling the house repeatedly to receive it.

While Wesley was prosecuting his travels during the present period, Grimshaw encountered with him a severe assault from a mob. They rode to Roughlee; again and again were they stopped on the way by their friends, who entreated them not to proceed, for the rioters were rising at Colne to meet them. They pressed forward, however, and arrived at Roughlee before the mob appeared. Wesley says he was afraid for Grimshaw; but his apprehensions were unfounded, for the heroic vicar was "ready to go to prison or death for Christ's sake." Wesley took his stand and began to preach. Before he ended his sermon the mob reached the town, and camo pouring down the hill-side like a torrent. He consulted with their leader, by whom he was borne off with Grimshaw to Barrowford, two miles distant, where "the whole army, led on with music, drew up in battle array" before the house in which they had been placed. On the way one of the rioters struck Wesley a severe blow in the face, another threw a stick at him, and another brandished a club over his head with threatening oaths. While the mob raged around the house the magistrate met Wesley and Grimshaw within, and endeavored to extort from them a pledge that they would no more visit the neighborhood. Wesley replied that he would sooner cut off his right hand than give the required promise. He and the magistrate went out at one door, Grimshaw and a friend at another; but the mob immediately crowded upon the latter, "tossed them to and fro with the utmost violence," and covered them with dirt and mire. Grimshaw was knocked down, but rose again and joined Wesley. At their request the leader of the mob undertook to conduct them back to Roughlee. They were followed by the rioters and pelted with stones and dirt. Wesley was once felled to the ground. Some quiet people who were his friends attempted to follow at a distance, in order to render him any aid that might be in their power, but they were driven away by a shower of stones. Some were trampled in the mire and dragged by the hair, others were struck with clubs. One was forced from a rock, ten or twelve feet high, into the river. Wesley and his companions reached Roughlee at last, and the next morning rode away; but one of their number was knocked from his horse while they were escaping. The news of their sufferings excited sympathy for them in the neighboring towns. "At Widdop," says Wesley, "it made us all friends;" and the same day he addressed at Heptonstall bank a vast congregation, "serious and earnest." "I lifted up my hands," he says, "and preached as I never did in my life!"[14]

Charles Wesley traveled and preached during this period as diligently as John, making several excursions to the north of England, to Wales, and to Ireland. In Cornwall he was surprised, as had been his brother, at the salutary effects of Methodism among the mining population. They crowded the Gwennap amphitheater to hear him. He examined the members of the society there separately, and found it in confirmed prosperity. "Their sufferings," he writes, "have been for the furtherance of the Gospel. The opposers behold and wonder at their steadfastness and godly conversation."[15] Four exhorters had been raised up among them. "Both sheep and shepherds," he adds, "had been scattered in the late cloudy day of persecution, but the Lord gathered them again, and kept them together by their own brethren, who began to exhort their companions, one or more in every society." At a still later date he says of Cornwall: "The whole county finds the benefit of the Gospel. Hundreds who follow not with us have broken off their sins, and are outwardly reformed; and though persecutors once, will not

[14] Journal, Anno 1748. [15] Jackson's Charles Wesley, chap. 13.

suffer a word to be spoken against this way." At St. Ives he writes that "the whole place is outwardly changed. I walk the streets scarce believing it is St. Ives. It is the same throughout all the country. All opposition falls before us, or rather is fallen, and not suffered to lift up its head again." At Sithney fierce persecution had prevailed against the society, and women and children had been struck down and beaten in the streets; now one hundred of the former rioters gathered about him to fight for him against a threatened mob from a neighboring town. At St. Just the society had been overwhelmed by repeated riots. A clergyman, who was also a magistrate, was the instigator and his brother the captain of the mob. During eighteen months the rabble had raged and apparently conquered all before them. Methodist preaching had been entirely suppressed in the town, but Charles Wesley now began it again by "crying in the street to about a thousand hearers, 'If God be for us who can be against us?'" No voice was raised against him. "The little flock," he writes, "were comforted and refreshed abundantly. I spake with each of the society, and was amazed to find them just the reverse of what they had been represented. Most of them had kept their first love even while men were riding over their heads, and they passed through fire and water. Their exhorter appeared a solid, humble Christian, raised up to stand in the gap and keep the trembling sheep together. Here is a bush in the fire, burning, and yet not consumed! What have they not done to crush this rising sect? but lo, they prevail nothing! For one preacher they cut off, twenty spring up. Neither persecutions nor threatenings, flattery nor violence, dungeons nor sufferings of various kinds can conquer them. Many waters cannot quench this little spark which the Lord hath kindled; neither shall the floods of persecution drown it."

Leaving Cornwall, he went with Edward Perronet, a son of the vicar of Shoreham, to the north of England. Young Perronet, who afterward entered the Methodist ministry, was initiated, during this excursion, into the persecutions and other trials of an itinerant preacher's life. Though mobs had subsided at their former centers, they still broke out occasionally with fierceness in other places. Perronet, however, showed good courage, and sometimes intercepted blows and missiles aimed at Wesley by receiving them himself. On their route they saluted Grimshaw, who was sick; "his soul," writes Wesley, "was full of triumphant love. I wished mine were in its place. We prayed believingly that the Lord would raise him up again for the service of his Church." They visited Newcastle and most neighboring towns, preaching in the new chapels, in cockpits, in the streets, and in the fields, and witnessing almost everywhere the prosperity of their cause. From Newcastle they passed into Lincolnshire. At Grimsby they were attacked by a mob of "wild creatures, who ran about the room striking down all they met." The uproar lasted nearly an hour. Several caught at Wesley to drag him down. He put his hand on the leader of the riot, "who sat down like a lamb at his feet," and the rest soon fell upon each other and fought themselves out of the house, leaving the preacher to proceed with his discourse. At Darlaston, the scene of former and terrible riots, he preached before a house which had been pulled down by the mob. "The persecutors in this place," he writes, "were some of the fiercest in Staffordshire. I saw the marks of their violence, and thereby knew our people's houses as I rode through the town. Their windows were all stopped up. The word was a two-edged sword. The ringleader of the mob was struck down and convinced of his lost estate. I preached again with double power."

Joined by Rev. Mr. Meriton, they set out for Bristol. At Devizes they were assailed by a terrific mob, in the midst of which the parish clergyman was conspicuous as a chief actor. It was a day, writes Wesley, never to be forgotten. The rioters broke open and ransacked a dwelling, searching for him and his companions. They were in another house, where, however, the mob soon gathered; during four or five hours the storm raged. The mayor rode out of the town in sight of the rioters, thereby indirectly encouraging them. His wife, however, sent her maid to Wesley, entreating him to escape disguised as a woman. Her heart had been touched by the conversion of her dissipated son, who had intended to desert his home for the seas, but had been reclaimed by the Methodists of the town, and was now a member of their society. Wesley declined the doubtful mode of escape which she proposed; and meanwhile the mob brought an engine, and, breaking in the windows, flooded the rooms, and spoiled the goods of the house. They demanded that Wesley should be delivered up to them, to be thrown into the horse-pond. A leading member of the society was dragged away and cast into it, and was saved from death only by the courage of one of his brethren, who ran through the mob into the water and rescued him. The tumult raged more and more around the house; the rioters got upon the roof and were tearing up the tiles; "we saw not," says Wesley, "any possible way of escape," but when the rabble seemed on the point of breaking into the dwelling, their most "respectable" leaders became alarmed for the consequences and deterred them. After a cessation of an hour or more the tumult was renewed, and more than a thousand men joined in the assault. The horses of the preachers were driven into the pond, and left up to their necks in the water. The house was again attacked front and rear. "Such threatenings, curses, and blasphemies," writes Wesley, "I had never heard." He recalled the Roman Senate, sitting in the forum, when seized by the Gauls, but told his companions there was a fitter posture for Christians. They should be taken on their knees. They knelt down and waited in prayer, believing they should "see the salvation of God." "They were now," he writes, "close to us on every side, and over our heads untiling the roof. We expected their appearance, and retired to the furthermost corner of the room; and I said, 'This is the crisis.' In that moment Jesus rebuked the winds and the seas, and there was a great calm." It lasted three quarters of an hour before any person came to inform them of the reason of the sudden change. A constable then appeared, demanding a pledge that they would visit the place no more. It was manfully refused; but they were conducted through the mob out of the town, and went on their way rejoicing to other fields of conflict and conquest.

In a few months Charles Wesley was traversing Ireland, and before the Conference of 1750 he repeated his visit. He met there, as will hereafter be shown, outrages similar to those he had so successfully braved in England, but succeeded in planting Methodism in many parts of the island.

Amid these scenes of labor and strife, the Wesleys enjoyed not a few reliefs and consolations. They had established their cause throughout the land; and it had already visibly changed the moral aspect of much of the nation, elevating the most degraded classes of its population. Tens of thousands, rescued from virtual heathenism, blessed them as they passed along their extended ministerial routes. They had, connected with their principal chapels at London, Bristol, Kingswood, Newcastle, and other places, preachers' houses or parsonages for themselves and their assistants, which, if destitute of every luxury, were nevertheless comfortably furnished, and supplied with books. They cultivated the tastes of scholars. Charles was habitually indulging his love of lyric poetry; he composed immortal odes as he rode along the highways from town to town, and mob to mob, and published several volumes during the present period. John, though preaching twice or thrice a day, beginning at five o'clock in the morning in winter as in summer, and traveling, mostly on horseback, at a rate more than equal to the circumference of the globe every five years,[16] remarked that few men enjoyed more solitude than himself. He read continually as he journeyed, not only in theology, but still more in his favorite studies of history, antiquities, and the classic poets. Both the brothers had hitherto, with brief exceptions, enjoyed good health. Charles found relief to his constitutional sadness in

[16] He traveled five thousand miles a year.

habitual travel. John, after one or two attacks of illness, was confirmed by the same salutary means in almost unvarying bodily vigor[17] and mental serenity. He assures us, about this time, that ten thousand cares were of no more inconvenience to him than so many hairs on his head, and his continually changing intercourse with families on his routes had become to them a welcome occasion, not only of religious instruction but of refreshing cheerfulness. A contemporary, who was both an eloquent scholar and a good man, and knew Wesley for more than twenty years, says that his countenance as well as conversation expressed an habitual gayety of heart, which nothing but conscious virtue and innocence could have bestowed—that he was in truth the most perfect specimen of moral happiness he had ever seen, and that his acquaintance with him taught him better than anything else he had "seen or heard or read, except in the sacred volume, what a heaven upon earth is implied in the maturity of Christian piety."[18] Extremely economical, the limited means of the brothers met all their wants. A bookseller valued their publications at this early period at £2,500. Perronet, of Shoreham, says this was not half their value.[19] The growth of Methodism had unexpectedly opened an indefinite market for their literary works. Such, however, was Wesley's charitable use of this source of income, that it is estimated he gave away in the course of his life more than a hundred and fifty thousand dollars; and such, meantime, was his Christian, not to say philosophic simplicity and frugality, that when, by order of Parliament, the Commissioners of Excise sent out circulars, demanding from families an account of their taxable plate, and addressed

[17] His severest sickness was during the next year.

[18] Alexander Knox, Esq. See his "Remarks," addressed to Southey, on Wesley's Life and Character: Appendix to Southey's Wesley. See also Knox's allusions to Wesley in his "Thirty Years' Correspondence with Bishop Jebb." Knox says Wesley was always the presiding mind at dinner parties, as well by the good-humor as the good sense of his conversation.

[19] Letter to Madam Gwynne. Jackson's Charles Wesley, chap. 16.

him a letter, saying, "We cannot doubt that you have plate for which you have hitherto neglected to make an entry," his laconic reply was, "I have two silver teaspoons at London, and two at Bristol: this is all the plate which I have at present, and I shall not buy any more while so many around me want bread."[20] In his Appeal to Men of Reason and Religion, he had said: "Hear ye this, all you who have discovered the treasures which I am to leave behind me: If I leave behind me ten pounds, (above my debts and my books, or what may happen to be due on account of them,) you and all mankind bear witness against me that I lived and died a thief and a robber." The state of his affairs at his death, nearly half a century after, fully verified this pledge.[21]

The Wesleys found domestic shelter not only at their "Preachers' Houses," but in many comfortable homes among their people; and at Shoreham with Perronet; at Bexley with Piers, its Methodist vicar, under whose roof they wrote many publications; at Haworth with Grimshaw, and occasionally with Lady Huntingdon at Donnington Park. In Wales they were entertained at the opulent mansion of Marmaduke Gwynne, a magistrate of Garth. His princely establishment usually comprised, besides his nine children and twenty servants, a chaplain, and from ten to fifteen guests. The inmates of the household formed a good congregation in the domestic worship, and the Wesleys

[20] Moore's Life of Wesley, VII, 3.

[21] Wesley was a good example of "Systematic Beneficence." He remarked in early life that he had known but four men who had not declined in religion by becoming wealthy; later in life he corrected the remark, and made no exception. He himself, therefore, guarded scrupulously against the danger. When his own income was but £30 a year he gave away £2; when it was £60 he still confined his expenses to £28, and gave away £32; when it reached £120 he kept himself to his old allowance, and gave away £92. The last insertion in his private journal, written with a trembling hand, reads thus: "For upward of eighty-six years I have kept my accounts exactly. I will not attempt it any longer, being satisfied with the continual conviction that I save all I can and give all I can; that is, all I have. J. Wesley, July 16, 1790."

preached to them daily while seeking repose amid their liberal hospitality. Mr. Gwynne zealously promoted their peculiar views. He was one of the first influential citizens of Wales who had befriended Howell Harris in his evangelical labors. When Harris was first expected to preach near Garth Mr. Gwynne was determined to arrest him, not doubting from the current reports that he was a madman, or "an incendiary in Church and state." He went out with the Riot Act in his pocket, but said to his lady as he left her: "I will hear him for myself before I commit him." The sermon, however, was so orthodox and powerful that the magistrate was deeply affected, and "thought the preacher resembled one of the apostles." At its conclusion he stepped up to Harris, took him by the hand, and expressing his favorable disappointment, asked his pardon, bade him Godspeed among the people, and, to the surprise of the assembly, invited him to accompany him back to Garth to supper. The Principality owes to his munificent zeal much of the evangelical improvement which Methodism, Calvinistic and Arminian, has effected among its population.[22] He traveled with and protected the evangelists, and his name is printed in Wesley's early Minutes as a lay member of one of his Conferences.

On the eighth of April, 1749, Charles Wesley married Sarah Gwynne, a daughter of this excellent family. The good vicar of Shoreham had advised the marriage, and promoted it by letters to her parents. John Wesley approved it, and consecrated the ceremony. He describes the scene in his Journal as one "which became the dignity of a Christian marriage." Charles said his brother "seemed the happiest person among us." Their union was in all respects a fortunate one; neither of the parties ever had any reason to regret it. They established a comfortable, but simple home at Bristol, where Mrs. Wesley hospitably

22 "The authority and countenance of Mr. Gwynne and his family now became highly important to the cause of religion." Life and Times of Selina Countess of Huntingdon," etc., chap. 7.

entertained the lay preachers on their journeys; and notwithstanding her cultivated tastes, learned to admire as among the noblest of men, Nelson, Downes, Shent, and their heroic fellow-laborers.[23] To the end of her life, it is said, she spoke with emotion of these humble, but, in many respects, genuinely great and apostolic evangelists. Her religious temper was in harmony with that of her husband. She often accompanied him in his ministerial travels. She was not only admired but beloved by her humbler sisters of the societies, and throughout her husband's life rendered his home a sanctuary of repose from his labors, and of sympathy for his affections.

John Wesley himself found it not impossible, at this stage of Methodism, to hope for the blessed consolations of conjugal life. He had designed to marry, in 1749, Mrs. Grace Murray, his housekeeper at Newcastle, a lady every way fitted for him. She was, however, previously engaged to John Bennet, one of his lay preachers, and by the counsels of Charles Wesley, Whitefield, and others, adhered to her first engagement. Wesley felt profoundly his disappointment, and afterward contracted a marriage which was the severest misfortune of his life.[24]

[23] Jackson's Charles Wesley, chap. 16.

[24] The anonymous author of "Life and Times of Lady Huntingdon," (vol. i, chap. 3,) says of Grace Murray that "she possessed superior personal accomplishments, with a mind cultivated by education, and an imagination brilliant and lively in the highest degree. She was employed by Mr. Wesley to organize his female societies, and for this purpose she traveled through various parts of both England and Ireland. Mr. Wesley used to call her his right hand."

CHAPTER III.

INTRODUCTION OF METHODISM INTO IRELAND.

Religious Problem of Irish History — Wesley comprehended it — Bishop Berkeley on Irish Evangelization — Wesley arrives at Dublin — His Views of the Irish Character — Charles Wesley in Ireland — Mobs and Murders in Dublin — "Swaddlers" — Power of Methodist Music — Second Visit of John Wesley — He itinerates in the Country — Second Visit of Charles Wesley — Riotous Persecutions at Cork — Presentment by the Grand Jury against Charles Wesley — Triumphs of Methodism — Singular Conversions — John Smith at Glenarm — Persecution and Death of John M'Burney — Hard Fare of the Preachers — Robert Swindells — Thomas Walsh — Sketch of his Life — His Conversion from Popery — His Biblical Learning — Instances of the Power of his Preaching — He is mobbed and imprisoned.

The religious condition of Ireland has been the most singular anomaly of European history since the Reformation. That great revolution had a more positive effect on Scotland than on England itself; on Ireland it had scarcely any other than a disastrous influence. Ireland refused the Reformation, and has ever since been blighted under the retributive consequences of its pertinacious adherence to the Church of Rome. It is the only country, it has been said, in which the Reformation produced nothing but evil.[1] Its obstinate tenacity for Popery prevented its assimilation with the rest of the empire, and thence have chiefly arisen those abuses in its political administration which have filled its history with oppression, tumult, and wretchedness. These have again exasperated and confirmed its Papal proclivities, and have thus acted and reacted in its continual degradation.

Wesley on his first visit to Ireland comprehended the problem of its religious history; he observed that at least

[1] Southey's Life of Wesley, chap. 23.

ninety-nine in a hundred of the native Irish remained in the religion of their forefathers. The Protestants, whether in Dublin or elsewhere, had almost all been transplanted from England. "Nor is it any wonder," he adds, "that those who are born Papists generally live and die such, when the Protestants can find no better ways to convert them than penal laws and acts of Parliament."[2]

Twelve years before Wesley's arrival an Irish Protestant prelate published a work[3] in which he suggested, as the best means for the conversion of the country, substantially the same measures which Methodism provided—Lay instructors taken from the common people, and thereby the better able to reach them. The clerical gradations of the Church of Rome, from Cardinals down to Mendicants, suited, he remarked, her ministrations to all ranks of men; her poor clergy were very useful in missions, and of "especial influence with the people;" and he asked the questions whether, in default of abler missionaries, persons conversant with low life and speaking the Irish tongue, if well instructed in the first principles of religion and in the Popish controversy, though for the rest on a level with the parish clerks or the schoolmasters of charity schools, might not be fit to mix with the poor illiterate natives, and bring them over to the Established Church; whether it were not to be wished that some parts of the Liturgy and Homilies should be publicly read in the Irish language, and whether with these views it might not be desirable to train up some of the better sort of children in the the charity schools to be missionaries, catechists, and readers.[4]

[2] Journal, August 15, 1747.

[3] Berkeley's Querist. Southey's Wesley, chap. 23.

[4] Southey admits "that what Berkeley desired to see, Methodism would exactly have supplied, could it have been taken into the service of the Church; and this might have been done in Ireland, had it not been for the follies and extravagances by which it had rendered itself obnoxious in England at its commencement." The latter remark is altogether gratuitous. It was not the "follies," or rather what Southey considers "the follies of Methodism," that repelled it from the Church in England. The Wesleys and Whitefield were excluded from the pulpits of the Establishment before they adopted out-door preaching, or any other novelty which

If the progress of Methodism has not been as rapid in Ireland as elsewhere, notwithstanding its adaptation in these respects, the fact is owing mostly to temporary and political causes, which have perpetuated to our day the resentments and Papal prejudices of the people. It is claimed, however, by Methodist writers, that it is doubtful whether even the forms of Protestantism would at this day be extant in most of the country, had it not been for the energy which was infused into the Irish Protestant Churches by Wesley and his associates,[5] so universally enfeebled and tottering was the Establishment in Ireland at that time. With the political reliefs and social ameliorations of the island, Methodism has been obtaining ampler sway, and its history is important for at least its prospective results.

Wesley arrived in Dublin on Sunday the ninth of August, 1747. The bells were ringing, and he went immediately to St. Mary's Church, and in the afternoon, by arrangement with the curate, preached to "as gay and careless a congregation" as he had ever seen. The curate treated him politely, but was immovably prejudiced against his employment of lay preachers, and assured him that the archbishop was equally opposed to so extraordinary a novelty. Wesley sought the archbishop, and had an interview with him ten miles from the city. Two or three hours were spent in the consultation, during which the prelate advanced, and Wesley answered "abundance of objections." Had Berkeley been the bishop Methodism would probably have taken possession of the Church. Wesley gives us no information of the result of the interview; he immediately began, however, his usual course of independent labors.[6]

A lay preacher from England, Thomas Williams, had formed a society in Dublin in 1747.[7] Wesley found in it

Southey would call a "folly." The zealous and home directed style with which they preached the doctrines of the English Articles and Homilies arrayed the clergy and church-wardens against them, and this opposition compelled them to their "follies and extravagances," so called.

[5] Jackson's Life of Charles Wesley, chap. 15.

[6] Journal, August 11, 1747. [7] Myles's Chronological History, p. 56.

nearly three hundred members. He examined them personally, as was his habit in the principal societies at London, Bristol, and Newcastle; for none of his "assistants" or successors has been more minute and faithful in such pastoral labors.[8] He found them "strong in faith," and admired their docile and cordial spirit. He pronounced the Irish the politest people he had ever seen. "What a nation," he exclaims, "is this; every man, woman, and child, except a few of the great vulgar, not only patiently, but gladly suffers the word of exhortation." He had not yet fully learned their character; the "roaring lion," as he afterward found, "shook himself here also."

He preached repeatedly and without molestation at the society's chapel, which had been a Lutheran church. The house and its yard were crowded with respectful hearers; many wealthy citizens were present, and his reception contrasted strikingly with what it had been in most places in England. "If," he wrote, "my brother or I could have been here for a few months, I question if there might not have been a larger society in Dublin than even in London itself." The excessive cordiality of the people soon became a reason of some solicitude to him; "on that very account," he says, "they must be watched over with the more care, being equally susceptible of good or ill impressions." Having spent two weeks among them he preached his farewell discourse to an immense assembly, many of whom could not hear him, and took passage for England on Sunday, the 23d of August.

In about two weeks Charles Wesley arrived in Dublin, accompanied by Charles Perronet, another of the sons of the Shoreham vicar, and remained more than half a year in

[8] Smith (History of Methodism, II, 8) says: "The steady and zealous attention of Wesley to the character, conduct, and spiritual state of the individual members of his societies is truly remarkable. In 1745 he carefully examined the society in London one by one, and wrote a list of the whole with his own hand, numbered from one to two thousand and eight. In 1746 he repeated this operation, and wrote another list, in which the number was reduced to one thousand nine hundred and thirty-nine."

the country. During the brief interval since the visit of his brother, the "roaring lion" had raged in Dublin. A Papist mob had broken into the chapel, and some storehouses which appertained to its premises, destroying furniture, stealing goods, making a bonfire of the seats, window cases, and pulpit in the streets; wounding with clubs the members of the society, and threatening to murder all who assembled with them. It was, in fine, a thoroughly Irish riot, bristling with shillalahs and triumphant with noise. The mayor was disposed to protect the Methodists, but was powerless before the great numerical force of their persecutors. The grand jury threw out bills brought against the rioters, and thus gave indirect encouragement to their violence. Wesley met the society privately, but was followed through the streets to his lodgings by a retinue of the rabble, who complimented him with shouts of derision.

John Cennick had preached a Christmas sermon in Dublin on "the babe wrapped in swaddling clothes, lying in a manger." A popish hearer, who knew little or nothing of his Bible, deemed the text a ridiculous Protestant invention, and called the Methodists "Swaddlers," a title which was immediately adopted by the mob. "Swaddler! swaddler!" was shouted against Wesley by the children in the streets. "The word," he says, "sticks to us all, not excepting the clergy."[9] He faced the persecutors with his usual courage. Meeting privately with the society, and weeping with and comforting them, he went forth also daily to the public parks, and preached the word amid shouts and showers of stones. After having been more than a week in Dublin, struggling daily against the fiercest odds, he writes: "Woe is me now, for my soul is wearied because of the murderers which the city is full of." The mob, he says, seldom parted without killing one or more persons. A Methodist was knocked down, cut severely in several places, and thrown into a cellar, where stones were cast

[9] Jackson's Charles Wesley, chap. 14.

upon him. One of Cennick's Calvinistic brethren, a feeble man, was so abused by his neighbors, who prostrated and stamped upon him, that he died. The murderers were tried, but acquitted, "as usual," says Wesley. A woman was beaten to death by the rioters in one of his open-air assemblies. A constable, who was present to protect him, was knocked down, dragged on the earth till dead, and then hung up with triumph, and no one was called in question for the deed. Wesley himself was in the midst of perils, but escaped without a blow, except once, when he was stoned through the length of a street or two, and though screened by young Perronet, who interposed his own person as a shield for him, was struck by a missile. Their firmness, however, could discourage even an Irish mob. They were heard at last on the public green with quiet; and Wesley was able finally to record that never had he seen a more respectful congregation at the Foundry in London than at the Dublin green and in the society meetings at night. The word, he writes, came with power irresistible, and the prayers and sobs of the people often drowned his voice. Additions were almost daily made to the band of converts, and the "bulk of the communicants" at St. Patrick's were usually Methodists, led forward to the altar by Wesley himself. He preached continually, and sometimes five times a day. He collected subscriptions, and erected a better house of worship, and addressing the afflicted but growing company of believers for the last time before they left their chapel in Marlborough-street, he encouraged them from the appropriate text: "These are they that came out of great tribulation." It was, he writes, a day of "solemn rejoicing in hope of His coming to wipe all tears from our eyes." Thus, while the Gospel reclaimed them, did persecution bind them together in common sympathy under their common sufferings, and augment among them the fervor, simplicity, unworldliness, and mutual tenderness, which marked so distinctly the primitive character of Methodism, compelling even their enemies to wonder, and exclaim, See how these Christians suffer and love!

Several preachers had been sent out into the country, and news came of great "awakenings" in various places. Wesley set out for the interior. He heard the Methodist tunes sung or whistled by Catholic children on his route.[10] At Tyrrell's Pass the town crowded out to hear him. "Never," he writes, "have I spoken to more hungry souls. They devoured every word. Some expressed their satisfaction in a way peculiar to them, and *whistled* for joy. Few such feasts have I had since I left England. It refreshed my body more than meat or drink. God has begun a great work here. The people of Tyrell's

[10] The Wesleyan singing was a source of great power to early Methodism. Charles Wesley's hymns, with simple but effective tunes, spread everywhere among the societies; and hundreds of hearers who cared not for the preaching, were charmed to the Methodist assemblies by their music. It secured them much success among the susceptible Irish. A curious example of its power is told by one of the Irish preachers. At Wexford the society was persecuted by Papists, and met in a closed barn. One of the persecutors had agreed to conceal himself within it beforehand, that he might open the door to his comrades after the people were assembled. He crept into a sack hard by the door. The singing commenced, but the Hibernian was so taken with the music that he thought he would hear it through before disturbing the meeting. He was so much gratified that at its conclusion he thought he would hear the prayer also; but this was too powerful for him; he was seized with remorse and trembling, and roared out with such dismay as to appal the congregation, who began to believe that Satan himself was in the sack. The sack was at last pulled off of him, and disclosed the Irishman, a weeping penitent, praying with all his might. He was permanently converted. (Arminian Magazine, 1781, p. 474.) Southey remarks that "this is the most comical case of instantaneous conversion that ever was recorded; and yet the man is said to have been thoroughly converted." A tavern-keeper, relishing music, went to one of the meetings merely to hear the singing. He was afraid of the preaching, and that he might not hear it, sat with his head inclined, and his fingers in his ears. But a fly lit upon his nose, and at the moment he attempted to drive it away with one of his hands the preacher uttered with power the text: "He that hath ears to hear, let him hear." The word took hold upon the publican's conscience, and he found no relief till he became a converted man. (Sketches and Incidents, etc., p. 335.) Such anecdotes abound in the publications of Methodism, and are not without historical significance as illustrations of its *modus operandi.*

Pass were wicked to a proverb—swearers, drunkards, Sabbath-breakers, thieves, etc., from time immemorial. But now the scene is entirely changed. Not an oath is heard, nor a drunkard seen among them. They are turned from darkness to light. Near one hundred are joined in society, and following hard after the pardoning God." At Athlone he was mobbed and struck with a stone, while one of his companions was knocked from his horse, and severely wounded. The mob had been roused by a Roman priest; many Protestants turned out in favor of the Methodists, and the encounter became so perilous that the dragoons had to interfere. Wesley walked through the agitated mass to the market-house, but it could not accommodate a third of his hearers. He took his stand, therefore, in the window of a dilapidated building, and proclaimed his message to them. At Moat he preached amid weeping listeners, while the mob threw stones, and tried to drown his voice with drums. At Phillipstown he was welcomed by a party of dragoons, who "were all turned from darkness to light," and had been formed into a Methodist society. Returning to Dublin, he found that continual accessions were made to the society. His brother having arrived, Charles Wesley left for England with the benedictions of hundreds who had found his word "the power of God unto salvation." Methodism had entered Ireland never to be overthrown there.

John Wesley reached Dublin on his second visit, in company with his clerical friend, Meriton, and Robert Swindells, a lay preacher, March 8, 1748. He entered the new place of worship in Cork-street while his brother was conducting the devotions of the society, and immediately proceeded to preach. But such was their joy on seeing him again among them, that, he writes, his "voice could hardly be heard for some time, for the noise of the people in praising God." He found nearly four hundred persons united in the fellowship of the Classes. He preached daily, beginning at five o'clock in the morning, a measure unheard of among the dilatory Irish, but successful wherever he went. He was undisturbed on the public green, for the Dublin mob had, at last, been conquered. He passed rapidly among the country towns. At Phillipstown he confirmed the society of Methodist dragoons, and preached in a street full of attentive hearers; at Tullamore, to most of the inhabitants of the place; at Clara, to a vast congregation, many being wealthy families in their coaches; at Athlone, from the window of the unoccupied house where his brother had stood, to an assembly immense but perfectly respectful. "I scarce ever saw," he says, "a better behaved or more attentive congregation. Indeed, so civil a people as the Irish in general I never saw, either in Europe or America." So large an assembly as he addressed there the next day had never, he says, been seen in Athlone, and most of them were Papists. He was still astonished at their Irish cordiality. "Most of the congregation," he says, "were in tears." Indeed, almost all the town appeared to be moved, being full of good-will and desires for salvation, but, he adds, "the waters spread too wide to be deep; I found not one under very strong conviction, much less had any attained the knowledge of salvation in hearing thirty sermons." He now, in fine, perceived the real Irish character, and formed no very sanguine hopes of the immediate success of Methodism, though he knew that, could it be generally established in the country, it would ultimately achieve there its noblest results. He was astonished at the simple frankness of his converts, and had some difficulty in restraining it within decorous limits. Examining one of the classes, he says he found a surprising openness among them. He asked one of them in particular how he had lived in time past; the honest man spread abroad his hands and said, with many tears, "Here I stand, a gray-headed monster of all manner of wickedness," "which," says Wesley, "I verily believe, had it been desired, he would have explained before them all." Much in the same manner spoke one who came from Connaught, but with "huge affliction and dismay."

Traveling rapidly from town to town he soon returned to Athlone, where he again addressed a vast congregation, most of whom were Romanists. Their priest came among them and drove them away before him like a flock of sheep. Wesley admired their friendly attention, but could perceive none of the profound effects which attended his discourses among the sturdier sinners of England. He therefore preached in the evening on a threatening text; a fact which, so far as can be traced in his Journal, had occurred seldom, if at all, since his conversion in 1738. "I preached," he writes, "on the terrors of the Lord in the strongest manner I was able; but still, they who are ready to eat up every word do not appear to digest any part of it." At a subsequent visit he saw, however, some good results from his labors, for a society had been formed, and he preached in the market-place to a large congregation of Papists as well as Protestants. He describes them as "an immeasurably loving people," and it was difficult for him to escape from them. When he thought he had effectually done so he found, at a mile's distance from the town, a multitude awaiting him on a hill-top over which the road passed. They opened the way for him till he had reached their midst, then closed, and would not let him proceed till he had united with them in singing several verses. When he left, men, women, and children lifted up their voices and wept as he "never heard before;" his heart was touched by their affectionate simplicity; "yet a little while," he said, "and we shall meet to part no more, and sorrow and sighing shall flee away forever." At Tullamore the next day the people would not cover their heads in a hail-storm while he preached, though he requested them to do so. At Edinderry he found much good had been done by his lay assistants, but it was not as profound or vivid as he had expected; "I see," he remarks, "nothing yet but drops before a shower."

After spending three months in traversing Ireland, he returned to England. Numerous societies had been formed, and a corps of preachers distributed through the country. In about two months Charles Wesley again visited Dublin, where the society had greatly prospered. He left it quickly for Cork, where the lay preachers had met with much success. He was astonished to observe the impression which they had produced. A visible reformation had taken place in the morals of the populace; "swearing was seldom heard in the streets," and the churches and altars were crowded, to the astonishment of opposers.[11] He took the open field and preached to ten thousand hearers, Protestants and Papists, high and low. Two hundred members were enrolled in the society, yet he had occasion to repeat his brother's complaint of the superficiality of their religious character, for "all seemed awakened, but not one of them justified." The door appeared wide open for him, however, and he writes that even at Newcastle the awakening had not been so general. The city clergy turned out to hear him with unexpected favor; he was astonished at his multitudinous congregations, but asked himself, "How few will own God's messengers when the stream turns?" He knew human nature too well to suppose that this hearty good-will, natural as it was to the Irish character, could long resist the capricious mutability which is equally natural to it; and as soon as he began to gather genuine converts into the society, he prepared for the usual outbreaks of hostility. "Hitherto," he says, "they seem asleep, but the witnesses of Jesus are rising to rouse them."

Hardly had he returned to England when the storm gathered and burst over Cork. During about three months the mob, led on by a ballad-singer by the name of Butler, and indirectly sanctioned by the mayor, kept the city in excitement by a series of riots against the Methodists. Butler arrayed himself in a clerical gown, and with his ballads in one hand and the Bible in the other, went about pretending to preach against them. The excited people, armed with swords and clubs, fell upon them without mercy; men, women, and children were knocked down in the streets, and

[11] Jackson's Charles Wesley, chap. 15.

not a few of them dangerously wounded. Their houses were assailed; a member of the society, who was a well-known merchant, applied to the authorities for protection, but was sent away without redress; another member, whose house the mob were pulling down, ran to the mayor, who accompanied him to the spot, but amid the rioters cried out to the helpless Methodists, "It is your own fault for entertaining your preachers; if you will turn them out of your houses, I will engage that no harm shall be done, but if you will not you must take the consequences." A respectable Methodist citizen replied, very relevantly, that this was extraordinary usage for a Protestant government; that had he a Roman priest saying mass in every room of his house it would not be touched. The only response of the mayor was that the priests were protected, but the Methodists were not. The crowd, hearing the reply, huzzaed, threw stones faster than ever, and attacked the house until midnight.

The pusillanimous conduct of the authorities continued to inspirit the mob. Butler ranged the streets, armed with ballads and the Bible, and followed by drunken throngs shouting "Five pounds for the head of a swaddler." An Amazonian woman, indignant at the cowardice of the magistrates, attempted to interfere, but was carried away and inclosed in Bridewell. Twenty-eight depositions were presented to the grand jury at the Assizes against these disgraceful proceedings, but they were all thrown out, and the jury made "a remarkable presentment," which still stands on the city records, and which declares that "we find and present Charles Wesley to be a person of ill-fame, a vagabond, and a common disturber of his majesty's peace, and we pray that he may be transported." Nine of his associates were denounced in the same terms. All were preachers except one, whose crime was his hospitality in entertaining the itinerants. Butler and his crew were now more triumphant than ever; but at the Lent Assize all the preachers who were in the kingdom, or at least all who had been in Cork, presented themselves in a body before the court. They had now to deal with a higher authority, the king's judges. Butler was the first witness; to the question, What is your calling? he responded, "I sing ballads." "Here," exclaimed the judge, lifting up his hands indignantly, "here are six gentlemen indicted as vagabonds, and the first accuser is a vagabond by profession!" The second accuser replied he was "an anti-swaddler," and treated the court with such disrespect that he was ordered away for contempt. The preachers were triumphantly vindicated, but the reign of the mob was not over. John Wesley returned to Cork in 1750, and was assailed with terrible violence. The furniture, windows, and floor of the chapel were torn out and burned in the street. He went to Bandon to preach, but the Cork mob followed him thither in grand procession and hung him in effigy.[12] During nearly a week the rioters prevailed, unchecked if not encouraged by the mayor. They patrolled the streets with shouts and menaces, and one of them affixed an advertisement at the Exchange, subscribed with his name, proposing assaults on the houses of "Swaddlers," or of any citizens who dared to entertain them. But the excitement exhausted itself at last; many of the soldiers in garrison at Cork attended the Methodist preaching; soldiers made stanch Methodist converts in those stormy days, and the mob became afraid of them. Butler then went to Waterford and raised similar riots there, but in a quarrel with his associates lost an arm, and lingered out the remainder of his life disabled and miserable.

John Wesley afterward visited the city without molestation. Methodism took permanent root there; a spacious chapel was soon erected, and there are few places, says his Irish biographer,[13] where religion has prospered more than in Cork; "Being reviled for the name of Christ, the spirit of glory and of God has rested upon them, and many have been there the living and dying witnesses of the power of true religion." On a subsequent visit Wesley was received at the mansion-house by the mayor, and his presence

[12] Moore's Life of Wesley, VI, 1. [13] Ibid.

was considered an honor to the city. So advanced, in fine, did Methodism become in its social position in Cork, that five years later Wesley dreaded that city as the Capua of his preachers.[14]

It spread, meanwhile, rapidly over the country. It was permanently founded about this time, not only in the three southern counties, but also among the mountains of Ulster, where it found sympathy, and wrought its usual good effects, among the poorer classes of Protestants. Circuits were formed and regularly supplied, and several effective native preachers were raised up. The peculiar susceptibility of the Irish character afforded continually striking cases of conversion. "Are there any drunkards here?" cried an itinerant, as he preached amid a mongrel multitude. "Yes, I am one," replied a sobbing Irishman, who, returning intoxicated toward his home had stepped aside to the assembly, supposing it was witnessing a cock-fight, and from that day he was not only reclaimed from his long-confirmed vice, but became a genuine Christian.[15] Some poor natives who could not understand the English language of the itinerants, were awakened and effectually turned to a religious life by the force of their earnest manner of address. A deaf mute of the county of Antrim was thus reclaimed from a life of excessive profligacy in the twenty-fifth year of his age. He had been notoriously addicted to cock-fighting, horse-racing, drunkenness, and other vices, but became an upright citizen, a devoted member of the Methodist society, and its successful promoter among his townsmen. Unable to speak the word of exhortation to his neighbors, he preached by his exemplary life, and whenever the preacher or class-leader was expected in the town, he watched for his arrival, and hastened from house to house to summon the people to the place of prayer. His business had required him to work on the Sabbath, but on becoming a Methodist he would no more do violence to the Lord's day. Unable to read, he nevertheless learned, by the aid of his Christian brethren, the

[14] Journal, Anno 1755. [15] Arminian Magazine, 1781, p. 478.

precious promises, and their place in the sacred volume, and would often turn to them with "a wild screaming voice and floods of tears."[16]

In some towns Methodism secured a permanent lodgment in the most unexpected manner. John Smith, a zealous preacher, who had been rescued from desperate vices, felt "pressed in spirit" to preach in Glenarm, a neglected town among the mountains of the north. As he rode up to make his evangelical assault on the place he met a young lady who was riding with a servant. In reply to his inquiries, she warned him that it was a very wicked community. "Are there no good men there?" inquired the Methodist. "Yes, there is one, Wilber Hunter," was her only encouragement. Riding into the town, he inquired for the house of the one pious townsman. At the door he met a young woman, and directed his horse to be taken to the inn; "and tell every one you meet," he added, "that a visitor at your house has good news to tell all at seven o'clock." At the hour the house was filled. The eccentric evangelist was heartily welcomed by the warm-hearted Irishmen. They detained him nine days, preaching to them twice daily, and a society was then formed which continues to the present time. When he was about to depart he had but threepence in his pocket. He asked his landlady what he was to pay for his horse? "Nothing, sir," she replied; "a gentleman has paid all, and will do so if you stay a month." The whole incident was genuinely Irish.[17]

Mobs, however, continued for some time to alternate with such semi-humorous scenes of Hibernian good-nature, and they occasionally assumed a frightful and perilous severity. Another of them at least was fatal, and afforded Methodism

[16] Arminian Magazine, 1794, p. 439.

[17] Coke's and Moore Life of Wesley, III, 1. This work must be distinguished from Moore's Life of Wesley, a later production, which does not contain the facts referred to. The zealous John Smith died in the faith in 1772. Myles (Chron. Hist.) says: "He was a remarkably useful man; many hundreds were converted by his instrumentality, upward of twenty of whom became preachers."

its first Irish martyr. John M'Burney deviated sometimes from his circuit to preach in the market-place at Clones. Many people attended, and much good was done; but the Papists took alarm, and, assembling the rabble, persecuted the assembly so violently that it was feared the worship must be abandoned, especially as no magistrate would interfere. When about to give up, a singular incident occurred to restore confidence to the worshipers. A veteran military pensioner astonished the preacher and his friends by taking his post at a tree in the market-place, musket in hand, and proclaiming with a terrible oath that he would shoot the first man who should pass the tree to disturb the meeting. He was a Scotchman, wicked, but with high hereditary notions of religious decorum, and good courage to maintain them. "His word," says a contemporary writer, "was certainly attended with power of some kind, for not one of the rioters, although they shouted from a distance, attempted to pass the prescribed limits." The stanch old soldier mounted guard at the tree regularly at every visit of the preacher for several weeks, until he had completely won the field. "What strange instruments," writes a Methodist preacher who recorded the case on the spot, "what strange instruments are sometimes raised up to prevent or defeat the designs of hell!"[18] But the cowed rioters sought revenge elsewhere. M'Burney attempted to preach near the neighbouring village of Enniskillen. While the congregation was singing, the mob, armed with clubs, rushed in, breaking the windows and violently thrusting out men and women. The preacher was knocked down and dragged on the earth. He lay for some time senseless under the blows of the rioters. On becoming conscious he attempted to rise, but staggered and fell again. A ruffian set his foot upon his face, swearing he would "tread the Holy Ghost out of him." "May God forgive you, I do," exclaimed the sufferer, as soon as he could speak. He was then placed upon his horse, and one of the rioters

[18] Life of Rev. Henry Moore, p. 48.

mounting behind him, drove him impetuously down the mountain side to the town, where he was rescued by a hospitable citizen. Preaching as long as he had strength, and rejoicing that he had been counted worthy to suffer for Christ, he died at last of the injuries thus received, and claims in the history of Irish Methodism the honorable rank accorded to Thomas Beard in that of England.

Notwithstanding their frequent riots, Wesley always contended that the Irish were the politest people he had ever met; and that in their wretched cabins could be seen as thorough courtesy as at the courts of London or Paris. "The damp, dirty, smoky cabins of Ulster," said one of the preachers, "were a good trial; but what makes double amends for all these inconveniences, to any preacher who loves the word of God, is, that our people here are in general the most zealous, lively, affectionate Christians in the kingdom." "I had many an aching head and pained breast," wrote another, "but it was delightful to see hundreds attending to my blundering preaching with streaming eyes and attention as still as night." [19]

Methodism won many converts from Popery, and from among them secured one of its most distinguished early preachers, an extraordinary man, whose name, fragrant with saintly associations, still lingers as a household word among its families in both hemispheres. While Robert Swindells, a devoted lay preacher,[20] who, as we have seen, accompanied

[19] Southey's Wesley, chap, 24.

[20] Swindells was one of Wesley's best lay itinerants; he began to preach in 1741, and died in the Itinerancy in 1783. (Myles's Chron. Hist. of the Methodists, p. 297.) In the obituary of the Minutes for 1783, Wesley says: "He had been with us above forty years. He was an Israelite indeed. In all these years I never knew him to speak a word which he did not mean, and he always spoke the truth in love. I believe no one ever heard him speak an unkind word. He went through exquisite pain (by the stone) for many years, but he was not weary. One thing was almost peculiar to himself, he had no enemy; so remarkably was that word fulfilled, 'Blessed are the merciful, for they shall obtain mercy.'" (Arminian Magazine, 1784, p. 621.) Besides his connection with the conversion of Thomas Walsh, this good man did important service for

Wesley to Ireland in 1748, was addressing a large congregation on the parade ground at Limerick in 1749, a young man who had been trained a strict Roman Catholic, but whose intelligent and melancholy aspect betrayed an unsettled and inquiring mind, took his stand amid the throng, attracted among them not more by the novelty of the scene than by the hope that some words appropriate to his religious anxieties might be uttered by the humble preacher. The needed word was uttered, for the text of the itinerant was: "Come unto me all ye that labor and are heavy laden and I will give you rest." Twenty years later John Wesley wrote, respecting this Irish youth, that he knew a young man who was so thoroughly acquainted with the Bible that if he was questioned concerning any Hebrew word in the Old, or any Greek in the New Testament, he would tell, after a brief pause, not only how often the one or the other occurred in the Bible, but what it meant in every place. Such a master of Biblical knowledge he says he never saw before, and never expected to see again. His name was Thomas Walsh. His parents were rigorous Romanists; when a child they taught him the Lord's Prayer and the Ave Maria in Irish, (his native tongue,) and also the one hundredth Psalm in Latin. He learned English in his eighth year, and afterward the Latin grammar, under the tuition of his brother, a school teacher, designed for the Papal priesthood, but who, by reading the Scriptures, had discovered reasons for abandoning the faith of his family. Young Walsh, whose temper was constitutionally serious, if not melancholy, had deep religious solicitudes in his childhood. He describes himself as often terrified by his apprehensions of death and the future state, and as strict in his religious exercises, but "a small part of them only was addressed to God, the rest to saints and angels."[21] From his fourteenth

Methodism in Ireland. He deserves a fuller notice, but I have been unable to find any available records for it.

[21] Life of Thomas Walsh, composed in great part from his own accounts, by James Morgan. New York, 1843.

to his sixteenth year he was more than ever devoted to the requirements of his faith, particularly the Mass. He was scrupulous against most ordinary vices, especially profanity, except the petty forms of it, with which the native Irish language abounds more than any other tongue. Meanwhile his religious impressions deepened and became intense. "The arrows of the Almighty," he says, "stuck fast in me, and my very bones trembled because of my sins." He confessed to his priest, who advised "many prayers," but seemed not to comprehend his case. He strove to divert himself by recreations, but "a hell," he says, "opened in my breast." He fasted rigorously and prayed incessantly, and in his agony sometimes threw himself upon the ground, tearing the hair from his head. He records with morbid scrupulosity his failings and sins; the Confessions of Augustine scarcely surpass these brief records in candor and compunction; yet he says he "was as one who beateth the air," as he had not the Bible to instruct him.

In his eighteenth year the conversations of his brother led him to serious doubts respecting the pretensions of Popery. It had afforded his awakened mind no satisfactory relief, and his intelligence revolted from its manifest absurdities In an appointed interview with his brother and other Protestant friends, at which the Bible and Nelson's Feasts and Fasts of the Church of England were consulted and discussed till midnight, he was constrained, he says, "to give place to the light of truth." About one o'clock in the morning he returned to his lodgings, fell upon his knees, and for the first time prayed to God alone. No saint or angel was ever again invoked by him, for he was now convinced that "*there is but one God, and one mediator between God and man, the man Christ Jesus.*" He resolved, he says, to suffer no man to beguile him again into a voluntary humility in worshiping either saints or angels. His father attempted to reclaim him, but could not answer his arguments. His candid reading of the Scriptures entirely overthrew the sophisms by which the invocation of saints and the other errors of Popery were sustained. His quick, discerning intellect was surprised at the total absence of any intimations of these errors in the divine records.

He formally abjured the creed of his family, and united with the Established Church. But his sincere heart was full of charity; he speaks of the Papists in language which is unusual to such converts: "I bear them witness," he writes, "that they have a zeal for God, though not according to knowledge. Many of them have justice, mercy, and truth, and may, (notwithstanding many errors in sentiment, and therefore in practice, through invincible ignorance,) be dealt with accordingly, since as is God's majesty so is his mercy." He believed that after his enlightenment he could not be saved among them, but that earnest men who had not been thus convinced, would be accepted of God in their communion; and he dismisses the subject with a pathetic prayer in their behalf, which might well be substituted for much of the severity and dogmatism with which they are commonly treated. His renunciation of Popery relieved him of many superstitious troubles of mind, but deepened his religious anxiety. His conscience, he says, still condemned him; "There was no rest in my bones, by reason of my sin." It was in this state of mind that he heard Robert Swindells proclaim on the parade-ground at Limerick, "Come unto me all ye that labor and are heavy laden."

The evangelical itinerants soon penetrated to his native village of Newmarket. He welcomed them and joined the little Methodist society there; and now, he says, a purer light began to dawn upon him, for he saw not his "guilt only, but the all-sufficiency of Christ." The itinerants, true to the genius of Methodism, wrangled not about ecclesiastical or dogmatic questions with even Papists, but proclaimed the vital doctrines of personal religion. In one of their assemblies, "I was divinely assured," he says, "that God for Christ's sake had forgiven me all my sins; the Spirit of God bore witness with my spirit that I was a child of God. I broke out into tears of joy and love;" and a friend by his side received the same consolation at the same hour.[22] He lived now, writes his biographer, as in another world. A more saintly life than he exemplified from this time down to his death cannot be found in the records of either Papal or Protestant piety. The life of Thomas Walsh, says Robert Southey, "might indeed almost convince a Catholic that saints are to be found in other communions as well as in the Church of Rome." He saw in Methodism a genuine reproduction of the apostolic Church, and he gave himself to study that he might the better promote its marvelous mission. Besides his native Irish language, he mastered the English, Latin, Greek, and Hebrew; the latter was especially a sublime delight to him, as the tongue with which God himself had originally spoken to man. He rose at four o'clock, and continued to do so the remainder of his life, to study it, and he read it often upon his knees. "O truly laudable and worthy study!" he exclaims, "whereby a man is enabled to converse with God, with holy angels, with patriarchs and prophets, and clearly to unfold to men the mind of God from the language of God!" He believed even that a divine inspiration helped him in these sacred studies; and such was his success with them, that probably no man ever excelled him in the knowledge of the word of God. His memory was a concordance of the entire Bible. No Catholic saint ever pored more assiduously or devoutly over his Breviary than did this remarkable man over the original Scriptures during the rest of his life. His studies were intermixed with ejaculations of praise and supplication. "Turning his face to the wall, and lifting up his heart and countenance to heaven, with his arms clasped about his breast, he would stand for some time before the Lord in

[22] Southey (chap. 23) refers to the passage of Scripture at the utterance of which Walsh's mind was relieved, as affording to the psychologist "a curious illustration of Methodist conversions." It was, "Who is this that cometh from Edom, with dyed garments from Bozrah; this that is glorious in his apparel, traveling in the greatness of his strength?" Southey was evidently ignorant of the evangelical application which commentators and Walsh himself gave to the sublime text.

solemn recollection, and again return to his work."[23] Meanwhile his cry was, "I fain would rest in Thee! I thirst for the divine life. I pray for the Spirit of illumination. I cast my soul upon Jesus Christ, the God of glory, and the Redeemer of the world. I desire to be conformable unto him, his friend, servant, disciple, and sacrifice!" Such was this good, this sublime man, a noble trophy won by the illiterate preachers of Methodism from the abject superstitions of Popery. In reading the brief record of his life, we seem to have before us a combination and impersonation of the Hebraic grandeur of the old prophets, the mystic piety of the papal saints, and the Scriptural intelligence and purity of Protestantism.

He contemplated with a sentiment of awe the responsibility of the Christian ministry, and entered upon it with a trembling hesitancy and humility. "Lord Jesus!" he prayed in view of it, "Lord Jesus, I lay my soul at thy feet, to be taught and governed by thee. Take the vail from the mystery, and show me the truth as it is in thyself; be thou my sun and star by day and by night." Once in the ranks of the lay ministry no contemporary member of it became more eminent for zeal, labors, or sufferings. He walked thirty miles to his first appointment, which was in a barn, and amid the contradictions and mockery of some, and the tears of others, preached with an effect that demonstrated the genuineness of his mission. He proclaimed his message with remarkable power every day for some weeks at Limerick; and his awakened hearers sometimes could not be induced to leave the spot where they heard him till they received the peace of God. He went like a flame of fire through Leinster and Connaught, preaching twice and thrice a day, usually in the open air. Multitudes of all denominations attended his ministrations, and before long he was known all around the country. His command of the Irish tongue gave him great advantage with the native Papists. They flocked to

[23] Life, etc., chap. 12.

hear their own rude but touching language; they wept, smote their breasts, and invoked the Virgin with sobbing voices, and declared themselves ready to follow him as a saint over the world. The beggars would gather around him as he passed, and, melting under his words, would kneel down in the streets and weep and pray. A Papist who had saved his earnings to leave to a priest or friar, for masses for his soul when he should be dead, called upon Walsh, begging him to take the money and the responsibility of praying his soul out of purgatory. "No man can forgive your sins," said the preacher; "the gift of God cannot be purchased with money; only the blood of Christ can cleanse from sin." The astonished Romanist was deeply affected, and cried earnestly to God, while Walsh knelt by his side, and prayed for him in Irish. A native, with whom he was conversing in English, became enraged at his religious warnings, and declared that "although he should be shot for it he would have satisfaction," adding, with an oath, "thou shalt never deceive another, for I am resolved to be the death of thee just now." Walsh immediately reproved him in Irish. "Why didst thou not speak so to me in the beginning?" exclaimed the excited man. "The lion became a lamb," says the preacher, "while I let him know in Irish what Christ had done for sinners. He departed with a broken heart."[24] When preaching in Irish, hearers who did not understand his speech were, nevertheless, sometimes smitten by his earnest and affecting manner, and an instance is related of a man who, hearing him in Dublin, was thus "cut to the heart."

It is admitted that no man contributed more than Walsh to the diffusion of Methodism in Ireland.[25] The Roman priests were alarmed at his success, and instigated mobs against him. On his way to Roscrea he was assailed by

[24] "It is an old maxim in Ireland," says Southey, "When you plead for your life, plead in Irish." "It has a peculiarly affecting expressiveness, particularly with reference to the things of God." Morgan's Life of Thomas Walsh.

[25] Southey's Wesley, chap. 23.

seventy-eight men armed with clubs; he was surprised at their illogical but Hibernian generosity, for they proposed to bring a clergyman of the English Church and a Roman priest to convert him to either faith, as he pleased, and then to let him depart in peace. He told them that he came not to discuss opinions, but to preach against the wickedness of any or all parties. This seemed incomprehensible to them. They, nevertheless, offered him his liberty if he would swear not to come to Roscrea again; but he would have suffered martyrdom rather than make such a pledge. They hurried him away, therefore, raging like wild beasts, to put him into a well, which they had secured for the purpose; but his calm and courageous bearing excited the admiration of some of the mob, and while one party cried vehemently that he should go into the water, another swore he should not. The parish minister interfered, and had him taken to an inn. The mob brought him out again, and it being market-day, he bravely took his stand among the throng in the street and began to preach; but some of the crowd seizing him by the back, hurried him out of the town. He at last got upon his horse, and, taking off his hat, prayed for some time in their midst, and then addressed them in a persuasive exhortation. "I came off from them at length," he writes, "in peace of conscience and serenity of mind." They had not conquered him; he resumed his labors in the town, and Methodism was securely planted there.

He traveled toward Cork, proclaiming the Gospel as he went. In a town near that city, sergeants, sent by a magistrate, arrived to seize him as he was about to preach beneath a tree. He opened his Bible at the text, Job xxi, 3: "*Suffer me that I may speak, and after that I have spoken, mock on.*" The officers, interested at first by the singularity of the text, and afterward by his eloquence, heard him attentively through the sermon. They then conducted him to the magistrate, who demanded a promise that he would preach there no more. He asked if there were no swearers, drunkards, and Sabbath-breakers in the town. "There are," was the reply. He refused to give the required promise, but intimated that if no reformation ensued among such offenders after he had preached there a few times, he would trouble them no more. This, however, was not satisfactory, and he was sent away to prison. The whole town seemed moved on his behalf, for his remarkable character and talents impressed all who heard him. Several persons accompanied him into the prison, where they spent the time in singing hymns. The inhabitants of the town sent bedding and provisions for him, and he preached to a multitude without, which extended as far as his voice could reach through the grated window. He afterward revisited the place repeatedly, as he had declared he would; and years later, his biographer records that there were yet remaining on the spot living fruits of his labors and sufferings. In the north of Ireland he was still more severely treated by Protestant assailants; his life was periled several weeks with a fever, occasioned by exposures in his attempt to escape his Christian persecutors.

His name became well known among the Roman Catholic churches throughout the country. The common people would hear him notwithstanding the remonstrances of their priests, and many were turned not only from Popery, but from flagrant vices to repentance and a holy life. All kinds of derogatory reports were spread abroad to deter them from his preaching. In Clonmel the priest assured his congregation that the eloquent itinerant had been a servant boy to a certain priest, and that having stolen his master's books, he had by that means learned to preach, and was now availing himself of his newly-acquired art for a better living. At Cork the Papists crowded to hear him, and many were converted; the priests were greatly irritated, and one of them affirmed publicly that "as for that Walsh, who had some time before turned heretic, and went about preaching, he had been dead long ago, and he who then preached in this way was the devil in his shape." Such was the only manner in which they could account to the ignorant multitude for the power of his discourses. The people, nevertheless, ran after him, and wept and cried aloud under his word as he proclaimed it on mountains and highways, in meadows, private houses, prisons, and ships. They often followed him when the sermon was concluded, begging for further instruction. They would come to his rooms to entreat his counsels and prayers, and kneeling down under his exhortations, would begin to call with tears upon the Virgin and Apostles, till he could check them and teach them better.

As it was Wesley's habit to transpose his preachers often, Walsh was sent to London, where he did much good among his Irish countrymen. He addressed them in their own language in Moorfields and at Short's Gardens, and they crowded to hear their native tongue so eloquently used. He preached constantly twice a day, and with such fervor that one of his intimate friends says it is scarcely possible to enable a stranger to conceive of the glow of his soul, and the energy of his spirit on these occasions; "such a sluice of divine oratory ran through the whole of his language as is rarely to be met with."[26] Wesley called him "that blessed man;" "wherever he preached," he adds, "the word, whether in English or Irish, was sharper than a two-edged sword. I do not remember ever to have known a preacher who in so few years as he remained upon earth was an instrument of converting so many sinners."[27] In London he had frequent discussions with the Jews. He attended their synagogues, and his intimate knowledge of Hebrew enabled him to reason with them out of their own original Scriptures.

During nine years did this remarkable man pursue his tireless and luminous course. It was closed at last, as we shall hereafter see, by a death of singular mental anguish, but final triumph, presenting a startling lesson well worthy the study of the best of men.

[26] Morgan's Life of Walsh, chap. 15. [27] Myles's, Chron. Hist., p. 64.

The Methodist itinerants in Ireland, visited frequently by the Wesleys, and stimulated, if not, indeed, led on, by this talented and flaming native preacher, planted their cause in most of the country. It was destined to pass through many vicissitudes, and to show its energy at times as much by endurance as by progress; but its root struck ineradicably into the soil, and it is not perhaps too much to say that it saved Protestantism in many parts of the island. Persecutions subsided; Wesley in later life was received with veneration as an apostle; "the scandal of the cross," he wrote, "has ceased, and all the kingdom, rich and poor, Papists and Protestants, behave with courtesy, nay, with good-will." He rejoiced at last over a larger society in Dublin than anywhere else in the United Kingdom, except London. He directed his course toward the island always with a peculiar interest, and the time he spent there in his numerous visits amounted to at least six years.

CHAPTER IV.

LABORS OF THE CALVINISTIC METHODISTS: 1744–1750.

Whitefield's third Visit to America — His dangerous Sickness in Maine — Testimonials against him — His Success — The Cape Breton Expedition — His Reception at Philadelphia — Singular Religious Interest in Virginia — Maryland — He goes to Bermuda — He embarks for England — Labors of Howell Harris — The Countess of Huntingdon traveling in Wales — Whitefield arrives in London — Rev. John Newton — Whitefield in Scotland — His Travels in England — Remarkable Conversion — Bishop Lavington's Attacks — Charles Wesley and Whitefield preaching amid the Alarms of Earthquakes in London.

WHILE Wesley and his Arminian colaborers were successfully spreading Methodism during the present period, Whitefield and the other Calvinistic agents of the movement were hardly less active. Whitefield re-embarked for America in August, 1744. He arrived at York, Maine, in disabled health, after a passage of eleven weeks. Three weeks he lingered between life and death, but preached repeatedly though he had to be carried like a child. After one of his sermons he was taken home and laid near the fire; his friends wept around him, and he heard them say, "He is gone." He supposed himself dying, but "recollecting," he says, "the life and power which spread all around, while expecting to stretch into eternity I thought it was worth dying for a thousand times."[1] The venerable Moody, pastor of York, still remembered for both his piety and his humor, attended him, and welcomed him in the name of "all faithful ministers in New England." But on arriving at Boston he found the good pastor's welcome not entirely veri-

[1] Philip's Life and Times of Whitefield, chap. 14.

fied. Harvard College had issued a "testimony" against him, and not a few clergymen opposed him in a similar manner. Hostile "testimonies" signed by ministers came out almost every day.[2] Fifteen pastors, assembled at Taunton, Mass., published a testimony in his favor. "But," he writes, "amid all this smoke a blessed fire broke out; the awakened souls were as eager as ever to hear." He was admitted, though with reluctance, to the pulpits of Coleman, Sewall, Webb, and Gee. He began to expound at six o'clock in the morning, as he had done in Scotland, and though this hour was now before full daylight in that latitude, he usually had two thousand hearers. He found occasion also to rejoice over the results of his former labors. Twenty pastors at least acknowledged that they had not been converted till he came among them. Tennent had been abroad itinerating since his last visit, and so extensive had been the "awakening," that many supposed the latter-day glory had come, and that a nation was to be born in a day. Fanatics marred the good work, and hence the reaction at Harvard College and elsewhere.

Whitefield's presence and eloquence could not long be resisted anywhere. Some favorable incidents also occurred to help him at this visit. An accomplished wit of the city used to entertain his convivial friends over the bottle with scraps from his sermons and imitations of his manner. He was present in the church one day to get new specimens, but when supplied could not make his way out through the crowd. The word, meanwhile, took effect on his conscience. He went afterward to one of the city pastors, "full of horror;" and seeking Whitefield, begged his pardon. Other equally remarkable conversions deepened the popular interest. The expedition against Cape Breton was preparing in the city; such at last was Whitefield's power over the populace, that Sherburne, one of the commissioners, insisted on his favoring it publicly, as "otherwise the serious people would be discouraged from enlisting." He gave them a

[2] Gillies's Memoirs of Whitefield, chap. 12.

motto for their flag,[3] after "which great numbers enlisted." They wished him to become one of their chaplains, but he had better work. He preached a sermon to them, and sent them to the North with the enthusiasm of crusaders. In six weeks news came of the fall of Louisburgh, when he delivered a thanksgiving sermon to a great multitude, who flocked from all quarters. The spirit of the Puritan commonwealth still survived in New England, and Whitefield evidently relished it.

He had now reconquered the people, if not their pastors. It was proposed to build him "the largest place of worship that was ever seen in America," but he left them for other fields: for the Eastward as far as Casco Bay; for Cape Cod as far as North Yarmouth; for Rhode Island and Connecticut; preaching twice a day to thousands. "And though," he writes, "there was much smoke, yet every day I had more and more convincing proof that a blessed Gospel fire had been kindled in the hearts of both ministers and people."

At Philadelphia he was heartily welcomed. The society which occupied the house that had been erected for him at his former visit, wished to settle him there, and offered him a salary of four hundred pounds per annum, and half the year for his itinerant labors. He found that his previous visit had left a profound effect; Gilbert Tennent's "feet were blistered" in walking to and fro visiting the awakened.[4]

He was gratefully surprised on reaching Virginia to learn that a volume of his sermons had produced an extraordinary religious interest. A gentleman who had obtained a copy invited some of his neighbors to hear them read at his house. Soon it could not accommodate the throng who gathered for the purpose every Sunday, and they erected a "meeting-house merely for reading." No one dared to offer public prayer on these occasions, as none had ever been accustomed to do so; yet deep religious convictions spread

[3] *Nil desperandum, Christo duce:* Fear nothing while Christ is Captain.
[4] Philip's Life and Times of Whitefield, chap. 14.

among them, and "they could not keep from crying out and weeping bitterly." The reader was invited abroad with his volume, and the "awakening" extended to several towns. Tennent and Blair visited them soon after; a pastor by the name of Robinson took charge of them for some time, and in 1747 there were four chapels in the neighborhood of Hanover which had sprung from this singular excitement.[5]

Whitefield passed on rapidly to his Orphan House at Bethesda, near Savannah, but paused not long there. Returning northward, his preaching was attended with great success in Maryland. "The Gospel is moving southward," he writes; "the harvest is promising; the time of the singing of birds has come." His travels in that region, including some excursions into Pennsylvania, comprised three hundred miles. "Thousands and thousands are ready to hear the Gospel," he says, "and scarce anybody goes out but myself. Now is the time for stirring!" It is not surprising that when he arrived in Philadelphia again he wrote that he had almost continually a burning fever. Yet he expresses great regret that he omitted one night, (to oblige his friends,) and purposes to do so once more, that they might not charge him with self-murder. "But," he adds, "I hope yet to die in the pulpit, *or soon after I come out of it.*" They were prophetic words.

At New York he preached with his usual power and success, and wrote, "I shall go to Boston as an arrow from a bow, if Jesus strengthen me." He was soon there, and found all opposition subdued. He wrote to Tennent that "the arrows of conviction flew and stuck fast," and that he was "determined to die fighting, though it be upon his stumps." This was enthusiasm, doubtless, but it was such

[5] Morris's Narrative. Philip's Whitefield, chap. 14. Samuel Morris was the gentleman who obtained and read the sermons. He and his associates were called Lutherans. They were required by law to attend the Established Church or take some dissenting designation. They knew not at first what title to assume, but at last chose the great Reformer's name.

enthusiasm as makes heroes. The world disdains it nowhere but in religion, where it is most befitting and most needed. With Whitefield it was no spasmodic impulse; it had lasted now more than ten years, and was to sustain him in scarcely diminished labors during a quarter of a century more, till, in accordance with his expressed hope, he should descend from the pulpit to die.

He traveled during the first tour of his present American visit about eleven hundred miles; but we cannot trace, by the slight data that remain, his repeated excursions northward and southward. They were, however, incessant. His passage among the colonies seemed as the flight of an archangel, beheld with delight and awe by the wondering people.

In 1748 he departed for the Bermudas on account of his health. Before leaving he wrote from North Carolina: "I am here hunting in the woods, these ungospelized wilds, for sinners. It is pleasant work, though my body is weak and crazy." "Pray for me," he adds, "as a dying man; but O pray that I may not go off as a *snuff*. I would fain die blazing, not with human glory, but with the love of Jesus." But never did "a dying man" seek health as did Whitefield among the Burmudas. He spent more than three months on the islands, preaching almost daily twice or thrice, sometimes in the churches, sometimes in the open air. One week, he says, it being rainy, he preached only five times in private houses; "'faint, yet pursuing,' must be my motto yet." He was entertained with much respect and hospitality by the island dignitaries, civil and clerical, and the common people soon appreciated his remarkable talents with enthusiasm, as they had done wherever he had been. The churches were crowded, while hundreds usually thronged about the doors and windows. There was a visible improvement in the people from Sabbath to Sabbath; they were "affected as in the days of old at home." One week he preached, besides the Sabbath services, two funeral sermons and five discourses in private houses. He went, in fine, from island to island, church to church, house to house, laboring as if the judgment day were immediately to be revealed; and when he preached his farewell sermon, the whole audience wept aloud, as if parting from an old and endeared pastor. He could hear the crowd of negroes outside sobbing with grief, and wept himself, unable to resist the general and contagious sorrow. "Surely," he exclaimed, as he left them, "a great work has been begun in some souls at Bermuda." A hundred pounds were spontaneously raised for his Orphan House, and the ship in which he departed was supplied by the grateful islanders with a superabundance of provisions for his comfort on the passage. He had extended the movement of Methodism to these isles of the sea; in a few years more Wesley's assistants were to follow him, and to spread it through all the British colonies of the West Indies. He embarked for England in June, 1748.

Meanwhile Howell Harris was pursuing his missionary itinerancy in Wales. He was, says Wesley, a powerful orator, both by nature and grace; but he owed nothing to art or education.[6] He was also an apostle in labors, travels, and trials. Persecutions and mobs opposed him in Wales, as they had Wesley in England. In Brecknockshire and Carmarthenshire especially, the Methodists "were hunted like partridges." Harris gives an account of a single "round" of his travels in South and North Wales, in which he had gone, during nine weeks, over thirteen counties, traveled one hundred and fifty miles each week, and preached twice a day, and some days three or four times; in this journey he had not taken off his clothes for seven nights together, being obliged to meet the people, and preach at midnight, or very early in the morning, to avoid persecution. Many of his followers were carried before the magistrates and fined for assembling together. Near the town of Bola, where he was almost murdered at a former visit, he was again attacked, and struck on the head with a

[6] Journal, Anno 1756.

stone, but escaped unhurt. "I never," he writes, "saw such crowds come to hear. Many hearts and doors have been opened lately."[7]

In May, 1748, Lady Huntingdon started on a tour through Wales, accompanied by two noble but devout women, Lady Anne and Lady Frances Hastings. They were met at Bristol by the leading Welsh evangelists, Howell Harris, Griffith Jones, Daniel Rowlands, and Howell Davies. They journeyed by brief stages, stopping at almost every village for a public religious service. Two of the preachers proclaimed the word every day as they went, and thus scattered the seed of the truth over a large range of the country. At Trevecca, afterward noted as the seat of her "school of the prophets," she passed several days. Some eight or ten clergymen and lay evangelists met her there, and preached four or five times daily to great congregations gathered from all the surrounding country. "The influence of the Spirit of God," writes Lady Frances Hastings, "was evidently afforded with his word, and many were added unto the Lord."[8] Rowlands's sermons seem especially to have been attended with extraordinary effect; immense assemblies were moved by the truth, as a forest by the wind, and prayed aloud for the Divine mercy. The societies were encouraged and fortified by this seasonable visit. "On a review of all I have heard and seen during the last few weeks," wrote the countess on her return, "I am constrained to exclaim, 'Bless the Lord, O my soul; and all that is within me bless his holy name!' Many on these solemn occasions, there is reason to believe, were brought out of nature's deepest darkness into the marvelous light of the all-glorious Gospel of Christ."

She arrived in London with Howell Harris and Howell Davis in time to receive Whitefield, who, after an absence of four years, reappeared among his old friends flaming with

[7] Letter of Howell Harris. Life and Times of Selina, Countess of Huntingdon, chap. 7.

[8] Ibid. chap. 6.

unabated zeal. He was received with enthusiasm, and the Tabernacle was soon again thronged. John Newton, one of the ministerial notabilities of the last century, and the well-known friend of Cowper, describes the scene there as quite marvelous. He used to rise at four o'clock in the morning to hear the great orator at his five o'clock service, and says he has seen Moorfields as full of the lanterns of the worshipers before daylight as the Haymarket was full of flambeaus on opera nights. "I bless God," he adds, "that I have lived in his time."

He now began his chaplaincy at Lady Huntingdon's residence, but could not long be content with the city. In September, 1748, he departed on his third visit to Scotland; Bateman, the Methodist vicar of St. Bartholomew's, and both the Wesleys supplying his place at the countess's mansion till his return. His zeal and eloquence again prevailed against all opposition in the North. Two synods and one presbytery discussed the propriety of discountenancing him. All unfavorable rumors were canvassed before them, but only to his advantage, for a more disinterested, guileless man than Whitefield never lived. At Edinburgh and Glasgow he was greeted by congregations almost as vast as had gathered about him at Moorfields and Kennington Common. Grateful groups came to inform him of his former usefulness in their conversion. At Cambuslang the old scenes of interest were revived. The pertinacious "Seceders" still complained that he did not "preach up the Solemn League and Covenant." "I preach up the covenant of grace," replied Whitefield, and sped his way, superior to all partisan and polemic strifes.

He returned to England, where he was attended by his old triumphs. There was, he wrote to Lady Huntingdon, a great stirring among the dry bones at Birstal and Kingswood. At Plymouth, the scene of former persecutions, a "tabernacle" had been built for him, and the city "seemed quite a new place." Kinsman, afterward distinguished in England as a successful evangelist, was one of his converts there. A youth had climbed a tree to hear and mimic him. Whitefield, attracted by his outrages, cried, "Come down, Zaccheus, come down, and receive the Lord Jesus Christ." The appeal was effectual, and the young man became not only a convert but a zealous preacher.

At Tavistock he was mobbed. A bull and dogs were brought and set upon the assembly while he was praying. He prevailed over the rabble, however, and delivered his message. At Exeter a persecutor came to the field-preaching with his pocket full of stones to throw at him; he stood with one in his hand, ready for the convenient moment, but the word struck his conscience; he dropped his missiles and made his way to the preacher, contritely acknowledging, "Sir, I came here to break your head, but God has broken my heart." He became a genuine Christian and an ornament to the Church.[9]

Having traversed the west of England to the extent of six hundred miles, spreading through all his course a marvelous sensation, he returned to London in March, 1749. He and Wesley now exchanged pulpits. They were bound together by their common Christian spirit, their common success, and their common persecutions. It was about this time that Lavington, Bishop of Exeter, sacrificed the dignity of his office by assailing them with merciless severity in his pamphlet, entitled, "The Enthusiasm of Methodists and Papists compared," to which both the evangelists wrote replies. Soon after his elevation to the see of Exeter, Lavington delivered a charge to his clergy, which was said to reflect severely on the Methodists. A forgery, pretending to be this address, was printed in London. The prelate charged the counterfeit on the Methodist leaders in a public "Declaration." They denied it peremptorily, and its printer afterward confessed the fraud, and exonerated them from any direct or indirect collusion with him. Lady Huntingdon communicated this confession to Lavington, and demanded a retraction of his Declaration. He treated her appeal with

[9] Gillies's Whitefield, chap. 14.

silent contempt till she threatened to make public the actual state of the case, when he sent her a note "apologizing to her ladyship and the Messrs. Whitefield and Wesley for the harsh and unjust censures which he was led to pass on them, from the supposition that they were in some measure concerned in and had countenanced the late imposition on the public." He even requested them to "accept his unfeigned regret at having unjustly wounded their feelings, and exposed them to the odium of the world."[10] This acknowledgment was not, however, made by him publicly, as it should have been in order to counteract his hasty "Declaration." The countess herself gave the recantation to the public. The bishop would not pardon this necessary act, and vented his indignation in relentless attacks on the Methodists. His tracts on their "Enthusiasm" exaggerated their real faults, and imputed to them many that were monstrous fictions. The historian of the times cannot show a greater kindness to his memory than to pass these flagrant publications with the least possible allusion. They are known in our day only by the triumph of the cause they impeached, a cause whose early incidental defects the Christian world is not willing to set off against its beneficent results.[11]

Whitefield could not remain long in London; he was feeble in health there, and soon unable to hold a pen. Again he started on his old routes. At Portsmouth he preached to a great assembly amid clamorous outcries; but before he closed the leader of the opposition was subdued, and "received him into his home with tears of shame and joy."[12] He passed into Wales, and had a triumphant progress

[10] See his letter in Lady Huntingdon's Life and Times, chap. 7. "Such," says the author of this work, "was the recantation of this wily prelate. but it was only in the language of hypocrisy."

[11] Wesley showed his characteristic kindness of heart when, some years later, while at Exeter, he wrote in his Journal: "I was well pleased to partake of the Lord's Supper with my old opponent, Bishop Lavington. O may we sit down together in the kingdom of our Father!" (Journal, Anno 1762.)

[12] Philip's Whitefield, chap. 16.

through its towns and villages. "Jesus," he wrote, "rides on in the chariot of the everlasting Gospel." He preached, mostly out of doors, in eight counties, and to more than a hundred thousand hearers. Throughout eight hundred miles he had conquered all opponents; "not a dog stirred a tongue." Magistrates and people beheld him with respect, if not with awe. Twenty thousand people were sometimes present, and many prayed and wept aloud under his sermons. "I think," he says, "we had not one *dry* meeting." Returning, he went to Exeter, not to answer Lavington's slanders, but to counteract them by the preaching of the Gospel. He proclaimed it there in the fields with great power. At one of his sermons the prelate and some of his clergy stood near, gazing on an assembly of ten thousand of the common people, many of whom trembled under the word, while others threw stones at the head of the preacher. He went into Yorkshire and preached for Grimshaw at Haworth to six thousand hearers, and administered the Lord's Supper to a thousand. Wesley's preachers and people invited him to Leeds, where he addressed an assembly of ten thousand. Charles Wesley met him on the highway and took him to Newcastle, where he preached repeatedly in the Wesleyan chapel, but finding the crowd too great turned out into the fields. Many were his converts through all these regions, some of whom afterward laid the foundations of the Dissenting Churches which now flourish there.[13]

He returned frequently to London, where "thousands on thousands crowded to hear," and conversions were continually occurring. In the early part of 1750 repeated earthquakes alarmed the metropolis. Charles Wesley and Whitefield were in the city, and presented a sublime example of ministerial faithfulness amid the general trepidation. On the 8th of March, while the former was rising in the pulpit of the Foundry to preach, at five o'clock in the morning, the earth moved through all London and Westminster with a strong, jarring motion, and a rumbling noise like distant thunder.

[13] Philip's Whitefield, chap. 16.

The walls of the Foundry trembled; a great agitation followed among the people; but Wesley cried aloud to them, "Therefore will we not fear though the earth be moved, and the hills be carried into the midst of the sea, for the Lord of Hosts is with us, the God of Jacob is our refuge." His heart, he says, was filled with faith, his mouth with words, "shaking their souls as well as their bodies."[14] The subterranean shocks recurred during several days. Multitudes flocked to the early Methodist service in deep alarm. The Westminster end of the metropolis was crowded with coaches and people flying precipitately, and London "looked like a sacked city." Throughout a whole night many of the alarmed people knocked at the Foundry door, entreating admittance, though "our poor people," writes Wesley, "were calm and quiet as at any other time." During one of those terrible nights Tower Hill, Moorfields, and Hyde Park were filled with lamenting men, women, and children; Whitefield stood among them in Hyde Park preaching at midnight. A deep moral impression followed these events. They gave origin to many tracts and sermons, and the courage and labors of the Methodist evangelists could not fail to secure the reverence of the people.

On the morning in which Charles Wesley stood preaching amid the trembling walls of the Foundry, John Wesley assembled the Conference of 1750 in Bristol—a date at which opens a new period of our narrative.

[14] Jackson's Charles Wesley, chap. 17.

CHAPTER V.

DEVELOPMENT OF OPINIONS AND ECONOMY BY THE CONFERENCES, FROM 1745 TO 1750.

The Conference of 1745 — Its Composition — Its Theological Discussions — Is the Witness of the Spirit invariable in Conversion? — Sanctification — Terrible Preaching — Church Government — Wesley's High Church Views — Lord King's Primitive Church — Wesley still designed not to form a permanent Sect — The Session of 1746 — Laymen admissible — Progress of Opinion — Faith and Works — Necessity of the Lay Ministry declared — Its Divine Right acknowledged — Ordination anticipated — Exhorters recognized — Importance of Local Preachers and Exhorters — First List of Circuits — Session of 1747 — Its Members — Private Judgment and Free Discussion — Relation of Faith to Assurance — Correction of Wesley's Opinion on the Subject — Cautions respecting Sanctification — What is a Church? — Divine Right of Episcopacy denied — Session of 1748 — Number of Circuits — The Formation of Societies resumed — Conference of 1749 — A Scheme of General Union — Assistants distinguished from Helpers — Quarterly Meetings ordered — Book Distribution — Session of 1750 — Extraordinary Results of the first Decade of Methodism.

THE second Conference was held in Bristol, August 1st, 1745. John Hodges, rector of Wenvo, Wales, was the only regular clergyman who was present besides the Wesleys. One layman, Marmaduke Gwynne,[1] and seven lay preachers, Thomas Richards, Samuel Larwood, Thomas Meyrick, James Wheatley,[2] Richard Moss, John Slocombe, and Herbert Jenkins, met with them. The deliberations related to questions of theology and church economy. As at the first conference, all dogmatic subjects not immediately concerned in personal religion were avoided; Justification, Sanctification, and the

[1] See page 268.

[2] Wheatley's name is omitted by Smith. (Hist. of Meth.) Myles gives it. (Chron. Hist., p. 34.)

Witness of the Spirit were especially discussed. It was asked, Is assurance absolutely necessary to our being in the favor of God? or may there possibly be some exempt cases? We dare not positively say there are not, was the answer.[3] "Is it indispensably necessary to final salvation? Suppose in a Papist, or in general among those who never heard it preached? Love hopeth all things. We know not how far any of these may fall under the case of invincible ignorance. Does a man believe any longer than he sees a reconciled God? We conceive not. But we allow there may be infinite degrees in seeing God, even as many as there are between him who sees the sun when it shines on his eyelids closed, and him who stands with his eyes wide open in the full blaze of his beams. Does faith supersede (set aside the necessity of) holiness or good works? In nowise; so far from it that it implies both, as a cause does its effect. When does inward sanctification begin? In the moment we are justified. The seed of every virtue is then sown in the soul. From that time the believer gradually dies to sin and grows in grace. Yet sin remains in him, yea, the seed of all sin, till he is sanctified throughout in spirit, soul, and body. Is it ordinarily given till a little before death? It is not to those that expect it no sooner, nor consequently ask for it, at least not in faith. But would not one who was thus sanctified be incapable of worldly business? He would be far more capable of it than ever, as going through all without distraction."

It was also asked whether some of the assistants did not preach too much on the wrath and too little on the love of God, and answered: "We fear they have leaned to that extreme, and hence some of their hearers may have lost the joy of faith. Need we ever preach the terrors of the Lord to those who know they are accepted of him? No, it is folly so to do; for love is to them the strongest of all motives."

While the conference thus avoided as much as possible

[3] Minutes of the Wesleyan Conferences, etc., vol. i, p. 22. London, 1812.

unessential polemics—the polemics, however, which have most engrossed theological parties, and most distracted Christendom—it showed a decided progress of opinion on ecclesiastical questions.[4] It was providential, perhaps, that Wesley's sentiments on Church order and ecclesiastical prerogatives were at first somewhat rigid, and known to be so, otherwise he might have suffered more seriously in his relation to the national Church, and swung away, with his increasing followers, into perilous ecclesiastical novelties and experiments. It was as providential, however, that with the advancing necessities of Methodism he was led to increasing liberality on such questions, until finally he was prepared, when the great exigency which required the special organization of American Methodism arrived, to practically disown the most important High-Church prejudices by the most important ecclesiastical act of his life—an act which has given to the world an example of Apostolic Episcopacy without the usual adventitious dignities or pretensions of prelacy, or even a claim of Apostolic Succession, or of any Scriptural or other authority higher than that of practical expediency itself.

At the present Conference it was asked: "Is not the will of our governors a law?" The answer was emphatic: "No; not of any governor, temporal or spiritual. Therefore, if any bishop wills that I should not preach the Gospel, his will is no law to me. But what if he produce a law against your preaching? I am to obey God rather than man." To the question, "Is Episcopal, Presbyterian, or Independent Church government most agreeable to reason?" a reply was given which presents the true rationale of Church order. "The plain origin of Church government," says this answer, "seems to be this: Christ sends forth a preacher of the Gospel. Some who hear him, repent and believe the Gos-

[4] The bound, or "octavo Minutes," as they are usually called, contain only the theological part of the deliberations of this conference. For the remainder of its proceedings we are indebted to the "Disciplinary Minutes," lately discovered. See note on page 211.

pel. They then desire him to watch over them, to build them up in the faith, and to guide their souls in the paths of righteousness. Here, then, is an independent congregation, subject to no pastor but their own, neither liable to be controlled in things spiritual by any other man or body of men whatsoever. But soon after, some from other parts, who are occasionally present while he speaks in the name of Him that sent him, beseech him to come over to help them also. Knowing it to be the will of God, he consents, yet not till he has conferred with the wisest and holiest of his congregation, and with their advice appointed one or more who has gifts and grace to watch over the flock till his return. If it please God to raise a flock in the new place before he leaves them, he does the same thing, appointing one whom God has fitted for the work to watch over these souls also. In like manner, in every place where it pleases God to gather a little flock by his word, he appoints one in his absence to take the oversight of the rest, and to assist them of the ability which God giveth. These are Deacons, or servants of the Church, and look on the first pastor as their common father. And all these congregations regard him in the same light, and esteem him still as the shepherd of their souls. These congregations are not absolutely independent. They depend on the pastor, though not on one another. As they increase, and as their Deacons grow in years and grace, they need other subordinate Deacons or helpers, in respect of whom they may be called Presbyters or Elders, as their father in the Lord may be called the Bishop or overseer of them all. Is mutual consent absolutely necessary between the pastor and the flock? No question. I cannot guide any soul unless he consent to be guided by me. Neither can any soul force me to guide him if I consent not. Does the ceasing of this consent on either side dissolve the relation? It must in the very nature of things. If a man no longer consent to be guided by me, I am no longer his guide. I am free. If one will not guide me any longer, I am free to seek one who will. But is the shepherd free to leave his sheep, or the sheep to leave their shepherd? Yes, if one or the others are convinced it is for the glory of God and the superior good of their souls." The more direct question, How shall we treat those who leave us? was answered by the advice, first, "Beware of all sharpness, or bitterness, or resentment; second, Talk with them once or twice at least; third, If they persist in their design consider them as dead, and name them not except in prayer."[5]

Notwithstanding the liberality of these views, Wesley still believed in the Apostolic Succession, in the priestly character of the Christian ministry, and the essential distinction of its three orders. He explicitly affirmed this belief in a letter written at the end of the present year.[6] His opinions, however, were evidently fast being unsettled by study, and by the practical difficulties which they presented in the momentous work opening before him. In about three weeks after the letter alluded to, he recorded in his Journal that he had recently read Lord King's Account of the Primitive Church. "In spite," he says, "of the vehement prejudice of my education, I was ready to believe that this was a fair and impartial draught; but if so, it would follow that bishops and presbyters are (essentially) of one order, and that originally every Christian congregation was a Church independent on all others." That irrefutable work made a profound impression on his mind, and, as we shall hereafter see, thoroughly dispelled his High-Church errors.

It is evident from the Minutes of this Conference that Wesley had as yet no settled purpose of maintaining a per manent organization of his followers. He still hoped that the general revival of religion would prepare the Established and Dissenting Churches to take charge of them, and obviate any such necessity. It was therefore suggested that his assistants should preach without forming any more new societies in large towns, particularly in Wales and Corn-

[5] Smith's History of Methodism, II, 8.
[6] It is given in his Journal, 1745.

wall. In the preceding Conference, as has been shown, he opposed any unnecessary increase of the lay ministry; and declared that "its employment at all was allowable only in cases of necessity." In fine, the ambition of founding a new sect, so heedlessly imputed to him by some of his critics, had not entered his mind; his one purpose was the reformation of religion and morals throughout the land; and his policy, pertinacious even with High Church prejudices, aimed to effect this reformation as far as was at all practicable within the pale and under the auspices of the national Church.

The third Conference assembled at Bristol on the twelfth of May, 1746. John Wesley, Charles Wesley, John Hodges, Samuel Taylor, Jonathan Reeves, Thomas Maxfield, Thomas Westall, Thomas Willis, and Thomas Glascot were present. These annual assemblies were yet designed to be quite informal, and to include, besides regular clergymen and lay preachers, such prominent laymen as might be within convenient reach. At the preceding session Marmaduke Gwynne attended, as we have seen, and on the present occasion, to the question, Who are proper persons to attend any Conference? It was replied, that besides the preachers conveniently at hand, the most prudent and devoted of the Band-leaders of the town where the session might be held, and any pious and judicious stranger who might be in the town, should be invited.[7]

The deliberations lasted but two days. They related, as at the previous sessions, exclusively to questions of personal religion, and to ministerial arrangements. An important advancement in the theological development of Methodism was marked here. It was asked, "Wherein does our doctrine now differ from that we preached when at Oxford?" and answered, "Chiefly in these two points: First, We then knew nothing of the righteousness of faith in justification; nor, second, Of the nature of faith itself, as implying consciousness of pardon."

7 "Disciplinary Minutes." Smith's History of Methodism, II, 3.

To the question, Is not the whole dispute of salvation by faith, or by works, a mere *strife of words?* it was answered: "In asserting salvation by faith we mean this: First, That pardon (salvation begun) is received by faith, producing works; second, That holiness (salvation continued) is faith working by love; third, That heaven (salvation finished) is the reward of this faith. If you, who assert salvation by works, or by faith and works, mean the same thing, (under standing by faith the revelation of Christ in us; by salvation, pardon, holiness, glory,) we will not strive with you at all. If you do not, this is not a *strife of words*, but the very essence of Christianity is the thing in question."[8]

Wesley's conviction of the importance and necessity of the lay ministry had been deepened since the last session. Providential circumstances every day rendered it more evident that the great religious interest which had begun in the land must be conducted forward chiefly by that agency, or be generally abandoned. Next to revelation itself, such providential indications were decisive of Wesley's judgment. The lay ministry was then God's own means, because the only means provided, for the prosecution of the growing work. But much discrimination was necessary to ascertain the fitness of untrained men for such a momentous responsibility. How shall we try those who think they are moved by the Holy Spirit, and called of God to preach? was an anxious question asked at this session. Three tests were given in the answer: Have they grace, gifts, and fruits? "First, Do they know God as a pardoning God? Have they the love of God abiding in them? Do they desire and seek nothing but God? And are they holy in all manner of conversation? Second, Have they gifts (as well as grace) for the work? Have they (in some tolerable degree) a clear, sound understanding? Have they a right judgment in the things of God? Have they a just conception of salvation by faith? And has God given them any degree of utterance? Do they speak justly, readily, clearly? Third, Have they

[8] Wesleyan Conferences from the first, etc., vol. i, p. 29.

fruit? Are any truly convinced of sin, and converted to God by their preaching?" "As long as these three marks concur in any, we believe," affirmed the Conference, "that he is called of God to preach. These we receive as a *sufficient proof* that he is *moved thereto by the Holy Ghost*;" a decision which has never been essentially modified by the rapid progress of ministerial improvement within the pale of Methodism, and which has incalculably tended to its success by the great variety and consequent adaptation and efficiency of the natural talent embodied in its ministry. Many directions, prescribing the studies and other habits of the lay ministry, were adopted at this session, but they will more appropriately come under consideration elsewhere.

It is evident also from the proceedings of this Conference, that though Wesley still believed, as he did through the rest of his life, in the *appropriateness* of ordination, and the usual orderly distinctions of the Christian ministry, *they were no longer essential requisites* in his estimation. His lay assistants were "moved of the Holy Ghost," and "called of God" to their work; they were, therefore, by Divine right as legitimate preachers of the word as any priest or bishop of the land. Yet he did not ordain them, nor by any analogous ceremony set them apart for their office; but with the reason assigned for this course was given also a distinct intimation that a more formal consecration might sooner or later become desirable. To the question why they did not use more form and solemnity in receiving a new laborer, it was answered that the Conference purposely declined it: "First, Because there is something of stateliness in it; second, Because it was not expedient to *make haste;* we desire barely to follow Providence as it gradually opens."[9] At a later date, as we shall see, Wesley did ordain some of his assistants.

We meet in the Minutes of this Conference with the first intimation of another class of lay laborers, which has since been of no small influence in the progress of Methodism. It was provided that none should be allowed to exhort in

[9] Disciplinary Minutes. Smith's History of Methodism, II, 3.

the societies without a note of authorization from the preacher, and that this license, as it has since been called, should be renewed once a year. Thus arose the order of "Exhorters," a notable example of the manner in which Methodism appropriated all its resources of talent. The Local Ministry has usually graduated from the class of Exhorters, and the Itinerant Ministry from the class of Local Preachers, while men incompetent for either of these two offices have remained with usefulness in the subordinate rank of Exhorters. This process of graduation has always been a process of preparation. Thousands of able Local Preachers, whose modesty as laymen would never have allowed them to begin their ministerial labors in the pulpit, have effectually begun them in the vestry as Exhorters; and hundreds of itinerants, whose ability for the pulpit would never have been otherwise ascertained, either by themselves or their brethren, have disclosed it in the humbler labors of the Local Ministry, and gone forth from them as high priests of the Church. The history of Methodism teaches few lessons more emphatically than the importance of maintaining these practical processes and distinctions, so effective in its past progress, and so evidently essential to its genius and destiny.

We have already seen that Wesley, observing the necessity of repeating his labors in any given place in order to secure permanent results, had resolved to "strike no blow which he could not follow up." From that time he endeavored to methodize as much as possible the itinerant labors of both himself and his associates. The Minutes of the present Conference give us the first intimation of definitive circuits, though it is supposed they existed before.[10] The whole country was mapped into seven of these itinerant districts. Wales and Cornwall each constituted one. Newcastle, with doubtless many neighboring towns, was another. That of Yorkshire included seven counties. London, Bristol, and Evesham were the head-quarters of others.

[10] Smith's History of Methodism, II, 3.

The fourth Conference assembled at the Foundry in London, on June 16, 1747, and was numerically the most imposing session yet held. Besides the Wesleys, their venerable chief counselor, Perronet, (vicar of Shoreham,) Manning, (vicar of Hayes,) Bateman, (rector of St. Bartholomew the Great in London, where Wesley now often preached,) and Piers, (vicar of Bexley,) attended it. Howell Harris, the Methodist apostle of Wales, whose capacious soul suffered no loss of affection for Wesley by his alliance with Whitefield, was also a member. The other lay preachers present were Thomas Hardwick, Thomas Maxfield, John Bennet, John Downes, Thomas Crouch, Robert Swindells, and John Madden.[11]

The first question was how they should render the Conference "eminently" an occasion of "prayer, watching, and self-denial." They resolved to have a special care "always to set God before them," and to spend the intermissions of the sessions in devotions and in visiting the sick. The right of utterly free discussion, so distinctly stated in the first Conference, was asserted more emphatically than ever. Unanimous agreement was pronounced desirable, but in speculative matters each, it was affirmed, could only submit so far as his judgment should be convinced; in every practical point, so far as would not wound his conscience. It was asked, "Can a Christian submit any further than this to any man or number of men upon earth?" "It is," they answered, "undeniably plain he cannot, either to pope, council, bishop, or convocation. And this is that grand principle of every man's right to private judgment in opposition to implicit faith in man, on which Calvin, Luther, Melancthon, and all the ancient Reformers, at home and abroad, proceeded. Every man must think for himself, since every man must give an account for himself to God."

Two important theological themes were discussed: the

[11] Disciplinary Minutes. Smith's History of Methodism, II, 3. The "Octavo Minutes" do not mention the names of the lay preachers (except Harris and Hardwick) nor Perronet.

relation of Assurance to Faith in Justification, and the extent of Sanctification. It was admitted that sanctifying faith *is itself* a divine assurance, but not without evident hesitancy, as the Conference could not deny that some good men give abundant proof of Justification while they deny Assurance. "There may be exempt cases," say the Minutes; but they add, "it is dangerous to ground a general doctrine on a few particular examples."[12] To the question, What will become of them if they die in this state? it was replied: "This is a supposition not to be made. They cannot die in this state; they must go backward or forward. If they continue to seek they will surely find righteousness, peace, and joy in the Holy Ghost. We are confirmed in this belief by the many instances we have seen of such as these finding peace at the last hour; and it is not impossible but others may then be made partakers of like precious faith, and yet go hence without giving any outward proof of the change which God hath wrought." Wesley himself saw the vagueness and difficulty which prevailed in the deliberations on this subject, and in less than a month his reflections corrected his present opinion. In a letter to his brother he denies that "justifying faith is a sense of pardon." "Every one," he writes, "is deeply concerned to understand this question well, but preachers most of all, lest they should either make them sad whom God hath not made sad, or encourage them to say peace where there is no peace. Some years ago we heard nothing of justifying faith, or a sense of pardon, so that when we did hear of them the theme was quite new to us; and we might easily, especially in the heat and hurry of controversy, lean too much either to the one hand or to the other. By justifying faith I mean that faith which, whosoever hath it not is under the *wrath* and the *curse* of God. By a sense of pardon I mean a distinct, explicit assurance that my sins are forgiven. I allow, first, that there is such an explicit assurance; second, that it is the *common* privilege of *real* Christians; third, that it is the *proper Christian*

[12] Minutes of Wesleyan Conferences from the first, etc., vol. i, p. 634.

faith which purifieth the heart and overcometh the world. But I cannot allow that justifying faith is such an assurance, or necessarily connected therewith, because if justifying faith *necessarily* implies such an explicit assurance of pardon, then every one who has it not, and every one so long as he has it not, is under the *wrath* and under the *curse* of God. But this is a supposition contrary to Scripture, as well as to experience."[13] This matured view of the question he entertained during the rest of his life, but he always taught the blessing of assurance as the privilege and right of every true believer.

The doctrine of entire Sanctification was unreservedly asserted, but with several important cautions against its imprudent treatment either in the pulpit or in personal life. To the question, suppose one had attained to this, would you advise him to speak of it? it was replied: "Not to them who know not God; it would only provoke them to contradict and blaspheme: nor to any without some particular reason, without some particular good in view; and then they should have an especial care to avoid all appearance of boasting, and to speak more loudly and convincingly by their lives than they can do by their tongues." It was asked, "Does not the harshly preaching perfection tend to bring believers into a kind of bondage or slavish fear? It does. Therefore we should always place it in the most amiable light, so that it may excite only hope, joy, and desire." It was further asserted that "we may continue in the joy of faith even till we are made perfect. Since holy grief does not quench this joy, and since even while we are under the cross, while we deeply partake of the sufferings of Christ, we may rejoice with joy unspeakable." These cautions were pushed even further. It was insisted that to "teach believers to be continually poring upon their inbred sin, is the ready way to make them forget that they were purged from their former sins. We find by experience it is so, or to make them undervalue and account it a little thing. Whereas,

[13] Myles's Chron. Hist. of Methodism, p. 54.

indeed, (though there are still greater gifts behind,) this is inexpressibly great and glorious."[14]

Of the discussions on ecclesiastical questions we have no traces in the current Minutes, but in the "Disciplinary Minutes" are evidences of important progress. The term *church* is asserted to mean in the New Testament "a single congregation."[15] A "national church" is pronounced "a merely political institution." It is conceded that the "three orders" of deacons, presbyters, and elders, obtained early in the Church, but are not enjoined in Holy Scripture; that unformity of Church government did not exist till the age of Constantine, and was not taught by the sacred writers, for the reason that variety in ecclesiastical administration was necessary for the varied circumstances of different ages and countries. We have also positive proof that Wesley had abandoned his belief in the divine right of Episcopacy. He declares in these Minutes that it was not asserted in England till about the middle of Queen Elizabeth's reign; and that till then all bishops and clergy in England continually allowed and joined in the ministrations of those who were not episcopally ordained. The arguments of the "Irenicum" and "The Primitive Church" had now evidently prevailed with him, and not these so much, perhaps, as the providential arguments afforded by the increasing exigencies of his great work, and by his growing catholicity. He still, however, repels the charge of schism. "You profess," continue these Minutes, "to obey both the rules and the governors of the Church, yet in many instances you do not obey them. How is this consistent? It is entirely consistent. We act at all times on one plain uniform principle. We will obey the rules and governors of the Church when-

[14] By a singular error in the Bound Minutes (Minutes of the Methodist Conferences from the first, etc., London, 1812) the report on Sanctification is numbered as pertaining to the next Conference, held in 1748. There are no Minutes whatever of that Conference except in the recently discovered "Disciplinary Minutes." See Smith's Hist., II, 3. Myles (Chron. Hist.) gives it correctly.

[15] Smith's History of Methodism, II, 3.

ever we can consistently with our duty to God. Whenever we cannot, we quietly obey God rather than man. But why do you say you are thrust out of the churches? Has not every minister a right to dispose of his own church? He ought to have, but in fact he has not. A minister desires that I should preach in his church, but the bishop forbids him. That bishop then injures him, and thrusts me out of the Church." Still thus denied the churches, they resolved to limit less than ever their field-preaching; reasons were discussed for extending it, and after recording some sixty assistants as in the work, besides coadjutors among the regular clergy, they dispersed to exemplify these convictions in the length and breadth of the land.

On the second of June, 1748, the fifth Conference was held in the Tower-street Chapel, London.[16] John Wesley, Charles Wesley, William Felton, Charles Manning, Thomas Maxfield, John Jones, Thomas Meyrick, John Trembath, Edward Perronet, son of the vicar of Shoreham, Jonathan Reeves, Richard Thomas Bateman, John Green, William Tucker, Howell Harris, Samuel Larwood, James Jones, and William Shent were present. No theological question was examined, as the time was mostly employed in discussing the interests of Kingswood School. Nine circuits were reported: London with ten towns or counties, Bristol with thirteen, Cornwall with nine, Ireland with four, Wales with four, Shropshire with seven, Cheshire with five, Yorkshire with nine, and Newcastle with ten.

The Minutes of this session afford one, and but one, very important indication of the progress of Wesley's opinions respecting the distinct mission of Methodism. Taken in connection with his improved views on ecclesiastical questions, it has not a little significance. At a previous Conference it was resolved, as has been shown, to preach without forming new societies, especially in the larger communities.

[16] As the Octavo Minutes contain no records of this session, we are indebted for them exclusively to the "Disciplinary Minutes." Smith's Hist., etc., II, 3.

It was hoped that the Methodists might be thus kept in closer sympathy with the Established Church, and that tendencies to secession might be prevented. It was a concession to the many devout men who approved the opinions and usefulness of Wesley and his fellow-laborers, but who recoiled at the prospect of a Methodist sect, which, by its separation from the national Church, could not fail to carry with it the sympathy of a large proportion of the common people, and might in the future shake the very foundations of the Establishment. This policy was now abandoned. It had been tried, and was found to be pernicious. The clergy generally continued their hostility to Methodism. They neglected, and in many cases maltreated the thousands of converts which it sent to their communion altars, and proffered to their pastoral care. "We have preached," says the Minutes, "for more than a year, without forming societies, in a large tract of land from Newcastle to Berwick-on-Tweed, and almost all the seed has fallen upon the wayside; there is scarce any fruit of it remaining." Among the inconveniences arising from this course, it was affirmed that, first, the preacher could not give proper exhortations and instructions to those who were convinced of sin, unless he had opportunities of meeting them apart from the mixed, unawakened multitude; second, they could not watch over one another in love unless thus united together; third, nor could the believers build up one another, or bear one another's burdens. Wesley still, however, clung to the Church, though it was difficult for him, with even such concessions, to prevent many of his people from resenting, by open dissent, its stately and obstinate disdain of their laborious lay preachers, as well as of the Methodistic clergy, who were unimpeachably orthodox, and the most useful ministers of the realm.[17]

[17] At a later date, Wesley, in alluding to the arguments of Methodists who advocated open dissent, says: "I will freely acknowledge that I cannot answer these arguments to my own satisfaction. As yet we have not taken one step further than we were convinced was our bounden duty. It is from a full conviction of this that we have preached abroad, prayed *extempore*, formed societies, and permitted preachers who were not epis-

The Conference adjourned, counseling "a closer union of the assistants with each other."

About eighteen months later, November 16, 1749, it assembled again in London.[18] A measure was now suggested which would have tended to consolidate the societies, and sever them, practically, still more from the Established Church. It was proposed that the society in London should be considered the mother church; that every assistant in country circuits should send reports to the stewards of the London circuit, who should arrange a regular correspondence with all the provincial societies. With this scheme was to be combined an annual collection throughout the land for the relief of necessitous societies. Wesley was at first greatly pleased with the plan. "Being thus united," he said, "in one body, of which Christ Jesus is head, neither the world nor the devil will be able to separate us in time or in eternity." Its possible tendency toward a separation from the Established Church was probably his reason for not effectively adopting it. He proposed, however, to try it by appointing one of his "Helpers" on each circuit to take charge of its societies, giving him exclusively thereafter the title of "Assistant," a term which had hitherto been applied, interchangeably with "Helper," to all his lay preachers. Nine such were designated to the circuits, which still contin-

copally ordained. And were we pressed on this side, were there no alternative allowed, we should judge it our bounden duty rather wholly to separate from the Church than to give up any one of these points; therefore, if we cannot stop a separation without stopping lay preachers, the case is clear, we cannot stop it at all." Letter to Rev. Mr. Walker, September 24, 1755. Arminian Magazine, 1779.

18 The Octavo Minutes cannot be relied on for a distinct report of the proceedings of this session, for many of the proceedings attributed by that work to this year belong to other sessions. They are a compendium of the Minutes from 1748 to 1763, placed together for convenience, but without discrimination. For the real Minutes of 1749 we are indebted to a manuscript report appended to the recently-discovered "Disciplinary Minutes." (Smith's Hist. of Meth., II, 3.) As the Minutes were not usually printed, written copies alone were presented to new members of the Conference at their admission on probation. (Watson's Wesley, chap. 9.) This important manuscript is doubtless one of those copies.

ued to be of that number. The proposed relation to the London circuit was not, however, realized. The annual Conference became more appropriately the centre of unity to the societies.

A variety of minute regulations originated at this session. Quarterly meetings, which had been held in some sections, were ordered to be everywhere observed. Watch-nights and love-feasts were to be held monthly. Every circuit was to be supplied with books by the Assistant, and every society was to provide "a private room," and also books, for the Helper. A return was to be made quarterly of money for books from each society, and thus began that organized system of book and tract distribution which has secured to Methodism a more extensive use of the religious press than can be found in any other Protestant denomination of our day. Wesley had already issued many publications, from the one-page tract to the stout volume. He forthwith began his "Christian Library," in fifty volumes, and all his preachers were soon active "colporteurs." Tracts especially did he publish, and scatter both by his own hands and by his preachers. "A Word to a Smuggler;" "A Word to a Swearer;" "A Word to a Street-Walker;" "A Word to a Drunkard;" "A Word to a Malefactor;" "A Word to a Sabbath-Breaker;" such were the titles of small publications which he disseminated over the kingdom. "He thus," says his best biographer, "by his example, was probably the first to apply, on any large scale, this important means of usefulness to the reformation of the people."[19]

On the 8th of March, 1750, was held the seventh Conference. Only four months had passed since the preceding session; its proceedings seem not to have been important. Not a trace of its Minutes is preserved; nor have we the Minutes of any subsequent sessions, save two, before the year 1765, when their regular publication commenced.

A little more than ten years had passed since the recognized epoch of Methodism. The results thus far were cer-

[19] Watson's Life of Wesley, chap. 8.

tainly remarkable. A scarcely paralleled religious interest had been spread and sustained throughout the United Kingdom and along the Atlantic coast of America. The Churches of both countries had been extensively reawakened. The great fact of a Lay Ministry had been accomplished—great not only in its direct results, but perhaps more so by its reacting shock, in various respects, against the ecclesiasticism which for fifteen hundred years had fettered Christianity with bands of iron. It had presented before the world the greatest pulpit orator of the age, if not of any age; also one of the greatest religious legislators of history; a hymnist whose supremacy has been but doubtfully disputed by a single rival;[20] and the most signal example of female agency in religious affairs which Christian history records. The lowest abysses of the English population among colliers and miners had been reached by the Gospel. Calvinistic Methodism was restoring the decayed nonconformity of England. Wesleyan Methodism, though adhering to the Establishment, had taken an organic and permanent form; it had its Annual Conferences, Quarterly Conferences, Class Meetings, and Band Meetings; its Watch-nights and Love-feasts; its Traveling Preachers, Local Preachers, Exhorters, Leaders, Trustees, and Stewards. It had districted England, Wales, and

[20] The Presbyterian Quarterly for March, 1858, says: "We regard it as a great loss to the Presbyterian Churches of our country that so few, comparatively, of Charles Wesley's hymns should have been admitted into their collections. It may not be generally known that, not even excepting Dr. Watts, he is the most voluminous of all our lyrical authors, and it were only justice to add, that he is the most equal. . . . We have never read or sung a finer specimen than his well-known paraphrase of the 24th Psalm: Our Lord is risen from the dead, etc. There is another objective hymn by Charles Wesley which is among the finest in the language. We wonder that it has not found its way into American hymn books: Stand the omnipotent decree, etc. Well has this hymn been spoken of as being in a strain more than human. There is the noble hymn by Charles Wesley, Jacob wrestling with the Angel, concerning which Dr. Watts did not scruple to say that it was worth all the verses he himself had written. James Montgomery declares it to be among the poet's highest achievements. Never have we read a finer combination of poetic taste and evangelical sentiment."

Ireland into Circuits for systematic ministerial labors, and now commanded a ministerial force of about seventy men.[21] It had fought its way through incredible persecutions and riots, and had won at last a general, though not universal peace. Its Chapels and Preachers' Houses, or parsonages, were multiplying over the country. It had a rich Psalmody, which has since spread wherever the English tongue is used; and a well-defined Theology, which was without dogmatism, and distinguished by two notable facts, that could not fail to secure popular interest, namely, that it transcended the prevalent creeds in both *spirituality* and *liberality*—in its experimental doctrines of Conversion, Sanctification, and the Witness of the Spirit, and in the evangelical liberalism of its Arminianism. It had begun its present scheme of Popular Religious Literature, had provided the first of that series of Academic institutions which has since extended with its progress, and was contemplating a plan of Ministerial Education, which has been effectively accomplished. Already the despondent declarations of Watts, Secker, and Butler,[22] respecting the prospects of religion, might be pronounced no longer relevant. Yet Watts had been dead but two years, and Secker and Butler still survived.[23]

[21] There are no data for an estimate of the membership of its societies..

[22] See pages 28, 29.

[23] Watts had lingered in his hospitable retirement at Abney Park, whence he beheld with grateful surprise the religious revolution which was spreading through the country. He received there occasional visits from Charles Wesley, Lady Huntingdon, and other leading Methodists. Doddridge still survived, welcoming Whitefield and the Wesleys at Northampton and corresponding with them. He revised Whitefield's journals, and, in his occasional visits to London, found religious consolation among the Methodists at Lady Huntingdon's mansion.

BOOK IV.

PROGRESS OF METHODISM FROM 1750 TO THE DEATH OF WHITEFIELD IN 1770.

CHAPTER I.

METHODISM IN IRELAND: 1750–1760.

Wesley again in Ireland — John Jane — Progress of Methodism — Remarkable German Colony — It gives Birth to American Methodism — Methodism in the Army in Ireland — Duncan Wright, a Soldier, becomes a Preacher — Sketch of his Life — A Military Execution induces him to preach — He joins the Itinerancy — A converted Surgeon — Thomas Walsh — His Sickness — His saintly Character — His Dissent from Fletcher on the Death of Good Men — His own Mental Trouble in Death.

Immediately after the Conference of 1750 Wesley again started for Ireland, passing through Wales, and preaching with much success on his route. He was accompanied by Christopher Hopper, a man of note among the early Methodist itinerants. Wesley summoned John Jane, a self-sacrificing evangelist, to meet him and Hopper at Holyhead before they embarked. Jane gave an example of the usual heroic obedience of the lay preachers to their great leader's commands; he made the journey on foot with but three shillings for his expenses. The devoted man could not fail, however, to secure the interest of humble families on the route; he was entertained six nights out of seven by utter strangers, and arrived at Holyhead with one penny in his pocket. In a few months he sunk under excessive labors. The poverty of the Methodist itinerants seldom allowed them to use horses in those times, and John Jane usually traveled on foot; a long walk to a preaching place on a hot day produced a fever, under which he died with more than resignation—"with a smile on his face," said one of his fellow-laborers, leaving as his last utterance the words, "I find the love of God in Christ Jesus." Wesley concludes a notice of his death in his Journal with these remarkable words: "All his clothes, linen and woolen, stockings, hat, and wig are not thought sufficient to answer his funeral expenses, which amount to £1 17s. 3d. All the money he had was 1s. 4d., enough for any unmarried preacher of the Gospel to leave to his executors."[1] St. Francis himself, adds Robert Southey, might have been satisfied with such a disciple.

Wesley spent nearly four months in Ireland during this visit, traveling and preaching in every direction. At Dublin he found the societies in a more prosperous state than ever. In Cork the riots had not yet entirely subsided; their contagion had also spread to other towns; and he was frequently assailed while preaching in the open air in that part of the island. In Limerick the foundations of Methodism had been securely laid; sixty Highlanders of the army had joined the classes, "and by their zeal, according to knowledge, had stirred up many." At Newmarket, the former residence of Thomas Walsh, he met a prosperous society, and was so deeply affected among them as to be compelled by his emotions to stop short several times in his address. At Athlone, he says, it was such a night as he had seldom known; the stout-hearted were broken down on every side. In Longford a storm of rain could not drive the people from the out-door services; the word cut like a two-edged sword; several persons fell as if smitten with death, and some were carried away insensible. Others, he writes, would have gone away but could not, for the hand of

1 Wesley's Journal, Anno 1750.

the Lord pressed them to the earth. Yet such were his views of the Irish character that he exclaimed, amid these scenes: "O fair beginning! But what will the end be?" Similar effects attended his labors at Drumcree, and, indeed, throughout this prolonged visit. As he passed daily from town to town, preaching morning, noon, and night, among Papists and Protestants, he was almost everywhere cheered with evidences of the triumph of the Gospel. The work of God advanced, he writes, in the county of Cork, and at Waterford and Limerick, as well as in Mount Mellick, Athlone, Longford, and most parts of the province of Leinster. He had the satisfaction of observing how greatly God had blessed his lay fellow-laborers, by whom multitudes were saved from the error of their ways. Many of these had been eminent for all manner of sins; many had been Roman Catholics; and he supposes the number of converts among the latter would have been far greater had not the Protestant, as well as the Popish priests, taken pains to hinder them.[2] The dead Protestantism of the land was his chief obstacle. "O what a harvest might be in Ireland!" he writes, in the midst of these tireless labors, "did not the poor Protestants hate Christianity worse than either Popery or heathenism." Before leaving Dublin for England he was heard in the public green by larger congregations than he had ever addressed in the city.

In 1752 he was again in Ireland visiting most of the towns of his former route. He found equal reasons for encouragement. His preachers were now numerous enough in the country for him to hold an informal Conference among them. The mobs at Cork had ceased, and he projected a new chapel in that city. He repeated his visit in 1756, when all his assistants on the island met him at Dublin, and planned, with good courage, for still greater labors. Thomas Walsh accompanied him in his excursions among the towns, preaching in Irish with great

[2] Short History of the People called Methodists. Works, vol. vii, page 366. Am. ed.

effect. After visiting the societies in Leinster and Munster, they went into the province of Connaught, scattering the good seed broadcast. He visited also, for the first time, the province of Ulster, where he found that the labors of his preachers had been extensively useful. Churchmen, Dissenters, and reformed Papists constituted the societies, and there "was no striving among them except to enter in at the strait gate."

He had now traversed every part of Ireland except the county of Sligo, on the western coast. In 1758 he returned in order to visit particularly that section—the best peopled, he says, that he had seen in the kingdom. He preached in the market-place of the city several times to large congregations, and with great effect; and from that time, he adds, there have never been wanting a few in Sligo who worship God in spirit and in truth; and in many other parts of the county numerous converts had been gathered into classes.

He passed to Court Mattress, where he found a colony of Germans, whose fathers had come into the kingdom under Queen Anne, from the Palatinate on the Rhine. A hundred and ten families had settled in the town and in the adjacent hamlets of Killiheen, Ballygarrane, and Pallas, and their population was now numerous. Having no minister they became noted for drunkenness, profanity, and an utter contempt of religion; but they had changed remarkably since they had heard the truth from the Methodist itinerants; an oath was now rarely heard among them, nor a drunkard seen in their borders. They had built a large preaching-house in the middle of Court Mattress. Many times afterward Wesley preached among them, as did also his fellow-laborers, and with lasting effect. So did God at last provide, he remarks, for these poor strangers, who for fifty years had none that cared for their souls.

At a later visit, he says that three such towns as Killiheen, Ballygarrane, and Court Mattress could hardly be found elsewhere in Ireland or England; there was no profanity, no Sabbath breaking, no ale-house in any of them. "How," he exclaims, "will these poor foreigners rise up in the day of judgment against those that are around about them!"[3]

But the most extraordinary fact respecting this German colony thus found out and evangelized by the Methodist itinerants, was not yet apprehended by Wesley. It was destined to give birth to Methodism in the New World. During his visit to the island in 1752, he became acquainted with one of these German Irishmen, who was afterward licensed as a local preacher among them. Fourteen years later this young man resided with a small company of his countrymen in the city of New York. Strangers in a strange land, and deprived of the religious aids which Methodism had afforded them among their distant brethren, they had lost their religious zeal and strictness, and some of them were playing at cards, when a devout woman, a later emigrant from Ballygarrane, reproved them, and going to the local preacher entreated him to resume his Methodist labors. He was recalled to his duty by the seasonable appeal. He opened his own house, a humble one-story building, for worship, preached there, and formed there the first Methodist society in America. In two years more he dedicated the first American Methodist chapel, and thus founded that form of Methodism which was destined to become, within the lifetime of many then born, the predominant Protestant belief of the New World, from Newfoundland to California.[4]

On one of his visits to Ireland Wesley said that "the first call" of Methodism there was to the soldiers.[5] They de-

[3] Journal, Anno 1760.

[4] Wesley's Journal, 1758, 1760, 1762. Bangs's History of the Methodist Episcopal Church, vol. i, chap. 2. Wakeley's Lost Chapters Recovered from the Early History of American Methodism, chaps. 2, 3, 13. See also two letters by Rev. C. P. Harrower, in the Christian Advocate and Journal, (New York,) May 13 and 20, 1858.

[5] Journal, Anno 1756.

fended him and his people amid the mob at Cork, where they flocked to his preaching, and where the rioters, when they saw them in the assembly, lowered their shillalahs or retreated. Ordinary Methodists suffered persecution quietly; but these stout-hearted men felt that their Methodism ought not to deprive them entirely of the use of their professional license, and were quite ready to stop praying at times in order to fight a little for what they deemed the honor of religion. They gathered around Wesley at Dublin, where he often preached near their barracks for safety from the rabble. They liked him heartily, with the rough generosity of soldiers, as not only a good but a brave man. They made a way for him with their swords into an immense crowd in the public green of that city, and preserved order while he preached. There was a class in that city composed of nineteen of them who "were resolved," he says, "to fight the good fight of faith." At Phillipston they constituted the strength of his society. At Limerick he formed, as we have seen, a class of sixty. At Kilkenny they took him into the barracks, and had him preach to them, and "a few of both the army and the town met together" as a society. In another place the remnants of John Nelson's regiment gathered to hear him. At Kinsale they rallied around him, and many of them, he writes, "were good soldiers of Jesus Christ."

The army in Ireland afforded to Methodism, during our present period, one of its most useful early preachers. Duncan Wright, a brave Scotchman, had early a "bookish inclination," and in his childhood "read and wept often till his head ached" wishing to be a Christian, "and to be easy and happy, but not knowing how." He resolved to dissipate his anxieties by seeing the world in a military life, and enlisted in his eighteenth year in a regiment of foot. The next year he was in camp near Cashel, Ireland, but found no escape there from his religious impressions, for a good corporal preached frequently to the troops. Methodist fellow-soldiers disturbed his conscience when the regiment removed to

Limerick. He attended the Methodist society in that city, and at last sought the conversation of its members with eagerness, as the best guidance to his disturbed mind. He used to spend his wakeful hours at night in weeping and prayer, and it was on one of these "weeping nights," he says, "that the Lord brought him in an instant out of darkness into his marvelous light."[6]

During the ensuing two years he passed through many vicissitudes, inward and outward, and was deeply impressed with the thought that he should openly proclaim the truth to his comrades. He resisted the impression, however, until a melancholy event called him to his duty. The government, he says, had resolved to shoot a deserter in every city of Ireland as an example. A youth but twenty years old, in Wright's regiment, was among the condemned. The earnest Scotchman hastened with trembling to converse and pray with him, though he was surrounded by guards. He found the unfortunate young man "weeping as if his heart would break, and reading 'The Whole Duty of Man' with all his might, like a drowning man catching at anything to save himself." Wright spoke a few words of exhortation to him, and returned to him in the evening, though with reluctance, as there were many soldiers gazing upon them. He prayed with him, and exhorted all who were present. The doomed youth saw himself an undone sinner, without help, and almost without hope. Taking with him some of his comrades, Wright visited him twice or thrice a day, and four days before his execution he received the peace of God. From that time he witnessed a good confession to all who approached him. Every one that saw him go to the place where he was shot, could not but admire the serene joy that appeared in his countenance. He said but little; but his calm, happy death made a deep impression on many of the soldiers, for they could not fail to discern the difference between him and one they saw die shortly before at Dublin, who showed the greatest reluctance, the field-officer of the day being obliged

[6] Arminian Magazine, 1781, p. 368.

to ride up to him several times to tell him he *must* die, while this converted victim was not above ten minutes on his knees before "he dropped the signal and went to paradise."

The execution of this young man induced Wright to preach, and at last to enter the itinerant ministry. Every night, after the call of the roll, he held a meeting at his quarters for his fellow-soldiers, and soon formed a Methodist class among them. He at first only sang, prayed, and read with them; but his light usually went out early, and he was compelled to lay aside his book and exhort. He thus became known as the camp preacher. As his regiment moved from town to town he had opportunities of spreading the truth. He was, in fine, already an itinerant evangelist. He planted Methodism in Galway; no Methodist preacher had ever been there before him, yet he had many seals to his ministry in that city, and years later he wrote: "Some of them are a comfort to me to this day, and some are fallen asleep in Jesus." He did good service also in Dublin while there with his regiment.

His colonel endeavored to stop his preaching, but could not, and was at last glad to get him out of the army; and "thus it was," he says, "that the Lord thrust me into the harvest." He assisted at a great revival in Waterford, and proved himself a workman that needed not to be ashamed, so that Wesley soon sent him out as a traveling preacher.

His loss to the army was, however, in an unexpected manner supplied for a time. The surgeon of a regiment, who was the favorite wit of his comrades, went to hear a local preacher in order to procure new matter of merriment; but while leaning on his cane, and looking waggishly at the speaker through his fingers, the humble man's word pierced his heart like an arrow. He became a zealous Methodist, and preached to the soldiers wherever he could find opportunity, till on visiting some sick prisoners in the Dublin Newgate he contracted a malignant fever, and "finished his course rejoicing in God his Saviour."

Duncan Wright proved himself a good soldier of the Lord Jesus. He traveled extensively in Ireland, sometimes accompanying Wesley, though he had to acknowledge that, notwithstanding his own military training, Wesley's activity gave him "too much exercise," and he "had to give it up." Besides his useful labors in Ireland he preached in Scotland, and occupied important circuits in England, and after thirty years' service fell at his post.

While Methodism was thus advancing in Ireland, it was destined to suffer toward the close of the present period an irreparable loss. Wesley was in Limerick in the spring of 1758; he met there Thomas Walsh, "just alive." "Three of the best physicians in these parts," he writes, "have attended him, and all agree that it is a lost case. O what a man to be snatched away in the strength of his years? Surely Thy judgments are a great deep!" Thomas Walsh died a martyr, but he was self-martyred. His constitution was originally feeble, yet he used it in his mental and ministerial labors as if it were Herculean; he preached constantly twice, and often thrice a day, besides visiting his people from house to house, especially the sick and the dying, from some of whom it is said he was rarely a day absent while he was stationed in London. Meanwhile his studies were pursued as if they were alone the occupation of his time. He rose at four in the morning, and pored over his books late into the night; and preaching and pastoral work, assiduously as they were pursued, seemed but slight intermissions of the work of the brain. When advised to take more sleep, he replied, "Should a man rob God?" apparently not aware that his extreme self-denial was the most effectual robbery of God by the abbreviation of his usefulness and life. He walked the streets of great cities absorbed in introspection and prayer, and as unobservant of external things as if he were in the solitude of a wilderness. He spent much time reading the Hebrew and Greek Scriptures upon his knees. He seldom smiled, and perhaps never laughed after the commencement of his public ministry. This habitual self-absorption, added to excessive labor, produced the usual consequences of such errors; his health failed, and his nervous sensibilities suffered tortures which he too often ascribed to demoniacal agency.

In some of his inward combats he would rise at night, and prostrating himself with his face upon the floor would pray and weep before God with unutterable agony. He needed rest and relaxation, and the innocent refreshments of social life. Wesley, who, if not one of the wisest, was one of the most sagacious of men, knew what was requisite in a case like that of Walsh; he took prudent care of his own health, and wrote the best sanitary rules for his preachers; but when we remember that Walsh was frequently with him in Ireland, and labored at three different periods in London, the last time for nearly two years, residing there in Welsey's own house, we are surprised, we are more than surprised, that he did not interpose his authority, if his advice were unavailing, to rescue this young and splendid victim. Wesley seemed to regard him with a sentiment which could hardly be called respect; it was reverence, if not awe. Of no other one of his contemporaries, young or old, has he left such emphatic expressions of admiration as for this young man—a youth of hardly twenty years when he began his ministry, and but twenty-eight when he descended into the grave.[7] All contemporary allusions to him, found in Methodist books, express similar reverence, if not indeed wonder. Not merely his great learning, nor his talents in the pulpit, where he often seemed clothed with the ardor and majesty of a seraph, but something in his character, something of saintly dignity and moral grandeur, impressed thus his friends, and those most who were most intimate with him.[8] His

[7] In a letter to his brother Charles he says of Walsh: "I love, admire, and honor him! and wish we had six preachers in all England of his spirit." Works, vol. vi, p. 662.

[8] "He was a person of a surprising greatness of soul, for which the whole circumference of created good was far, far too little." Morgan's Life of Walsh, chap. 15.

Roman Catholic education and reading seemed to have given to his piety an ascetic tinge, which the confiding and joyous trustfulness of his Methodistic faith could not entirely correct. He fasted and denied himself excessively. At twenty-five he looked like a man of forty.[9] He persisted in preaching when "one would have thought he must drop down dead immediately after." His friends represent him as seeming not to belong to this world; nor could a person better conceive of him, they say, than by forming an idea of one who had returned from the happy dead to converse with men. "Thou knowest my desire," he wrote; "thou knowest there has never been a saint upon earth whom I do not desire to resemble, in doing and suffering thy whole will. I would walk with thee, my God, as Enoch did. I would follow thee to a land unknown, as Abraham did. I would renounce all for thee, as did Moses and Paul. I would, as did Stephen, seal thy truth with my blood!" One who from study of the Scriptures understood what manner of person a Christian approved of God must be, and who from his religious solicitude read, conversed, and thought of little else, says that in Thomas Walsh he saw clearly what till then he had only conceived; that in him his conceptions were truly exemplified. Prostrate upon his face, kneeling, standing, walking, eating—in every posture, and in every place and condition, he was a man mighty in prayer. "In sleep itself, to my certain knowledge," says one of his associates, "his soul went out (Cant. v, 2) in groans, and sighs, and tears to God. His heart having attained such a habit of tendency to its Lord, could only give over when it ceased to beat." He is represented as sometimes lost in mental absence on his knees, with his face heavenward, and arms clasped upon his breast, in such composure that scarcely could one hear him so much as breathe; as absorbed in God, and enjoying a calmness and transport which could not be expressed; while

[9] With the exception of his larger and more luminous eye, his portraits might be taken as fac similies of the current pictures of Jonathan Edwards, whom he resembled much in other respects.

from the serenity, and something resembling splendor which appeared on his countenance, and in all his gestures afterward, one might easily discover that he had been on the Mount of Communion, and had descended, like Moses, with the divine glory on his brow.

His public prayers were attended with such ardor, pertinence, and faith, that it appeared, says his biographer, "as though the heavens were burst open, and God himself appeared in the congregation."

He was sometimes rapt away, as from earth, in his devotions, being quite lost to himself, and insensible of everything around him, absorbed in the visions of God; and in these profound and solemn frames of mind he has remained for hours, still and motionless as a statue.

It has already been remarked that the death of this saintly, this seraphic man, was attended by circumstances deeply afflictive to his friends, and affording a suggestive lesson.[10] Bunyan shows his sagacity in representing his hero as beset with terrors and demoniacal mockeries before his final triumph, for the characters of neither good nor bad men can be inferred from their dying words. It pleases God usually to comfort exceedingly his children in the solemn crisis of death; and even the phantasies of the struggling and disordered mind generally then take their character from the habitually pious or godless course of the preceding life; but it is sometimes otherwise; disease and drugs have much effect on the shattered sensibilities, and Christian biography teaches that surviving friends should attach but little significance, whether saddening or consoling, to the last expressions of the dead. Life, not death, reveals the probable fate of the soul.

Thomas Walsh once heard Fletcher, of Madeley, preach in Wesley's Chapel, in London, on the dying trials of good men. Fletcher supposed that some comparatively weak believers might die most cheerfully; and that some strong ones, for the further purification of their faith, or for

[10] See page 296.

inscrutable reasons, might have severe conflicts. At the subsequent meeting of the Bands, Walsh opposed this opinion, and said he thought it bore hard against God's justice, faithfulness, and covenant love to his servants. Fletcher modestly observed that God's wisdom was sovereign and unsearchable; and though he was sorry he had given offense, yet he could not, with a good conscience, retract what he had said. With some degree of warmth Walsh replied: "Be it done unto you according to your faith; and be it done unto me according to mine!" and here the matter rested.[11]

Two years afterward Walsh needed in death the consolatory opinion of Fletcher. During some months he struggled with what were doubtless the agonies of a disordered nervous system. He was brought almost to the extremity of mental anguish, if not despair of his salvation. To his Christian brethren it was a mysterious spectacle, and public prayers were offered up for him in Dublin, London, and other places. "His great soul," says his biographer, "lay thus, as it were, in ruins for some considerable time, and poured out many a heavy groan and speechless tear from an oppressed heart and dying body. He sadly bewailed the absence of Him whose wonted presence had so often given him the victory over the manifold contradictions and troubles which he endured for his name's sake."

But as sometimes the clouds, thick on the whole heavens, are rent at the horizon the moment the sun seems to pause there before setting, and his last rays stream in and flood with effulgence and joy the entire sky, so was the darkness lifted from the last hour of this good man. After prayers had been offered in his chamber by a group of sympathizing friends, he requested to be left alone a few minutes that he might "meditate a little." They withdrew, and he remained in profound prayer and self-recollection for some time. At last he broke out with the rapturous exclama-

[11] Rev. Melville Horne: Appendix to Walsh's Life.

tion: "*He is come!—he is come!—my beloved is mine, and I am his;—his forever!*" and died.

Thus lived and thus, in his early manhood, died Thomas Walsh, a man whose memory is still as ointment poured forth in the sanctuaries of Methodism.[12]

Before the conference of 1760 Wesley again passed rapidly over much of Ireland. He found the societies in Dublin larger than they had ever been. Connaught enrolled more than three hundred members; Ulster about two hundred and fifty; Leinster a thousand; Munster about six hundred. Methodism, he remarks, had now successfully made its way into every county in Ireland, save Kerry, and many were its exemplary witnesses in most large towns, as well as in the rural districts. He doubted not, however, that there would have been double the number had it not been for the hostility of Protestants, who, with an infatuation which blinded them against their own interest, had endeavored to defeat the Methodistic movement in almost every important place of the kingdom.[13]

[12] The last mental sufferings of Walsh "spread a very strong sensation among his brethren," says Horne. Fletcher, whose wise remarks in London he had so hastily challenged, was deeply affected by his friend's sad verification of them. He wrote a heart-touching letter to Charles Wesley on the occasion, and expressed himself as despondent in view of his own death after such a fact; yet no more triumphant death is recorded in Christian biography than that which awaited the pious vicar of Madeley. See Melville Horne's remarks, Appendix to Walsh's Life. Horne's irrelevant supposition as to the cause of Walsh's despondence is sufficiently refuted by Jackson: Life of Charles Wesley, chap. 21.

[13] See his "Short History of the People called Methodists." Works, vol. vii, p. 373, Am. ed.

CHAPTER II.

ARMINIAN METHODISM IN ENGLAND AND SCOTLAND: 1750-1760.

Success in Cornwall — Wesley in Scotland — His slight Success — He itinerates in England — State of the Societies — Proselytism of the Baptists — Nathaniel Gilbert and Methodism in the West Indies — First African Methodist — Happy Deaths of Methodists — James Wheatley the first expelled Methodist Preacher — John Bennet's Secession — Grace Murray — Wesley's fraternal Disposition toward Calvinists — Whitefield — Wesley preaches and administers the Sacrament to the Calvinistic Leaders at Lady Huntingdon's House — Sketches of Thomas Lee and Christopher Hopper — Charles Wesley ceases to itinerate — Death of Meriton — Fletcher of Madeley — Wesley's Desire for Rest and Solitude — His unfortunate Marriage — His serious Sickness — His Epitaph — His Notes on the New Testament — James Hervey — Wesley's Address to the Clergy — His Views of Ministerial Qualifications.

AT the beginning of the present period of our narrative Wesley wrote to one of his preachers that from Newcastle to London, and from London to Bristol, God was everywhere reviving his work.[1] He visited Cornwall repeatedly during this time.[2] At St. Just he still found the largest of his societies in the west; so great a proportion of believers he had not seen in any other part of the nation, nor "any society so alive to God." He laid there the foundation of a new chapel, and when it was completed pronounced it the best in the country. Preaching-houses had begun to dot the west generally, but they were as yet very humble structures, and scarcely distinguishable as chapels.

He assembled at St. Ives the stewards of all the Cornish

[1] Letter to Joseph Cownley. Lives of Early Methodist Preachers, vol. i, p. 100.

[2] Journal, 1750, 1753, 1757.

societies in a quarterly meeting, and held with them the first Watch-night known in that region. Only slight and occasional attempts were now made at persecution, for Methodism had triumphed generally in this once degraded section of the land. "What now," wrote Wesley, "can destroy the work of God in these parts but zeal for and contending about opinions." He had as great an antipathy against doctrinal controversies as most theologians have zeal for them. Crowds of tinners attended him wherever he appeared. Gwennap assembled still its immense hosts. At Camelford he preached in the market-place, and had occasion to exclaim, "How are the lions in this town become lambs!" Port Isaac, long a barren soil, promised now to bring forth abundant fruit. At St. Agnes the knowledge of God had already "traveled from the lowest to the greatest." He was surprised at the talents of the Cornish local preachers; he heard extempore preaching from a reformed tinner as correct as "most men of learning could write." Some of the old persecutors in high life had become changed; and the one who imprisoned Maxfield no longer molested the Methodists nor allowed others to oppose them, but had become noted by his charities to the poor. At one place he found, in his usual pastoral examination of the society, that some of its members were in the practice of using, if not of dealing in "uncustomed goods," then a general vice on the Cornish coast. He stopped short in his inquiries, and told them they should see his face no more unless the accursed thing were entirely abandoned; and Methodism, more than any other means, has corrected the evil throughout Cornwall.[3] At St. Mewen and St. Austle his congregations were too large to be accommodated. At St. Ewe some fell to the earth under the preached word, and the whole assembly seemed awe-struck. At Redruth he addressed in the open street a crowd who wept around him. At Falmouth he found that the former riots were followed by reverent attention; the town was "quiet from one end to the other;" not

[3] It reformed also the barbarous cruelties of the wreckers on that coast.

only his chapel, but the yard and the neighboring houses were crowded with eager hearers. At Breage a great reformation had taken place; it had been noted for its violence against the Methodists; its clergyman instigated mobs and fabricated the basest slanders respecting Wesley and his societies, charging him with having been expelled from Oxford for a crime, and his people with extinguishing the lights in their private meetings like the ancient heathen. After bringing upon the inoffensive society much suffering by these reports, the clerical persecutor had sunk into despondence and hanged himself. The people now flocked around Wesley; he had not intended to stop among them, but they constrained him. He preached in the street, and gratefully recorded that "the lions of Breage too were now changed into lambs." Everywhere, in fine, on the west coast did he find the power of the truth prevailing.

In April, 1751, he first visited Scotland, accompanied by Christopher Hopper, who had returned with him from Ireland. It has already been stated[4] that Methodist dragoons from the regiment of John Haime, in Flanders, had founded societies at Dunbar and Musselborough. A colonel, now in quarters at the latter place, invited Wesley to the North. Whitefield warned him not to go, as his Arminian principles would "leave him nothing to do but to dispute from morning till night."[5] Wesley replied that he would go; that he would studiously avoid controverted points, and, according to his custom, keep to the fundamental truths of Christianity. He went, and was welcomed to Musselborough. He preached while the people stood as statues around him, respectful, but too cold for his Methodistic ardor; nevertheless, the prejudice which, as he says, the devil had been several years planting, was plucked up in an hour. A bailiff of the town and an elder of the kirk waited upon him with the request that he should stay with them for some time, or at least two or three days longer, and offered to fit up a larger place for his congregations. His engagements, however,

[4] See page 239. [5] Coke and Moore's Life of Wesley, III, 2.

called him away; but Hopper returned and preached among them to large congregations. This, says the lay itinerant, was the beginning of a good work in Scotland.[6] Still later Hopper preached at Edinburgh, Dunbar, Leith, Dundee, and Aberdeen. God, he wrote, blessed his word, "and raised up witnesses that he had sent us to the North Britons also."

In April, 1753, Wesley again entered Scotland. He was received courteously by Gillies of Glasgow. He preached early in the morning outside the town; the weather and the hour did not suit the Scotch, and his congregation was small; but at the service under a tent in the afternoon he had "six times as many," and his word was "in power." It rained the next day, and Gillies had the courage to open the kirk for him. A few years earlier it would have required equal courage on the part of Wesley to enter it, such had been his "High-Church principles." "Surely," he said at the close of the day, "with God nothing is impossible! Who would have believed, five and twenty years ago, either that the minister would have desired it, or that I should have consented to preach in a Scotch kirk!" His next congregation was too large for the church, and he addressed them in the open air. On the Sabbath more than a thousand people listened to him in a shower of rain, and at his last sermon the meadow on which he preached was filled from side to side. He believed that a great and effectual door was opened for Methodism in the north, but the apparent respectfulness of the Scotch was mostly indifference. Their cold courtesy denied to Methodism even the stimulus of riots. They did not persecute him, but they would not follow him. On another occasion he remarked that they *know* everything and *feel* nothing. It became, indeed, a problem to him "why the hand of the Lord, who does nothing without a cause, was almost entirely stayed in Scotland?"

He persisted, however, in his visits to the north. In 1757 he was again welcomed by Gillies to Glasgow, and the kirk could not accommodate his numerous but impassive congre-

[6] Hopper's Life. Lives of Early Methodist Preachers, vol. i, p. 30.

gations. A tent-pulpit was placed for him in the large and commodious yard of the poor-house, where a singular spectacle was presented. Around him stood the collected people; in front was the infirmary, with its windows crowded with the sick, while adjacent to it was the lunatic hospital with its inmates reverently listening. Amid these scenes he not only proclaimed his message, but what, perhaps, had never been done before by a Methodist preacher in Scotland, baptized several children. His congregations grew daily, notwithstanding the comparatively slight effect of his word. At one time his voice could hardly reach their outmost limit; at another two thousand people retired, unable to hear, though the evening was calm and clear. He discovered a small obscure society in the city, but, with the characteristic national taste, they met mostly to discuss some general or difficult point of religion. He directed them to confine their attention to matters of personal piety, after the example of the Methodists in England, and placed them under the care of Dr. Gillies. He was agreeably surprised to find the society founded by John Haime's fellow dragoons at Musselburgh, zealous for the faith; "and there," he adds, "the tree was known by its fruits; the national shyness and stubbornness were gone, and they were as open and teachable as little children." At Dunbar he met equal encouragement—"a little society, most of them rejoicing in God their Saviour." The men whose piety had been tried in the fires of Fontenoy had introduced into both these places the living faith.

Wesley traversed England during the present period in every direction, and found the societies almost everywhere advancing. His preachers were still occasionally mobbed, but he himself was generally, if not universally, received with a respect which was fast growing into a national sentiment of reverence. At Birmingham the chapel could not contain half his congregation, and he had to go into the street. "How has the scene changed here!" he writes; "the last time I preached at Birmingham the stones flew on every side; if any disturbance were made now the disturber would be in more danger than the preacher." In meeting the society there, he says, the hearts of many were melted within them, so that neither they nor he could refrain from tears. At Wednesbury and Darlaston, formerly the strongholds of the Staffordshire mobs, God had summoned away, by "a train of amazing strokes, most of the old persecutors, and those that remained were not only respectful but cordial." He preached to a large congregation in the open air at the former place, amid a rain storm, but every man, woman, and child stayed till the end of the discourse. Peace, however, had brought greater perils than persecution. It was necessary for him to sift out Antinomian and Anabaptist errors, which had been brought in among them from abroad. At a later visit to Wednesbury he found a new chapel erected, and remarked that few congregations exceeded this either in numbers or seriousness. At Wakefield, where, a few years before, the people were "as roaring lions," and the honest vicar would not allow him to preach in his yard lest the mob should pull down the house, he was now heard attentively in the church. At Hull he met a very different reception, for it was his first appearance there. As he landed on the quay it was crowded with staring and laughing groups inquiring "Which is he? Which is he?" An immense multitude, rich and poor, horse and foot, with many coaches, gathered to hear him in the fields, half a mile out of the city. He cried to them, "What shall it profit a man if he gain the whole world and lose his own soul?" Some thousands heard seriously, but "many behaved as if possessed by Moloch." Stones and clods flew on every side. When he had finished the mob followed him, throwing missiles into his coach windows. The house in which he was entertained was attacked until midnight, and its windows broken to the third story. Hull, however, speedily redeemed itself, and has ever since maintained the honor of Methodism. At his next visit he was respectfully heard by its best citizens; and even the rich, he says, had the Gospel preached unto them in the streets. At Sunderland he found John Nelson's society to be "one of the liveliest in the north of England." It included two hundred and fifty members. At Biddick a multitude of colliers stood to hear him in a drenching rain storm, and melted like wax under the word. At Barnard Castle he held his ground and preached through his discourse, though the mob played an engine upon the assembly. At Chester he saw the Methodist chapel in ruins; two days before his arrival the mob had pulled it down; but he took his stand near the wreck, and defended "the sect everywhere spoken against." The mob was subdued, and Methodism again reared its standard there never to be struck. At his next visit the scene was quite changed; "there was peace through all the city." At Bolton the society had doubled since his preceding visit; they were increased in grace as well as in numbers, "walking closely with God, lovingly and circumspectly with one another, and wisely toward those who were without." At Charlton he addressed a vast congregation gathered from all the towns and country for many miles around. Methodism had recently made its way into the neighborhood against the most discouraging odds. All the farmers had entered into a joint engagement to dismiss from their service any one who should dare to hear the itinerant preachers; but, providentially, the chief man of the combination was soon after smitten by the truth, and sent for these very men to preach in his house. Many of the other confederates came to hear, and their servants and laborers gladly followed their example; "so the whole device of Satan fell to the ground, and the word of God grew and prevailed." At Manchester Methodism still had severe struggles; the mob stood quiet and awe-struck while he preached in the street, but when he closed "raged horribly." He made his first visit to Liverpool, (April, 1755,) though he had now been itinerating over the realm for more than fifteen years; but that great commercial metropolis was yet in its infancy. He found there a Methodist chapel larger than that at Newcastle, and the hearts of the whole congregation "seemed to be moved before the Lord and the presence of his power." He spent nearly a week among them, preaching to crowds morning and evening.[7]

At Keighley, famous for riots, he preached without molestation; "such a change," he writes, "has God wrought in the hearts of the people since John Nelson was in the dungeon here." At York, which formerly repelled Methodism at every point, he now found the "richest society, number for number," which it possessed in England. At Sheffield, which had been unvisited by a Methodist itinerant since he himself had been there two years before, the little society had not only sustained itself, but had made progress in numbers and grace by its own efforts, under the guidance of its Class-leaders. As he passed and repassed Haworth, he frequently paused to preach for Grimshaw. He usually administered the Lord's Supper there to a thousand communicants, and preached in the church-yard to many thousands of hearers, gathered from all the adjacent towns and villages. At Placey Methodism had demonstrated its efficacy, as at Kingswood, and a society of redeemed colliers welcomed him. It was a "pattern to all the societies in England;" no member ever missed his band or class; they had no discord of any kind among them, but with one heart and one mind provoked each other to love and good works. At Hornby he found that the landlords had turned all the Methodists out of their houses; but it proved "a singular kindness," for they built small houses at the end of the town, in which

[7] His remarks on the growth and prospects of Liverpool are a curiosity in our day. He says: "Liverpool is one of the neatest, best built towns I have seen in England. I think it is full twice as large as Chester; most of the streets are quite straight. Two-thirds of the town, we were informed, has been added within these forty years. *If it continue to increase in the same proportion, in fifty years more it will nearly equal Bristol.* The people in general are the most mild and courteous I ever saw in a seaport town; as indeed appears by their friendly behavior, not only to the Jews and Papists who live among them, but even to the Methodists, (so called.) Many of them, I learned, were dear lovers of controversy; but I had better work. I pressed upon them all 'repentance toward God, and faith in our Lord Jesus Christ.'"

forty or fifty of them lived together, a little Christian community, as comfortable and devoted as a station of Moravians. At Wandsworth, "a desolate place," an effectual door was opened for him by a West India planter, several of whose negroes were present and awakened by the word. He baptized two of them, one a convert and the first regenerated African he had ever known. She returned to the West Indies with her master, and was the first of that innumerable host of her people which Methodism has ever since been leading into heaven from Africa and America. "Shall not his saving health be made known to all nations?" wrote Wesley, after preaching to them. The words were more prophetic than he supposed. This American gentleman was Nathaniel Gilbert, Speaker of the House of Assembly in Antigua. He became a local preacher, as we shall have occasion to notice, and introduced Methodism into the West Indies, where it has since spread among all the English colonies.

Such are but a few glimpses of Wesley's incessant travels and labors during this period. It would be impossible to follow him in their detail and in their results, without filling volumes. One interesting fact enhanced the encouragement of this general prosperity; Methodism had now been sufficiently long in progress to afford many ripe sheaves for heaven. It had been signalized by remarkable conversions; it had now become noted by triumphant deaths. "Our people die well," has always been a grateful remark of Methodists. As they were expected to maintain a good "assurance" of the Divine favor in life, it was hardly possible they should falter on entering into the eternal life. By the year 1751 good John Nelson had a catalogue of more than seventy who had ascended to their rest in triumph from his prosperous society at Birstal.[8] In Bristol, London, and Dublin, the societies now frequently recorded, with mournful joy, the departure of their brethren beloved into the "general assembly, and Church of the first-born which are written in heaven." The Journals of both the Wesleys

[8] Jackson's Charles Wesley, chap. 17.

abound in such notices. Charles Wesley especially took a melancholy pleasure in recording them, and in no place more than among the reclaimed colliers of Kingswood, as yet the most interesting field of the triumphs of Methodism over the barbarism of the British populace. Many of his elegies, written on such occasions, have an unearthly power; a sadness of the grave pervaded by the rapture of heaven. On the death of nearly every Methodist preacher, from Thomas Beard, the martyr, who was the first that died, till, with an elegiac verse on his lips, he lay down himself to die, he wrote not one only, but usually two or three of these affecting and beautiful memorials. His "Funeral Hymns," occasioned, with hardly an exception, by actual deaths, constitute the most perfect part of the Methodist psalmody, and for a hundred years and more these testimonials of the dying triumphs of their early brethren have been sung at the death-beds and funerals of Methodists throughout the world.

These encouraging evidences of prosperity in most of the land were contrasted, however, by frequent instances of discord and delusion. At Bristol serious disturbances occurred, and its nine hundred Methodists were diminished in 1757 to but half the number; but a day of fasting and prayer was observed, an extraordinary revival ensued, and the strength of the society was restored. The society at Norwich was rent and almost destroyed in 1751, by the defection and apostasy of James Wheatley, who fell into scandalous vices and has the peculiar distinction of being the first Methodist preacher expelled from the Connection. The secession broke to pieces; Wesley gathered its remnants together, incorporated them into his remaining societies, and left the latter nearly six hundred strong.[9] In Lancashire the classes were disturbed by the secession of John Bennet and a large part of the Methodists at Bolton. Bennet was a man of classical education and superior native talents. He had been

[9] Short History of the People called Methodists. Works vol. vii, p. 373. American Edition. My other data are from his Journal, from 1750 to 1760. Works, vol. iii.

led into the Methodist ministry by Lady Huntingdon. His correspondence with Wesley shows him to have been opposed to Calvinism, but at his defection he assailed the Methodists violently for their Arminianism, and imputed Papistical doctrines to Wesley. He had been a useful man in Lancashire, Derbyshire, and Cheshire, but his new course was proportionally disastrous.[10]

In many of the country towns Wesley's most onerous work was the administration of Discipline, especially along the coasts, where the crime of smuggling was hardly recognized by the common people as a vice. He showed it no forbearance. He nearly broke up whole Classes in order to suppress the evil, and his societies did more than all the police of the realm to abate it.

He was also compelled to labor indefatigably to reclaim his incipient Churches from doctrinal wranglings.[11] These he would not tolerate; Methodism disowned their import-

[10] He was the husband of Grace Murray, to whom Wesley had made overtures of marriage. He died in about eight years after his separation from the Methodists. His excellent wife lived for more than fifty years, in Christian retirement, near Chapel-en-le-Frith, honoring religion by her daily example. She remained partial to the Methodist usages to the last, and maintained a class-meeting in her house for many years. She died in 1803, aged 89. Her last words were, "Glory to thee, my God; peace thou givest me." Wesley undoubtedly loved her, and she deserved his affection and his name. See Life and Times of Lady Huntingdon, vol. i, p. 45.

[11] The catholic reader will, perhaps, be surprised to learn that Wesley's chief vexation in this respect was from the Baptists. He frequently refers to them as inveigling away his converts, or "making havoc" of his societies; and on one occasion (Journal, April 3, 1751) laments that he had to "spend near ten minutes in controversy with them," more than he had "done in public for many months, perhaps years before." Charles Wesley seldom alludes to the proselyting habits of these zealous people without a tinge of bitterness. They seem to have vexed his righteous soul more than any other class of Christians, except those lay Methodist preachers who favored Dissent. He calls them a "caviling, contentious sect, always watching to steal away our children." (Jackson's Charles Wesley, chap. 20.) How have the times changed since then, and who would now think of ascribing such a proclivity to a denomination which professes union, while it denies communion, with all the rest of the evangelical world, and whose reputation is so peculiar in respect to proselytism—the worst deformity of bigotry?

ance; it would not admit that dogmas, except the most fundamental and generally received, should be considered conditions of Christian communion, or of membership in its Classes. Calvinistic Antinomianism beset him at almost every turn, and ravaged his most promising societies. With the evangelical Calvinists of his day he maintained, however, the most harmonious relations. He ministered often during the present period in Whitefield's chapels, and Whitefield in his. After preaching in Whitefield's Tabernacle in Plymouth, he said: "Thus it behoveth us to trample on bigotry and party zeal. Ought not all who love God to love one another?" "Mr. Whitefield," he wrote, during a visit to London, "called upon me; disputings are now no more; we love one another, and join hand in hand to promote the cause of our common Master."[12] He met Whitefield and the Calvinistic leaders on all convenient occasions, and at one time preached and administered the Lord's Supper, at Lady Huntingdon's house in London, to Whitefield, Madan, Romaine, Downing, Venn, Griffith Jones, and others.[13] Tenacious as these good men were of what they called the "Doctrines of Grace" they could not well quarrel while they saw that the great "Work of Grace" was so triumphantly advancing through the country by the labors of both parties.

Though Wesley's reputation and years now commanded too much public respect to allow of frequent disturbances from mobs, his lay preachers had still often to encounter them, especially in towns and villages where they preached for the first time. Among the bravest of the brave of these heroic men was Thomas Lee. Few of his fellow-laborers endured severer "fights of affliction." From his childhood he had feared God, and maintained an admirable purity of conduct. He uttered an oath when but four years old, but felt such compunction for it that he never swore again throughout his life. As early as his tenth or eleventh year

[12] Journal, Anno 1755.

[13] Wesley's text on this occasion showed his spirit. It was 1 Corinthians, xiii, 13: "Now abideth faith, hope, charity, these three; but the greatest of these is charity."

he experienced deep religious impressions, and the words "everlasting" and "eternal" were much upon his mind. In his fifteenth year, while an apprentice to the "worsted trade," he gave himself with fondness to books, and spent much of his leisure in reading the Scriptures. He also found delight in prayer, and had many inward consolations, though he had never then heard any one speak of the comforts of the Holy Ghost. He was, in fine, one of those earnest, sensitive minds, numerous in all communities, present in nearly all congregations, who are ready to respond to the first faithful appeals of the pulpit, and who sprang forth everywhere with ardor on the first appearance of the Methodist itinerants of those times, recognizing their apostolic character, ready to weep at their feet, and to die with them in their persecutions. He heard Grimshaw, and made many good resolutions, which were revived and deepened when he heard some of the humbler Methodist evangelists. "From that time," he writes, "my heart was so united to them that I dropped at once all my former companions, and, blessed be God! I have not from that hour had one desire to turn back."

His scrupulous conscience was, however, a long time troubled with religious anxieties. He suspected that he was a hypocrite, and mentioned his fears to a friend, but got no comfort from the ambiguous reply given him. It was impossible, he says, to express the anguish he felt; he longed for death, though he believed himself unfit for it. But he omitted no religious duty; with the consent of his master, who had the good sense to esteem him highly, he prayed daily in the family, and soon conducted domestic worship in neighboring households. Being alone a great part of one day, and much engaged in meditation and prayer, he felt a persuasion that God was willing to receive him. He left his business immediately and went to his usual place of prayer; "in a moment," he says, "God broke in upon my soul in so wonderful a manner that I could no longer doubt of his forgiving love. I cried, 'My Lord and my God!'

And with the spirit I was then in, I could have praised, and loved, and waited to all eternity."[14]

His habit of praying in families had now prepared him to conduct prayer-meetings, and as Methodism pressed all its available talent into use, he was soon holding such services among his neighbors. He was invited to Harding Moor, Lingobin, and Thornton. No Methodist itinerant had yet appeared in these places, but the faithful young evangelist was enabled in a short time to deliver up a society in each of them to the traveling preachers. Working at his business half the time for his subsistence, and exhorting and praying up and down the country, he founded Methodism not only in the villages named, but also at Long Addingham, at Greenough Hill, at Hartwith, and other places. At Pateley Bridge he was initiated into the common lot of the Methodist evangelists, and received his first baptism of persecution from the clods, clubs, and stones of the mob. His meek and pure spirit was not weak, but displayed during this and later trials a heroism which John Nelson would have admired. "We have done enough," cried the mob, who were instigated by the parish clergyman; "we have done enough to make an end of him." "I did, indeed," he says, "reel to and fro, and my head was broken with a stone. But I never found my soul more happy, nor was ever more composed in my closet. It was a glorious time, and there are several who date their conversion from that day." Such tests were very salutary to the early Methodist ministry. They drove cowards quickly from the ranks and made heroes of all others. He went to a neighboring town, had his wounded head dressed, and the same day bravely preached in the street to a large crowd, many of whom had come with him from the scene of his sufferings. Some of the rioters had followed with them, but as their clerical leader was not present they were restrained, "and the Lord blessed us much," says the evangelist.

During four years did this good man travel about on foot,

14 Lives of Early Methodist Preachers, vol. ii, p. 196.

preaching and founding societies in neglected and obscure places. He was often, he says, thoroughly wet, and obliged to preach in his damp clothes from appointment to appointment. He worked at night that he might travel and preach by day. His appointments multiplied so fast that he was at last obliged to give up business, buy a horse, and take the field as an itinerant; it was much against his will, for though he had made full proof of his ministry his modesty shrunk from an honor so high, as he deemed it. The eccentric but generous Grimshaw could not fail to love such a man; driving about Yorkshire night and day on his evangelical tours, he witnessed the usefulness of Lee, and inspiriting him by his own example, sent him out on one of his extended circuits for a month. He thus appeared formally among the traveling preachers of the day, and never disappeared from their ranks until he was summoned away to his final rest.

We cannot, by tracing the travels of Whitefield and Wesley during this period, obtain a correct impression of the times. Their comparatively few persecutions would lead us to suppose that the populace had been almost universally subdued, but the subordinate laborers were still in many places confronting the fiercest mobs. It is incredible what trials Thomas Lee encountered during most of these years. In the winter of 1752 and 1753 the work of God prospered exceedingly, he writes, throughout his long routes in Yorkshire; "but persecution raged on every side." Wherever he went he was in perils, "carrying, his life in his hands." One day as he was going through Pateley the captain of the mob, who was kept in constant pay, pursued him, and pulled him from his horse. The crowd soon collected about him, and one or another "struck up his heels," he says, "more than twenty times upon the stones." They pulled him into a house by the hair of his head, then pushed him back with one or two upon him, and threw him upon the edge of the stone stairs. The fall nearly broke his back, and for many years he suffered from the injury. Thence they dragged him to the common sewer, rolled him in it for some time, and then drove him to the bridge and threw him into the water. When they drew him out he was unable to rise from the ground, his strength being quite spent. His wife, who, like Nelson's, was worthy of him, now came to his relief with a few friends. Seeing her helping him, some of the rioters asked, "What, are you a Methodist?" and giving her several blows, which made her bleed at the mouth, swore they would put her into the river. All this time he lay upon the ground, the mob being undetermined what to do with him. Some cried, "Make an end of him;" others were for sparing his life; but the dispute was cut short by their agreeing to put other Methodists into the river; and taking a number of them away for the purpose, they left him and his wife together. She endeavored to raise him up, but having no strength he dropped to the ground again. She again raised him, and supported him some distance, when by her assistance he was enabled to mount a horse, and made out to ride to the house of a friend, where he was stripped from head to foot and washed. He left his wet clothes, and rode courageously to Greenough Hill, where a congregation was waiting for him, and though "much bruised and very weak," he preached from Psalm xxxiv, 19: "Many are the afflictions of the righteous; but the Lord delivereth him out of them all." He was not to be discouraged, and the next day was again proclaiming his message. His brethren followed him to a neighboring appointment; but the leader of the mob came also, and with a long stick broke the glass of the windows while he preached. "This," he says, "made a little confusion at first, but afterward the Lord poured down his blessing in an uncommon manner. Almost all were in tears, and the people took joyfully the spoiling of their goods." Thence he rode to Hartwith, where, he writes, "we had peace, and the power of the Lord was with us;" but when the preaching of the day was over he was so bruised and sore that he could not undress himself without aid. Nearly a whole year "hot persecutions" prevailed around him. The Methodists were violently abused in the streets. They applied to the dean of Ripon for protection, but got none, for the Church would have suffered in the investigation. "But," remarks the persecuted preacher, "what made amends was, the members of the society loved each other dearly, and had exceedingly comfortable seasons together;" and after one of his days of sore trial, he says of their meeting, "it seemed to us little less than heaven; and though it was a hard day, it was a blessed one to my soul." In later life he wrote that he remembered that once, during these times of trouble, when his life continually hung in suspense, a demurring thought occurred to him—"It is hard to have no respite, to be thus perpetually suffering." Immediately it was impressed upon his mind: "Did you not, when you were on the borders of despair, promise the Lord that if he would give you an assurance of his favor you would count no suffering, sorrow, nor affliction too great to be endured for his name's sake?" This reflection at once silenced all murmuring, and thenceforth he bore whatever befell him with patience and joy, and felt willing to bear it as long as God saw meet, if it were to the end of his life.

During the remainder of this period Thomas Lee preached on the Birstal, Leeds, Lincolnshire, Newcastle, and Manchester Circuits. His labors were greatly effective, his circuits incredibly long. We may judge somewhat of the labors of the Methodist preachers of that day from the fact that his "Leeds round" comprehended Sheffield and York, and extended into Derbyshire on the south, to Hull on the east, and to Newton on the north. His Manchester Circuit included Lancashire, Cheshire, parts of Shropshire and of Wales, Staffordshire, and part of Derbyshire. Throughout most of these years he suffered from mobs; sometimes the pulpit was torn out of the preaching-house, and burned in the street; at others eggs, "filled with blood, and sealed with pitch," were thrown in upon the assemblies, "making strange work wherever they alighted." Mire, clods, and stones flew about him as he rode into or out of the towns; the rioters beat him and his horse, knocked him off his horse, dragged him on the earth, poured water upon him from his head to his feet, covered him with paint, "laying it on plenteously." Such was the treatment he received, particularly in Newark, in 1760. He was offered immediate relief if he would only promise to preach there no more; but this, he says, he could not do. He suffered on till he conquered, and could write: "Thus ended the trouble in Newark; since then the word of God has prospered greatly, and a convenient preaching-house has been built, in which numerous congregations meet without disturbance."

After years of such labors and trials, Thomas Lee wrote to Wesley: "If I this moment saw all the sufferings I have had for His name's sake; if they were now spread before me I would say, 'Lord, if thou wilt give me strength I will now begin again, and thou shalt add to them lions' dens and fiery furnaces, and by thy grace I will go through them all.' My life, though attended with many crosses, has been a life of mercies. I count it one of the greatest favors that he still allows me to do a little for him, and that he in any measure owns the word which I am able to speak in his name. I beg that I may be humble at his feet all the days of my life, and may be more and more like Him whom my soul loveth."[15]

One of the lay heroes of Methodism, especially in the north, during this period, was Christopher Hopper, a man distinguished through many years of faithful service. He describes his early life as especially wicked.[16] He was prone to anger and of a cruel disposition, and took, he says, a diabolical pleasure in hanging dogs, worrying cats, and

15 He died in 1786. Mary Lee, his devoted wife, who had stood by him amid mobs, wrote to Wesley of his last moments, that "he sobbed several times, looked up once and smiled, closed his eyes, and gently fell asleep." Wesley records his death in the Minutes of 1787, and calls him "a faithful brother, and a good old soldier of Jesus Christ."

16 Lives of Early Methodist Preachers, vol. i, p. 25.

killing birds and insects, wringing and cutting them to pieces. These, however, were the freaks of his misdirected childhood, for his heart was naturally tender, and his robust soul full of beneficent energy, and during his youth his religious impressions were frequent and sometimes intense. He endeavored to stifle them in singing, dancing, fishing, fowling, in hunting, cock-fighting, card-playing, racing, or "whatever the devil brought to town or country," but could not succeed. The universe appeared to him, he writes, as a vault wherein true comfort was entombed, and the sun itself as a lamp to show the gloomy horrors of a guilty mind. "I was not happy," he adds, "yet I believed there was something that could make me so, but I knew not what it was nor where to find it." His vigorous mind had meanwhile acquired no small amount of scientific knowledge, and he became a school-teacher. Wesley passed through his neighborhood; "he made a short blaze," says Hopper, "soon disappeared, and left us in consternation." But Hopper felt the impression of his sermon. "At this time there was a great bustle," he adds, "among all sorts and parties about religion, and I made a bustle among the rest. I said, I will read my Bible, say my prayers, go to the parish church, and reform my life." This, however, he soon perceived, was not sufficient to appease the moral cravings of his awakened spirit. Reeves, one of the heroic itinerants who had been indicted at Cork as a vagabond, passed through the town, and under his preaching the baffled penitent saw what he yet needed. "I am broken to pieces," he said; "I am sick of sin, sick of myself, and sick of a vain world. I will therefore look unto the Lord." In deep compunction he called upon God for relief, and soon found it. God, angels, men, and the whole creation, he writes, appeared then to him in a new light, and stood related to him in a manner he never before knew. This was what Wesley and the Methodists called conversion; the renovation of the soul, by which it is placed in harmony with all its just and pure relations to men and to God, and, in the consciousness of that harmony, has a peace which passes expression. Wesley made him a Class-leader. He began also to exhort with great success. His "poor old mother" was among the first fruits of his zeal. His brother and sister also soon acknowledged him the instrument of their conversion. Many of his former companions were reclaimed from their vices. The "fire kindled, and the flame spread," and he was called to Low-Spenn, Barlow, Woodside, Prudhoe, Newlands, Blanchland, Durham, Sunderland, and many other places, and before he was hardly aware what the result would be, he found himself preaching and itinerating. Persecutors attempted to seize and impress him for the army, but he escaped them in remarkable ways, sometimes leaving them to quarrel among themselves respecting him, and to end their disputes with "blows and bloody faces." Rectors and curates headed mobs to assail him, and answered his arguments with hard words and hard blows. He was indicted before a court, but nothing could be found against him. None of these things moved him; "I gave," he says, "my soul, body, and substance to my adorable Saviour, and I grieved I had no more to give."

Thus did Christopher Hopper do good service during these times, in founding and spreading Methodism in scores of towns and villages. He usually led a class every night, and preached three or four times every Sabbath. He made excursions to Newcastle, Sunderland, and Durham, and towns and villages around his home to the distance of twenty or thirty miles, preaching with great power. He did not, he says, regard much a little dirt, a few rotten eggs, the sound of a cow's horn, the noise of bells, or a few snow-balls in their season, but he found occasion sometimes to think more seriously of salutations from the mob in blows, stones, brickbats, and bludgeons. When he had to preach with a patch on his wounded head he gloried in it as a badge for his Lord. He spread Methodism greatly in Allendale, "where a glorious work broke out." He went from town to town, and from house to house, "singing, praying, preaching," and large multitudes followed him from place to place, weeping and praying. Whole congregations were sometimes melted into tears under his discourses, and "bowed down before the Lord as the heart of one man." He preached in barns, cock-pits, ale-houses, and wherever he could find a door open for him.

It would require many pages to detail the travels and labors of this faithful itinerant in England, Ireland, and Scotland; the many mobs he encountered, and the many societies he founded. He was the first Methodist lay preacher, as we have recorded, who went into Scotland; and all the north of England still cherishes his memory. He did much during our present period to extend Methodism in that part of the country. Cownley, who had been his fellow-laborer in Ireland, was also with him, and they formed several societies which continue to this day. On the banks of the Tyne, in Prudhoe and Nafferton, besides a variety of other places in that neighborhood, numbers were awakened and converted. They endured no little persecution also. In one of Cownley's excursions into the Dales he was assaulted by a mob, which was headed by a clergyman. Warm from the village tavern, this zealous son of the Church advanced to the attack with the collected rabble. Cownley was preaching near the door of an honest Quaker, when the minister insisted that he was breaking the order of the Church, and began to recite the canon against conventicles. "If I am disorderly," answered the preacher, "you are not immaculate;" and he reminded him of the canon "for sober conversation, and against frequenting ale-houses." Confounded with the pertinent reply the parson retired for a while; but mustering up his courage and his ale-house friends he returned, and with threats of prosecution began to take down the names of the hearers. A Quaker, who was one of the congregation, hearing the menace, stepped up and with unruffled gravity clapped the curate on the back and said, "Friend John, put my name down first." This ended the contest; quite disconcerted, the clergyman withdrew and left the field to the Methodist, and it was never afterward yielded.

Both these noted itinerants were chief founders of Methodism in the Dales. During these years they met formidable difficulties, but left the region to their successors covered with a rich harvest, and the "Dales" soon stood prominently on the list of circuits in the Conference Minutes.[17]

Of Charles Wesley's labors during the present decade we have but disconnected traces in fragments of journals and undated letters. His family resided at Bristol, and as Methodism had now spread over the country, and was generally settled and systematized, and its superintendence by his brother was almost ubiquitous, he ceased to itinerate in the latter part of 1756, and thenceforward mostly confined himself to its head-quarters in London and Bristol.[18] His passages between these cities were continual; his pulpit and pastoral labors in each more arduous, if possible, than when he traveled more at large. In the metropolis he had charge of four principal chapels, besides other preaching-places, and the communion was administered by him every Sabbath, beginning at five o'clock in the morning. After the expulsion of Wheatley he made an excursion over most of England expressly to ascertain the moral condition of the lay ministry. Wheatley had reported that his own private flagrancies were common among these laborious and devoted men. Charles Wesley himself was suspicious that they were at least becoming disaffected toward the national Church, his prejudices for which were now more strenuous by far than those of his brother. He assembled them in small conferences, at various points, and was surprised at their usefulness, integrity, and talents. He speaks of only two or three as deficient in abilities, and one he sent back to his secular employment as intellectually incompetent for the ministry; but he brought to London only favorable

[17] After laboring more than half a century in the itinerant ministry, Hopper died in 1802, aged eighty. While on his death-bed, the veteran said to a friend: "I have not a doubt, no, not the shadow of a doubt; and as for the enemy, I know not what has become of him. I have neither seen him nor heard from him for some time. I think he has quitted the field."

[18] Jackson's Life of Charles Wesley, chap. 21.

reports of the piety and ministerial decorum of them all.[19]

Wesley lost during the present period one of the earliest coadjutors which the Established Church had afforded him. Rev. John Meriton died on the 10th of August, 1753. He was a member of the first Wesleyan Conference, and attended most of the subsequent sessions down to the year of his death. He itinerated extensively in England, Wales, and Ireland. He was mobbed and imprisoned for the Gospel, and deserves a fuller record in the history of the great revival for which he labored and suffered so much; but no traces of his useful life remain, except in brief yet frequent allusions of contemporary Methodist documents. Even the place of his death is unmentioned, and we know nothing of his last hours. Charles Wesley, however, has embalmed his memory in an immortal elegy.[20]

His place in the Methodist ranks was more than supplied by another Churchman, who came to Wesley's assistance during the present period. In the "Short History of the People called Methodists," Wesley says: "March 13, 1757, finding myself weak at Snowsfields, I prayed that God, if he saw good, would send me help at the chapels. He did so. As soon as I had done preaching Mr. Fletcher came, who had just then been ordained priest, and hastened to the chapel on purpose to assist me, as he supposed me to be alone. How wonderful are the ways of God! When my bodily strength failed, and no clergyman in England was able and willing to assist me, he sent me help from the mountains of Switzerland! and a helpmeet for me in every respect! Where could I have found such another!" Fletcher thus comes upon the scene, and comes as an angel of light.

As the traveler sails along the North shore of the Lake of Geneva, Switzerland, interested in its rare scenery as

[19] Jackson's Charles Wesley, chap. 17.

[20] See it in Jackson's Charles Wesley, chap. 18, English edition. It is omitted in the American edition.

well as in the literary associations which Gibbon, De Stael, and others have left to Lausanne and Coppet, his eye is attracted by Nyon, a beautiful village between these towns. The large homestead of the Flecheres, descendants of a noble Savoyard house, stands prominently out among the humble dwellings of the villagers, and is still occupied by the family, who continue to maintain the name and religious reputation of their house. John William de la Flechere was born there in 1729.[21] He was early religiously inclined, and was designed by his parents for the Church. His superior intellect gave him distinguished success in the prize competitions of the University of Geneva. On completing his studies he abandoned his intention of entering the ministry, one of his objections being his Arminian sentiments, and his consequent inability conscientiously to subscribe to the Calvinistic doctrines of the Church of his country. He chose a military life, and going to Portugal, received a captain's commission for Brazil, but accidentally failing to sail at the appointed time, he departed for Germany; a similar disappointment there induced him to go over to England. In London he heard the Gospel faithfully preached, and became convinced that notwithstanding his strict religious habits he was yet an unregenerated man. "Is it possible," he wrote, "that I who have always been accounted so religious; who have made divinity my study, and received the premium of piety from my university for writings on divine subjects; is it possible that I should yet be so ignorant as not to know what faith is?" After a protracted struggle he was enabled to "believe with the heart unto righteousness." Never was the doctrine of faith as the condition of spiritual life, the potent element which "works by love," and secures both inward holiness and outward good works, more demonstrably exemplified than in the subsequent career of this rare man. At Wesley's instance he took orders in the national Church. On March 6, 1757, he was ordained a deacon, and on the

[21] Life of Rev. John William de la Flechere, etc., by Joseph Benson, chap. i.

following Sabbath a priest. He hastened the same day to Wesley at West-street chapel, and assisted him in his services. Thenceforward he was Wesley's most ardent coadjutor in the Establishment; his counselor, his fellow-traveler at times in his evangelical itinerancy, an attendant at his Conferences, the champion of his theological views, and, above all, a saintly example of the life and power of Christianity as taught by Methodism, read and known, admired and loved by Methodists throughout the world. Madeley, his vicarage, is familiar and dear to them next to Epworth itself. He will reappear often in our narrative, and always with a reflection of the glory of that Divine Presence with which he habitually lived in an intimacy and purity rarely if ever excelled by even the holiest men who have walked with God on earth.

Wesley could not but be deeply impressed at the present time by the remarkable results of the Methodistic movement. He began his career without an anticipation of its consequences, but the nation had now been, to a great extent, morally awakened, and the future was apparently pregnant with greater results than the past. Reflecting on the subject while in London, he says: "From a deep sense of the amazing work which God has of late years wrought in England, I preached on those words, Psalm cxlvii, 20: 'He hath not dealt so with any nation;' no, not even with Scotland nor New England. In both these God has, indeed, made bare his arm, yet not in so astonishing a manner as among us." This must appear, he argued, to all who impartially consider, 1. The number of persons who had been reformed; 2. The swiftness of the work in many, who were both convinced and truly converted in a few days; 3. Its depth in most of those, changing the heart, as well as the whole conversation; 4. Its clearness, enabling them boldly to say: "Thou hast loved me; thou hast given thyself for me;" 5. Its continuance. In Scotland and New England, revivals had occurred at several times, and for some weeks or months together; but the Methodist movement had lasted for about eighteen years without any observable intermission. Above all, he adds, let it be remarked that a considerable number of the regular clergy were engaged in the great revival in Scotland, and in New England above a hundred, perhaps as eminent as any in the whole province, not only for piety, but also for abilities; whereas in England there were only two or three inconsiderable clergymen, with a few young unlettered men, and these were opposed by well-nigh all the clergy as well as laity in the nation. "He that remarks this must needs own both that this is a work of God, and that he hath not wrought so in any other nation."

Wesley had now passed the middle period of life; his opinions had in some respects moderated, but not his earnestness nor his labors. An habitual cheerfulness marked his daily life. His continual intercourse with all classes of men made him at home with all. He relished a good story, and could tell one with zest; and his conversation was often anecdotal and playful. Both his religious feelings and natural temperament were exempt from gloominess. He loved children, and they never failed to love him. Books were his daily entertainment, and a relief to his increasing cares; he indulged in not only the graver kinds of reading, but in poetry, the drama,[22] fiction somewhat, and especially the curious and entertaining researches of antiquaries. But notwithstanding these reliefs, his natural love of retirement and of studious habits led

[22] The pious zeal of one of his preachers deprived him of the honor of taking rank among the numerous commentators of Shakspeare. John Pawson, a very holy man, had charge of City-Road Chapel after Wesley's death, and occupied the adjacent parsonage, Wesley's London home. He expurgated its library with iconoclastic zeal. Wesley's intimate friend and executor, Rev. Henry Moore, says that "among the books which Mr. Pawson laid violent hands on and destroyed, was a fine quarto edition of *Shakspeare's Plays*, (presented to Mr. Wesley by a gentleman in Dublin, *the margin of which was filled with critical notes by Mr. Wesley himself.*" The good man judged them, and the work itself, "as among the things which tended not to edification." Life of Rev. Henry Moore, p. 180. New York.

him often to long, amid his daily preachings and travels, and the care of all his Churches, for leisure and a place of rest. While hastening, like a courier, over Ireland, he paused on his way to Dublin in a village, amid "a little earnest company," and wrote: "O, who should drag me into a great city if I did not know there is *another world?* How gladly could I spend the remainder of a busy life in solitude and retirement!" Entering a solitary house on the romantic coast of Wales, where no other dwelling could be seen, he envied its humble tenants; "here I was," he wrote, "in a little, quiet, solitary spot, *maxime animo exaptatum meo!*—most heartily desired by me, where no human voice was heard but those of the family." Rest in this life he knew could never be his lot, but he still hoped for a home.

In 1749, as has been stated, he designed to marry Grace Murray, who would have made him a congenial wife; her natural amiability, her accomplishments and piety had evidently won his affection; and he felt profoundly his disappointment, but relieved it by pursuing, with undiminished energy, his accustomed labors.[23]

With the advice of his friend and counselor, Perronet, of Shoreham, he married in 1752 Mrs. Vizelle, a widow lady of wealth, of intelligence, and of apparently every

[23] Watson (Life of Wesley, chap. 10) gives an extract from an unpublished letter of Wesley, which proves both how deeply he felt, and how resolutely he bore his disappointment. "The sons of Zeruiah were too strong for me. The whole world fought against me, but, above all, *my own familiar friend*, [Charles Wesley.] Then was the word fulfilled: 'Son of man, behold I take from thee the desire of thine eyes at a stroke, yet shalt thou not lament, neither shall thy tears run down.' The fatal, irrevocable stroke was struck on Thursday last. Yesterday I saw my friend, (that was,) and him to whom she is sacrificed. But why should a living man complain, a man for the punishment of his sins?" Jackson (Life of Charles Wesley, chap. 17) says that several letters of Wesley to his termagant wife, during his worst trials from her, show "the utmost tenderness of affection, such as few female hearts could have withstood, and justify the opinion that had it been his happiness to be married to a person who was worthy of him, he could have been one of the most affectionate husbands that ever lived. Those who think that he was constitutionally cold and repulsive utterly mistake his character."

qualification necessary to render his home happy and exemplary. At his own instance, her ample property was secured, before the marriage, to herself and her children. She understood that he was not to abate his itinerant labors. He pursued them as usual, and in about two months after his marriage wrote in his Journal: "I cannot understand how a Methodist preacher can answer it to God to preach one sermon or travel one day less in a married than in a single state. In this respect surely, 'it remaineth that they who have wives be as though they had none.'" His wife traveled with him for some time, but soon very naturally grew dissatisfied with a life so restless and so incompatible with the tastes and convenience of her sex. Unwilling to travel herself, she became equally dissatisfied with her husband's habitual absence. Her discontent took at last the form of a monomaniacal jealousy. During twenty years she persecuted him with unfounded suspicions and intolerable annoyances, and it is among the most admirable proofs of the genuine greatness of his character that his public career never wavered, never lost one jot of its energy or success, during this protracted domestic wretchedness. She repeatedly deserted him, but returned at his own earnest instance. She opened, interpolated, and then exposed to his enemies his correspondence,[24] and sometimes traveled a hundred miles to see, from a window, who accompanied him in his carriage. At last, taking with her portions of his Journals and papers, which she never restored, she left him with the assurance that she would never return. His allusion to the fact in his Journal is characteristically laconic. He knew not, he says, the immediate cause of her determination, and adds: "*Non eam reliqui, non dimissi, non revocabo*"—I did not forsake her, I did not dismiss her, I will not recall her. She

[24] She resided in Wesley's parsonage at the Foundry. Charles Wesley, whose family still continued at Bristol, found it necessary to guard them against allusions to her, in their correspondence with him, as she opened his letters. Jackson's Charles Wesley, chap. 21.

lived about ten years after leaving him. Her tombstone commemorated her virtues as a parent and a friend, but not as a wife.[25]

To his domestic trials were added, in the latter part of 1753, the sufferings and anxieties of a perilous sickness. His symptoms—pains in the chest, cough, fever and debility—indicated a rapid consumption, and his physicians required an entire cessation of his labors and retirement in the country. The London societies became alarmed, and great anxiety soon spread among his people throughout the nation, for never before was his continued agency so apparently necessary to the stability of Methodism. Public prayers were offered for his restoration at the Foundry, and throughout the land as the afflicting intelligence extended. Charles Wesley hastened to the metropolis, hardly expecting to see him alive. Unable to sit on his horse, he was conveyed to the country in a coach. On one day his death was hourly expected by his attendants; he was conscious of his danger, and, to prevent "vile panegyric," wrote for his own epitaph this remarkable passage: "Here lieth the body of John Wesley, a brand plucked from the burning,[26] who died of a consumption in the fifty-first year of his age; not leaving, after his debts are paid, ten pounds behind him.[27] Praying God be merciful to me, an unprofitable sinner, he ordered that this, if any inscription, should be placed on his tombstone."

With his usual equanimity he pursued his literary labors during this season of general anxiety among his people. He finished the books which he designed to insert in his "Christian Library," transcribed a part of his Journals

[25] Southey is candid in his account of this case, (Life of Wesley, chap. 24.) Watson supplies additional and necessary facts. (Life of Wesley, chap. 10.) There is an intimation in Wesley's Journal as late as June 30, 1772, which seems to imply a temporary reconciliation. "Calling," he says, "at a little inn on the Moors, I spoke a few words to an old man there, as my wife did to the woman of the house." At her death she left him a ring. Coke and Moore's Life of Wesley, II, 4.

[26] See note on page 60.

[27] See page 268.

for the press, and retiring, by order of his physician, to the Hotwells near Bristol, began there his Notes on the New Testament, with a new version of the text; a work unrivaled among Biblical commentaries for its terseness, condensation, and pertinency, and a recognized standard of Methodist theology throughout his "Connection." In the spring he resumed his itinerant labors with renewed health and undiminished energy.

To his many other trials was added one during this period which, by its undeserved and unexpected severity, and its pernicious public influence, occasioned him no little suffering. Hervey, the author of the "Meditations" and "Contemplations," "Theron and Aspasio," and other works noted more for their meretricious style than for any intrinsic excellence, had been a member of the "Holy Club" at Oxford. Eminently pious, but feeble in health, he pursued, after leaving the university, a course of clerical labor in a retired parish; he continued, however, to maintain a deep interest in the progress of Methodism, and sharing the Calvinistic opinions of Whitefield, was in habitual correspondence with him and Lady Huntingdon. He acknowledged himself to be under the greatest obligations to Wesley till he entered the controversial lists against his Arminianism. He had admitted to his confidence William Cudworth, a man who was chiefly responsible for his alienation from the Wesleys, and at whose instigation he commenced his unfortunate "Eleven Letters." Hervey died in 1758; as his end approached he directed that the manuscript of this work should be destroyed. His brother, however, judged that it would be a desirable pecuniary speculation to publish it, and placed it in the hands of Cudworth to be finished, giving him liberty "to put out and put in" whatever he judged expedient.[28] Cudworth's Antinomian sentiments led him to abhor Wesley's opinions; he caricatured them relentlessly by his interpolations of Hervey's pages, and sent forth in Hervey's

[28] See Jackson's Charles Wesley, chap. 21; and Coke and Moore's Life of Wesley, III, 2.

name the first and most reckless and odious caveat against Methodism that ever emanated from any one who had sustained friendly relations to it. It was republished in Scotland, and tended much to forestall the spread of Methodism there. Wesley felt keenly the injustice and heartlessness of this attack, but his sorrow was mitigated by the knowledge that most of the abuse in the publication was interpolated, and that Hervey, who had delighted to call him his "friend and father," knew him too well to have thus struck at him from the grave. He answered the book; but time has answered it more effectually—time, the invincible guardian of the characters of great men.

Wesley had now the sympathy and co-operation of some zealous and able men among the regular clergy. He was still anxious that the momentous work on his hands should at last obtain the patronage and be continued under the auspices of the Church. He lamented the general lack of zeal, the inefficiency, the secular motives, the ignorance and stupidity which characterized many of its pastors. In 1756 he sent forth his "Address to the Clergy;" it pleads earnestly for the best intellectual qualifications of their office, and contends that without a knowledge of the original tongues of the Scriptures no clergyman can, "in the most effectual manner," expound and defend them; "for without a knowledge of the literal meaning of every word, verse, and chapter, there can be no firm foundation on which the spiritual meaning can be built." But not for Biblical knowledge only does he plead; Logic, History, and the Natural Sciences are advocated with much earnestness. He also insists upon the highest style of manners as necessary in the office; "all the courtesy of the gentleman joined with the correctness of the scholar." St. Paul, he says, showed himself before Felix, Festus, and Agrippa, "one of the best bred men, one of the finest gentlemen in the world." He rebukes with a tone of severe scorn the common remark of English families in high life, that "the son who is fit for nothing else will do well enough for a parson." But on no prevalent evil of the order does he spend more remark and force than on the practical simony with which preferment was conducted. Gain, as a motive to the office, beyond a comfortable subsistence, he reprobates as a disgrace to the profession, a profanation of its apostolic prestige, and a provocation of the ill-will of the people. The moral standard of qualification for the ministry he lifts to the highest altitude. He would have his clerical brethren return to the simplicity, self-sacrifice, and martyr-spirit of the first ages, and this he pronounced the great requisite of the times for the salvation of the Church and the nation. He would have them, in other words, become genuine Methodist preachers. "Is not," he asks, "His will the same with regard to us as with regard to His first embassadors? Is not His love and is not His power still the same as they were in the ancient days? Know we not that Jesus Christ is the same yesterday, to-day, and forever? Why then may not you be as burning and as shining lights as those that shone seventeen hundred years ago? Do you desire to partake of the same burning love? of the same shining holiness? Do you design it, aim at it, press on to this mark of the prize of the high calling of God in Christ Jesus? Do you constantly and earnestly pray for it? Then, as the Lord liveth, ye shall attain it!"[29] His hope of an evangelical clergy in the national Establishment was not, however, to be verified in his own day, and Methodism was compelled to take care of itself.

[29] Works, vol. vi, p. 217. American edition.

CHAPTER III.

CALVINISTIC AND MORAVIAN METHODISM: 1750-1760.

Whitefield "ranging" — His Good-Humor — His Health — His steady Zeal — The New Tabernacle — Cordiality between Welsey and Whitefield — Whitefield in America — In Ireland — Terrible Mob in Dublin — Distinguished Methodistic Churchmen — Berridge — Extraordinary Religious Interest at Everton — Singular Conversion — Romaine — His Persecutions — His Labors — His Writings — Madan — His Conversion — His Eloquence — His Labors — Venn — His Connection with the Methodist Founders — Moravian Methodism — Ingham — His Numerous Societies in Yorkshire — Their Discipline — Their attempted Union with Wesley — Their Overthrow by Sandemanianism — Wesley's Legislative Ability — Death of Lady Ingham — Ingham's Death and Character.

Early in 1750 Whitefield went forth from London "ranging," as he called it, through the land, and preaching with his usual power at Gloucester, Bristol, Exeter, Plymouth, Nottingham, Manchester, and other places, till he reached Edinburgh. "Invitations," he wrote, "came from every direction. . . . I want more tongues, more bodies, more souls for the Lord Jesus."[1] He preached on his route about one hundred sermons, to a hundred and fifty thousand hearers, in less than three months. It was amazing, he said, to see how the people were prepared for him in places which he had never visited before; the Methodist lay preachers had been over most, if not all the ground, had triumphed over persecutions, and had prepared the whole land for him.

His labors in Scotland at this visit are not minutely recorded, but are said to have left a deep impression; he preached from two to four times a day till his health yielded.

[1] Gillies's Whitefield, chap. 14.

Many, he wrote, were under conviction, and hundreds received benefit and consolation from the word. In a few months he was ranging through Wales, where he rode five hundred miles, preaching twice every day.

In 1751 he passed over to Ireland; he found in Dublin "many converted souls," and his congregations were large, and "heard for eternity." He hastened among the country towns, preaching daily, and in the most of the island he discovered that a great evangelical work had been advancing, though through prodigious opposition. Large numbers were converted not only from Popery, but to a truly spiritual life, at Athlone, Dublin, Limerick, Cork, and various other places. Wesley and his lay preachers had stood the brunt of the first mobs, and had at last conquered, so that at this visit Whitefield scarcely met with opposition. Hundreds prayed for him as he left Cork; and it is said that many Papists promised to leave their priests if he would stay among them. He preached eighty times during his short stay of less than two months, and left the island for Scotland, well satisfied with the brief retrospect. "Providence," he wrote, "has wonderfully prepared my way, and overruled everything for my greater acceptance. Everywhere there seems to be a shaking among the dry bones, and the trembling lamps of God's people have been supplied with fresh oil. The word ran and was glorified."

On reappearing in Glasgow, he was received with renewed enthusiasm. Thousands attended his services every morning and evening, and seemed never to be weary. He was followed from town to town; and many influential clergymen shared the popular enthusiasm, admiring his devout spirit, and delighting in his extraordinary eloquence and his social qualities; for in the latter respect one of them describes him as exceedingly entertaining, and as "reviving" as in his sermons. A playful humor, rich in evangelical sentiment, strange as the collocation may seem, enlivened his social intercourse, and especially his dinner-table converse. "One might challenge," says Gillies, alluding to this visit, "one might challenge the sons of pleasure, with all their wit, good-humor, and gayety, to furnish entertainment so agreeable."[2]

At Edinburgh, the longer he stayed the larger were his congregations. In about twenty-eight successive days he preached to nearly ten thousand hearers a day. It was during these excessive labors that we first hear of his habit of "vomiting blood" after preaching. It would have terrified and sent into retirement, or to a healthier climate, any ordinary man; by Whitefield it now came to be considered a relief to his over-excited system, and seems to have continued during most of the remainder of his life.[3]

He returned to London to embark again for America, where he spent the winter, laboring chiefly in Georgia and South Carolina. Unhappily we have no important records of this visit; but it was doubtless, like all the rest of his career, a series of unintermitted labors. The epistolary fragments which affords glimpses of his movements, palpitate with life. "I intend to begin," he wrote, on hearing of the death of Doddridge, "I intend to begin, for as yet I have done nothing; God quicken my tardy pace, and help me to do much work in a little time." In June, 1752, he was again in London, planning tours of the whole country. "O that I could fly from pole to pole publishing the everlasting Gospel!" he wrote, as he left the city to "range" through the west. At Bristol he stood up amid "Moorfields congregations," and saw the "old times revived again," and during a fortnight flew like a herald over Wales, preaching twenty times and traveling on horseback three hundred miles. We next hear of him in Scotland again, where he rejoices over immense congregations, and the news of "a dozen young men" who were awakened under his preaching ten years before, and were now useful preachers. But soon he is on his southern route, passing as "a flame of fire." The enthusiasm which had now borne him along as on wings

[2] Memoirs of Whitefield, note, chap. 15.

[3] Memoirs of Rev. Cornelius Winter, by Rev. William Jay.

for fifteen years suffered no abatement, but seemed rather to kindle into increased fervor. As he hastened southward, from town to town, he wrote at Sheffield: "Since I left Newcastle I have scarce known sometimes whether I was in heaven or on earth. At Leeds, Birstal, Haworth, and Halifax, thousands and thousands have flocked twice a day to hear the word of life. The word has run so swiftly at Leeds that friends are come to fetch me back, and I am now going to Rotherham, Wakefield, Leeds, York, and Epworth. O that I had as many tongues as there are hairs upon my head! Fain would I die preaching." In fine, the whole temperament and genius of the man, as well as his religious sentiments, were adapted to preaching, and the extraordinary course of life he had adopted. Preaching was as natural to him as flight to an eagle.

On the first of March, 1753, he laid the foundation-stone of the new Tabernacle, in London, on the site of the old structure which had been the theater of his eloquence and usefulness. Wesley loaned him the use of the Spitalfield's Chapel while the new edifice was rising, and their mutual harmony became more than ever manifest. Whitefield continually revealed, during these times, the magnanimity of his great soul by proofs of liberality toward his Arminian coadjutors. He visited Norwich at the crisis of the trouble of Wheatley, and Bolton at the defection of Bennet, and in both cases pleaded with the societies to maintain their union and their fidelity to Wesley. As he formed few societies himself, most of his preaching excursions were, in effect, recruiting tours for the Wesleyan societies and the evangelical Dissenters. When Wesley was sick he hastened to visit him, but first sent a letter, written from the fullness of his heart. "If," he said, "you will be in the land of the living, I hope to pay my last respects to you next week. If not, farewell! My heart is too big! Tears trickle down too fast; and I fear you are too weak for me to enlarge. May underneath you be Christ's everlasting arms! I commend you to his never-failing mercy, and am your most affectionate, sympathizing, and afflicted younger brother in the Gospel."

During this year he made what is supposed to have been his most successful campaign in England; we have not its details, but know that in three months he traveled twelve hundred miles, and delivered a hundred and eighty discourses to hundreds of thousands of hearers.[4] The Arminian Methodists welcomed him everywhere to their chapels, but no chapels could accommodate the people. At Leeds twenty thousand hung upon his word. All Yorkshire was roused with interest; the Methodists thinned out the Minster, and overawed the mob, says one of his biographers.[5] Glasgow and Edinburgh again poured their tens of thousands out upon the public green to hear his thrilling words, and London rallied its still greater hosts.

In March, 1754, he was again on the deck for America, accompanied by a score of poor children, who were to receive shelter in the Orphan House at his Bethesda, where he found a hundred and six persons in his family, "black and white." He was soon ranging northward. At Philadelphia and New York the former scenes of enthusiastic interest were again enacted. Everywhere, he wrote, "a Divine power accompanied the word; prejudices were removed, and a more effectual door opened than ever for preaching the Gospel." He projected a tour of two thousand miles to Boston, and back again to Georgia, and passed over it as on a triumphal march. In Rhode Island and Massachusetts he found "souls flying like doves to the windows," and opposition everywhere falling before him. President Burr accompanied him, and says that his magical eloquence attracted in the eastern metropolis weeping thousands every morning to his ante-breakfast sermons. Whitefield writes that he never saw a more effectual door opened for the truth. The godless were awakened, believers quickened, and enemies made at peace with him. Such was the eagerness of the crowd that it was often impossible for him

[4] Philip's Life and Times of Whitefield, chap. 19. [5] Ibid.

to get into the pulpit but by climbing into the windows. He went as far as Portsmouth, New Hampshire, where a cavalcade came out to meet him; and returning he preached two or three times a day through his entire route. It was perhaps his most effective campaign in America. The trumpet of the truth was sounded along its whole Atlantic coast, and the religious interest of all the colonies was roused. He himself regarded it as the most important of his evangelical expeditions: "What have I seen? Dagon falling everywhere before the ark; enemies silenced or made to own the finger of God; and the friends of Jesus triumphing in his glorious conquests. A hundredth part cannot be told. We had scarcely one dry meeting." On his southern route hearers flocked forty and fifty miles to the points at which he was to pass. Unquestionably these mighty labors did much to sustain and project forward those evangelical agencies which have since made the nation an arena of religious revivals and philanthropies. They were especially a fitting preliminary to the more systematic evangelization which Arminian Methodism was about to extend over the continent.

In May, 1755, he was again in London, and began to preach amid the uproar of mobs at Longacre, near the theaters; drums, bells, and yells saluted him whenever he appeared there. Foote caricatured him on the boards of the theater. Letters threatening his life were sent to him, and a ruffian came into the pulpit to attack him with clenched fist; but he persisted till at last he saw rise, as his battery at the West End, the Tottenham-court Chapel, subsequently renowned in the history of religion in London.

In 1757 he revisited both Scotland and Ireland; the former with a heartier reception than ever before, the latter with an Irish welcome of stones, clods, and shillalahs. The Lord High Commissioner at Edinburgh treated him with distinction, and the clergy invited him to a public dinner. They also flocked to hear him, and as many as a hundred were present at a time in his immense congregations. On passing from these hospitalities into Ireland, he expected the cordial treatment he had received at his preceding visit; but while preaching on Oxmantown Green, in Dublin, he received what was nearly, as he said, his "parting blow from Satan." He finished his sermon, but could not return to his lodgings by the way he came. It was barricaded by the solid mass of the mob, so that he had to go nearly half a mile from one end of the Green to the other, through hundreds of excited Papists. A soldier and four Methodist preachers accompanied him part of the way, but fled for their lives and left him to the mercy of the mob. Stones flew about him from all directions, and he reeled under them till he was breathless and dripping with blood. His strong beaver hat protected his head for some time, but was at last knocked off, and left it defenseless. He received several severe wounds, one near his temples. He thought of Stephen, he says, and as he believed that he received more blows than the ancient martyr, he had great hopes that like him he should "be dispatched, and go off in this bloody triumph" to the presence of his Lord; but he staggered at last to a door and was sheltered. Meanwhile the mob broke up his field-pulpit, and severely beat and wounded his servant with the fragments. Whitefield lay speechless and panting for some time in the house where he had taken refuge. A few of his friends had followed him, and now washed the blood from his wounds; but as soon as he revived, the family, fearing their house would be demolished, entreated him to leave them. As it was perilous for him to go out, a mechanic offered him his wig and cloak as a disguise. He put them on, but ashamed of such apparent cowardice threw them off with disdain, determined to face the populace in his proper habit. A Methodist preacher brought a coach to the door, Whitefield leaped in and rode unhurt, and with what he calls "Gospel triumph," through whole streets of Papists, who threatened him at every step of the way. None, he says, but those who were spectators of the scene could form an idea of the affection with which he was received by the weeping, mourning, but now joyful Methodists. A Christian surgeon was ready to dress his wounds, after which he went into the preaching-house, and having given a word of exhortation, "joined in a hymn of praise and thanksgiving to Him who makes our extremity his opportunity, who stills the noise of the waves and the madness of the people."

Under this memorable sermon John Edwards, one of Wesley's ablest preachers, received the truth, and afterward devoted himself to similar labors and trials. Whitefield escaped from Dublin, but immediately resumed his work, preaching with great power at Athlone, Limerick, and Cork, but soon left the island for more inviting fields and returned no more.

During the remainder of our present period he made several tours in England, Wales, and Scotland, and the public interest augmented with every visit; but in the north, with undiminished popularity, he had to adopt Wesley's lamentation over the moral insensibility of the Scotch. They crowded to hear him; "but it is a dead time," he wrote; "little or no stirring among the dry bones." He comforted himself, however, by his Calvinistic opinion of the Divine sovereignty. Wesley declined that consolation.

It was during these times that some of the most important coadjutors afforded by the national Church to the Calvinistic Methodists became prominently identified with the Methodistic movement. The names of Berridge, Romaine, Madan, and Venn are consecrated in its annals.

Rev. John Berridge, vicar of Everton, had been preaching for years without, as he believed, a true knowledge of personal religion. In 1758 he invited a visit from Wesley. "A few months ago," writes the latter, "he was thoroughly convinced that by grace are we saved through faith. Immediately he began to proclaim the redemption that is in Jesus, and God confirmed his own words, exactly as he did at Bristol in the beginning, by working repentance and faith in the hearers, and with the same violent outward symptoms."[6] These violent symptoms were, indeed, more extraordinary than had occurred under the preaching of either Wesley or Whitefield.

[6] Journal, Anno 1758.

Wesley has recorded them with much minuteness, and while it cannot be denied that they sometimes took an extreme and even fanatical form, yet they were but the concomitants, the human infirmities, of a profound and widespread religious reformation. The Rev. Mr. Hicks, vicar of Wrestlingworth, Berridge's neighbor, entered zealously into the excitement. The whole region round about was astir. Curious or anxious multitudes came ten, twenty, and even thirty miles, to hear these awakened clergymen, and witness the wonders which attended their labors, and few came who did not return to spread the excitement by a renewed religious life. Berridge's church was usually thronged, aisles, portals, and windows. The hearers crowded up the pulpit steps until the preacher was sometimes nearly stifled with their breath, and scores fell helplessly to the floor, and were carried to the parsonage. The assembly was often swayed with irrepressible emotion, sometimes crying out with groans and sobs, at others pervaded by a sound of "loud breathing, like that of people gasping for life." A spectator describes the faces of "all the believers present as really shining at times;" and he adds, "such a beauty, such a look of extreme happiness, and at the same time of Divine love and simplicity, did I never see in human faces till now." Berridge soon began to itinerate almost as energetically as Grimshaw, and Everton, like Haworth, became the center of an extensive range of evangelical labors. He often rode a hundred miles and delivered ten or twelve sermons a week. He preached much in the open air. At Cambridge, standing upon a table, he addressed ten thousand hearers. At Stafford, where he had been curate, he was determined to preach "a Gospel sermon," such as he declared he had never preached there when responsible for the souls of the people; he did so in a field to a host of wondering hearers. A robust man, who had been "chief captain of Satan's forces" in the town, and was noted for his profanity and readiness to horsewhip the Methodists, was suddenly seized with the "violent symptoms" which had before excited his mirth or his wrath. "I heard," says a correspondent of Wesley who was present, "a dreadful noise on the farther side of the congregation, and, turning thither, saw him coming forward, the most horrible human figure I ever saw. His large wig and hair were coal-black; his face distorted beyond all description. He roared incessantly, throwing and clapping his hands together with his whole force. Several were terrified and hastened out of his way. I was glad to hear him after a while pray aloud. Not a few of the triflers grew serious, while his kindred and acquaintance were unwilling to believe even their own eyes and ears. They would fain have got him away, but he fell to the earth, crying, 'My burden! my burden! I cannot bear it!' Some of his brother scoffers were calling for horsewhips till they saw him extended on his back at full length. His agonies lasted some hours; then his body and soul were eased."

It was estimated that during one year at least four thousand souls had been awakened in this revival. Wesley returned to the scene repeatedly to aid his two clerical brethren. He was startled at its marvels, and acknowledged the human infirmity which mixed with them, but accredited not only as a Christian, but as a Christian philospher, the inestimable good which attended the excitement. Its excesses subsided, but its blessings remained. At a visit after the novelty of the excitement had passed, Wesley preached for Berridge, and observed "a remarkable difference as to the *manner* of the work. None now were in trances, none cried out, none fell down. A low murmur was heard, and many were refreshed with the *multitude of peace.*"

Reviewing the case, he remarked that more or less of these outward symptoms had usually attended the beginning of a general religious interest. So it had been in New England, Scotland, Holland, Ireland, and many parts of England, but after a time they gradually decreased, and the revival proceeded more quietly. Those whom it pleases God to employ on such occasions ought, he adds, to be "quite passive in this respect; they should choose nothing, but leave entirely to him all the circumstances of his own work."

Berridge continued his zealous course during more than twenty years. His theological opinions allied him with Whitefield, and he became a notable champion of Calvinistic Methodism. He was rich, but liberal to excess, and rented preaching houses, supported lay preachers, and aided poor societies with an unsparing hand. He was a laborious student, and nearly as familiar with the classic languages as with his native tongue. Like most good men whose temperament renders them zealous, he had a rich vein of humor, and his ready wit played freely but harmlessly through both his public and private discourse.[7]

Romaine had distinguished himself at Oxford, and as curate in Devonshire and Essex. He had met Warburton in controversy on the "Divine Legation of Moses." In the metropolis he was appoined to the Lectureship of St. Botolph's, and that of St. Dunstan in the West, as also to St. George's, Hanover Square, where he was morning preacher. His discourses were original and powerful, and his eloquence, inspired as much by his earnestness as by his genius, soon attracted larger crowds than could be accommodated in his churches. He had caught the Methodistic spirit of the times, and was now found to be too zealous, too urgent a preacher, and too strict a pastor for the satisfaction of his patrons. At St. Dunstan, where he held two lectureships, clamorous opposition was raised against him, and his rector refused him admission to the pulpit. The dispute was brought before the Court of King's Bench, and one of his lectureships was taken from him by the decision; but the other was confirmed, and endowed with a salary of eighteen pounds a year, which, notwithstanding his exalted talents and devoted character, was his chief support from the Church. On being removed from

[7] Berridge died in 1793, aged 76. A host of evangelical clergymen had by that time appeared in the national Church, chiefly through the influence of Methodism. The venerable Simeon, of Cambridge, and several others of them, bore Berridge to the grave, with the tears of thousands.

Hanover Square, Lady Huntingdon appointed him one of her chaplains. He thus became openly connected with the Methodists, but retained some time the lectureship of West Dunstan, where, however, his evangelical zeal and doctrines gave such offense to the rector that he usually took possession of the pulpit before Romaine could finish the liturgy, and thereby prevented his preaching. Another ruse of his opponents was to keep the church doors closed till the latest moment, while the crowds congregated in the streets, and at last rushed into the doors so precipitately as to endanger their lives. The wardens sometimes refused to light the church, and often did Romaine address the multitude with but a single taper, which he held himself in one hand, while gesticulating with the other in those powerful appeals that sent trembling amid the multitude, and at once astonished and exasperated his enemies.

It was about the beginning of our present period that he entered the Methodist ranks as chaplain to Lady Huntingdon. He preached often with Whitefield, the Wesleys, Fletcher, and others at her mansion. He made frequent evangelical tours into the country, and proclaimed the word at all opportunities with signal effect. He first took his stand as an "open-air" preacher at Haworth with his friend Grimshaw. He labored with Ingham's Moravian Methodist societies in Yorkshire, and traveled extensively in Sussex and Hampshire with the Countess of Huntingdon, preaching incessantly. He accompanied Madan to Everton, and co-operated with Berridge amid the extraordinary scenes that occurred there and throughout the neighboring region. His opinions were strongly Calvinistic, and he was unreserved in his dissent from some of the peculiar sentiments of Wesley, but met him frequently in the catholic services of Lady Huntingdon's mansion, sharing in his prayers and preaching, and receiving from his hands the Lord's Supper. Romaine became rector of St. Andrew, Wardrobe, and St. Anne's, Blackfriars, and died a faithful adherent to the national Church. His numerous works —"The Life of Faith," "Walk of Faith," "Triumph of Faith," "Self-existence of Jesus Christ," "Sermons on the Hundred and Seventh Psalm," and others—are precious exponents of the resuscitated evangelical spirit of the times, and continue to have a salutary influence on the Calvinistic piety of England and America.

A young lawyer of brilliant talents and aristocratic relations was in the habit of meeting with his gay associates at a coffee-house in London. He was the wit of the company, and at one of their meetings, when Wesley was to preach in the neighborhood, his companions sent him to hear the intinerant apostle, in order to give them a mimicked specimen of his preaching. Just as he entered the place of worship Wesley announced as his text, "*Prepare to meet thy God!*" It struck the young man's conscience; he listened with emotion to the sermon, and thenceforward the career of his life was changed. On returning as a necessary courtesy to his company at the coffee-house, they asked him if he had "taken off the old Methodist?" "No, gentlemen," was his reply, "but he has taken me off," and he retired from their circle to return no more.

Lady Huntingdon was personally intimate with his mother, and the young convert found in the friend of his parent a religious guide; he became a faithful attendant at the devotional meetings which were held continually at the house of the countess. The possessor of an opulent fortune, he had no pecuniary motive to seek a lucrative position in the Church; and being a superior scholar, he had little need of preliminary training for the pulpit. He quickly owned his Methodistic principles, and sought ordination, not, however, without some obstructions, though his brother was a bishop. He preached his first sermon at Allhallows, London, to a large assembly, attracted mostly by the novelty of the fact that a lawyer had turned preacher. But his power as a pulpit orator was immediately revealed, and thenceforward could not fail to secure him crowds of hearers. Tall and commanding in stature, majestic in countenance, unusually dignified and graceful in manner, and, above all, profoundly impressed himself with the truth he delivered, his audience was struck with surprise, and his entrance upon the sacred office was "hailed with the acclaims of the friends of religion, who heard the doctrines of the Reformation nobly defended by an able advocate, whose knowledge was equal to his zeal."[8] Wesley had scarcely made a more notable convert, and had never given to his Calvinistic brethren a more important trophy. Such was Rev. Martin Madan. During the present decade of our narrative he was prominent in the Methodistic movement. He traversed much of the country with Romaine, Venn, Lady Huntingdon, and Wesley, proclaiming the truth with great effect. He continued to labor as an evangelist, and as chaplain to the celebrated Lock Hospital, till the publication of his "Thelypthora; or, Treatise on Female Ruin," a work of benevolent intention but of fallacious theories, which greatly diminished his usefulness.

Rev. Henry Venn was curate of Clapham, and served three lectureships in the metropolis. He heard Whitefield often in both places, and his intimacy with Bryan Broughton, one of the original Methodists at Oxford and a coadjutor and correspondent of Wesley and Whitefield, led him to sympathize with the great revival which Methodism was extending over the land. He accompanied Whitefield and Madan on an itinerant excursion into Gloucestershire, and was thus initiated into those "novel" methods of ministerial labor which distinguished his new friends, and which he pursued, as he found opportunity, the remainder of his useful life. Whitefield, in a letter to Lady Huntingdon, describes him as "valiant for the truth, a son of thunder; he labors abundantly, and his sincerity has been owned of the Lord in the conversion of sinners. Thanks be to God for such an instrument as this to strengthen our hands!" During more than thirty years he co-operated zealously with Whitefield, the Wesleys, and Howell Harris in many parts of England and Wales. He adhered steadfastly to the Church after the necessary secession of Lady Huntingdon's societies,

[8] Life and Times of the Countess of Huntingdon, chap. 10.

but continued the "irregularities" of his labors, preaching in private houses, barns, and sometimes in the open air, till the disabilities of age compelled him to retire.[9] Like Berridge and Grimshaw, he made his parish at Huddersfield the head-quarters of extensive labors in all the neighboring region. No less than thirteen young men, who had been converted by his instrumentality, entered the ministry, chiefly in Independent churches. Besides his regular Sabbath services, he usually preached eight or ten sermons each week in remote parts of his parish, and many of them were delivered in the open air. He found, he says, his "out-door preaching much owned of the Lord."[10] He was the correspondent as well as co-laborer of the Wesleys, and his name continually recurs on the pages of their Journals during these times. In the theological world he is noted as the author of "The Complete Duty of Man," an able attempt to correct the defects of the more famous "Whole Duty of Man."

Thus did an illustrious constellation of Churchmen—Fletcher, Grimshaw, Berridge, Thompson, Romaine, Madan, Venn, and others—gather around the elder lights of Methodism in this memorable decade of its history. They reflected much luster upon, but borrowed more from it; and they owe their chief importance in ecclesiastical history to the fact that they were Methodists as well as Churchmen.

We have contemplated the Methodistic movement thus far as advancing chiefly in two separate though nearly parallel lines—Arminian and Calvinistic. We have had occasional glimpses, however, of a third development of the great revival, one which reached a crisis, worthy of particular attention, toward the end of this period. Both the

[9] See page 171. The attempt of Venn's biographers (his son and grandson) to clear him from the noble reproach of Methodism is too futile to need remark. The reader will find it answered in Lady Huntingdon's Life and Times, chap. 17, and Jackson's Charles Wesley, chap. 18. The motive of his biographers was as reprehensible as their attempt was unsuccessful. Venn corresponded through thirty years with Lady Huntingdon, but not one of the letters is inserted in his Memoir.

[10] Letter to the Countess of Huntingdon: Life and Times, etc., chap. 17.

Arminian and the Calvinistic Methodist bodies suffered no little inconvenience from the English excesses of Moravianism, after the separation of Wesley and Lady Huntingdon from it in London. The most difficult cases of discipline in their respective communities came from this source. These excesses were temporary, however, and no desirable purpose could be promoted by a record of them in our pages. Ingham, one of the Oxford Methodists, and the companion of Wesley in Georgia, was impressed, like Wesley himself, on the sea and at Savannah, by the simplicity and moral beauty of the Moravian religious life. On their return to England he accompanied Wesley to Herrnhut, and so strong became his sympathies with this excellent people that he could not sacrifice his attachment to them when the Methodists revolted from the disorders of the Fetter-lane society. He went into Yorkshire, and with incredible itinerant labors, assisted by Moravian companions, he founded there what may be called a Moravian form of Methodism. Preaching stations were established throughout the county and in neighboring shires. At Birstal he took Nelson publicly by the hand, and gave him liberty to speak in all his chapels. The Wesleys, Whitefield, Madan, and Romaine often preached for his societies, and they seem to have been generally recognized by the Methodistic leaders as a legitimate branch of the great revival, notwithstanding Wesley's people in Yorkshire experienced many vexations from the eccentricities of individual preachers, who retained some of the London Moravian follies. The student of the contemporary Methodist documents is surprised at the frequent allusions made to these "Inghamite societies," and their numerical and moral importance. They multiplied till no less than eighty-four were reported. John Cennick joined them, after leaving successively Wesley and Whitefield. Grimshaw delighted to mount his itinerant steed and scour the country among them, for his great soul could never pause to consider merely geographical or ecclesiastical distinctions. Their preachers often accompanied Wesley in his travels in that part of the kingdom; two of them, Batty and Colbeck, stood with him, like good soldiers of the Lord Jesus, in the fiery fight of affliction which he and Grimshaw encountered from the Colne mob at Roughlee, and Grimshaw and Ingham had a severe conflict previously with the same rabble.

Count Zinzendorf and his son-in-law, Bishop Joannes de Watteville, visited them, and assisted in the organization of their discipline. On the accession of a new member he was presented with a ticket, by which he had admission to all their services, which consisted of public meetings, choir meetings of men and choir meetings of women, and many other peculiar occasions. They had circuits for preaching, which comprised Yorkshire, Westmoreland, Cumberland, and Lincolnshire, with portions of Cheshire and Derbyshire. Ingham was admitted to Wesley's Conference in Leeds, but the precise relation of his societies to the Wesleyan body was never defined. He had his own Conferences also, and at one of them was elected a *general overseer*, or bishop. Lady Huntingdon, who could not approve all the disciplinary features of his societies, attempted to promote a union of them with Wesley, and she sent Whitefield to Newcastle-upon-Tyne to meet the Wesleys for consultation on the subject. Charles assented, but John declined the overture. He was sagacious enough to perceive its dangerous liabilities, for he knew well the incoherent elements of the mongrel association, and the impossibility of subordinating them to the strict regimen which he had been able to establish among his own people, and by which alone these reclaimed multitudes could be kept together. Events soon confirmed his wise judgment.

In 1759 Ingham read "Sandeman's Letters on Theron and Aspasio," and "Glass's Testimony of the King of Martyrs." These works produced such an impression on his mind that he deputed two of his preachers to Scotland to learn more fully the views of their authors. At Edinburgh they met Sandeman, and Glass at Dundee. They returned converts to the Sandemanian principles, and immediately spread discontent and disputes among the societies. Ingham's authority could not control the partisan violence which soon broke out. He called in the assistance of his friends. The Countess of Huntingdon wrote them letters. Whitefield felt deeply for them, "wept and prayed," and used his influence to save them. Romaine hastened into Yorkshire, but could not restrain them. Ingham attempted to excommunicate the disturbers, but it was an endless task. The whole order was wrecked and sunk. Thirteen societies only remained from more than eighty which had flourished with all the evidences of permanent prosperity.[11]

Discipline and authority, such as Wesley alone among the Methodist founders seemed capable of establishing, were necessary to any enduring organization of the various and crude elements which Methodism gathered from the degraded masses of the English populace. The Countess of Huntingdon resembled him most in capacity for government. She attempted to give an organized unity to the Calvinistic Methodists, but her effort was too late to prevent the threefold division which at last took place among them, and their consequent declension.

The fate of Ingham's societies is one of the best vindications of Wesley's wisdom as an ecclesiastical legislator. The dispersion of these societies, however, left some good results. Many of them were merged in the Wesleyan or Dissenting bodies, especially in the class of Scotch Presbyterians called Daleites. Many of their preachers remained useful men, and the disaster was much relieved by the consideration that Wesleyan Methodism took general possession of Yorkshire, and that two Methodistic orders were hardly necessary at the time of Ingham's failure.[12]

[11] Sandemanianism was afterward introduced into New England, but failed by its own distractions. Sandeman died in Danbury, Connecticut. His tomb is still preserved there, and slight traces of Sandemanianism linger in the vicinity.

[12] I have found it difficult to trace the relations of Ingham's societies to the Moravian and Methodistic bodies. There seem to have been other and independent Moravian societies in Yorkshire besides his.

Ingham sank into temporary despondence after the breaking up of his societies. He deemed their overthrow a divine judgment upon himself, and seemed inconsolable for some time, but recovered his tranquillity at last. His wife, Lady Margaret Hastings, sister-in-law of the Countess of Huntingdon, and the instrument of introducing the latter to the Methodists, rapidly declined in health soon after these events, but her afflicted husband was comforted by the moral beauty with which the sun of her life went down. "Thanks be to God," she exclaimed in her agony, "Thanks be to God, the moment has come, the day is dawning!" and died. "When she had no longer strength to speak to me," wrote Ingham, "she looked most sweetly at me and smiled. On the Tuesday before she died, when she had opened her heart to me and declared the ground of her hope, her eyes sparkled with divine joy, her countenance shone, her cheeks were ruddy; I never saw her look so sweet and lovely in my life. All about her were affected; no one could refrain from tears, and yet it was a delight to be with her."[13] She occupies a conspicuous place among the "elect ladies" of early Methodism.

Four years later Ingham followed her into the rest that remaineth for the people of God. He is reported to have been in person uncommonly handsome—"too handsome for a man"—a gentleman in manners, a saint in temper, and an apostle in labors. He contributed greatly to the Methodistic revival, and, notwithstanding some errors, deserves an honorable record in its annals.

The text may need correction by better information. Ingham left the Moravians under Lady Huntingdon's influence.

[13] The pious Romaine wrote to a friend: "I got a good advancement by the death of Lady Margaret, and was led into a sweet path of meditation, in which I went on contemplating till my heart burned within me. . . . Many a time my spirit has been refreshed with hearing her relate simply and feelingly how Jesus was her life."

CHAPTER IV.

DEVELOPMENT OF OPINIONS AND ECONOMY BY THE CONFERENCES: 1750–1760.

Deficient Records of the Conferences — Salary of the Preachers — Prominent Members at the Session of 1753 — Separation of prominent Preachers —Tendency to Dissent—The Perronets—Charles Wesley's High-Church Prejudices — Critical Importance of the Session of 1755 — Question of Separation from the National Church — Charles Wesley's hasty Conduct —Was Dissent expedient at this Time? — Wesley writes his "Twelve Reasons against a Separation from the Church of England" —Wesley as a Reformer — His Opinion of John Knox — Historical Importance of his Conservatism — His Ecclesiastical Opinions at this Time — Subsequent Sessions—Conference Examination of Character introduced.

Conferences were held annually, and oftener during the present period, but no authentic Minutes remain of any sessions except two, and of these our accounts are very meager.

To the session of 1750 allusion has already been made. Respecting that of 1751, held at Bristol, Wesley expressed much anxiety; many of his preachers were tired of his forbearance with the national clergy, and of the dependence of the Methodist societies upon them for the sacraments, and some of both preachers and societies were eager for open Dissent. He also suspected, though erroneously, other grievances. He says: "My spirit was much bowed down among them, fearing some of them were perverted from the simplicity of the Gospel; but I was revived by the sight of John Haime and John Nelson, knowing they held the truth as it is in Jesus, and did not hold it in unrighteousness. The more we conversed the more brotherly love increased. I expected to have heard many objections to our first doctrines, but none appeared to have any; we seemed to be all of one mind, as well as one heart."[1] He held a second Conference the same year at Leeds; thirty preachers were present; he particularly inquired "concerning their grace, gifts, and fruits, and found reason to doubt of one only."

At the Conference of 1752 an attempt was made to provide better support for the preachers. Hitherto their only pecuniary claim was for the payment of their traveling expenses by the Stewards of Circuits; their board was gratuitously given by members of the societies as they passed along from town to town; any other assistance was in the form of donations, and was scarcely enough to provide them with clothing and books. It was now ordained that each preacher should be supplied with twelve pounds per annum. For many years, however, this meager allowance was seldom provided, and the self-denying itinerants had to be content with what partial payments their brethren could make.

We have a list of the members present at the tenth Conference, held May 22, 1753, at Leeds. Grimshaw, Hopper, Shent, Walsh, Nelson, Hampson, Edward Perronet, John Haime, with many others, attended. Twelve local preachers and four laymen were also recognized as members. At this session it was resolved that the Conference should thereafter sit successively at London, Bristol, and Leeds. Some suggestions were adopted respecting the best modes of suppressing discords in the societies which were occasioned by Moravian and Calvinistic influences.[2] The eleventh session was held in London, May 22, 1754. Wesley says: "The spirit of peace and love was in the midst of us. Before we parted we all willingly signed an agreement not to act independently of each other, so that the breach lately made has only united us more closely than ever." Five able preachers, Jonathan Reeves, John Edwards, Samuel Larwood, Charles Skelton, and John Whitforth, had retired from the itinerancy. The lack of pecuniary support for their families seems to have been the chief motive for their secession. Reeves became a useful minister of the Established

[1] Journal, Anno 1751. [2] Smith's History of Methodism, II, 3.

Church; the others were settled as Independent pastors. The written pledge mentioned by Wesley seems to have been designed as a guard against any future liability of the kind.

The ensuing year was attended by new difficulties. Some of the ablest of the lay preachers were disposed to concede the reasonable demand of the people for the sacraments from their own pastors. In many cases the national clergy, upon whom the societies were dependent for these means of grace, were flagitiously immoral; they had been often found at the head of mobs attacking the Methodists who were to receive the Eucharist from their hands the next Sabbath. In not a few instances the Methodists were denied the right of communion. Wesley himself had been repelled from the sacramental altar by the drunken curate of Epworth; his brother had been treated in like manner in Wales; his adherents were so treated in Bristol, Leeds, and parts of Derbyshire. Neither the good temper nor the good sense of his people could require them to submit to this privation and such outrages. Joseph Cownley, whom Wesley considered one of the best preachers in England, demanded for himself and his brethren the right, as legitimate ministers of the Gospel, to supply their persecuted people with the sacraments; Thomas Walsh, and Edward and Charles Perronet, joined him in this demand, and actually began to administer them.[3] Charles Wesley, whose mind, less noble than his heart, was perpetually fettered by his High-Church sentiments, became alarmed. His influence over his brother on any disputed question was feeble, and deservedly so, for on ecclesiastical questions especially he seemed incapable of progress, only because, through his strong prejudices, he was incapable of logic. He endeavored to influence his brother by correspondence with his friends. Walter Sellon, who had been a Methodist itinerant, but was now a curate in Leices-

[3] Edward Perronet afterward ceased to travel, through his opposition to Wesley's adherence to the Church. He settled at Canterbury as a Dissenting pastor, and wrote a severe satire against the Establishment, entitled *The Miter*. Charles Perronet continued in the itinerancy till 1776, when he died at his post.

tershire, and retained much influence with Wesley, was employed by Charles to defeat the new tendencies.[4] Charles also meanwhile remonstrated with his brother. He knew that John had declared his belief in the equality of presbyters and bishops, and suspected that he had, as a presbyter, secretly ordained some of the malcontent preachers.

As the Conference of 1755 approached much anxiety was felt for the decision which might be reached on the question. It was likely to be an important crisis in the history of Methodism, and the correspondence between Charles Wesley and Sellon became eager. The latter was to attend the Conference and plead for "the Church;" Grimshaw was to be present only to take leave of them if they took leave of the Church. The session began on the 6th of May, 1755, at Leeds. Its prospective importance brought together no less than sixty-three preachers, the largest number that had yet assembled at any Conference. The main question proposed for discussion was whether they ought to separate from the Establishment. It was debated through three days. John Wesley records the result; whatever was advanced, he says, on the one side or the other, was seriously and calmly considered; and on the third day they were all fully agreed in the general conclusion that, whether it was lawful or not, it was no way expedient to separate from the Church.[5] Walsh and his associates consented, for the sake of peace, to cease to administer the sacraments. John Wesley said that when he reflected on their answer he admired their spirit and was ashamed of his own. He acknowledged that though he "did not fluctuate, yet he could not answer the arguments" on their side of the question; but his brother seemed incapable of understanding his liberality. "I have no fear about this matter," wrote John; "I only fear the preachers' or the people's leaving, not the Church, but the love of God and inward or outward holiness. To this I press them forward continually. I dare not in conscience spend my time and strength on externals. If, as my lady

[4] Jackson's Charles Wesley, chap. 19. [5] Wesley's Journal, Anno 1755.

says, all outward establishments are Babel, so is this establishment. Let it stand, for me; I neither set it up nor pull it down. But let you and I build up the city of God."

In another letter, alluding to the excommunication of a clergyman by the Bishop of London for preaching "without license," he wrote: "It is probable the point will now be determined concerning the Church, for if we must either *dissent or be silent, actuam est.* We have no time to trifle." "Church or no Church," he again wrote, "we must attend to the work of saving souls."[6] This was as generously as it was bravely said; and especially does it appear so when we consider the coolness of his temper and the tenacity of his attachment to the Church.

Though Charles Wesley had secured his main design, he perceived that it was a concession made by the Christian spirit of the discontented preachers. Their manly good sense had not yielded to new convictions respecting the right they claimed. Some of them were as able men as the pulpits of England could present. They and their people had borne long and patiently the maltreatment of the Established clergy; they could make out an unanswerable argument from the best ecclesiastical authorities of the Anglican Church for their new claim; they proved both their good sense and good temper by suspending it for the sake of peace; but Charles Wesley saw clearly enough that it was only suspended, that such men could not always be treated as children, and unwilling, if not incapable, through his obstinate "Churchmanship," of sharing their generous spirit of concession, he had no sooner secured his purpose than he retired from the Conference and left the town without taking leave of even his brother. "I took French leave this morning," he wrote to his family: "the wound is healed—*slightly.*" And at a subsequent date he declared himself "done with Conferences forever," a rash assertion, which he afterward practically recalled. The pertinacity and precipitancy of his conduct in this whole affair is in unfortunate contrast with

[6] Smith's History, etc., II, 3.

the charitable and considerate course of the lay preachers. Methodism owes inestimable obligations to Charles Wesley for the unrivaled Psalmody which he gave it, and for his eloquence, his travels, and his sufferings in its behalf. His ecclesiasticism, however, continually retarded its development, and had he ultimately prevailed he would have defeated one of the most momentous measures in its history—its American organization. While the moderation of the lay preachers cannot fail to command our admiration, its expediency is not unquestionable. Had Methodism taken a more independent stand at this early period, when it had so many intolerable provocations from the Establishment, and the popular mind so little ground of sympathy with the Clergy, it is the opinion of not a few wise men that it might before this time have largely superseded the Anglican hierarchy, and done much more than it has for the dissolution of the unscriptural connection of the Church and state. The measure demanded by its lay ministry at this Conference, and by many of its societies, it was compelled subsequently to adopt, but at so late a date, and with such precautions, that it has ever since, wisely or unwisely, maintained an ambiguous relation toward both Churchmen and Dissenters.

The thirteenth annual Conference was held at Bristol August 26, 1756. Fifty preachers were present, including Charles Wesley, notwithstanding his precipitate retirement from the preceding session and his equally hasty resolution to attend no more. The propriety of adhering to the Church, and of treating "the clergy with tenderness," was again considered. God gave us all to be of one mind, says Wesley. The Rules of the Society, of the Bands, and of Kingswood school, were examined and confirmed, and the Conference was adjourned with a declaration from both the Wesleys of their purpose never to separate from the Church.

To confirm this conclusion Wesley wrote at this time his "Twelve Reasons against a Separation from the Church of England," though they were not published till 1758. They are a remarkable example of his terse style, his precise habit of thinking, and his large charity. He dreaded the controversies which a separation would occasion, and his consequent diversion from his better work; the offense it would give to many devout minds; the scorn it would provoke among gainsayers; the difficulties of constructing an independent Church, and the internal discords, experiments, and excesses it might induce among his own people and preachers. Moving as Wesley did amid mobs and tumults, no man in public life ever maintained more self-recollection or a finer sense of order. He abhorred disputation, and even controversy. He contemned the vulgar idea that rudeness is essential to energy, or an anarchical spirit to the heroism of great reformers.[7] He repressed with calm but prompt determination any appearance of such a spirit among his associates. When, in Scotland, viewing the ruins of Aberbrotheck, "God deliver us," he exclaimed, "from reforming mobs." He acknowledged the usefulness of John Knox, but reprobated his spirit. "I know," he wrote, "it is commonly said the work to be done needed such a spirit. Not so; the work of God does not, cannot *need* the work of the devil to forward it. And a calm even spirit goes through rough work better than a furious one. Although, therefore, God did use, at the time of the Reformation, some overbearing, passionate men, yet he did not use them *because* they were such, but *notwithstanding* they were so. And there is no doubt he would have used them much more had they been of a humbler, milder spirit."

If his temper in this respect led to too much moderation in the present instance, it was, nevertheless, of great importance to the future course of Methodism; it infused into the system that spirit of conservatism which, without neu-

[7] One of his critics, Isaac Taylor, has rightly estimated him in this respect at least. "It is a fact worthy of all regard, that when Heaven sends its own chosen men to bring about needed reformations at the cost of a momentary anarchy, it does not give any such commission as this to those who by temper are anarchists. . . . The Wesleys present a notable illustration of this principle. Great innovators indeed they were, but anarchists they were not." Wesley and Methodism, p. 58.

tralizing its force, has preserved it from the peril of those incongruous elements which it has necessarily gathered under its extended sway. The proverbial conservatism of Methodism, notwithstanding its equally proverbial energy, has been owing almost as much to the impression which Wesley's personal character has left upon its ministry, as to the discipline which he gave it. His fidelity to the Church is the more striking, as it was not at this date the result of any ecclesiastical opinion, but of that expediency which with him was always a moral law. He had been convinced, as we have seen, that the recognized distinction between the orders of bishops and presbyters was a fallacy, that the apostolic succession was a "fable," and that the doctrine that "none but episcopal ordination was valid" was "an entire mistake," as proved by Bishop Stillingfleet.[8] Admirable, then, if even mistaken, was the caution with which he avoided every violent measure not forced upon him by absolute necessity, and the unswerving self-control by which he controlled all around him.

The fourteenth session was held on August 4, 1757. We have no trace of its Minutes. Of the fifteenth session, held at Bristol on August 10, 1758, we have but a single sentence: "It began and ended in perfect harmony." The sixteenth, held in London on August 8, 1759, was equally harmonious. We have no intimation of its proceedings, except that the time was almost entirely employed in the personal examination of the characters of the preachers, a usage which has ever since been annually maintained in Methodist Conferences throughout the world. The seventeenth session was held at Bristol, August 29, 1760. Wesley arrived late in the week from Ireland, and the deliberations continued but two days. "The love and unanimity" of its members, he says, "was such as soon made me forget all my labors." Such is its brief, its only record.

[8] A Letter to a Friend: Works, vol. vii, p. 301. "I firmly believe I am a Scriptural *episcopos*, as much as any man in England, or in Europe. For the uninterrupted succession I know to be a fable, which no man ever did or can prove." Ibid., p. 312.

CHAPTER V.

ARMINIAN METHODISM FROM 1760 TO 1770.

Great Revivals — The Doctrine of Sanctification — Writers on the Subject — Disturbance in the London Society — George Bell's Delusions — Thomas Maxfield's Separation from Wesley — Fanaticism respecting the End of the World — George Story — Fate of Bell and Maxfield — Wesley itinerating — His large Congregations in England and Ireland — He visits Scotland — Christopher Hopper — Cudworth's Letters of Hervey — Thomas Taylor — Sketch of his Life — His Adventures in Scotland — Duncan Wright among the Highlanders — Dissent among Wesley's Societies — Death of Grimshaw — Death of Coates, the oldest Lay Preacher of the Connection — Wesley and Warburton — Fletcher at Madeley — His Persecutions — His Liberality — His Pastoral Habits — His Preaching — His Piety — Wesley at Madeley — Condition of Methodism in 1770 — It is introduced into America — Barbara Heck — Philip Embury — Wesley's Regard for Military Men — Captain Webb.

The year 1760 was signalized by a more extraordinary religious interest than had hitherto prevailed among the Methodist societies. "Here began," says Wesley, "that glorious work of sanctification which had been nearly at a stand for twenty years. From time to time it spread, first through various parts of Yorkshire, afterward in London, then through most parts of England, next to Dublin, Limerick, and through all the south and west of Ireland. And wherever the work of sanctification increased, the whole work of God increased in all its branches."[1] It con tinued to advance with deepening effect for several years. In 1762 he remarks that his brother had some years before said to him that the day of the Methodist Pentecost had not fully come; but he doubted not it would, and that then they should hear of persons sanctified as frequently as they had thus far heard of them justified. "It was now fully come,"

[1] Myles's Chronological History of the Methodists, p. 72.

adds Wesley. His Journal for successive years records the spread of this higher Christian experience, and its salutary effects on all the interests of his societies. Wherever he went he preached on the subject as particularly appropriate to the present development of the Methodistic movement. In March, 1761, he called many of his preachers together at Leeds, and inquired into the state of the societies in Yorkshire and Lincolnshire; they were pervaded by the new interest. He found, he writes, the work of God increased on every side, particularly in Lincolnshire, where there had been no such interest since he had preached at Epworth on his father's tomb.[2] At Manchester he exhorted the societies to "go on unto perfection," and a flame was kindled which he trusted neither "men nor devils would ever be able to quench." In London all the societies were revived; "many believers entered into such a rest as it was not in their hearts before to conceive;" the congregations were increased, and while Christians sought a more entire consecration, the godless were awakened more numerously than ever. At Bristol he made the same record; the society was larger than it had been for many years. "God was pleased to pour out his Spirit this year," he writes, "on every part of England and Ireland, perhaps in a manner we had never seen; certainly not for twenty years." At Liverpool prevailed such a religious excitement as had never been known there before.[3] In 1762 he ascertained that there were about four hundred witnesses of sanctification in the London societies, and on his visit to Ireland the same year he found the classes almost everywhere quickened with the same aspirations after holiness. Such times were never before in Limerick, wrote one of his Irish correspondents; "the fire which broke out before you left us is now spreading on every side. Blessed be God, his word runs swiftly."[4] Wesley records his opinion that this great revival was more remarkable in Dublin than even in London, far greater in proportion to the members in the societies, and more exempt

[2] Journal, Anno 1761. [3] Journal, August, 1762. [4] Ibid, July.

from objectionable features; none there were headstrong or unadvisable; none were wiser than their teachers; none dreamed of being infallible or above temptation; none were whimsical or enthusiastic; "all were calm and sober-minded." At the close of the year 1763 he says: "Here I stood and looked back on the late occurrences. Before Thomas Walsh left England God began that great work which has continued ever since without any considerable intermission. During the whole time many have been convinced of sin, many justified, and many backsliders healed. But the peculiar work of this season has been what St. Paul calls *the perfecting of the saints.*" Many persons, he adds, in London, in Bristol, in Yorkshire, and in various parts both of England and Ireland, experienced so deep and universal a change as it had not entered into their hearts to anticipate. After a deep conviction of inbred sin, they had been so filled with faith and love that sin vanished, and they found from that time no pride, anger, or unbelief. They could rejoice evermore, pray without ceasing, and in everything give thanks. "Now," he continued, "whether we call this the destruction or suspension of sin, it is a glorious work of God; such a work as, considering both the depth and extent of it, we never saw in these kingdoms before."

Some, he admits, had lost the blessing; a few, "very few compared to the whole number," had given way to enthusiasm and separated from their brethren; but though these errors formed a serious stumbling-block, yet the work went on, "nor has it," he says, "ceased to this day in any of its branches. God still convinces, justifies, sanctifies. We have lost only the dross, the enthusiasm, the offense. The pure gold remains, faith working by love, and we have reason to believe increases daily." And as late as 1768 he writes to a friend, blessing God that if a hundred enthusiasts were set aside, they were still encompassed with a cloud of witnesses who have testified, and do testify in life and in death, the Perfection he had taught for forty years.[5]

[5] Journal, August, 1768.

It was indeed remarked that the professors of santification were generally, as at Dublin, distinguished more than other Methodists as "calm and sober-minded." Quietness without "quietism" became a characteristic of them as a class, and, among preachers and people, they were considered by Wesley to be his most prudent, most reliable coadjutors. During forty years he had been preaching, as he says, this doctrine of Christian Perfection, and throughout that period many exemplary witnesses of it had lived and died in his societies. While at Oxford, as we have seen, he became convinced that the Mystic writers, with all their errors, had apprehended a great truth of Christianity in this tenet. The sketch of a perfect Christian by Clemens Alexandrinus had excited his ardent aspirations. Bishop Taylor had irradiated that ideal of religious character by his rare eloquence. William Law had written ably upon it. Thomas à Kempis and other Catholic saints had taught and exemplified it. Fenelon had been an illustrious example of it in both his writings and life. Wesley translated the life of Fenelon's friend, Madam Guyon, and gave it to his people as a practical demonstration of the great truth. He also published in his Christian Library the essay of Dr. Lucas on Religious Perfection,[6] as presenting generally the Scriptural view of the subject. The Scriptural phrases "Sanctification," "Perfection," "Perfect Love," would, independently of these authorities, have suggested to him a pre-eminent standard of spiritual life, but these writers had given a specific and even technical character to the words. Their opinions, glowing with the very sanctity of the Gospel, and aspiring to what most men deemed an altogether preter-human virtue, have been rendered familiar to the Methodist itinerants throughout England, and later throughout the world, in the writings of Law, Fletcher, and Wesley. Every one of them, at his reception into the traveling ministry, avowed his belief in the doctrine, and that he was "groaning after," if he had not already attained, this

[6] The third part of "An Inquiry after Happiness," by Dr. Lucas, prebend of Westminster.

exalted grace. Perhaps no single fact affords a better explanation of the marvelous success of Methodism. Wesley observed and declared that wherever it was preached revivals usually prevailed. "It is," he said, "the grand depositum which God has given to the people called Methodists, and chiefly to propagate this, it appears, God raised them up. Their mission was not to form a religious party, but to spread holiness over these lands." The doctrine of personal sanctification was, in fine, the great potential idea of Methodism. It not only gave it life and energy, by inspiring its congregations with devout and transforming aspirations, but it was the precise sentiment needed as the basis of its ministry. Nothing short of entire self-sacrifice could consist with the duties and privations of that ministry; and according to their doctrine of Perfection, entire consecration was the preliminary of entire sanctification. These holy men, then, in making an entire public sacrifice of themselves, did so as a part of an entire consecration to God, for the purpose of their own entire personal sanctification, as well as their usefulness to others. What ideal of ministerial character and devotion could be more sublime or more effective? And this ideal they realized in the exceeding labors and purity of their lives, and the martyr-like triumphs of their deaths.

Wesley defined this Scriptural truth more clearly than any other modern writer. Evangelical theologians cannot deny his definition of the doctrine. They can dissent from him only in respect to the time in which entire sanctification may be practically reached by the believer. All admit it as at least an ideal, yet Scriptural standard of spiritual life, to be habitually aspired to by good men, though attained, with rare exceptions, only at death. Wesley claimed it as, like justification, an attainment of Faith, and practicable at any moment.[7]

[7] Alexander Knox, Esq., the friend and correspondent of Bishop Jebb, says, (Thirty Years' Correspondence with Bishop Jebb, Letter XIX.,) "Nay, the very point you aim at in them, I mean their view of Christian Perfection, is in my mind so essentially right and important, that it is on

The "enthusiasm" to which Wesley alludes as having marred this special revival, was mostly limited to London, where George Bell, a life-guardsman and an honest madman, had become one of his local preachers. Bell supposed he had effected a miraculous cure; he attempted another on a blind man, but pronounced in vain the *Ephphatha*. His failure in the last case did not correct his delusion respecting the first. It arose, he argued, from the patient's want of faith. His language became fanatical in public meetings. He asserted that his "Perfection" rendered him infallible, above temptation, and superior to the instructions of all persons who were not perfect, and to the rules of the Bands and of the United Society.[8] Wesley admonished him, and visited London repeatedly to restrain him. His forbearance shows the kindness of his heart, but was injudicious.

Fanaticism is always infectious. In this instance it spread rapidly, and Wesley was surprised to learn that Thomas Maxfield was allied with the enthusiasts. Maxfield had been converted under his preaching at his first visit to Bristol. He ranked as his earliest lay preacher, and Wesley had promoted his welfare in all possible respects. He introduced him, in London, to a social position above his birth, by which he had secured an advantageous marriage; and obtained ordination for him in Ireland from the Bishop of Londonderry, who favored Wesley's labors in that country, and who, in laying hands on Maxfield, said: "Sir, I or-

this account particularly I value them above other denominations of the sort. I am aware that ignorant individuals expose what is in itself true by their unfounded pretensions and irrational descriptions; but with the sincerest disapproval of every such excess, I do esteem John Wesley's stand for holiness to be that which does immortal honor to his name. . . . In John Wesley's views of Christian Perfection are combined, in substance, all the sublime morality of the Greek fathers, the spirituality of the Mystics, and the divine philosophy of our favorite Platonists. Macarius, Fenelon, Lucas, and all of their respective classes, have been consulted and digested by him, and his ideas are essentially theirs." See also Knox's Essay on Wesley's Character, addressed to Southey. Appendix to Southey's Wesley.

[8] Wesley's Journal, February, March, and April, 1763.

dain you to assist that good man, that he may not work himself to death." Maxfield was not naturally an enthusiast, and how far he shared the fanaticism of Bell and his associates it is difficult to ascertain. He seems to have been, perhaps unconsciously, inclined to side with them more from discontent with Wesley's authority, than from any sympathy with their errors. Being now an ordained clergyman, well married, and with good resources, it was natural that he should dislike his subordinate position and wish an independent one. Whatever was his motive, he took side with the enthusiasts and really became their head, though Bell continued to furnish by his ravings the chief stimulus of their extravagances.

Wesley was compelled at last to expel the latter, and to disclaim, in the provincial newspapers, a prophecy which he had spread that the world would end on a given day. A great panic arose from this prediction. The news of it extended into the interior, injuring the reputation of the Methodists, till Wesley's disclaimer could follow and counteract it. George Story, one of Wesley's best itinerants, reached Darlington on the predicted day, and found many of the people terrified, and others indignant and threatening to tear down the preaching-house and kill the first preacher who should appear in the neighborhood. Story was a dispassionate man, and telling the mistress of the house that if she would venture the building he would venture himself, he confronted the mob with the newspaper containing Wesley's advertisement in his hand. He could not otherwise have prevailed over the uproar and delivered his sermon.

In London, meanwhile, the terror of the people was too great for the logic of even Wesley, though he endeavored day and night to dispel the delusion. Scores of members withdrew from the societies, giving up their tickets. "Blind John," they exclaimed, "is incapable of teaching us; we will keep to Mr. Maxfield." On the dreaded day Wesley preached against the prophecy, but many, he says, were afraid to go to bed. Some betook themselves to prayer-meetings, which were continued through the night; and others went out into the fields, believing that if the world was not destroyed, London at least would be by an earthquake.

The failure of the prediction did not wholly disconcert Bell's party, for insanity in the form of fanaticism has a subtle shrewdness at sophistry. Prayers might have prevailed to avert the threatened doom, or it might have been postponed for some new reasons; or the prophecy might have been designed as a trial of the faith of believers, like the demand for the sacrifice of Isaac. In the course of time, Bell lost his religious ardor. From being a fanatic, he became a skeptic; he turned politician, was rampant for ultral opinions, and died at an extreme age a "Radical Reformer."

Maxfield gathered round him the alienated members of the London Society, and opened an independent chapel in Moorfields, where he continued to labor for about twenty years. He became Calvinistic in his opinions, and published a severe pamphlet against Wesley. Some of the Methodists who seceded with him continued with him to the last, but most of them returned.[9] Wesley treated him throughout this disturbance with extreme forbearance, and when he chose the alternative of preaching for the followers of Bell, rather than for the Methodists at the Foundry, went thither himself from Westminster, and preached with deep affliction from the text, "*If I am bereaved of my children I am bereaved.*"

If Wesley's treatment of these disturbances was at first too indulgent, his final course was characteristically decisive, and soon extinguished the evil. He then went forth traversing the land, and found the societies flourishing, the revival extending into many new places, and his congregations larger than ever before. In some towns even his five o'clock morning assemblies were so great that he had to leave the chapels for the open air. The Birstal hill was thronged with twenty thousand hearers. At Leeds his out-door assembly was almost as large, and surpassed all preceding congregations there. At Newcastle, he says, he knew

[9] Coke and Moore's Life of Wesley, II, 4.

not that he had ever preached to three such congregations in one day as met him at the outside of Pandon Gate; he was obliged to speak to the utmost reach of his voice from the first to the last word. On Carlton Hill, at Edinburgh, he addressed the largest throng he had ever seen in the kingdom, and the most deeply affected. Throughout Cornwall the interest of preceding years was unabated. His congregations, in some instances, were too large to be able to hear him, and in his favorite amphitheater at Gwennap he preached to thousands, whom he supposed no human voice could reach on any level ground.

In Ireland he was greeted with similar encouragements. At Cork many of the chief of the citizens, clergy as well as laity, were present at his street preaching. "What a change," he writes; "formerly we could not walk through these streets but at the peril of our lives." At Kilfillan nearly all the town, Irish, English, Germans, Protestants and Papists, gathered around him in the market-place, and many followed him to his lodgings, where he continued to pray with and exhort them till bedtime; and the next day, as early as four o'clock, the "town seemed all alive," and audible sobs and ejaculations were heard from "old and young, on the right hand and on the left." At Limerick he addressed, "amid a solemn awe," the largest congregation he had ever seen there; and in Dublin he preached, in Barrack-square, to "such a congregation as he never saw in Dublin before." "What a change," he adds, "since Mr. Whitefield a few years ago attempted to preach near this place!"

He visited Scotland several times during this period, with better success than in former years, but with none comparable to that which attended him in other parts of the realm.

Christopher Hopper had not labored in vain in Edinburgh. "Many poor sinners," says this noted lay preacher, "were converted to God," and a society was formed. He extended his labors to Dundee, Musselburgh, Leith, Aberdeen, and other places, and when Wesley arrived he saw a better prospect for Methodism in the North than at any earlier period.[10] In 1764 the society at Aberdeen was able to lay the foundation of its first chapel, "the Octagon," as the preaching-houses were then called from their peculiar architecture. The next year a similar building arose at Edinburgh. A Scotch edition of Cudworth's Letters of Hervey was extensively circulated, and damaged the influence of Methodism seriously. The devoted lay preachers, attending to their one work, and indisposed to waste their time in polemics, were met at all points and deeply afflicted by the influence of this unfortunate book. "O," wrote one of them, "the precious convictions which these letters have destroyed! Many who have often declared the great profit they have received under our ministry were by these induced to leave us. This makes us mourn in secret places."[11] Hervey himself, were it possible, shared their mourning in heaven over the heedless and heartless stratagem.

The opposition, however, gave way, though slowly. A new champion entered the field, one who had been well tried in itinerant labors and sufferings, and who could not be intimidated by the adversities which so peculiarly beset Methodism in Scotland. Thomas Taylor was a Yorkshire man, a fact of considerable significance in the history of a Methodist preacher of those days. His parents died in his infancy and his education was neglected. He was early of a turbulent and daring disposition. At seven years of age he was habitually profane in his language, and being of a passionate temper—"O that I could write this in tears of blood," he says—he frequently swore "in a most dreadful manner," nor did he "stick at lying." One of his brothers took him to his house and attempted to teach him the business of a clothier; but he disliked work, and ran away several times, suffering severely from cold and hunger in his wanderings. As he advanced in youth his evil habits strengthened, and his "mouth was fraught with oaths, lies, and deceit." He became a dexterous gambler, and having much pride and little money, was the more intent on furnish-

[10] Early Methodist Preachers, vol. i. [11] Coke and Moore's Wesley.

ing himself with resources by that art. He was, in fine, one of those reckless cases of early vice which Methodism alone seemed at that day adapted to reach. Whitefield passed through his neighborhood about his seventeenth year; there was an immense multitude of hearers; the great preacher's "voice was like a trumpet," and the discourse was attended with "an amazing power" to the conscience of young Taylor. He made the best resolutions; but they soon failed, and left him in such wretchedness that he sought relief by attempting to enlist in the army, but fortunately he was half an inch too short for the standard of the recruiting service.

He afterward heard a sermon from an earnest Independent preacher, which revived and sealed upon his conscience the impressions of Whitefield's discourse. While under deep religious convictions he met with a Methodist layman, who maintained a public meeting in his own house every Sunday evening, and who instructed him respecting his religious duties. His reformation was at once visible to all, but he had many inward conflicts before his awakened conscience found rest. While in retirement, reading his Bible and praying, one evening, he was enabled to apprehend by faith the atonement. "I saw," he says, "the Lord hanging upon the cross, and the sight caused such love to flow into my soul that I believed that moment, and have never since given up my confidence. I was enabled to cast my soul upon that atoning sacrifice which I saw was made for my offenses."[12]

Thus introduced into the Christian life, Thomas Taylor soon began to travel about Yorkshire, preaching the Gospel to rustic assemblies, as John Nelson had done before him. He heard Thomas Hanby, a veteran of the early Methodist ministry, and was so impressed by the evangelical character of his preaching and the heroism of the "Itinerancy," that he resolved to join it. Walking to London, he was received at the Conference in 1761, and sent into Wales. Two years he traversed the mountains of the Principality, enduring hardships from hunger and cold, from journeys among bleak

[12] Lives of Early Methodist Preachers, vol. iii.

and almost trackless hills in winter, and at times from mobs; but his success was great; he formed numerous societies, and proved himself one of the best of the Methodist itinerant host.

In 1763 he was sent to Ireland, where he labored two years, suffering not a little from Papists whose tenets his Yorkshire hardihood led him to attack imprudently, as he confesses. He preached abroad in towns and villages, sometimes depending upon the troops for protection. His fare was often very hard, and he lost for a time his speech and hearing, and came near losing his life, through sickness occasioned by sleeping in damp beds. At Cork he was especially successful; he preached abroad in every part of the city, and the society was greatly enlarged.

During his laborious ministry thus far he had, by his diligence and that systematic improvement of time which Wesley continually enjoined upon his preachers, gathered a large amount of valuable knowledge, and acquired the use of the Latin, Greek, and Hebrew languages.

It was in 1765 that he entered Scotland. Wesley sent him to introduce Methodism into Glasgow. Thoroughly tried as he had been by the hardships of the itinerant ministry in Wales and Ireland, he says that his new field in Scotland presented tests severer than any he had yet known. The winter was at hand; he was in a strange land; there was no society, no place for the preacher's entertainment, no place even to preach in, and no friend to consult. He took a private lodging, and gave out that he would preach on the Green, a public resort hard by the city. A table was carried to the place, and at the appointed time he found two baker's boys and two old women waiting. His soul sunk within him. He had traveled by land and by water, near six hundred miles, to this city, and such was his congregation! At length, however, he mounted his table and began the singing, which he had entirely to himself. A few more hearers crept together, all seemingly very poor people, till at length he had about two hundred around him. His natural energy, as well as his Christian zeal, was not to be defeated, and the night following he had a more promising congregation. The third night it rained violently; this quite cast him down. "The enemy," he says, "assaulted me sorely, so that I was ready to cry out, 'It is better for me to die than to live.' But God pitied my weakness." The next day the sky cleared up, and he took the field again and kept it steadily every day for about three months. He soon rallied large congregations, and on one occasion the largest assembly he had ever seen gathered to hear him. He mounted his table, but found it too low; a chair was then set upon it, but even this did not enable him to command the vast multitude. He then ascended a high stone wall and cried aloud, "The hour is coming, and now is when the dead shall hear the voice of the Son of God; and they that hear shall live." He conceived great hopes from the effects of this appeal, as the multitude stood rapt in silence and attention; but when he concluded he was astonished to see them quietly open a lane for him through their midst, and stand calmly staring at him as he walked through it, no one inquiring, "Where dwellest thou?" "I walked home," he says, "much dejected." His ardent Yorkshire nature could not at first interpret this Scotch apathy. He solved the problem afterward, however, for he discovered that the most important part of a Scotchman's religion is his creed, and the popular creed was thoroughly Calvinistic, notwithstanding Socinianism prevailed among the upper classes. The Scotch wept aloud and fell like dead men under Whitefield's preaching, for Whitefield was a good Calvinist, though he cared little about the "League and Covenant." But Wesley, whose preaching was attended in England with more such phenomena than Whitefield's, was powerless among them except to command their phlegmatic attention.

Hervey's Eleven Letters, garbled by Cudworth, met Taylor at Glasgow. They carried gall and wormwood wherever they went. Arminianism was a fatal heresy, and the best disposed of his hearers seemed perplexed with the difficult problem that so much zeal and devotion as he and his fellow-itinerants showed could co-exist with such amazing heterodoxy.

A generous instance of ministerial conduct involved the persevering Yorkshireman in still greater difficulties. A Scotchman was condemned for murder; Taylor visited him in prison, and attended him to the gallows, where, according to the barbarous law of that day, the unfortunate man's right hand was struck off with an ax, and attached on the gibbet before he himself was suspended; Taylor had reason to believe that "the Lord had plucked him as a brand from the burning," and published an account of his case. The popular theology revolted at this charity for a penitent malefactor. "It is amazing," says the itinerant, "what a cry was raised against me for saying that God had mercy on such a sinner." Scurrilous papers were cried up and down the streets against him, and a zealous Scot commenced a weekly publication to oppose him. His case, he says, was now deplorable, for he had famine within doors and plenty of reproach without. He was compelled to practise the closest economy to save himself from extreme want. He sold his horse to pay for his lodging, yet he shared his little stock of funds with a poor brother preacher, who, passing through Glasgow for Ireland, had lamed his own horse, and had not money enough left to bear him forward. Taylor confesses that he never kept so many fast days either before or afterward. It was important, but next to impossible, for him to keep up his credit. He resorted to a little artifice to do so: frequently requesting his landlady not to prepare his humble dinner, he would dress himself before noon and walk out till after dinner time, and then return to his "hungry room with a hungry stomach," his hostess supposing he had dined elsewhere.

For some time it seemed, indeed, that he was attempting a hopeless task. The severe weather was approaching, and his funds were diminishing. He was beset also with characteristic examples of Scotch economy, which confounded his own frugal experiments. Though his voice was poor he had to do his singing mostly alone, as the Scotch did not know the Methodist hymns or tunes. One of his hearers proposed to become his precentor, after the Kirk custom, and "lead the psalms." Taylor supposed it was an act of Christian compassion, and the experiment proceeded very well for a time, but he was surprised at last by a bill from his precentor for "thirteen shillings fourpence, which was just fourpence a time." Taylor dismissed him and the Scotch psalms together, and began again to sing the Methodist melodies, "the people liking them right well." They soon became familiar, and have never since ceased to be heard in Glasgow.

A few stout mobs and downright persecutions would have suited the evangelist better than these vexatious trials; but though he was perplexed he could not be discouraged. He continued to preach in the streets night and morning till the November weather rendered it impossible. Throngs gathered to hear him, to scent out his heresy if for no other purpose; but some were awakened and converted, and at last the obstinate opposition gave way so far that when no longer able to preach abroad a room was provided for his meetings, and furnished by his hearers with seats and a pulpit. His labors now began to yield fruit; his friends continually increased; the Methodist Society of Glasgow was formed, and Methodism founded there, never, he trusted, to be overthrown, however feebly it had to struggle against the formidable odds which still encompassed it. It is a curious fact, however, that not till the society had increased to forty or fifty members did any one inquire how he was maintained. They then asked him if he had an estate, or supplies from England. "I told them," he says, "I had neither; but having sold my horse, I had made what little I had go as far as I could. I then explained our custom to them. I told them of the little matter we usually received from our people. The poor souls were much affected, and they very liberally supplied my wants, as also those that came after me." He labored mightily with them during the ensuing winter, and left them in the spring with seventy members. He had fought a good fight, and he had also kept his faith, for during the severest period of his sufferings a new kirk was opened in Glasgow, an influential member of which had appreciated his fine talents, and offered to settle him as its pastor, with a good salary. "It was," he says, "honor and credit on the one hand, and hunger and contempt on the other;" but to accept it appeared a "betrayal of the trust which was reposed in him" by his brethren. The sentiment of honor was higher among these noble men than honor itself.

Such were Thomas Taylor's "adventures" in Glasgow;[13] such the history of the origin of Methodism in that city. He went elsewhere in Scotland, laboring for some years with similar trials and success. At Edinburgh he preached usually in the "Octagon" in the morning, and on Castle Hill in the evening. Between Edinburgh and Glasgow he formed a circuit, including Burrowstounness, Linlithgow, Falkirk, and Kilsyth. Thomas Olivers and other itinerants came to his help, and through many obstacles made some progress.[14]

After Taylor's partial success in Glasgow the Methodist itinerants penetrated to the Highlands, and at his next visit Wesley preached at Inverness, where a society was formed which continues to this day. His reception was now cordial

[13] So Southey not unjustly calls them. He refers to them with his usual invidiousness, but with evident admiration of the heroic Methodist.

[14] During fifty-five years did Taylor pursue his itinerant ministrations in Scotland, England, Wales, and Ireland, encountering mobs, founding societies, and enduring all kinds of hardships. He was a thorough disciplinarian, a great economist of time, an indefatigable student, and a powerful preacher. He was among the first, if not the first after Wesley's death to introduce the sacraments among the Methodists, and to break away from the disadvantageous custom till then strictly maintained among their societies, (except in London, where Charles Wesley officiated as a Churchman,) of never assembling during "Church hours" on the Sabbath. He was nearly eighty years old when he died, honored and beloved as a veteran throughout the connection. In a sermon a short time before his decease he raised his venerable form in the pulpit, and said with great emphasis: "I should like to die like an old soldier, sword in hand." He was soon after found dead in his chamber. Montgomery's well-known ode, "Servant of God, well done," etc., was writter on his death.

everywhere, and his "High-Churchism" had so far relaxed that he "laid aside his last portion of bigotry,"[15] and shared in the communion of the Lord's Supper at the West Kirk, Edinburgh. At a subsequent visit the magistrates of Perth and Arbroath conferred upon him the freedom of those cities.

In 1769 the Methodist preachers pushed their labors with much energy among the Highlanders. Alexander MacNab, followed by Duncan Wright, formed many classes. Wright reacquired the Erse language, and traveled over the country preaching from town to town three times a day in houses, and usually once a day in the open air. "Though by this means," he writes, "I had many an aching head and pained breast, yet it was delightful to see hundreds of them attending with streaming eyes, and attention still as night, or to hear them in their simple way singing the praises of God in their own tongue. If ever God said to my heart, *Go, and I will be with thee*, it was then. I extol the name of my adorable Master that my labors were not in vain. How gladly would I have spent my life with these dear souls."

While Wesley and his fellow-laborers were thus extending their cause in all the land, they were called to bear, during the present decade, not a few adversities which were severer than any local inhospitalities or mobs. The societies were in many places distracted by disputes respecting the propriety of dissent from the national Church. Members who had joined them from among Dissenters, especially, could not approve Wesley's extreme loyalty to the Establishment, which still disowned and often persecuted his measures and his people, and such members had the peculiar inconvenience of being under the necessity of going for the sacraments back to the sects which they had left, or to the Church, which many of them had never attended. Some of his preachers, tired out by his persistence in this questionable policy, deserted him to take charge of independent churches, where they could maintain their self-respect as genuine ministers of the Gospel by administering the sacraments

15 Coke and Moore's Wesley, III, 2.

to their hearers, and in not a few places discontented Methodists resorted to their ministry.

He was called also to mourn over the death of some of his most esteemed fellow-laborers. In 1762 the eccentric but indefatigable and useful Grimshaw died in the peace of the Gospel. Wesley felt deeply his loss, and devotes several pages of his Journal to an affectionate notice of him—more than to the death of any other one of his friends. "In sixteen years," says Wesley, "he was only once suspended from his labor by sickness, though he dared all weathers upon the bleak mountains, and used his body with less compassion than a merciful man would use his beast. His soul at various times enjoyed large manifestations of God's love, and he drank deep into his Spirit. His cup ran over, and at some seasons his faith was so strong, and his hope so abundant, that higher degrees of spiritual delight would have overpowered his mortal frame." Besides his unusual labors in his own parish, he preached about three hundred times a year in other places. He fell at last a victim to his pastoral labors during an epidemic fever. His old friend Jeremiah Robertshaw, a veteran Methodist preacher, approached him on his death-bed; "God bless you, Jerry," he said; "I will pray for you as long as I live, and if there is praying in heaven I will pray for you there also." "I am as happy as I can be on earth," he declared to another, "and as sure of glory as if I were in it." "*Here goes an unprofitable servant,*" were his last and characteristic words. It would have been impossible for such a man not to have thrown himself, soul and body, into the Methodist movement. A loyal Churchman, he was imbued nevertheless with the catholic spirit of Methodism. While driving about his circuits, like a horseman on the field of battle, he co-operated with all good men who came upon his track. "I love Christians," he used to say, "true Christians of all parties; I do love them, I will love them, and none shall make me do otherwise."

At his own request his remains were carried to the residence of his son at Ewood, a parish of Halifax, where they were followed by a vast and weeping procession to Luddenden church. According to his dying wish, the mourning crowd sang as they bore his corpse along on the highway. Venn preached his funeral sermon in the churchyard, as the multitude could not be accommodated in the church. He repeated it the next day at Haworth, where thousands assembled from all the neighboring country, and wept as at the death of a parent. Romaine lamented him in an eloquent funeral discourse at St. Dunstan's, in London. Both Calvinistic and Arminian Methodists universally felt that a prince and a great man had fallen in Israel.[16]

In 1764 died John Manners, a humble laborer who had spent five years of great usefulness in the lay ministry. Wesley said that he seemed expressly raised up for the extraordinary revivals of 1760, 1761, and 1762. During these three years he preached in Dublin, amid a religious interest seldom or never equaled in that city. He was not eloquent, but rather rude in speech, yet he labored with his might, and walked intimately with God. "The way is quite clear," he said, as he descended into the valley and shadow of death. "My soul is at liberty."[17]

The next year Alexander Coates, the oldest lay preacher then in the Connection, departed to his rest, venerable with years and usefulness. He had preached about a quarter of a century. His pulpit talents are said to have been very extraordinary; he was exceedingly popular, and his conversation "wonderfully pleasant and instructive." He always called Christ his "Master." He was one of

[16] He left an only son, who, notwithstanding his strict religious education at Wesley's school in Kingswood, became a drunkard. He revered, however, the example of his parent's piety. While riding home drunk on the old circuit horse of his deceased father, he used to say, "Once thou carried a saint, but now thou carriest a devil." Such recollections and the many prayers that ascended for him at last prevailed. He repented with bitter anguish, and died exclaiming, "What will my father say when he sees that I have got to heaven?"

[17] Myles's Chronological History of the Methodists, chap. 4.

the many humble founders of Methodism, who left no account of their laborious lives, but whose record is on high. One of his brethren inquired, a short time before he ceased to breathe, if he had followed cunningly devised fables? "No! no! no!" was his emphatic reply. "Do you see land?" he was then asked. "Yes, I do," he answered, and "after waiting a few moments at anchor, he put into the quiet harbor." His old friend and faithful co-laborer, Christopher Hopper, says, with an affection and pathos which only such fellow-laborers and fellow-sufferers could feel, "I saw him fall asleep in the arms of our adorable Saviour without a doubt. Farewell, my brother, for a season. But we shall meet again to part no more."[18]

Wesley continued to be attacked with fierceness through the press. He had effectually answered Lavington; during the present period he replied to a more able and influential prelate, Warburton, bishop of Worcester. Warburton had assailed him in a tract "On the Office and Operations of the Holy Spirit." It was remarkable chiefly for its personal misrepresentations of Wesley, and the indication which it affords of the low standard of religious opinion at the time among the highest functionaries of the national Church. The bishop's theology appears but little above the ethics of natural religion. He cites whatever his rationalistic sagacity could detect in Wesley's writings as liable to be construed into credulity or enthusiasm; and the frankness with which Wesley recorded extraordinary facts, afforded abundant materials for his invidious purpose.[19]

Wesley is classed as "special among modern fanatics,"

[18] Wesley's Journal, Anno 1765; Early Methodist Preachers, vol. 1.

[19] It is noticeable that Wesley records in but comparatively few instances, his own opinion of the many marvels related in his Journal. Never was a more Baconian record made of such phenomena; they are usually given circumstantially as facts, for the examination of the learned or the curious, and are of no small value in this respect. He has, however, given us sufficient evidence of his belief respecting supernatural agency in physical phenomena; this fact has already been shown in the text, and will be further examined in its appropriate place.

and as "claiming almost every apostolic gift in as full and ample a manner as they were possessed of old." His reply not only "fairly meets the attack," as Southey admits,[20] but fairly refutes it in the most essential points. Wesley could not, either as a Christian or as a philosopher, agree with the prelate's Deistical views of Scriptural phenomena, and contends, with what his friends should esteem admirable frankness, though his enemies would call it weakness, for several remarkable facts which he had recorded, and which Warburton condemned as impossible, unless they were miraculous, and incredible if they were claimed to be so. Wesley was vague if not contradictory in his judgment respecting the swoons and convulsions of his hearers at Bristol, Newcastle, and other places. He was, as has been shown, not a little perplexed by them. At Newcastle he ascribed them mostly, if not entirely, to demoniacal agency. At Everton he seems to have supposed some of them to be the effect of divine influence. Warburton had advantage from these facts; but the phenomena were new to Wesley; they have been more common in our day, yet even our later science is baffled by them. Wesley's "Letter" to the bishop was long and elaborate, and remarkable for its candor and respectfulness. It is a fine example of both his style and logic, though it consists chiefly of citations and concise comments.

Fletcher was zealously at work during the present period. He had joined a Methodist class in London, and his first public exercise, after his ordination, had been, as we have seen, in one of Wesley's chapels. He continued some time in the metropolis assisting Wesley, and preaching and administering the Lord's Supper at Lady Huntingdon's mansion. On returning to Tern Hall, Shropshire, his liberal patron, in whose family he had been tutor, offered him the living of Dunham; the parish was small, its labor light, and its income good being £400. But Fletcher had previously preached several times in the

[20] Southey's Life of Wesley, chap. 24.

populous and degraded parish of Madeley, and had conceived such sympathy for its wretched inhabitants that he declined the offer of Dunham as affording "too much money and too little work." His patron then proposed to give Dunham to the vicar of Madeley, and secure the latter for him. He thus, by an act of self-sacrifice, became settled in the obscure parish which his name has rendered familiar in all the Protestant world. Few places in England needed more the labors of such a man. It was a region of mines and manufactures. Its population was debased, and its congregation small. For months he went about his parish early on the Sabbath morning, with a bell in his hand, to awake such parishioners as excused their neglect of worship by alleging that they could not wake early enough to prepare their families for the service. The vicious began to be reclaimed, and persecutions arose. Sometimes his public services were interrupted by outbreaks of scurrilous language from offended hearers. A bull-bait was attempted on one occasion, near the spot where he had announced a public service, and a part of the rabble was appointed to "bait the parson; to pull him from his horse, and to set the dogs upon him." He escaped only by a providential detention at the funeral of a parishioner. His preaching against drunkenness aroused all the malt men and publicans of the town against him. A magistrate threatened him with his cane and with imprisonment, and many of the neighboring gentry and clergy joined his persecutors. A clergyman posted on the church door a paper, charging him with schism and rebellion. Some of his friends were arrested. He was, in fine, subjected to the usual treatment of the Methodist clergy of the times, and he labored with their usual zeal and success. Like Grimshaw and Berridge, Thompson and Venn, he established preaching appointments, at Madeley Wood, at Coalbrook Dale, and most other places within ten miles of his parish, and Madeley became, like Haworth, Everton, St. Gennis, and Huddersfield, a radiating point of Methodist influence and labors for the whole region around it. With incessant preaching he combined the most diligent pastoral labors. He went from house to house, sympathizing with the afflicted, helping the poor, ministering to the sick, and admonishing the vicious. His liberality to the poor is said, by his successor in the parish, to have been scarcely credible.[21] He led a life of severe abstinence that he might feed the hungry; he clothed himself in cheap attire, that he might clothe the naked; he sometimes unfurnished his house that he might supply suffering families with necessary articles. Thus devoted to his holy office, he soon changed the tide of opposition which had raged against him, and won the reverence and admiration of his people, and many looked upon their homes as consecrated by his visits.

His preaching is described as greatly effective. He spoke the English language not only with correctness, but with eloquence. There was, says Gilpin, who heard him often, an energy in his discourse which was irresistible; to hear him without admiration was impossible. Powerful as are his writings, his preaching was mightier; his "living word soared with an eagle's flight; he basked in the sun, carried his young ones on his wings, and seized the prey for his Master."

Meanwhile his devout habit of mind quickly matured into saintliness itself. We look in vain through the records of Roman or Protestant piety for a more perfect example of the consecration of the whole life, inward and outward. For a time he erred by his asceticism, living on vegetables and bread, and devoting two whole nights each week to meditation and prayer, errors which he afterward acknowledged. He received Wesley's doctrine of Perfection, and not only wrote in its defense, but exemplified it through a life of purity, charity, and labor, which was as faultless, perhaps, as was ever lived by mortal man.[22] Even in theological controversy his spirit was never impeachable.

[21] Gilpin's Biographical Notes in Fletcher's "Portrait of St. Paul."

[22] Southey says: "No age or country has ever produced a man of more fervent piety or more perfect charity; no Church has ever possessed a more apostolic minister." Life of Wesley, chap. 25.

"Sir, he was a luminary," said Venn to a brother clergyman; "a luminary, did I say? He was a *sun*." "I have known," he added, "all the great men for these fifty years, but I have known none like him."[23]

It was during our present period (in 1768) that the theological school of Lady Huntingdon, at Trevecca, was opened, and Fletcher appointed to its presidency. Benson, the Methodist commentator, and its head master, says that Fletcher was received there at his frequent visits as an angel of God. Sober and reserved as was the usual style of Benson, his pen glows when he writes of those occasions. "The reader," he says, "will pardon me if he thinks I exceed; my heart kindles while I write. Here it was that I saw, shall I say, an angel in human flesh? I should not far exceed the truth if I said so. But here I saw a descendant of fallen Adam so fully raised above the ruins of the fall, that though by the body he was tied down to earth, yet was his whole *conversation in heaven;* yet was his life from day to day *hid with Christ in God.* Prayer, praise, love, and zeal, all ardent, elevated above what one would think attainable in this state of frailty, were the elements in which he continually lived. Languages, arts, sciences, grammar, rhetoric, logic, even divinity itself, as it is called, were all laid aside when he appeared in the school-room among the students. And they seldom hearkened long before they were all in tears, and every heart caught fire from the flame that burned in his soul."

Closing these addresses, he would say: "As many of you as are athirst for the fullness of the spirit of God follow me into my room." Many usually hastened thither, and it was like going into the Holiest of Holies. Two or three hours were spent there in such prevailing prayer as seemed to bring heaven down to earth. "Indeed," says Benson, "I frequently thought, while attending to his heavenly discourse and divine spirit, that he was so different from, and superior to, the generality of mankind, as to look more like Moses

[23] Life and Times of Lady Huntingdon, chap. 30.

or Elijah, or some prophet or apostle come again from the dead, than a mortal man dwelling in a house of clay!"

Besides his labors in Madeley and the region round about, and his important services among the ministerial candidates at Trevecca, Fletcher made preaching visits to London, Bath, Kingswood, Bristol, Wales, and Yorkshire. He sometimes accompanied Wesley and Lady Huntingdon in their travels, attended the annual Conferences, was indefatigable in the use of his pen for the promotion of Methodism, and took rank as one of its most conspicuous representatives. Madeley became one of Wesley's favorite stopping places in his ministerial travels. The church could not contain the congregation which flocked to hear him there, and, as in his visits to Grimshaw, at Haworth, he had to stand on a platform in one of its windows, preaching to them within and without. "I found," he says on one of his visits, "employment enough for the intermediate hours in praying with various companies who hung about the house, insatiably hungering and thirsting after the good word. Mr. Grimshaw, at his first coming to Haworth, had not such a prospect as this. There are many adversaries indeed, but yet they cannot shut the open and effectual door."

Wesley had passed, during the present decade, through many trials: domestic troubles which would have made life a burden to most men; disturbances in some of his societies which had thus far no parallel in their history; persecutions from the mob which, if less severe toward himself personally, were more so toward his lay preachers than ever; and travels and labors which surpassed those of any preceding years of his life. But he closed this period, at the Conference of 1770, with results and prospects such as had never before cheered him. He could hardly now fail to perceive that Methodism was to be a permanent fact in the religious history of his country. Without design on his part, its disciplinary system had developed into consistency and strength; its chapels dotted the land; its ministerial plans formed a net-work of religious labors which extended over England, Wales, Ireland, a part of Scotland, and reached even to North America and the West India islands. Seven years before, when the number of its circuits was first recorded, they were but thirty-one; they now amounted to fifty. Its corps of lay itinerants included one hundred and twenty-one men, besides as many, perhaps more, local preachers, who were usually diligent laborers in their sectional spheres. The membership of its societies was nearly *thirty thousand* strong.

Toward the close of this period he was further cheered by an extraordinary opportunity for the enlargement of his great work, one which has been attended with its grandest results. A new sign appeared in the western sky, and was hailed by the Conference with thanksgiving, with prayers, and contributions of men and of money. The little colonies of German "Palatines," which Methodism had redeemed from gross demoralization in Ireland, had been mostly dispersed. Wesley, as he year after year passed over that country, lamented their gradual disappearance, but he saw not then the special design which divine Providence was to accomplish by them. In 1760 some of them, among whom was Philip Embury, emigrated to New York.[24] Subsequently another company arrived, among whom was Barbara Heck,[25] through whose instrumentality Embury and his Methodist associates were led, in 1765, to resume in the New World the Methodistic discipline and labors which they had adopted in Ireland. Some years before Captain Webb, of the British army, had been converted under Wesley's preaching in Bristol. Wesley had a strong regard for military men; he liked authority, obedience, methodical habits, and courage; he found that soldiers had made good Methodists in Ireland

[24] Not 1765, as heretofore stated in Methodist publications. See letter to the author from Dr. G. C. M. Roberts, of Baltimore, in the Christian Advocate and Journal for Sept. 2, 1858.

[25] Not Hick, as she is called in all former Methodist books which mention her. The name appears to have been changed by her son, and her descendants call themselves Hick. A portion of the Heck family emigrated to Canada, and retain the original name.

and Scotland, as well as in Flanders, and that Methodist soldiers made good preachers, and especially good disciplinarians, as in the example of John Haime, Sampson Staniforth, Duncan Wright, and others.[26] Captain, then Lieutenant Webb was therefore soon licensed by him as a local preacher. Being sent on military duty to New York, he preached in his uniform, and with great success, for the newly-organized society. He sent a call to Wesley for preachers, two of whom were dispatched from the Conference of 1769. Previous to the Conference of 1770 Wesley received letters from these messengers, reporting a society in New York of about one hundred members, and a chapel which accommodated seven hundred hearers, and yet only a third part of those who crowded to the preaching could get in. "There appears," wrote one of the newly-arrived preachers, "such a willingness in America to hear the word as I never saw before."[27] Whitefield had spread the influence of the Methodist revival in the American Churches from Maine to Georgia, but his mission was ending, he was dying in New England. The great work of Arminian Methodism in the New World had begun, and already two young men, Francis Asbury and Richard Whatcoat, who were to be among its earliest bishops, were traveling circuits in England.

[26] Wesley advised the Methodists to learn the military exercise, that they might the better defend their country when the French threatened to invade it in 1756. (Jackson's Charles Wesley, chap. 20.) He made an offer to the Government, "when the kingdom was in imminent danger," to raise troops among his people. (Works, vol. vii. p. 81.) He was a stanch English patriot, and believing that fighting was sometimes necessary, believed also that none were fit for it but such as were fit to die. Like Uncle Toby, he thought soldiers, above all other men, should be saints.

[27] See the correspondence of Pilmoor and Boardman, in Coke and Moore's Life of Wesley, III, 3.

CHAPTER VI.

CONFERENCES FROM 1760 TO 1770.

The Greek Bishop, Erasmus — Wesley's Proposition of Union with Evangelical Clergymen —Twelve of them meet at the Conference of 1764 — They decline his Terms — Proceedings of the Session of 1765 — Tickkets — First Temperance Societies — Reports of Members first made in 1766 — Wesley's Views of his own Authority — He requires his Preachers to Study — Whitefield, Howell Harris, and Laymen present at the Session of 1767 — Its Statistics — The Circulation of Books —Term of Circuit Appointments — The Conference of 1768 — Its Statistics — The Preachers required to abandon secular Business — John Nelson and William Shent — Origin of Methodism at Leeds — Books— Field Preaching — Early Rising — Sanctification — Session of 1769 — Preachers sent to America—First Provision for Preachers' Wives—Wesley laments the Unwillingness of the Regular Clergy to co-operate with him — He proposes a Plan for the Perpetuation of his Lay Ministry — Session of 1770 — Its Minute on Calvinism.

It has already been stated that no Minutes remain of the Conferences held in the present decade before the year 1765. Of the session of August 29, 1760, Wesley gives but a passing intimation in his Journal. His allusion to that of September 1, 1761, is but a sentence. That of August 9, 1762, was held at Leeds.[1] It is an interesting proof of the mutual good understanding of the Calvinistic and Arminian Methodists, that most of the leaders of the former were present with Wesley at this Conference. Lady Huntingdon, Whitefield, Romaine, Madan, and Venn attended it.[2] Wesley only says of it: "Our Conference began on Tuesday morning, and we had great reason to bless God for his gracious presence from the beginning to the end." It is evident, however, that the demand of both

[1] Not at Bristol, as Smith says: History of Methodism, II, 3. See Wesley's Journal, and Myles's Chronological History, chap. 3.

[2] Life and Times of the Countess of Huntingdon, chap. 17.

people and preachers for a more general administration of the sacraments in their societies had by this time become still more urgent, for early in the next year Wesley obtained the ordination of Dr. Jones, one of his preachers, and classical teacher at Kingswood school, from a Greek bishop by the name of Erasmus, who was traveling at the time in England. Several other lay preachers received ordination from him also, and some clamor arose from the fact, but their sufficient apology was that the prelates of the national Church still refused them this courtesy.[3] Charles Wesley, however, would not recognize the ordination of Dr. Jones, nor share with him in the administration of the sacraments. Jones, who was a man of piety and learning, was justly offended by this ungenerous treatment, and left the Connection.

The Conference of July 19, 1763, was held at London, amid the ferment occasioned by Maxfield's secession. "It was a great blessing," says Wesley, "that we had peace among ourselves, while so many were making themselves ready for battle." The circuits now numbered twenty in England, two in Scotland, two in Wales, and seven in Dublin; in all thirty-one. At this session the first provision for "old, worn-out preachers" was made, by the establishment of a general fund, to which each preacher contributed ten shillings. It was the beginning of that

[3] Toplady attacked Wesley severely on this occasion. Thomas Olivers conclusively answered the attack. See Myles's Chron. History, chap. 3. Southey affects, without reason, to doubt the episcopal character of Erasmus. It was satisfactorily ascertained by Wesley before the ordinations. Compare notes to Southey's Wesley, chap. 26, with Myles, as above. It is one of the characteristic blunders of the author of "The Life and Times of the Countess of Huntingdon" that he says: "Wesley was accused of a breach of the oath of supremacy by thus availing himself of the powers of a foreign prelate; and accused also of pressing the prelate to make him—Wesley—a bishop. The former charge was denied by Mr. Olivers, and the latter justified," etc. This statement is absolutely false; Olivers denied the latter accusation on the authority of Wesley. Wesley himself, in reply to an attack from Rowland Hill, declared: "I never entreated anything from Bishop Erasmus, who had abundant unexceptionable credentials as to his episcopal character. Nor did he ever 'reject any overture' made by me. Herein Mr. Hill has been misinformed. I deny the fact; let him produce the evidence." Works, vol. vi, p. 196.

series of "Connectional Funds" which has since become so extended and effective among British Methodists.[4]

To the session of August 6, 1764, Wesley devotes but three brief sentences in his Journal. "The great point," he says, "I now labored for, was a good understanding with our brethren of the clergy who were heartily engaged in propagating vital religion." Seven years before, Walker, of Truro, a devout man but rigid Churchman, had proposed that he should abandon all his societies in parishes over which evangelical clergymen presided. Wesley's good sense led him to see that this course would soon result in their extinction, and the defeat of the great work for which God had thrust him out. He desired their continued connection with the Church; he desired the co-operation of pious clergymen in their local management, for thereby he could secure the sacraments in a manner satisfactory to most of them, but he could not abandon his own responsibility for them; for how few of even the evangelical clergy, if disposed, were capable of sustaining them in the special work to which they were providentially designated, and what certainty could he have that their successors would do so? He therefore declined the proposition of Walker. A more prudent and important act had hardly occurred in his history. He was, however, still intent on the union of all evangelical clergymen in the great revival which he was conducting, and on the steadfast union of his people with the Church. He therefore addressed a circular letter to many of the most evangelical clergy of the Establishment, proposing, not any concession of opinions, for "they might agree or disagree touching absolute decrees on the one hand and perfection on the other," but a more catholic spirit, and better co-operation with him, as a member of the Church of England, in

[4] It was during this year that the Minutes of preceding Conferences from 1748 were compiled and placed in the "Octavo Minutes," with the date of 1749, (see page 212,) a fact which has inextricably confused their data. I have chosen, therefore, to use whatever material they may afford for the historical illustration of Methodism, in distinct chapters on its doctrines and economy.

the spread of true religion throughout the land.[5] It is to this correspondence that he refers in the brief allusion of his Journal to the present Conference. Though only three clergymen had responded to his overtures, no less than twelve met him at the session, but not in the catholic spirit which he himself had manifested. They insisted, in fine, upon the very course which Walker had proposed and Wesley had rejected seven years before. It was a momentous juncture to Methodism; and to Wesley's calm steadfastness subsequent generations owe the fact that it was not then absorbed into the Establishment, and that the organic consolidation which it had been for some time assuming was not effectually counteracted. Charles Wesley himself had the indiscretion to take side with these clergymen against him, and the heedlessness to declare that if he were a parish minister the lay itinerants "should not preach in his parish."[6] The lay preachers showed both their good sense and self-respect by unanimously agreeing with Wesley; and as the clerical visitors would not unite with him, except on their own conditions, he determined to pursue his providential course without them. And thus was another step taken forward toward the legitimate independence and permanence of Methodism.

With the twenty-second Conference, held at Manchester August 30, 1765, began the regular annual publication of the Minutes. They now assumed more than ever the form of business-like documents. Theological and ecclesiastical questions are seldom discussed in them, as these subjects had already been settled with sufficient definiteness for the present progress of the body. The names of Preachers admitted on trial, of the Assistants, Helpers, and Circuits, the appointments for the ensuing year, and financial arrangements, with singularly minute rules of discipline for the societies as well as for the preachers, make up their substance.

At the session for this year were reported twenty-five circuits, with seventy-one preachers, in England; four, with

[5] See the whole correspondence with Walker and others in Coke and Moore's Life of Wesley, II, 4.

[6] Myles's Chron. History, chap. 4.

four preachers, in Scotland; two, with two preachers, in Wales; and eight, with fifteen preachers, in Ireland, making thirty-nine circuits and ninety-two lay itinerants, besides the Wesleys, their clerical coadjutors, and a numerous corps of local preachers, many of whom effectively devoted a large portion of their time to itinerant labors. The title of "Superannuated Preachers" occurs this year for the first time in the Minutes, and the financial plan for their relief was further matured. The certificate, or "Ticket," by which members of the societies could, in removing, transfer their membership to their new places of residence, was adopted, and became a permanent custom. In 1749 the chapels had been legally settled upon trustees. A person was now appointed to examine their deeds, and see that vacancies among their trustees were filled. It was ordered that men and women should sit apart, that field-preaching should be maintained wherever possible,[7] and love-feasts not be continued longer than an hour and a half, as "every person should be home by nine o'clock." Preachers were directed to "exhort all that could, in every congregation, to sing," and to see that they were taught to sing by note; to enjoin upon the heads of families the duty of family prayer, with the reading of the Scriptures, night and morning, and to recommend them to be good "economists." The phrases "brother" and "sister" were to be used "*prudently*;" tobacco and drams were not to be touched by preachers on "any pretense," and were to be denounced among the people.[8]

The twenty-third session was held in Leeds, August 12, 1766; forty circuits were reported. For the first time we now have an attempt at a census of the societies, but it is too imperfect to afford an aggregate estimate of their members. Ireland and Wales, as also London and other circuits,

[7] Wesley wrote to one of his preachers: "If you desire to promote the work of God you should preach abroad as often as possible. Nothing destroys the work of the devil like this." Letter 678; Works, vol. vii.

[8] "So that in fact the Methodist societies were the first temperance societies." Watson's Life of Wesley, chap. 9.

made no returns; Cornwall reported over twenty-two hundred; Grimshaw's Haworth circuit more than fifteen hundred; Nelson's Birstal circuit nearly fourteen hundred; Leeds more than one thousand; Newcastle eighteen hundred; Lancashire seventeen hundred and forty-two; Edinburgh one hundred and five, and Dundee three hundred and twenty-one.

During several years subscriptions had been made for the relief of suffering societies. The amount reported at the present year was seven hundred pounds, one hundred and fifty of which were sent to Aberdeen and Edinburgh. The whole debt of the societies for their chapels and preachers' houses was £11,383. "We shall be utterly ruined," said Wesley, "if we go on at this rate;" and it was ordered that no building should be undertaken till two thirds of the necessary money should be subscribed. It was again asserted that the Methodists were not Dissenters; they were recommended to attend the Church service every Sabbath, and the preachers were directed to hold their Sunday worship at five o'clock in the morning, and the same hour in the evening, to avoid interference with the Church worship.

In a concluding address, remarkable for its length and pointedness, Wesley stated the grounds of his power as providentially placed at the head of the Arminian Methodist societies, and exhorted the preachers to more faithfulness, detailing, as reasons, the prevalent faults of their people.

After describing the unavoidable manner in which the societies and Conferences had involved him in his present responsibility, and the impossibility of his now abandoning it with a good conscience, he remarked: "I did not seek any part of this power; it came upon me unawares; but when it was come, not daring to bury that talent, I used it to the best of my judgment. Yet I never was fond of it; I always did, and do now, bear it as my burden, the burden which God lays upon me, and therefore I dare not yet lay it down. But if you can tell me any one, or any five men, to whom I may transfer this burden, who *can* and *will* do just what I do now, I will heartily thank both them and you." "Preaching twice or thrice a day," he added, "is no burden to me at all; but the care of all the preachers and all the people is a burden indeed." As he advances in his exhortations to the preachers his sentences grow ardent with earnestness. He insists on increased pastoral labor, visits from house to house, and the instruction of the children of their people. After answering the objection that this thorough work would preclude all study, he proceeds to complain of their want of diligence in the latter respect and of their desultory habits of reading. "Why are we not more knowing?" he asks; "we talk, talk, read history, or what comes next to hand. We must, absolutely must, cure this evil or give up the whole work.[9] But how? Read the *most useful* books, and that regularly and constantly. Steadily spend all the morning in this employment, or at least five hours in twenty-four. 'But I have *no taste* for reading.' Contract a taste for it by use or return to your trades. 'But different men have different tastes.' Therefore, some may read less than others, but none should read less than this."

He finally urges them to go "into every house and teach every one therein, young and old;" to spend at least an hour twice a week with the children of the societies wherever ten of them could be assembled; to rise at four in the morning; to observe five o'clock in the afternoon for private prayer, and to bear in mind that any time for this duty is no time. "O let us," he concludes, "stir up the gift of God that is in us! Let us no more sleep as do others! But whatsoever our hand findeth to do *let us* do it with our might!"

On August 18, 1767, was held in London the twenty-fourth annual Conference.[10] The continued harmony of the two sections of Methodism is indicated by the fact that both Whitefield and Howell Harris were present. Several lay

[9] It is worthy of notice that this sweeping declaration was uttered by him in the same address in which occurs the much-abused passage: "Gaining knowledge is a good thing, but saving souls is better."

[10] It is numbered by mistake as the twenty-third in the Octavo Minutes, edition of 1812: London.

itinerants and local preachers also attended it. Nine new preachers were "admitted on trial," among whom was Francis Asbury, afterward the chief founder of American Methodism. Two desisted from traveling, and six probationers were admitted to full membership. Forty circuits were reported. Their number, however, does not show the extent of the field, for they were continually changing, and two or three were often combined in one. England had twenty-five, Ireland nine, Scotland five. All Wales was this year included in one. Twenty-five preachers were designated to those of England, nineteen to those of Ireland, seven to Scotland, and three to Wales. There were 22,410 members in the English societies, 2,801 in the Irish, 468 in the Scotch, and 232 in the Welsh. The comparatively small number reported from Wales arose from the fact that while Calvinistic Methodism formed but few societies in the rest of the country, it had begun in Wales, under Howell Harris, by their organization, and as Wesley disowned dogmatic terms of membership, and recognized the whole Methodistic revival as a unit, the Welsh converts of his preachers very naturally resorted to the societies of Harris. It seems never to have occasioned a demur on his part.

The membership of the societies amounted to 25,911:[11] London circuit reported 2,180; Bristol 1,177; Cornwall, 2,038; Staffordshire, 1,994; Lancashire, 2,000; Leeds, 1,088; Bristol, 1,476; Haworth, 1,356; Newcastle, 1,910.

The examination of the characters of preachers, now an invariable part of the proceedings, seems to have occupied most of the time of the session, as but few other important items of business are recorded. Among these was the better circulation of books; a means of usefulness which began almost at the origin of Methodism, and may thus be considered the commencement of the popular and systematic use of the religious press by evangelical Protestantism. Hitherto books had been sold on all the circuits; the

[11] This is Myles's estimate. (Chron. Hist.) The aggregate given in the Octavo Minutes is 26,341.

Assistants were now instructed to "give them away prudently," and beg money from the rich to pay for them for the poor.

A singular apprehension had been expressed by the trustees of the Wednesbury Society, that the conference might impose the same preacher upon them for many years. They seem to have prized the itinerancy, and the Conference, to relieve their fears, allowed to be inserted, in the deeds of "Preaching Houses," the promise "that the same preacher shall not be sent ordinarily above one, never above two years together." English Methodists afterward found it convenient to change the term to three years. Quarterly fasts in all the societies were ordered at this session. "Love and harmony," says Wesley, "reigned from the beginning to the end."

The twenty-fifth Conference was held at Bristol, August 16, 1768. Eleven probationers were admitted to membership, and twelve candidates were received on trial, among whom was George Shadford, another name known in American Methodist history. Two desisted from traveling. The contributions toward the payment of debts on chapels and preaching houses were £5,666, besides the collection of £173 for Kingswood school. The financial system which has since been a distinguishing characteristic of English Methodism, had already begun to take efficiency under the systematic genius of Wesley. The whole debt remaining in England, Ireland, and Scotland, was £7,728. Forty circuits were reported, and 27,341 members, showing a gain of 1,430 over the returns of the preceding session.

While some circuits returned an increase, others reported a declension, and an inquiry was made why the preachers were not more effective. The reason most discussed was the fact, hitherto quite general, of their partial devotion to secular business. This had been to some extent necessary, their support by the societies having been quite deficient. John Nelson, as we have stated, worked as a mason during the day and preached at night. William Shent, one of the earliest and noblest of the itinerants, who had been impressed for a soldier, at whose feet Grimshaw once fell, saying, "I am not worthy to stand in your presence," and whom Lady Huntingdon called a guileless Israelite, had maintained himself by a humble craft in Leeds.[12] He kept it up by hiring assistants, and by returning frequently to his shop from his distant fields of labor, and at last was compelled to give his entire time to it, excepting such intervals as he could spare for preaching excursions in the vicinity.

Wesley now saw that the time had come to correct this inconvenience. He did not deny its necessity under some circumstances, as in the case of St. Paul, but the keeping of shops, or dealing in merchandise, he pronounced "an evil in itself, an evil in its consequences." Those views of their character, as legitimate preachers of the Gospel, which he had already expressed, were again indicated by the fact that he applied to them the passages of Holy Scripture which assert the right of Christian pastors to a pecuniary support from the Church. He even appealed to the office of Ordination in the Liturgy of the national Church as relevant to the case, thereby classing his itinerants, in this respect, with the regular clergy. "Therefore," he concludes, "give up all, and attend to the one business, and God will recompense you a hundred fold in this world as well as in the world to come."

The increased circulation of books was urged as a means of checking the lamented declension. Wesley, from the very beginning of his public career, seemed to have a sublime idea of the power of the religious press; he used it continually, and never ceased to exhort his preachers to circulate books and tracts. "Carry them with you in every round," he said; "leave not a stone unturned." They were to be presented everywhere among the people, and even portions

[12] Three female members of his family were the first Methodists of Leeds, and are still held in affectionate remembrance there as "the three Marys." On hearing of the fame of John Nelson, when he began to exhort among his neighbors at Birstal, they went thither to see him, and soon after opened the way for him at Leeds. He preached his first sermon there in front of Shent's shop.

of them read by the preachers in the congregations, in order to promote their sale.

Field preaching was to be kept up diligently, and it is evident that Wesley intended it should never be abandoned, never, at least, while any considerable portion of the population neglected the house of God. The morning five o'clock preaching was to be maintained wherever twenty persons could be found to attend it. This he deemed absolutely necessary for the success of Methodism; "it is," he says, "the glory of the Methodists. Rising early is equally good for soul and body. It helps the nerves better than a thousand medicines; and in particular preserves the sight, and prevents lowness of spirits more than can well be imagined."

He exhorted them to give more attention than ever to the doctrine of sanctification. "I ask, once for all, Shall we defend this perfection or give it up? You all agree to defend it, meaning thereby, as we did from the beginning, salvation from all sin by the love of God and our neighbor filling the heart. The Papists say, 'This cannot be attained till we have been in purgatory.' The Dissenters say, 'It will be attained as soon as the soul and body part.' The old Methodists said, 'It may be attained before we die, a moment after is too late.' You are all agreed we may be saved from all sin before death. The substance then is settled." As to the question, Is the change instantaneous or gradual? he agues that it is both; that from the moment of justification there may be a gradual sanctification, a daily growth in grace; but that, if sin ceases before death, there must, in the nature of things, be an instantaneous change; there must be a last moment wherein it does exist, and a first moment wherein it does not. But should the preacher insist upon both one and the other? Certainly, he replies; he should insist on the gradual change, and that earnestly and continually. But there are reasons why he should insist on the instantaneous one also. If there be such a blessed change before death, all believers should be encouraged to expect it, because the more earnestly they expect it, the more steadily and swiftly does the gradual experience of grace go on in their hearts, the more watchful are they against all sin the more zealous of good works; whereas the contrary effects were usually observed when this expectation ceased. They are *saved by hope;* by this hope of a total renovation saved with a gradually increasing salvation. Destroy this hope, and that salvation usually stands still. Therefore, he concludes, whoever would advance the gradual salvation of believers should strongly insist upon the instantaneous one.

On the first day of August, 1769, began at Leeds the twenty-sixth Conference. The number of circuits reported was forty-six, showing a gain of six. The aggregate of members was 28,263, showing an increase of 922. Ten probationers were admitted, and twelve candidates received on trial. Six ceased to travel.

It was at this Conference that the first appeal for Methodist preaching from America was presented by Wesley. "Who is willing to go?" he asked. Richard Boardman and Joseph Pilmoor responded, and were appointed to the distant field. The occasion could not fail to produce a deep interest in the assembly. Methodism had already begun its work in the West Indies by Nathaniel Gilbert, who had formed a society of two hundred negroes in Antigua. Whitefield had spread it in spirit and power among the independent churches of North America, where he was about to die. It was now to take an organic form in the New World by the agency of Wesley's lay preachers. "What can we do further in token of our brotherly love?" he asked, after the appointment of Boardman and Pilmoor. "Let us now make a collection among ourselves," was the prompt response, and the liberal sum of £70 was collected among these generous men, most of whom were habitual sufferers from want. Twenty of the seventy pounds were appropriated for the voyage of the two missionaries, and fifty were sent toward paying the debt of "Wesley Chapel," the first that ever bore that name, and the first Methodist church of the Western hemisphere.

As measures had been adopted at the preceding Conference to relieve the preachers from dependence upon secular business for a maintenance, another step forward for their support, and toward the permanent organization of the lay ministry, was now taken by the enactment of a regular circuit collection for an "allowance" to their wives. Only about one third of them seem yet to have been married men; but as these had thus far been appointed only to the wealthiest circuits, in order that their families might not unnecessarily suffer, the effective operation of the itinerant system had been seriously restricted, and its talents distributed not so much according to the need of the societies as to the necessities of the preachers. The allowance now made for a wife was small, being but ten pounds a year; but it was the beginning of a better provision, which in our day has secured to Wesleyan preachers and their families a more competent and more reliable average support than is afforded perhaps by any other religious community of England, not excepting the national Church itself.

Wesley was now sixty-six years old. It was prudent to think of the means necessary to perpetuate the unity of his preachers and people after his death. He read a paper to the Conference on this subject. He referred to the failure of all his efforts to secure the co-operation of even the "evangelical" portion of the clergy of the Establishment, and the fact that from among the fifty or sixty to whom he had addressed his circular letter on the subject only three had responded. "So I give this up," he said, with undissembled grief: "I can do no more. They are a rope of sand, and such will they continue." But it was otherwise with his own traveling fellow-laborers. They were one body, acting in concert and by united counsels. And now was the time to consider what could be done in order to continue this union. As long as he lived there would be no great difficulty, for he, under God, was a center of union to them. They all knew him, they all loved him for his work's sake, and therefore, were it only out of regard to him, would continue connected with each other. But by what means might this connection be preserved when God should remove him?

He proposed that on notice of his death all the preachers in England and Ireland should repair to London within six weeks; that they should seek God by solemn fasting and prayer; draw up articles of agreement, to be signed by those who chose to act in concert; dismiss in a friendly manner those who should not so choose; select by votes a *committee* of three, five, or seven, each of whom was to be a *moderator* in his turn—to do what he did: "propose preachers to be tried, admitted, or excluded; fix the place of each preacher for the ensuing year, and the time of the next Conference."

It was further proposed that a document should be signed by all who agreed to these suggestions, pledging them, first, To devote themselves entirely to God; denying them selves, taking up their cross daily; steadily aiming at one thing—to save their own souls and the souls of their hearers; secondly, To preach the *old Methodist doctrines*, as contained in the Minutes, and no other; thirdly, To observe and enforce the whole *Methodist discipline* as defined in the Minutes."

It was finally ordered that this plan should be issued in the Minutes, and submitted to the consideration of the preachers, many of whom were not present at the session. It was held in suspense by Wesley during several years, but was brought up for consideration at the Conferences of 1773, 1774, and 1775, and signed by all the preachers present at those sessions, amounting to one hundred and one. The arrangement was afterward superseded by Wesley's Deed of Declaration, but it is worthy of this passing notice, as a proof of his growing conviction that Methodism would be compelled, sooner or later, to take an independent and permanent form.[16]

The twenty-seventh Conference was held in London, August 7, 1770. Eighteen candidates were received on probation, and sixteen probationers admitted into membership. Five members ceased to travel. Fifty circuits were reported, being an increase of four. The last in the list is es-

[16] Myles's Chron. Hist., etc., chap. 5.

pecially significant; it reads: "Fiftieth, *America*, Joseph Pilmoor, Richard Boardman, Robert Williams, John King." Volumes of history were anticipated in that brief sentence.

The returns of members of societies amounted to 29,466, showing a gain of 1143. The payments on society debts amounted to £1700, but the sum remaining unpaid was nearly £7000. A resolution, characteristic of Wesley's strict economy, was adopted, putting a stop to all building for the ensuing year. No new house was to be erected, no alteration nor addition made in any old ones, unless the societies concerned should defray the expense, without lessening their yearly collections.

Forty-three preachers' wives were to be provided for during the ensuing year, and the former regulation respecting them was re-enacted. The children of preachers were to be supported by the circuits on which their fathers labored. An illustration of the financial condition of the ministry is afforded by the fact that only twelve pounds a year were allowed for a preacher's wife, and four pounds for each of his children; and the latter sum was to be paid for boys only till their eighth year, when they were to be sent to Kingswood school; and for girls till their fourteenth year, after which no provision was yet made for them.

To prevent scandal, it was enacted that in all cases of insolvency among members of the societies, a committee should examine their accounts, and bankrupts were to be immediately "expelled," if their failure should be seen to have occurred from any unjust causes.

While the Minutes showed an increase of members, ten circuits reported a decrease. It was therefore urgently asked: "What can be done to revive the work of God where it has decayed?" And the preachers pledged themselves anew to pastoral diligence, visiting from house to house, to increased care of the religious training of the children of their societies, to field preaching, early morning services, and the circulation of religious books.

This session was memorable for the occasion which it

gave for the revival of the Calvinistic controversy. In the Conference of 1744 it was declared that they had "leaned too much toward Calvinism." No man of his age possessed or preached clearer views of the great doctrine of the Reformation—Justification by faith—than John Wesley. But he knew its liability to Antinomian abuse. As early as 1738 he guarded it against this perversion, with no little emphasis, in his sermon before the University of Oxford, and in his first Conference he admonished his preachers against it. He believed that the Calvinism of his day tended to it, and the "leaning toward Calvinism," to which he objected, was such a representation of the relation of works to faith as tended to supersede the former by the latter. The doctrine of the "imputation of Christ's righteousness," upon which American Calvinists have in latter years very largely adopted his opinions, was particularly, as he thought, abused by contemporary Calvinists, and the theological world owes him no small obligation for the discrimination with which he guarded the Methodistic movement against this Antinomian tendency.

The Minute on the question at the present Conference was not designed as a popular view of the subject; it was liable itself to abuse in that respect; but as a brief, dogmatic statement, made for his preachers as students of theology, it is safe and Scriptural. It produced the most violent theological controversy known in the history of Methodism, in which Shirley, Toplady, Hill, Fletcher, and Olivers were the champions. It has tended, more than any other occasion for a hundred years, to fortify evangelical Arminianism in the Protestant world. It forecast, perhaps irrevocably, the theological character of Methodism, and, by Arminian Methodists, at least, must be considered one of those special providences which have developed and determined its character. As this memorable controversy did not take place till the next Conference, and forms one of the most interesting facts in our narrative, the Minute which produced it will be given at that period.

CHAPTER VII.

CALVINISTIC METHODISM FROM 1760 TO 1770.

Mutual Relations of the Calvinistic Methodist Societies — Position of the Countess of Huntingdon — She itinerates with her Preachers in Yorkshire — They attend Wesley's Conference — Venn — Grimshaw — Fletcher — Sketch of Captain Scott — Adventures of Captain Joss — The Countess and her Preachers at Cheltenham — Lord Dartmouth — A great "Field Day" — "Quadruple Alliance" between the Wesleys and Whitefield and Lady Huntingdon — Trevecca College — Expulsion of Methodist Students from Oxford — Scenes at Trevecca — Whitefield's Declining Health — He again Visits America — Returns to England in 1765 — Last Interviews with Wesley — Last Voyage to America — Happiness of his Religious Frame as he approached his End — His Excursion up the Hudson — Last Sermon — Character — Results.

It would be difficult if not impossible to define the mutual relations of the Calvinistic Methodist societies. Calvinism has always tended, by some occult law, to ecclesiastical independence, and has thereby favored freedom of thought rather than effectiveness of organization. Whitefield and Howell Harris were the apostles of Calvinistic Methodism; Romaine, Madan, Venn, and Berridge, their coadjutors; the Countess of Huntingdon was their most important center of union. Her good sense, the influence of her social position as a member of the British aristocracy, (an important consideration to the English mind,) and, still more, her munificence, upon which most of the Calvinistic chapels were more or less dependent, enabled her to centralize their sympathies around her own person, and she never abused the moral power which she thus commanded. No formal conferences were held; few, if indeed any, representative consultations were had; but the Calvinistic evangelists naturally resorted to her house for counsel with each other, and always with her. Most of their leaders were her chaplains, a fact which gave her a paramount influence. Severely practical, and never whimsical in her judgments, she added to her other sources of power a moral authority to which all reverently deferred.

While really directing the whole Calvinistic movement of Methodism, she never transcended what was deemed the propriety of her sex by any activity in the public assemblies of her societies. She often "itinerated" among them, but was always accompanied, not by Whitefield, for his movements were too rapid for her, but by Harris, Romaine, Venn, Fletcher, or Madan, they preaching, while she maintained her womanly decorum as a hearer, planning their labors and counseling the societies privately.

Her excursions among them were frequent during the present period. In 1760 she went into Yorkshire with Romaine and Venn, and was joined there by Whitefield.[1] One object of their visit was to harmonize the distracted societies of Ingham. In 1762 she again visited that county, and, with Venn, Romaine, Madan, and Whitefield, was present at the Conference at Leeds. Their attendance seems to have been purely one of courtesy and Christian fellowship. No dissentient opinion disturbed the deliberations; Wesley expressed in his Journal thankfulness to God for "his gracious presence, which attended it from the beginning." The occasion must have been one of deep interest, presenting, as it did, an imposing representation of the whole Methodist movement, in the persons of most of its great leaders, and crowded by an unusual attendance of local preachers, class-leaders, and stewards.

After the session Whitefield went to Scotland, rousing the towns and villages in his course. The countess hastened to Knaresborough, where she had frequent meetings with the evangelical clergy of the shire, inspiriting them to more energetic labors. Romaine continued with her, preaching daily and with powerful effect. Venn, who had

[1] Life and Times of the Countess of Huntingdon, chap. 17.

charge of the parish of Huddersfield, wrote to her, after her departure, with an overflowing heart, respecting the "light and life" which her visit had spread among the Yorkshire Churches. The catholic-minded Grimshaw, who was evangelically the archbishop of Yorkshire, and was now about to depart to the Church triumphant, rejoiced to see any new laborer enter his great Methodist diocese. He wrote to the countess, after her visit, that the "Lord's work prospers amazingly among us," and that the societies were everywhere in a good state. So pure at this time was the charity, so fervent the zeal of both classes of Methodists, that it was indeed difficult for either themselves or their enemies to distinguish between them. Grimshaw wrote, with a sort of rapture, of the blessings showered by the Lord upon them all while the countess and her chaplains were in Yorkshire. "How," he says, "did our hearts burn within us to proclaim his love and grace to perishing sinners. Come and animate us afresh; aid us by your counsels and your prayers; and stir us up to renewed activity in the cause of God. All the dear apostles go on well; all pray for your dear ladyship, and all long for your coming among us again." He had been, he continues, a "long round" since she was with them, and had seen Ingham, Venn, Conyers, and Bentley "all alive, and preaching Christ crucified with wonderful success." Nelson, Grimshaw, Ingham, and Venn had kindled a flame of Christian charity and zeal in Yorkshire which still glows over their graves. Not only these early and beautiful examples of religious fellowship, but the abiding results of Methodism in that region are among its best vindications.

Fletcher proposed, at the next visit of the countess to Yorkshire, to accompany her to that "Goshen of the land, to learn the love of Christ at the feet of his brethren and fathers there." She was also attended by Whitefield, Venn, Howell Harris, Townsend, Dr. Conyers, and Lady Anne Erskine, daughter of Lord Buchan; and Madan joined them afterward. They had public worship twice a day, Fletcher being the chief preacher, as Whitefield left them early for Wales. They paused at Venn's parish, in Huddersfield, where Fletcher preached twice to large congregations and with manifest effect. They also entered the parish of Grimshaw, who had now gone to his rest. Fletcher and Townsend addressed thousands there who had assembled from the towns and villages round about. Madan, Fletcher, and Venn, assisted by several Yorkshire clergymen, preached incessantly for some weeks, not only in that county, but in the adjacent shires to vast multitudes. It was, in fine, a religious jubilee throughout that part of England. Whitefield again joined them, and spread widely the public interest. The Churches were quickened, hundreds if not thousands of hearers were awakened, and the whole region aroused.

Two interesting laymen, one a military man, Captain Jonathan Scott, and the other a mariner, Captain Torial Joss, were conspicuous among the Calvinistic laborers about this time. The former was with the catholic band in Yorkshire, where he preached with great usefulness and popularity. Whitefield had said of them that God, who sitteth upon the flood, can bring "a shark from the ocean, and a lion from the forest, and make them to show forth his praise." Methodism hesitated not to use any talent which Providence thrust in its way, though it took good caution against eccentricities which were not well guarded by prudence and piety. Both these remarkable men became powerful laborers in its field, and never betrayed its confidence. Their personal histories are striking illustrations of the manner in which the Methodistic revival reached all classes of men, and turned to account all kinds of talent.

Captain Scott was descended from an ancient and opulent family in the county of Salop. He was well educated, and in his seventeenth year adopted a military life as a cornet, but was soon promoted to the rank of captain of dragoons. He fought in the battle of Minden in 1759. Of vivid temperament, courageous and ambitious, he was, nevertheless, addicted to religious reflection, and in the midst of battle saw the folly of bravery itself, when it is without moral fitness for its perilous contingencies. He desired to be a genuine Christian, but knew not the power of faith as "the victory which overcometh the world." He read punctiliously the Psalms and Lessons of the Liturgy, and his fellow-officers usually accosted him with the pleasantry, "Well, Scott, have you read your Psalms and Lessons to-day?" Persisting, against the banter of his comrades, in these honest attempts to make himself righteous, he felt, nevertheless, from day to day, that he had no success. While quartered near Oathall, he was overtaken, on a shooting excursion, by a storm that drove him into a farm-house, the humble tenant of which was a Methodist and conversed with such good sense on religious subjects that Scott inquired where he had got his information. Pointing to a neighboring hall, the farmer replied that a famous man, Mr. Romaine, was now preaching there. The next Sunday the officer was present, and was struck by the devout order of the assembly, but still more by the text: "*I am the way.*" It was precisely what he needed, and led him at last to a saving faith in Christ.

During some time he remained in the army, but while in Leicester with his regiment, he began openly to preach to his men. A good but eccentric man having observed his ability and usefulness, one day shut him in an apartment alone with his God, a Bible, and a hymn-book, and declared that he must inevitably preach there that evening. He did so, and thus took his commission as an embassador of Christ. From this hour he never swerved, but zealously preached in his regimentals wherever he moved with his troops. The novelty of the sight of a military officer preaching in costume, excited the liveliest interest among the common people. Nearly all Leeds turned out to hear him, and he addressed "amazing crowds." Wherever he labored with Lady Huntingdon's clerical attendants, during her present visit to Yorkshire, he was a center of attraction to the multitude. He accompanied the countess to Madeley, where, as he could not canonically occupy the church, he preached at the invitation of Fletcher twice on Sunday from the horse-block at its door to an immense assembly, and the next day in Madeley Woods to a still larger concourse. Fletcher wrote of him as "a captain of the truth, a bold soldier of Jesus Christ. God had thrown down before him the middle wall of bigotry, and he had boldly launched into an irregular usefulness. For some months he had exhorted his dragoons daily, for some weeks he had preached publicly at Leicester, in the Methodist meeting-house, in his regimentals, to numerous congregations with good success." "The stiff regular ones pursue him," he adds, "with hue and cry, but I believe he is quite beyond their reach. I believe his *red coat* will shame many a black one. I am sure he shames me."

Whitefield could not but rejoice in such a fellow-laborer. He gave a public account of him in London. "I have invited the captain," he added, "to bring his artillery to the Tabernacle rampart, and try what execution he can do here." Scott went to the metropolis, and a great assembly welcomed him in the Tabernacle. The brave man's heart melted as he rose before them; he burst into tears, and lost the control of his voice; but recovering his composure, he delivered a discourse which produced a lasting impression, and rendered him thenceforth one of the most popular preachers of the city. He sacrificed for the Gospel flattering prospects in the army, sold his commission, and gave himself to the Christian ministry. During more than twenty years he was one of the most successful supplies of Whitefield's Tabernacle, and went to and fro through the country preaching in both Calvinistic and Arminian chapels.

Captain Joss was another example of the Methodistic spirit of the times. He was an energetic Scotchman, and trained to maritime life. He was early inclined to religion, but being discouraged at home, he hid his Bible out of the house, and reading it clandestinely, received from it impressions which he never lost. He was sent to sea when quite young; it was at a time of war, and being taken by the enemy, he was carried to a foreign port and suffered a severe imprisonment. Returning to Scotland during the Stuart rebellion, he was immediately impressed and sent on board an English ship of war. He made his escape, and connected himself with a coasting vessel which belonged to Robin Hood's Bay, in Yorkshire. Wesley records, in his Journal, frequent visits to this place, where he preached in the market square and on the Quay till he succeeded in founding a society. Joss, who had strictly maintained his morals, and even his religious scrupulousness, in all his adventures, and had been a diligent student during the winter suspensions of navigation, joined the Methodists, and became noted in the town for the ability of his exhortations. Wesley discerned his talents and encouraged him. He retained his Scotch Calvinism, but as he did not dispute about it, it was no obstacle among his brethren.

Still pursuing his sea-faring life, he preached on board his vessel, and became known as an evangelist in all the harbors which he frequented. His first regular sermon was delivered at Boston, Lincolnshire, where he produced an extraordinary impression. On being appointed to the command of a ship, he established regular worship among his crew, and became at once captain and chaplain, and soon trained a band of his converted tars to exhort and pray publicly.

He was a good sailor, and had accumulated enough property to become owner, in part, of his ship, with a fair prospect of wealth. But now disasters beset him continually, as if providentially to drive him from the seas. He made unfortunate voyages, and was repeatedly wrecked. At one time he lost his ship, and with difficulty saved himself and his crew; but, courageous against all odds, he went to Berwick for the purpose of building a still larger vessel. While there he preached to great crowds, and when about to leave, the common people mourned as at the loss of a faithful pastor. After he had sailed, a friend wrote, without his knowledge, to London, respecting his successful labors in Berwick during the preceding nine months. The letter came under Whitefield's eye, and when he heard of the arrival of the preaching captain in the Downs, he announced in his Tabernacle that Joss would preach there the next Saturday evening, and dispatched a messenger to the ship, which had already received among sailors the name of "The Pulpit," to summon him to London. His modesty was startled at the unexpected honor, and he refused to go, but the messenger would not leave the deck till he consented. Amid wondering throngs the sailor proclaimed the Gospel from Whitefield's pulpit, not only on Saturday but on Sunday, and Whitefield insisted that he should at once abandon the chart and compass, and give himself wholly to the ministry. He shrank from the proposition, but on his next voyage met with an accident which Whitefield deemed a warning. On his return to London still greater crowds gathered to hear him. Whitefield again urged him to confine himself to preaching, but he again resisted the call, and his following voyage was attended with a still worse disaster. On his third arrival at London his word was heard by yet greater throngs, and with still greater effect. While in the city his brother, a pious young man, fell overboard and was drowned in the Thames. "Sir," said Whitefield, "all these disasters are the fruits of your disobedience, and let me tell you that if you still refuse to hearken to the call of God, both you and your ship will soon go to the bottom." He yielded at last, and after his fourth voyage gave up the deck and took the pulpit. In 1766 Whitefield had the happiness to recognize him as his colleague at the Tabernacle and Tottenham Court, and Captain Joss became the Rev. Torial Joss, of famous memory in the religious history of the times.

During thirty years he was Whitefield's associate pastor of the London Calvinistic Methodist societies, and his popularity was only second to that of Whitefield himself. The crowd ran after him, and his word, delivered with great native eloquence, was successful in the conversion of multitudes of souls. Berridge called him "Whitefield's Archdeacon of Tottenham." He not only spread Methodism extensively in the metropolis, but made preaching excursions into the country. He usually spent four or five months of each year in itinerating in England and Wales. The Welsh especially delighted in his simple eloquence. Many came twenty miles on foot to hear him, and wherever he went he left seals of his ministry. He was a good man, mighty in the Scriptures, and faithful to the end. After preaching the Gospel more than thirty years, he was smitten down by sudden disease. "O the preciousness of faith!" he exclaimed to the groups around his death-bed. "I have finished my course. My pilgrimage is ended. O thou Friend of sinners, take thy poor old friend home!" As if rapt in visions of the celestial world, he at last uttered the word "Archangels," and expired.[2]

Thus did Methodism gather its trophies from the sea and the land, and while the "regular" clergy treated with scorn its "irregularities," and bishops wrote diatribes against its "enthusiasm," but failed to save the heathen masses around them, it went forward, redeeming the people.

In 1768 the Countess of Huntingdon made excursions into Gloucestershire and neighboring counties, attended by a corps of regular and irregular preachers whose ministry spread a great sensation throughout their course. "A remarkable power from on high," wrote the Countess, "accompanied the message of His servants, and many felt the arrows of distress."[3] Shirley, Romaine, Madan, Venn, and Maddock were with her, and Whitefield joined them at Cheltenham. They preached in the churches when they could obtain permission; when it was denied they betook themselves to Methodist and Dissenting chapels, to churchyards, to highways, and fields. At Cheltenham the church was refused them by its rector and wardens, but Lord Dartmouth, noted as a Methodist himself, opened his mansion for them. Downing, his chaplain, was a Methodist evangelist, and had done much good in the neighborhood. His lordship hoped to obtain the church for

[2] Gillies's Whitefield, ch. 19; Life, etc., of Lady Huntingdon, ch. 12.
[3] Life and Times of the Countess of Huntingdon, chap. 25.

Whitefield, but when the latter arrived it was denied to him also. An immense assembly had been attracted by the fame of the preacher and the exertions of the earl; finding the church door closed, Whitefield mounted a tombstone and cried aloud, "Ho! every one that thirsteth come ye to the waters!" A singular spectacle was it—the closed church, the graves covered with thousands of the people, and such churchmen as Venn, Madan, Shirley, Maddock, Talbot, Rowlands, and Whitefield, ordained and gowned, and yet proscribed for preaching to the famishing multitudes the doctrines of the Anglican Reformation; and this, too, while a peer of the realm, a nobleman distinguished for his wealth and dignity, admired by the king, the first Lord of Trade, sworn of the Privy Council, and Principal Secretary of State for the American Department, stood with his family among them, their friend and patron.[4] Such was the treatment of Methodism by the Established Church of the land.

Venn spoke of this "field day," and those which immediately ensued, as remarkable for interest and success beyond what his "powers could describe." He says he was overwhelmed by a sense of the awful power and presence of Jehovah; that the effect of Whitefield's discourse was so irresistible that some of the hearers fell prostrate upon the graves, others sobbed aloud, some wept in silence, and almost the whole assembly seemed struck with awe. When the preacher came to the application of his text to the ungodly, "his word cut like a sword." Many cried out with anguish. At this juncture Whitefield made an "awful pause" of a few seconds, then burst into a flood of tears. Madan

[4] America still respects the name of the noble Methodist at the college (Dartmouth, Hanover, N. H.) which he patronized. It was to him that Cowper alluded in the verses:

"We boast some rich ones whom the Gospel sways,
And one who wears a coronet and prays."

"They call my Lord Dartmouth an enthusiast," said George III.; "but surely he says nothing on religion but what any Christian may and ought to say." There was a vein of outright good sense running through the insanity of the aged king.

and Venn stood up during this short interval and exhorted the people to restrain as much as possible their emotions. Twice afterward they had to repeat the same advice. "O with what eloquence," writes Venn, "what energy, what melting tenderness did Whitefield beseech sinners to be reconciled to God, to come to him for life everlasting, and rest their weary souls in Christ the Saviour." When the sermon was ended the people seemed spell-bound to the ground. Madan, Talbot, Downing, and Venn found ample employment in endeavoring to comfort those who had broken down under a sense of guilt. They separated in different directions among the crowd, and each was quickly surrounded by an attentive audience still eager to hear the word of life.

Turned away from the church, the evangelists found shelter at Lord Dartmouth's mansion. Whitefield administered the sacrament there the same evening. Talbot "exhorted," and Venn closed the day with prayer and thanksgiving. The next day was equally interesting. Whitefield addressed "a prodigious congregation" in the church-yard, and Talbot preached at night at the earl's residence, where all the rooms and the adjacent grounds were crowded. A table was brought out before the door, and Whitefield mounting it, again addressed them with overwhelming effect. Intelligence of these extraordinary scenes soon spread abroad, and the next day Charles Wesley, and many Methodists from Bristol, Gloucester, Tewkesbury, Rodborough, and their adjacent villages, arrived and shared in the Pentecost; but all "loud weeping and piercing cries had subsided, and the work of conversion went on, and much solid good was done."

On leaving Cheltenham Madan and Talbot itinerated through Wiltshire, Oxfordshire, and Northamptonshire. "They went," says Hervey, who met them, "like men baptized with the Holy Ghost and with fire," and through all those regions, as well as Gloucestershire and Worcestershire, they sounded the alarm day and night, and woke up slumbering thousands. These proceedings seemed, indeed, disorderly to grave Churchmen, but Whitefield expressed the just view of them: "This order undoes us. As things now stand we must be disorderly or useless."

It is supposed that there were about forty clergymen of the Establishment publicly known about this period as "evangelical."[5] Wesley had tried in vain to introduce among them some plan of co-operation which should not compromise their opinions. With Whitefield and Lady Huntingdon he had better success. He frequently met them in London, and preached at the residence of the Countess amid throngs not only of the aristocracy, but of the Calvinistic Methodist ministers; he occupied their pulpits, also, in his travels through the country. About 1766 the Countess, Whitefield, and the two Wesleys cemented their Christian harmony by something like a formal, "a quadruple alliance," as Charles Wesley called it.[6] They agreed to meet as often as convenient and co-operate in their common work.

Lady Huntingdon prized highly Wesley's counsels. She could not fail to perceive his peculiar ability as an ecclesiastical administrator, and, more than any other leader of Calvinistic Methodism, shared his legislative and executive genius; but her sex did not admit of its exertion to the extent needed by her societies. She consulted him often on important occasions. In 1767 she submitted to him, and also to Venn, Romaine, and her other conspicuous associates, a plan for the education of preachers, from which arose her Trevecca College. Wesley heartily approved the scheme; it was, in fact, the exemplification of a design which he himself had propounded in his first and second Conferences.

A provision of this kind was the more needed as it had become manifest that the Methodists could expect no treatment, compatible with their self-respect, for their ministerial candidates at the English universities. About the time that Lady Huntingdon and Wesley were consulting respecting Trevecca, a conclusive motive for the project was given at Ox-

[5] Life and Times of the Countess of Huntingdon, chap. 27.

[6] See his letter (tinged not a little with his characteristic discontent toward his brother) in the Life of Lady Huntingdon, chap. 27.

ford. Methodism had again revealed itself within its learned cloisters, as also at Cambridge; in the latter the noted Rowland Hill headed a band of devout youth who were stigmatized by the title. At Oxford, Holward, of Worcester College, led a little company who were reproducing "The Holy Club," to the dismay of its clerical and literary dignitaries. Hill and Holward were in constant correspondence; Whitefield, also, had influential relations with them, and the new revival began to assume much prospective importance when it was summarily arrested by the collegiate authorities of Oxford. Six students of St. Edmund's Hall were cited to trial "for holding Methodistic tenets, and taking upon them to pray, read, and expound the Scriptures in private houses."[7] Dr. Dixon, Principal of St. Edmund's, defended the accused students from the Thirty-nine Articles, and spoke in the highest terms of their piety and exemplary lives; but his motion for their acquittal was overruled, and they were expelled. The proceeding produced a general sensation in religious circles throughout the country. Sir Richard Hill dedicated to the Earl of Litchfield, Chancellor of the University, a pungent pamphlet, entitled "Pietas Oxoniensis." Horne, afterward Bishop of Norwich, entered into the controversy in favor of the expelled young men. Macgowan, who had been a local preacher among the Methodists, but was now a Baptist pastor in London, published against the University a satirical sermon, famous in that day, under the title of "The Shaver," which, with Aristophanic humor, but scathing logic, showed the Oxford proceedings to be not only impious but supremely ridiculous; many thousands of the publication flew over the land. Whitefield addressed a published and forcible letter to the Vice-Chancellor. Most, if not all these young men had been sent to Oxford under the auspices of Lady Huntingdon; and the Oxford authorities, as also the public journals, accused her of "seducing young men from

[7] St. James's Chronicle. Philip's Whitefield, chap. 27. The chief charges against one of them was that "he had been instructed by Mr. Fletcher, a decided Methodist," and had "associated with Methodists."

their respective trades and avocations and sending them to the University, where they were maintained at her expense, that they might afterward skulk into orders." It was time, therefore, that Trevecca should be opened. In three months it was dedicated by Whitefield, several of the persecuted students resorted to it, and most of them became useful ministers in the national Church or among the Dissenters.

In August, 1769, a remarkable scene was exhibited at Trevecca. It was the celebration of the first anniversary of the college; and so catholic was yet the whole Methodist movement, that both its Calvinistic and Arminian leaders met there in harmony, and gave an example of Christian charity which should never be forgotten by their successors. Nearly a week before the celebration many of the most distinguished evangelists had arrived, and vast congregations, sermons, exhortations, prayers, and conversions, in the court-yard of the castle, marked these preliminary days. Early in the morning of the anniversary the Eucharist was administered, and shared by Methodists of all opinions. Its administrators were Wesley and Shirley, the exponents of the Calvinism and Arminianism of the day. A large company of clergymen first partook of it, then the students, and afterward the countess, and a train of "elect ladies," mostly of high rank, followed by the people. Fletcher preached in the court at two o'clock, and was succeeded by a sermon in Welsh, after which all the clergymen dined with Lady Huntingdon, while bread and meat were distributed from ample baskets to the multitude without. In the afternoon Wesley preached, and Fletcher followed with a second sermon. The evening was devoted to a "love-feast," the primitive Agape, derived, in a simplified form, through the London Moravians; it was an occasion of extraordinary interest; all classes sat "together as in heavenly places in Christ Jesus." Howell Harris, with a band of his Welsh converts, took part in the exercises in their own language, and narratives of Christian experience, prayers, and hymns occupied the hours. Wesley, always on the wing, left the next day; but Fletcher, Shirley, and other clergymen tarried several days in brotherly devotions, preaching from a platform in the court-yard to the multitudes who still lingered with them in deep religious interest.

But let us return, and for the last time, to the hero of Calvinistic Methodism. It pleases God, in accommodation to the infirmities of our fallen humanity, that his most eminent servants should not be entirely exempt from its common imperfections, otherwise they could not so well command our common sympathies, and do us the good for which they are sent; but often, as their appointed work is closing, does he put upon their brows an unearthly glory, as if crowning them among men for their admission among angels. Even in private life, when the aged pilgrim, or the long-suffering saint, or sanctified childhood itself, seems preparing to depart, it is often thus; but still more among the good and noted, of public Christian usefulness. Whitefield has appeared and reappeared amid the scenes of our narrative with continually increasing interest—an interest which the historian, while he may well apprehend that he shall be suspected of exaggeration, knows equally well to be short of the original reality. We come now to follow him to his grave, or rather to the scene of his ascension; and as we trace him through his last days, and behold his eloquence, his devotion, his heroism, taking a character of sublimity from the approach of death, we shall find that the ground upon which we tread becomes more holy, and should be walked with unsandaled feet.

We parted from him last in 1760. His health was feeble; the asthma oppressed him, and his chronic hemorrhage, "vomiting of blood," was considered by him a fortunate relief after the excitement of his discourses. In 1761 he was reduced almost to extremity, and expected death. Berridge, Romaine, Madan, and his other associates, had to sustain the services of the Tabernacle and Tottenham Chapel, and for the first time in his ministerial career he preached not for several weeks. In 1762 he considered it a sign of some improvement that he could resume his "ranging," and preach some "five times a week." He could "take the open field" occasionally. "O for power equal to my will!" he wrote; "I would fly from pole to pole publishing the everlasting Gospel of the Son of God." He made a voyage to Holland for his health this year, and on his return was soon again in Scotland, and could write: "All my old times have returned." Edinburgh, Glasgow, Cambuslang, again rejoiced under his ministrations. On returning to England, it is recorded that he was able to preach "*but once* a day," in extreme weakness.

In 1763 he was again on the ocean. It was his sixth expedition. At Philadelphia he preached twice a week, though still very feeble. Forty preachers, of various denominations, who had been regenerated in the American revival, congratulated him on his arrival. He passed through New York, Connecticut, and Rhode Island, to Boston, welcomed by tens of thousands. At New York he wrote that such a flocking of all ranks he never saw before. At Boston his reception was more cordial than ever. Even Harvard College, which had issued its "testimony" against him, voted him thanks for his Journal and other books, and received him as an embassador of Christ. On leaving the city for the south, messengers were sent after him; he went back and preached to immense crowds for several weeks.

In his southward tour the whole population on his route seemed swayed with interest. On reaching New York he wrote: "It would astonish you to see above a hundred carriages at every sermon in the New World." Before the end of 1764 he reached his beloved Bethesda, near Savannah, having preached all along his course from Boston to innumerable multitudes.

In the spring of 1765 he again swept over the colonies northward as far as New York. It would be impossible to estimate the influence of his powerful discourses on the Churches, and the religious interests of the Atlantic settlements generally. The population, from the highest to the lowest, gathered at all the prominent points of his passage. Hundreds of thousands heard the highest evangelical truths uttered with an eloquence probably never equaled. Writing from Philadelphia, he says: "All along from Charleston to this place the cry is, 'For Christ's sake, stay and preach to us.'"

In July, 1765, he again landed in England. He was still broken in health, but as ardent as ever with the devout enthusiasm which had borne him through unflagging labors for nearly thirty years. "O to end life well!" he wrote on his arrival; "methinks I have now but one river to pass over, and we know of One that can carry us over without being ankle deep." During the ensuing four years he itinerated in England, Scotland, and Wales, repeating his excursions whenever his health rallied sufficiently to allow him to mount his "field-throne," as he called his out-door pulpit. The enthusiasm of the people to hear him increased with the increased fame which years had given him. They gathered by ten thousands and twenty thousands around him, and he speaks of "light and life flying in all directions."

Cornelius Winter, a distinguished Calvinistic Methodist, gives us some glimpses of his more personal life about this period. He was avaricious of time, and his expectations generally went before the ability of his assistants to perform his commands. He was very exact to the time appointed for his meals; a few minutes' delay would be considered a great fault. He was irritable, but soon appeased. Not patient enough one day to receive a reason for his being disappointed under a particular occurrence, he hurt the mind of one who was studious to please him; he discovered it by the tears it occasioned, and, on reflection, he himself burst into tears, saying, "I shall live to be a poor peevish old man, and everybody will be tired of me." He never indulged parties at his table; a select few might now and then breakfast with him, dine with him on a Sunday, or sup with him on a Wednesday night. In the latter indulgence he was scrupulously exact to retire early. In the height of a conversation he would abruptly say, "But we forget ourselves," and rising from his seat, and advancing to the door, add, "Come, gentlemen, it is time for all good folks to be at home." Whether by himself, or having but a second person at his table, it must be spread elegantly, though it presented but a loaf and a cheese. It never presented much variety. A cow-heel was his favorite dish, and he has been known cheerfully to say, "How surprised would the world be, if they were to peep upon Dr. Squintum,[10] and see a cow-heel only upon his table." He was fastidiously neat in his person and every thing about him. Not a paper could be out of place or put up irregularly. Every part of the furniture must be in order before he retired to rest. He said he did not think he should die easy if he thought his gloves were out of their place. There was no rest in the house after four in the morning, nor sitting up after ten in the evening. He never made a purchase without paying the money for it immediately. He was truly generous, and seldom denied relief. He often dined among his friends, when he usually connected a comprehensive prayer with his thanksgiving at the table, noticing particular cases connected with the family: he never protracted his visit long after dinner. He often appeared tired of popularity, and said he envied the man who could take his choice of food at an eating-house, and pass unnoticed. He apprehended he should not glorify God in his death by any remarkable testimony, and was desirous to die suddenly.

His wife died in 1768; he writes of her with regret, but suffered scarcely an intermission of his labors by the event. His marriage was not as unfortunate as that of John Wesley, nor as fortunate as that of Charles.[11] If it yielded him no great happiness it did not interfere with

[10] One of his eyes was defective. See p. 92.

[11] Winter, who lived in his family, represents it as unhappy. (Winter's Memoirs, by Jay.) Philip (Life of Whitefield, chap. 11) attempts an elaborate and plausible, if not successful defense.

the great work to which everything else had to bend. At the death of his only child, his friends united in the request that he should decline preaching till it was buried; but he preached twice the day after its death, and once the following day, and the bell was tolling for the funeral before he left the pulpit; this was zeal, but not a lack of tenderness, for in a few minutes he was on his knees by the side of the corpse, shedding "many tears, though tears of resignation." The next day he was again in the pulpit. Never was there a man so entirely of one work as Whitefield.

This, his last sojourn in England, was of incalculable advantage to Methodism. He consecrated new chapels, provided by the Countess of Huntingdon; he promoted the success of the college at Trevecca; he stimulated his fellow-laborers, Romaine, Venn, Berridge, Madan, and their associates; he called out Scott, Joss, Rowland Hill, and other extraordinary laborers into his London pulpits, and spread renewed interest through most of the land. Meanwhile his generous spirit, fast ripening for heaven, sought every opportunity of promoting the catholicity of the great revival. He not only attended, and drew his most eminent associates to Wesley's Conferences, but met him often in private interviews. Wesley's equally charitable heart was touched by these Christian courtesies, and by the reminiscences of their long and common labors and sufferings. He saw that his eloquent friend was hastening to his rest, and that the opportunities for such brotherly amenities should be prized as soon to be had no more. In 1769 he records in his Journal that he spent "a comfortable and profitable hour" with Whitefield in "*calling to mind the former times*," and the manner in which God had prepared them for "a work which it had not entered into their hearts to conceive." Whitefield was at this time sinking fast. Two years earlier Wesley speaks of breakfasting with him, and of his appearing to be "an old, old man, fairly worn out in his Master's service." In February, 1769, he says: "I had one more agreeable conversation with my old friend and fellow-laborer, George Whitefield. His soul appeared to be vigorous still, but his body was sinking apace."

In September, 1769, the mighty apostle was again on the deck for America. He took affectionate leave of Wesley in a farewell letter as he embarked. After a tedious and perilous voyage, he was cheered to find Bethesda in unprecedented prosperity. For about thirty-two years he had cherished it as one of the fondest objects of his life. It was almost clear of debt, with two new wings, each nearly one hundred and fifty feet in length, and smaller buildings in much forwardness, and the whole executed "with taste and in a masterly manner." The governor and council of the colony received him with public ceremonies, and adopted his plans for the re-organization of the institution as a college. He seemed never more contented. "I am happier," he wrote, "than words can express." "O Bethesda! my Bethel! my Peniel! my happiness is inconceivable!" This year he was to die, and it was well that his last days were not to be clouded by an anticipation of the fate which awaited this his favorite project.[12] He felt a momentary temptation to repose in its tranquil retirement, "but all must give way to Gospel ranging, divine employ!" and soon he was again moving northward. Early in the morning on which he started he wrote the prophetic words: "This will prove a sacred year for me at the day of judgment. Hallelujah! Come, Lord, come!"

This last tour befitted his whole religious history. He was in improved health; never did his spirit soar more loftily; never did such frequent ejaculations of zeal and rapture appear in his correspondence. "Hallelujah! hallelujah!" he wrote to England; "let Chapel, Tabernacle, heaven, and earth resound with hallelujah! I can no more; my heart is too big to speak or add more!" To Charles Wesley he wrote: "I can only sit down and cry, 'What hath God wrought!' My bodily health is much improved, and

[12] It was destroyed by fire two or three years later, and scarcely a trace of its ruins remains.

my soul is on the wing for another Gospel range. Unutterable love! I am lost in wonder and amazement!"

In May he appeared again among the enthusiastic crowds of Philadelphia, preaching twice on Sunday, besides three or four times during the rest of the week. All ranks flocked to hear him, and now even the Episcopal churches were all open to him. The salutary effects of his former labors were everywhere obvious. He made an excursion from the city over a circuit of a hundred and fifty miles, preaching every day. So many doors were open, he wrote, that he knew not which way to turn. He turned finally to New York, where he preached "to congregations larger than ever." He passed up the Hudson River, and made a tour of more than five hundred miles, preaching at Albany, Schenectady, Great Barrington, and many other places. He had reached the New York frontier of that day; for as late as the Revolution the white population west of the Hudson scarcely extended back sixty miles to Cherry Valley, Johnstown, and some scattered settlements in Otsego, Montgomery, and Herkimer counties; and such was still the power of the Indian tribes, that during the war Schenectady itself was likely at one time to become the prominent point of the Western boundary of the state. "O what new scenes of usefulness are opening in various points of this world," wrote Whitefield, as he returned. He saw the gates of the Northwest opening, those mighty gates through which the nations have since been passing, as in grand procession, but he was not to enter there; the everlasting gates were opening for him, and he was hastening toward them. The last entry in his memoranda relates to his labors on this tour up the Hudson: "I heard afterward that the word ran and was glorified. Grace! grace!" He had preached with his usual zeal, and at every possible point, in churches, in streets, in fields, and at one time on the coffin of a criminal, beneath the gallows, to thousands of hearers; "Solemn! solemn!" he wrote; "effectual good, I hope, was done. Grace! grace!"

From New York he went to Boston, and wrote in one of his latest letters that never was the word received with greater eagerness than now, and that all opposition seemed to cease. He passed on to Newbury, where he was attacked with sudden illness; but recovering, he resumed his route to Portsmouth, N. H. During six days he preached there and in the vicinity every day. Returning he addressed a vast assembly in the open air at Exeter. His emotions carried him away, and he prolonged his discourse through two hours. It was an effort of stupendous eloquence—*his last field triumph;* the last of that series of mighty sermons which had been resounding like trumpet blasts for thirty-four years over England and America.

He departed the same day for Newburyport, where it was expected he would preach on the morrow. While at supper the pavement in front of the house, and even its hall, were crowded with people, impatient to hear a few words from his eloquent lips; but he was exhausted, and rising from the table, said to one of the clergymen who were with him, "Brother, you must speak to these dear people; I cannot say a word." Taking a candle he hastened toward his bed-room, but before reaching it he was arrested by the suggestion of his own generous heart that he ought not thus to desert the anxious crowd, hungering for the bread of life from his hands. He paused on the stairs to address them. He had preached his last sermon; this was to be his last exhortation. It would seem that some pensive misgiving, some vague presentiment touched his soul with the saddening apprehension that the moments were too precious to be lost in rest; he lingered on the stairway, while the crowd gazed up at him with tearful eyes, as Elisha at the ascending prophet. His voice, never, perhaps, surpassed in its music and pathos, *flowed on until the candle which he held in his hand burned away and went out in its socket!*[13] The next morning he was not, for God had taken him!

[13] This final scene in his ministry is given in none of his memoirs. It was related by a daughter of Rev. Mr. Parsons, in whose house he died.

He died of an attack of asthma, September 30th, 1770, as the Sabbath sun was rising from the neighboring sea. The effulgence of the eternal day had risen upon his beneficent, his fervid, his consecrated life. He had slept comfortably till two o'clock in the morning, when he awoke his traveling attendant, and told him that his "asthma was coming on again." His companion recommended him not to preach so often as he had. "I would rather wear out than rust out," he replied. He had expressed a desire to die suddenly, and now realized his wish. He sat in his bed some time, praying that God would bless his preaching, his Bethesda school, the Tabernacle congregation, and "all connections on the other side of the water." He attempted again to sleep, but could not; he hastened to the open window, panting for breath. "I am dying," he exclaimed. A physician was called, but could give him no relief. At six o'clock he "fetched one gasp, stretched out his feet, and breathed no more."

While at the dinner-table of Finley, at Princeton, he had remarked: "I shall die silent. It has pleased God to enable me to bear so many testimonies for him during my life that he will require none from me when I die." The only words he uttered during his agony were, "I am dying."

Many hundreds followed him to the grave. All the bells of the town were tolled; the flags of the shipping in the harbor were hung at half mast, and mourning guns were fired from their decks. Funeral sermons were preached in the principal cities of America. The magistrates of Georgia assembled in mourning at the State House, and led a procession to hear his funeral sermon at the church, which was hung in black; and it is said that all the cloth suitable for mourning in the stores of the colony was bought up.

The news of his death reached London early in November. The Methodist chapels were hung with mourning drapery. He left Wesley a mourning ring, and had appointed him to preach his funeral sermon. Wesley pronounced the discourse at the Tabernacle, and repeated it at

Tottenham Court, Greenwich Tabernacle, Deptford, and elsewhere, remarking in his Journal: "In every place I wish to show all possible respect to the memory of that great and good man." Charles Wesley published an elegy on his death, which does as much credit to his own genius and heart as to the character of his friend.

Whitefield's remains rest beneath the pulpit of the Federal-street Church, Newburyport. A massive marble cenotaph commemorates him near the altar. Many pilgrims visit the venerable church to honor his memory. Passing into an adjacent vestry, the visitor descends, with his guide and lanterns, through a door in the floor into a cript, and thence, by a side door, into the vault, extending under the pulpit, where, between two ancient pastors of the church, lies the open coffin of Whitefield. The bare and decaying bones lie upon a slight bed of mold formed of the dust of the body. As the thoughtful spectator gazes upon the full-orbed cranium, or takes it into his hands, many an eager inquiry is startled within him. What thoughts of power and grandeur emanated from this dome of the mind, thoughts that have stirred the depths of hundreds of thousands of souls, and will quicken their immortality! What were the attributes of his character; what the sources of his wonderful power?

Sufficient has already been said, in the course of this volume, to answer somewhat these questions; but we may well pause at the grave of so conspicuous a character in our narrative, the man who was the herald of Methodism, sounding the trumpet before its march in both hemispheres, and ask again, whence was his unrivaled power?

Whitefield was a man of no great intelligence, and of less learning, but of unquestionable genius; perhaps the greatest known, in the greatest or at least the rarest power of genius—eloquence.

He was born an orator. The qualities of the orator made up his whole genius; they were the first mental manifestations of his childhood, but were pent up in his heart, a magazine of energies, until kindled by the influence of religion, when they broke forth like the fires of a volcano. He was a man of boundless soul. He was a host of generous sympathies; and every sympathy in him was a passion. This was the secret of his eloquence. The Athenian orator said that action was eloquence. Perhaps antiquity has given undue authority to the saying. The pantomime is not eloquent; but strong passion always is, and always would be, had it the expression of neither hand nor feature, but only the tremulous tones of the excited voice coming from an unseen source upon the ear. There is no eloquence without feeling. Even the histrionic orator must feel—not affect to feel, but, by giving himself up to the illusion of reality in ideal scenes, actually feel. Whitefield's whole Christian course showed the prevalence of mighty feelings.

While eloquence is the rarest if not the greatest power of genius, pathos is the greatest if not the rarest power of eloquence. And remarkable, indeed, is the fact that a quality so rare, and therefore so precious, in oratory and literature, should be the most common of the sensibilities of the popular mind, the masses with whom the pulpit orator pre-eminently has to do. The strength of the natural affections, the prevalence of common sufferings among the common people, keep sacred within them the sense of sorrow and of pity even when most other virtues are gone; and the rudest natures usually weep the most readily, as they do the most sincerely.

Precisely in this greatest power of eloquence did Whitefield most excel. His thoughts, his whole mighty soul, flowed in his tears. He paused often in his sermons to weep, the people, meanwhile, sobbing aloud, or sinking to the earth under insupportable emotions.

While pathos, from its relation to the natural affections and to the common sorrows of men, affords to any orator his chief power, from its congeniality with the religious affections—contrition for sin, habitual trust in an atonement made by suffering, sympathy with erring men and periled souls, and the tenderness which essentially belongs to all religious affections—it is in a special manner the great power of pulpit eloquence; infinitely more so than terror, which, while a less general susceptibility, is related to but a single religious idea. The profound religious feeling of Whitefield was therefore an important element of his pulpit power. There was in him a remarkable combination of the unction from above, the "Holy Ghost and power," with intense natural sensibility. He was "full of faith and the Holy Ghost." In him religion was from the time of his conversion till his death a continual impulse; zeal for the conversion of men an unbroken spell. All his theological opinions, his ideas of sin and holiness, of heaven and hell, were not merely thoughts but sentiments; not speculations, but unquestionable realities. They were appreciated by him as directly as sensible facts are by ordinary men. This vivid spirituality inflamed his entire soul. A spiritual unction seemed to drip down his whole person, like the anointing oil that "went down to the skirts of Aaron's garments." Hervey has left a remarkable testimony to his Christian character. "For my part," he says, "I never beheld so fair a copy of our Lord; such a living image of the Saviour; such exalted delight in God; such enlarged benevolence to man; such a steady faith in the Divine promises, and such a fervent zeal for the Divine glory; and all this without the least moroseness or extravagance, sweetened with the most engaging cheerfulness, and regulated by all the sobriety of reason and wisdom of Scripture."[14]

And it is an extraordinary fact that the fervor of his zeal suffered no appreciable abatement throughout his long ministry of thirty-four years; not even the effect which age and disease might naturally have had upon it. His last year showed more zeal, if possible, than any before it; his last sermon, two hours long, in the open air, was more powerful than his first one at Bristol; like the sun, he went down with undiminished force, as majestically as he rose.

He was an enthusiast, doubtless, but in the best sense, and in no sense a fanatic. His whole soul seemed incandescent

[14] Gillies's Whitefield, chap. 20.

with a divine fire; yet the most remarkable thing about him, when we consider the natural constitution of his mind, is the perfect good sense with which he prosecuted a career so long, so fervid, and so novel. When he started at Bristol on his ministerial course, or took the open field at Kingswood, a severe prudence would have predicted some signal folly or failure in his life; some perilous extravagance of opinion or conduct. But what one can be recorded against him; what more than the common and petty defects of the best of men?[15] Without apparent sagacity, or even usual caution, the simplicity and entire purity of his conscience supplied him with protections which the most consummate wisdom seldom so well affords, and no extravagance can be imputed to him, except a boundless charity and a zeal which enabled him to reach the maximum capacity of his life for labor and travel.

He had not only the soul of eloquence, but also the art. Elocution is not eloquence; a speaker may be eloquent without it; he may have it in perfection, and not be eloquent. But Whitefield, while possessing the moral and intellectual elements of the orator, neglected not the practical principles of the art. It is said that he studied and privately practiced the prescribed rules of public speaking. His gestures are reported to have been remarkably appropriate; Franklin, who heard him often, says that each repetition of the same sermon showed a studied improvement, and that

[15] In even his controversy with Wesley his faults are excusable, if not admirable, on account of the occasions they afterward afforded for the exercise of the generosity and tenderness of his noble heart. When he was departing on his first American voyage, Wesley admonished him not to go, because of a warning which Wesley himself had received by sortilege. In the Calvinistic controversy Whitefield published the confidential fact; but perhaps no event in his life called forth more magnanimous and affecting expressions of regret and self-condemnation. He says of it, in his reply to Lavington: "For this I have asked both God and him pardon years ago, and although I believe both have forgiven me, yet I believe I shall never be able to forgive myself." Sortilege was not an uncommon folly of that day. See a ludicrous example of it on the part of Berridge, in the Life and Times of Lady Huntingdon, chap. 22.

several repetitions were necessary to perfect it; Foote and Garrick said that his eloquence advanced up to the fortieth repetition before it reached its full height.[16] His voice was laboriously cultivated, and became astonishingly effective. Garrick, who delighted to hear him, said that he could make his audience weep or tremble merely by varying his pronunciation of the word Mesopotamia. His style, both of language and gesture, was natural, and it perfectly comported with his strong natural feeling. Though he studied the art of eloquence, he was not artificial. The ornate, the florid style, so commonly received from the pulpit as eloquence, was never used by him. No one studying his genius can conceive for a moment that it was possible for him to use it; he was too much in earnest, too intent on the object before him. His language is always simple and colloquial, not fitted for books, but, therefore, the better fitted for speech, abounding in abrupt transitions, and strongly idiomatic; such language, in fine, as a sincere man would use in earnestly entreating his neighbor to escape some impending disaster. Though he did not like his reported sermons, they are evidently fac-similes of his style; direct, abrupt, full of local allusions, and presenting scarcely a single ornamented passage, the very speech of the common people. It would appear homely, even meager, did not the reader supply, in his imagination, the conversational manner, the tears, and the entreating voice of the speaker. It would be folly to say that a more refined style is not appropriate to the pulpit, popular as should be its address; but, let its refinement be what it may, it should have these characteristics of simplicity, point, and colloquial directness. This is the style of true eloquence; ornament pertains to imagination, and imagination belongs to poetry; but poetry and oratory are distinct. Genuine oratory is too earnest to admit of much ornament. Its figures are few and always brief. Its language is the language of the passions, not of the fancy, and the passions never utter themselves in embel-

[16] Philip's Life, etc., chap. 22.

lished phrases, but always directly, pungently. It is the great mistake of modern oratory, especially in the pulpit, that it confounds eloquence with poetry, but it was never the mistake of this greatest of preachers.

There was a species of humor, or rather popular aptness, in his discourse, which could not fail to interest the common people; for nowhere else can be found more mother wit, or readier repartee, than in large popular assemblies. Pulpit buffoons, however, can never claim sanction from his example; it is doubtful whether he ever made a con gregation laugh; but the oddity of his illustrations, the appositeness of his local or casual allusions, the colloquial familiarity of his address, the hearty "human nature" of his habitual tone of mind, and his abundant anecdotes, kept the compact thousands in an attitude of eager interest and charmed attention. They felt that though he had come down to them from the Mount of Transfiguration, and was shining with its glory, yet he had gone up to it from among themselves, and was still one of them. Through all his unusual forms of expression and surprising illustrations, was heard distinctly the undertone of his pathos and solemn earnestness. Vulgarity was, with him, next impossible to profanity itself. Cornelius Winter, who accompanied him in his last voyage to America, says that sometimes he wept exceedingly, stamped loudly and passsionately, and he was frequently so overcome that for a few seconds it seemed he never could recover; and when he did, nature required some time to compose herself. He hardly ever ended a sermon without weeping more or less. Winter adds that he has known him avail himself of the formality of the judge putting on his black cap to pronounce sentence. With eyes full of tears, and his heart almost too big to admit of speech, he would say, after a momentary pause, "I am now going to put on my *condemning* cap. Sinner, I must do it! I *must* pronounce sentence!" Then, in a strain of tremendous eloquence, he would repeat our Lord's words, "Depart, ye cursed," and not without a powerful description of the nature of that curse. But it was only by hearing him, and by beholding his *attitude and tears*, continues this writer, that any person could conceive of the effect.[17]

This dramatic power was another of his extraordinary talents. Not only every accent of his voice, remarks Gillies, spoke to the ear, but every feature of his face, every motion of his hands, every gesture spoke to the eye, so that the most thoughtless found their attention involuntarily fixed. Hume reports that once, after a solemn pause, he exclaimed: "The attendant angel is just about to leave the threshold of this sanctuary and ascend to heaven. And shall he ascend and not bear with him the news of one sinner among all this multitude reclaimed from the error of his ways?" To give the greater effect to this exclamation, he stamped with his foot, lifted up his hands and eyes to heaven, and cried aloud, "Stop, Gabriel, stop, ere you enter the sacred portals, and yet carry with you the news of one sinner converted to God." "This address," says Hume, "was accompanied with such animated yet natural action, that it surpassed anything I ever saw or heard in any other preacher."

At Lady Huntingdon's he was once illustrating the perils of the sinner who is led on by inadequate views of religion; he drew the picture of a blind beggar, guided along the brink of a deep precipice by a string around the neck of his dog; the dog escapes; the blind man lifts his foot over the precipice—"Heavens! he is gone!" shouted Chesterfield, leaping up before the assembly.[18] As though it were no dif-

[17] Memoirs of Winter, by William Jay.

[18] The effect of his eloquence on polished or shrewd minds seems to have been as irresistible as on the common people. Franklin's example is well known, but deserves requoting. He went to hear him in Philadelphia: "At this sermon," he says, "there was also one of our club, who, being of my sentiments respecting the building in Georgia, and suspecting a collection might be intended, had, by precaution, emptied his pockets before he came from home; toward the conclusion of the discourse, however, he felt a strong inclination to give, and applied to a neighbor, who stood near him, to lend him some money for the purpose. The request was fortunately made to, perhaps, the only man in the company

ficult matter, remarks Winter, "to catch the sound of the Saviour praying, he would exclaim: 'Hark! hark! do not you hear him?' You may suppose that as this occurred frequently, the efficacy of it was destroyed; but, no; though we often knew what was coming, it was as new to us as though we had never heard it before. That beautiful apostrophe, used by the prophet Jeremiah, 'O earth, earth, earth, hear the words of the Lord,' was very subservient to him, and never used impertinently."

Newton, of Olney, said: "As a preacher, if any man were to ask me who was the second I ever had heard, I should be at some loss; but in regard to the first, Mr. Whitefield exceeded so far every other man of my time that I should be at none. He was the original of popular preaching, and all our popular ministers are only his copies."[19]

Such was the man; the results of his influence on his age and ours it would be impossible to estimate, not only because he did not give them any aggregate form by the general organization of societies, but because of their great extent. It has been shown that he led the Methodistic movement over the first barriers in its way, and by field and itinerant preaching, broke open for it an unrestricted career. While in England he was almost as ubiquitous as Wesley, and in scarcely a section of the island did he fail to give impulse and energy to that evangelical reanimation which continues to our day. Writers who are not Methodists admit that Methodism saved the Nonconformity of England,[20] and Whitefield was its chief representative, and promoter among the Nonconformists. The whole evangelical Dissent of England feels his power to-day.

In Scotland, where his fellow-laborers in the revival had but slight agency, and where the Established Kirk was spiritually dead, and the zeal of the Seceders was more the

who had the firmness not to be affected by the preacher. His answer was, 'At any other time, friend Hopkinson, I would lend to thee freely, but not now; for thee seems to me to be out of thy right senses.'"

[19] See his letter in Lady Huntingdon's Life and Times, chap. 7.

[20] See page 30.

result of tenacity for opinions than of spiritual fervor, he may be considered the first great agent of that resuscitation of religion which, since the date of Methodism, has effectually counteracted the Socinian and semi-infidel tendencies which were once prevalent there, and has infused new and universal life into its Churches.

Wales is inscribed all over with the signatures of his usefulness. Griffith Jones, and Howell Harris had begun its evangelical regeneration, but their labors were disconnected, and, if we except Jones's itinerant schools, without definite scope. Whitefield's Calvinism gave him power in the Principality; he brought the two Welsh evangelists into co-operation with each other, and into communion with Methodism, and thence, in connection with Wesleyan Methodism, has arisen that extraordinary religious progress by which the thirty Dissenting Churches of 1715 have increased to twenty-three hundred; by which a chapel now dots nearly every three square miles of the country, and over a million people, nearly the whole Welsh population, are found attending public worship some part of every Sabbath.[21]

The Calvinistic Methodists, who had generally recognized in Lady Huntingdon's patronage and superintendence a bond of unity, were resolved, after Whitefield's death, into three sects: The first was known as Lady Huntingdon's Connection; it observed strictly the liturgical forms of the English Church, and its ministry ceased to itinerate; it possesses in our day about sixty chapels; Cheshunt College, in Hertfordshire, belongs to it, and was substituted for Trevecca, when the lease of the latter expired. The second was called the Tabernacle Connection, or Whitefield Methodists. Some of its churches used the national Liturgy, but many adopted the forms of the Congregational Independents, and most of them have been absorbed by the latter denomination. The third is known as the Welsh Calvinistic Methodists; it has continued to prosper down to our day. Its chapels are found in almost every village in Wales, and are alone equal to

[21] See pages 119, 120.

more than two-thirds the number belonging to the Establishment. Its first Association was held in 1743; in 1785 it was more thoroughly organized by Rev. Thomas Charles, whose legislative genius has thus perpetuated in effective vigor the usefulness of Griffith Jones, Howell Harris, and their Calvinistic Methodist coadjutors. According to the official statistics of the British Government respecting Wales, for 1857, there were in the Principality, Calvinistic Methodists, 52,670 communicants, 462 preachers, and 794 churches; Wesleyan Methodists, 19,014 communicants, 424 preachers, and 400 churches.

The extent of Whitefield's influence in America is still less appreciable, but perhaps still greater. The "Great Awakening" here had commenced before his arrival, but it was comparatively local, and its visible interest at least had mostly subsided. Edwards and some of his ministerial associates were yet praying and writing respecting it in New England; and the Tennents, Blairs, Finley, Rowland, and others, were devotedly laboring, in detail, in the Middle States, against the moral stupor of the times; but Whitefield's coming at once renewed the revival and gave it universality if not unity.[22] He alone of all its promoters represented it in all parts of the country, and at every repeated visit renewed its progress. In the South he was almost its only laborer; his preaching, and especially his volume of sermons, read by Morris,[23] founded the Presbyterian Church in Virginia; for before that period there was not a Dissenting minister settled in the colony.[24]

In the Middle States Whitefield's labors had a profound effect. He was an apostle to Philadelphia; he rallied around him its preachers, and stimulated them by his example. In New Jersey and New York he exerted a similar influence,

[22] For an account of the schisms and other troubles of the American Churches about this time, see Tracy's Great Awakening, etc., *passim*.

[23] See page 301.

[24] Letter of President Davies to Rev. Mr. Bellamy, now in the Old South Church Library, Boston; see Tracy's Great Awakening, chap. 19.

and the frequent repetition of his visits through about thirty years did not allow the evangelical interest of the Churches to subside. The ministers in the synod of New York more than tripled in seven years after his first visit.[25] In New England the effects of Edwards's labors were reproduced and rendered general by Whitefield's frequent passages. One hundred and fifty Congregational Churches were founded in less than twenty years;[26] and it has been estimated that between thirty thousand and forty thousand souls were converted in New England alone.[27]

The effects of the great revival, of which he had thus become the ostensible representative, have been profound and permanent. In fine, the Protestantism of the United States has taken its subsequent character from it, and the "Holy Club" at Oxford may be recognized as historically connected with the evangelical Christianity of all this continent, not only by the later influence of Arminian Methodism, but still more variously, if not more intimately, by the agency of Calvinistic Methodism. Wesley's charitable prediction that the breach between him and Whitefield, on account of Calvinism, would be a providential blessing, stands verified throughout the American Republic.

The effect of the Awakening on the character of the ministry was one of its greatest results. Since that period the "evangelical" character of the American pastorate has not, as before, been exceptional, but general. Twenty clergymen in the vicinity of Boston alone acknowledged, as we have seen, to Whitefield, at his third visit, that he had been the means of their conversion.

The Baptist denomination in the colonies received new energy from the "Great Awakening." Benjamin Randall was converted through the last sermons and death of White-

[25] Tracy's Great Awakening, chap. 19.

[26] Such was the estimate of President Styles. See Tracy, chap. 20.

[27] Trumbull (History of Connecticut) gives this estimate for only two or three years; others place the number at fifty thousand. Any such numerical estimates can be of little importance.

field,[28] and soon after founded the Free-Will Baptist Church, now fifty thousand strong in the United States.

Whitefield's labors prepared the way for Wesley's itinerants. They had arrived before his last visit; he gave them his blessing, as he passed through Philadelphia, and it has never failed them.

The revival had a salutary effect on education. It gave origin to Princeton College and its distinguished Theological Seminary,[29] and also to Dartmouth College. Whitefield's fellow-laborers founded both, and the Methodists of England contributed their money to both.

One of its most important blessings was its influence on the discipline of the Church, and especially on its relation to the state in New England. It banished the "Halfway Covenant," which had filled the eastern Churches with unconverted members; it made personal regeneration a requisite among the qualifications for the Christian ministry, and it introduced that general and profound conviction of the essential spirituality of religion, and the necessary independence of Church and state, which soon after began, and has since completed, the overthrow of all legal connection between the two throughout the country.[30]

Thus lived and died, and in the results of his labors lives still and will live forever, George Whitefield, the "Common Drawer" of the Bristol Inn, the "Poor Scholar," or Servitor of Pembroke College, the "Methodist" of the Holy Club of Oxford and the "Prince of Preachers." In proportion as the historian of his times should, by the soberest study of facts, approximate an exact estimate of his life and its consequences, would he incur the suspicion of exaggeration. It is not only questionable whether any other one man ever addressed by the voice so many of his fellow-men,

[28] "The death of Whitefield slew Randall," says a late writer, (Christian Review, April 1858.) The last sermons of Whitefield, at Portsmouth, N. H., impressed him deeply; but the death of the great preacher sealed the impression, and resulted in his conversion.

[29] Tracy's Great Awakening, chap. 20.

[30] Ibid.

but whether any other ever swayed them more irresistibly. It has been estimated that he preached eighteen thousand sermons, which would be ten a week for the thirty-four years of his ministry. He crossed the Atlantic thirteen times. The preaching tours he made through the colonies, from Maine to Georgia, would, with our modern means of travel, signalize before the country any clergyman's life; but the inconvenience and labor which they then involved can scarcely now be conceived. He has the grand distinction of having traveled more extensively for the Gospel, preached it oftener, and preached it more eloquently, than any other man, ancient or modern, within the same limits of life. A nobler eulogy could not crown his memory.

And here we may appropriately drop the curtain on the first act of this extraordinary drama in the modern history of religion. But the paramount man of the great movement was still abroad; a long period of life was yet to be allotted him; he was to survive nearly all his early fellow-laborers; to preach under trees which his own hands had planted at Kingswood, to the second and third generations of his people; and by his farther labors, to give to Methodism an organic form, which should secure efficiency and perpetuity to its mission. In turning from the grave of Whitefield we shall meet the fullest and noblest life of Wesley.

END OF VOL. I.

www.ingramcontent.com/pod-product-compliance
Lightning Source LLC
LaVergne TN
LVHW020928110826
845150LV00004B/799

* 9 7 8 1 4 2 5 5 5 4 1 0 1 *